Alamo Sourcebook

1836

Alamo Sourcebook 1836

A Comprehensive Guide to the Alamo and the Texas Revolution

Including the Siege and Final Battle . . .
the armies . . . their weapons, uniforms and equipment . . . the flags . . .
biographies of leaders of both sides . . . Alamo movies and music . . .
organizations to join . . . places to visit . . . and more!

Text by Tim and Terry Todish
Art by Ted Spring

EAKIN PRESS ★ AUSTIN, TEXAS

FIRST EDITION

Published in the United States of America
By Eakin Press
An Imprint of Sunbelt Media, Inc.
P.O. Drawer 90159 ★ Austin, TX 78709-0159
e-mail: eakinpub@sig.net

9 8 7 6 5 4 3 2

ISBN 1-57168-152-3

Todish, Timothy J.
Alamo sourcebook, 1836 : a comprehensive guide to the Alamo and the Texas Revolution / by Timothy J. Todish and Terry Todish ; illustrations by Ted Spring.
p. cm.
Includes bibliographical references and index.
ISBN 1-57168-152-3 (alk. paper)
1. Alamo (San Antonio, Tex.) — Siege, 1836 — Handbooks, manuals, etc. 2. Texas — History — Revolution, 1835-1836 — Handbooks, manuals, etc. I. Todish, Terry. II. Spring, Ted. III. Title.
F390.T64 1997
976.4'04--dc21 97-14503
CIP

DEDICATION

TO ALL OF THE MEN AND WOMEN, PAST, PRESENT, AND FUTURE,
WHO FREELY PUT THEIR LIVES ON THE LINE
FOR THE DEFENSE AND PROTECTION OF THEIR FELLOW MEN—
THE SOLDIERS, SAILORS, AIRMEN, MARINES,
POLICE OFFICERS, FIREFIGHTERS,
AND ALL THE OTHERS—
THIS BOOK IS RESPECTFULLY DEDICATED.

AN IRONIC TWIST OF FATE, AND A SPECIFIC DEDICATION

Since we wrote the above dedication, we have learned of an incident that illustrates all too well the very real dangers that these individuals face. On June 23, 1990, the paths of two of our French & Indian War historian friends crossed in a cruel way. Timothy Titus, then the interpretive programs assistant at the Crown Point State Historic Site in New York, and also a volunteer fireman, responded to an alarm at the home of Nicholas Westbrook, who is the director of nearby Fort Ticonderoga.

Although Nick's house was saved, Tim suffered permanent injuries to his right arm while battling the blaze. We would like to specifically dedicate this book to Tim Titus for his selfless sacrifice on behalf of our fellow historian and friend, Nick Westbrook.

FREEDOM IS NOT FREE

Freedom isn't free,

someone's paid for you and me,

and some died 'cause they believed,

the price of freedom is not free.

—Theme from the IMAX movie *ALAMO . . . The Price of Freedom*
(Written by Clint McAlister; performed by
Sergio Salinas; copyright Rivertheater Associates, Ltd.)

Contents

Preface

Few historical events are as widely known as the Siege and Battle of the Alamo. This is true not only in the United States, but also throughout much of the rest of the world. The idea of a small band of men choosing to fight and die, in the face of overwhelming odds, for the cause of liberty, has wide appeal.

References to the Alamo appear in very unlikely places, which just confirms the grip that the Alamo has on the imaginations of people from all walks of life.

Bob Becker, the sports editor for the Grand Rapids (Michigan) *PRESS,* devoted his July 4, 1991 sports column to the Alamo. He captured the true importance of the stand made by the Texians when he wrote:

> Just over 150 years ago, close to 200 men locked themselves into a crumbling fort and defended it against overwhelming odds for almost two weeks. . . .
>
> This wasn't a firefight, an ambush where soldiers react rather than think. They had almost two weeks to think about what they were doing, two weeks to decide whether to stand or run. And because they knew that there was no help coming, a decision to stand was also a decision to die.
>
> But stand they did, as so many others in our history have done. And it's because of them that today we are able to celebrate with ball games, picnics, parades, and fireworks.

The men, and also the women and children of the Alamo, faced a conscious choice. Up until virtually the end, they could almost certainly have slipped away to safety, but they did not. Today, some revisionists might characterize their fight as that of American imperialism against Mexico, but that was not how they saw it in 1836. The Texians and Tejanos in the Alamo believed that they were fighting for the cause of liberty over Santa Anna's tyranny. They felt that without their stand, the cause might fail, and so they chose to stay and fight regardless of the consequences.

Some of those who fought at the Alamo had indeed emigrated from the United States, but many others had not. A number of the Texians came from a variety of European countries, with the hope of fulfilling their dreams. A significant number of the Mexican citizens of Texas — the Tejanos — also cast their lot with the Texians. They had the most to lose of all of the rebels, yet they were willing to risk it all rather than live under the cruel and oppressive rule of the Mexican dictator, Santa Anna.

In the eyes of the people of 1836, this was truly a fight of good against evil. In our book, we will tell their story as fairly and as accurately as we can. Nothing is ever all black or all white, and this is especially true of the Mexican side of the Texas Revolution. In spite of what Santa Anna was, there were many brave, dedicated Mexicans who believed that they were fighting for their country, just as much as the Texians believed that they were fighting for freedom. We will make a special effort to recognize the dedication and sacrifices of the common Mexican soldier. We will also pay tribute to the many Tejanos who sided with the Revolution, and without whose help the Revolution may well not have succeeded.

In the *Alamo Sourcebook,* we not only tell the story of the Siege and Battle of the Alamo, but also give an overview of the events surrounding it. We cover the soldiers, and their uniforms, weapons and equipment, in detail that other books rarely go into. We provide a variety of information for modern day students of the Alamo — information about organizations to join, places to visit, and movies to see. We also include a comprehensive bibliography, so that interested readers can dig even deeper into the information presented here.

Much information about the Alamo is confusing and contradictory. In some cases, important information just plain does not exist, or at least has not yet been discovered. We have made every effort to use the best information available at the time of our writing. We also have consulted with, and had our text reviewed by, some of the best Texian historians working today.

Still, there were times when we had to make a choice about what version, or in some cases, versions, of the facts to present. Future research may well force us to revise our thinking in certain areas. We do not fear this, we welcome it! While we do not subscribe to the "political correctness" that motivates some historians today, we believe that the study of history must always include the search for new facts. There are also times when it is legitimate to reinterpret just what the facts really mean, but it must be done with caution, common sense, and a realistic evaluation of the facts.

We sincerely hope that you enjoy our book, and gain from it a greater appreciation for the courage and dedication of those who took part in these historic events.

Tim J. Todish
Terrence S. Todish
Grand Rapids, Michigan

Ted Spring
Nicoma Park, Oklahoma

Acknowledgments

The authors and the artist are deeply indebted to many people who helped to make this book a reality. We have utilized information from many sources, and truly appreciate the efforts of those whose published and unpublished works appear in the bibliography. While many of the facts concerning the Siege of the Alamo are subject to spirited debate, we feel that most of the authors have made an honest effort to record the truth as they see it, and we respect their differing opinions.

In our work, we often had to choose between conflicting versions of what happened, and we tried to do so using reason and common sense. In some cases, we present the different sides of an argument, so that the reader can make his or her own choices. We do not subscribe to any particular "side" or bias, but have tried to relate the true facts as accurately and honestly as we could.

In gathering and analyzing the vast amount of material covered in this book, we have received invaluable assistance from many people. We gratefully acknowledge and thank them for their help, and hold them blameless for any faults that the book might have.

Without the unselfish help, encouragement, and friendship of the following four people, this book truly could never have been written. Words alone cannot express how much we owe them!

Charles Lara, of Lakehills, Texas. Alamo historian, historical reenactor, past president of the San Antonio Living History Association, and founder of the Alamo Legacy & Missions Association.

Peter Stines, of Anahuac, Texas. Texas historian, artist, gunsmith, and historical reenactor.

Kevin Young, of San Antonio, Texas. A professional historian, author, movie advisor, and historical reenactor, Kevin began helping us when he was director of the San Antonio IMAX Theater, and continued to do so after several subsequent career moves.

Gary Zaboly, of New York City. Multi-talented artist, author, historian, and friend of some twenty years.

The following individuals also shared their knowledge and rendered other valuable assistance, encouragement, and friendship. We owe all of them a sincere debt of gratitude:

Roger Borroel, East Chicago, Indiana, author.

Reyes Carrasco, Grand Rapids, Michigan, helped with our understanding of the Spanish language and the Mexican culture.

Wallace O. Chariton, Plano, Texas, who has researched and published a tremendous amount of difficult to find information about the Texas Revolution, especially his excellent book *100 Days in Texas: The Alamo Letters* (Wordware Publishing).

Bill Chemerka, East Hanover, New Jersey, president of the Alamo Society, publisher of *The Alamo Journal,* and historical reenactor.

Doug Cohen, Davie, Florida, Alamo historian and collector, historical reenactor, and extra in John Wayne's *The Alamo.*

Gary Foreman, Racine, Wisconsin, movie producer, Alamo historian, and historical reenactor.

Bill Groneman, Racine, Wisconsin, author and Alamo historian.

Dr. Todd E. Harburn, Okemos, Michigan, author, Alamo historian, and historical reenactor.

John C. Jaeger, Flat Rock, Michigan, firearms expert, and historical reenactor.

Bob Lancaster, Newaygo, Michigan, an authority on British medals who helped us look into the "mystery of Edward Edwards."

Barry A. Lewis, Corunna, Michigan, an expert on muzzleloading artillery, who helped us with the "artillery" section.

Jerry Olson, Dearborn, Michigan, firearms expert, historical reenactor and outstanding analyst of historical facts and theories.

Frank Thompson, Burbank, California, author and authority on Alamo movies.

Colleen and Tim R. Todish, wife and son of Tim J., with their knowledge of the mysteries of Word Perfect and IBM computer systems, helped us to save time and avoid much frustration. Tim R. also analyzed the biographical data on the Alamo defenders, and did most of the data entry for Chapter Nine.

H. David Wright, Gallatin, Tennessee, artist and living historian who helped by sharing his vast knowledge of frontier accoutrements.

THE DEFENDERS OF THE ALAMO

by
Ted Spring

Most of them were young.
For the most part, they had little money or property.
Many had young wives and little children . . .
They had everything to lose!

Yet, on a cold March morning in 1836,
This ragtag group of men stood together heel to toe,
With a firm resolve to be free men.

They burned a page in Texas history,
And sent a message to would-be tyrants everywhere . . .
They reminded us all that
FREEDOM IS NOT FREE!

This is their story . . .

CHAPTER ONE

The Impossible Dream

PART 1: THE PROMISED LAND

"It is necessary to keep in mind that a new independent power exists now on this continent. It has been founded by an active, industrious, aggressive people . . . . it would be an unpardonable error not to take all necessary steps to check their territorial advance."

Jean Gasoit
Spanish Indian Agent, 1783
(Time Life: *The Spanish West,* 93)

MAYBE IT ALL BEGAN when Moses decided to lead his people to the Promised Land. Moses Austin, that is. The Promised Land was the Spanish province of Texas.

Moses Austin had been born in the United States, and had failed in some business ventures there. In 1798 he took his family and crossed the Mississippi into what was then Spanish Louisiana, where he prospered. Following the Louisiana Purchase, Austin again became subject to United States trade regulations. In the Panic of 1819, he had more economic difficulties. Seeking greener pastures, he set off for the Spanish holdings in Texas.

In trying to convince Spanish authorities that Americans could make good colonists, Austin faced a formidable challenge. Spain viewed the growing republic to the north as a threat, and had discouraged immigration from the United States. Spanish authorities were quite concerned that if too many Americans ventured across the border, while still maintaining close ties to their former country, the vast northern province might be lost. Texas was important not only because it added extensively to Spain's holdings in North America, but also it served as a buffer against hostile Indians and Americans.

The largely unsettled province was not working out well as a buffer, however. In August of 1812 a combined force of Americans and Mexican rebels, called the Republican Army of the North, had invaded Texas, determined to free the province from Spanish rule. Fulfilling Colonial Spain's worst fears, the force was recruited by Mexican radical Bernardo Gutierrez de Lara, and commanded by a former officer of the United States Army, Augustus Magee. The Tejano rebels were former followers of the executed priest and independence fighter Miguel Hidalgo y Costilla, and the Americans were adventurers and outlaws called filibusters by the Spanish and Mexican Royalists.

These revolutionaries were quite successful in their battles with the Spanish troops. Eventually they captured La Bahía, also known as Goliad, and San Antonio de Bexar, the provincial capital of Texas. Whether out of respect or fear or both, the rebels were treated fairly well by the Tejano citizens. In San Antonio de Bexar, the nearby mission-turned-fort called the Alamo became the revolutionaries' headquarters, and for the first time a rebel flag flew over its ramparts.

A Spanish counterforce, led by Maj. Gen. Joaquin Arredondo, spent the summer of 1813 retaking the province. On August 18 they met the main rebel force at the Battle of Medina. Several hundred of the rebels were killed outright, and many more were taken prisoner and brutally executed. Then the Royalist army inflicted a brutal retribution on the citizens of the San Antonio area for their kindness to the rebels. Many of the men were executed, many of the women violated.

In an ironic foreshadowing, there was a young Mexican officer in the Spanish service who was decorated for his actions in subjugating rebellious foreigners and Tejanos. He was nineteen years old, and his name was Antonio López de Santa Anna Perez de Lebron. He was called Lieutenant Santa Anna.

There was another attempt to "liberate" Texas, in 1818. A largely American force led by James Long captured Nacogdoches. The invaders were eventually defeated, and Long was executed in Mexico City. One of his youngest volunteers escaped, only to go on to a more noteworthy death at the Alamo. His name was Jim Bowie.

Eventually, Moses Austin convinced the Spaniards that if the right sort of Americans were brought in, they would be a help, not a danger. He proposed a settlement of hardworking, virtuous farmers and ranchers with families, who would take the oath of allegiance to Spain, accept the Roman Catholic faith, and serve as militia along with the presidial troops to keep the Comanches and other Indians at bay. Also, it would be in the colonists' best interests to help keep out less desirable Americans, who were a threat to the peace of their new country.

Once his proposal was accepted, Austin returned home to begin recruiting. Exhausted from his efforts, he took ill and died. Like his biblical namesake, he never saw the Promised Land settlements he had struggled to establish. That task fell to his son, Stephen.

Following his father's death, Stephen F. Austin journeyed to San Antonio de Bexar to make final preparations for the new colony. Hiring a *ranchero* from La Bahía named Manuel Becerra to guide him, Austin set out to select the land for his colony, traveling to the lower reaches of the Colorado and Brazos rivers. Austin dismissed Becerra from service and returned to La Bahía sooner than expected. In his journals Austin claimed that the *caballero* had become lost. However, Becerra had visited the area in question before, and in his journal he expressed concerns about the American's sincerity. In the end, Austin chose an area on the Brazos River about 15 miles inland from the Gulf Coast and 175 miles from San Antonio de Bexar to be used as the center of his colony. The town would be called San Felipe de Austin.

Despite a number of setbacks and challenges, the colony began to grow. Then, in March 1822, Austin decided to travel to San Antonio de Bexar to clear up some land title claims and report on the colony's progress to the governor. Shocking news awaited him there.

Arriving in San Antonio de Bexar, Austin found that the Mexicans had finally driven out the Spaniards and declared their independence. Austin's grants were nullified, and he would have to reapply to the new government in Mexico City. Disguised as a beggar in order to avoid the many *banditos* on the 1,200-mile trip, he journeyed south. In April he arrived in the revolution-convulsed capital city. There was still no constitution, no effective government, and no one to give Austin a straight answer regarding the fate of the proposed colony.

As in most revolutionary regimes, there were numerous groups and parties promoting their own agendas, and the frequent shifting of personal allegiances. The major split was between the Federalists and the Centralists. As their titles suggest, the Federalists tended to be more liberal, and wanted to invest most power in the old provinces, now called states. The Centralists were more conservative, and favored a strong central government. In May of 1822 the Centralists gained control and named Augustin Iturbide emperor of Mexico.

The following October, Iturbide shut down the Congress and established a military *junta* to govern Mexico. A colonization law was signed by Iturbide in January 1823, and Austin thought his troubles were coming to an end. Then Iturbide was thrown out. His laws, including the colonization law, were overturned, and Austin had to start all over again. It was not until April, a year after Austin's arrival, that the new Mexican Congress finally established a colonization policy.

Perhaps, though, the wait was worth it. According to the policy approved by the Mexican Congress, the average settler was to receive over 4,500 acres, and all land title claims were to be cleared. No taxes were to be assessed for six years, and there was to be no payment for the land, only a small charge for registering titles. Austin was given 100,000 acres for his own use and allowed to charge a minimal fee per acre to cover surveying and other costs. Austin was made the chief official of the colony with the title of civil commandant. As the founder of the colony he was also known as *empresario.* Only two of the old Spanish prerequisites to land ownership remained. Colonists had to become Mexican citizens, and at least nominal members of the Catholic church.

During Austin's seventeen-month absence, the colony had fallen on hard times, but the *empresario's*

FILIBUSTERS AND REVOLUTIONARIES: OTHER REVOLUTIONS IN TEXAS

In 1845 the United States *Magazine* and *Democratic Review* coined the term "Manifest Destiny" to describe the belief that it was God's will that the United States extend its borders from the Atlantic to the Pacific oceans. Although not defined until the mid-1840s, historians have long recognized that this belief was strong in the states many years before that date. As the slavery debate grew in intensity, both factions used the patriotic call to extend the country's boundaries to further their own social and political ends. This is reflected in the arguments that swept the country over involvement in Texas during both the Texas Revolution and the Mexican War. While many saw these wars as a crusade, some, including such noteworthy statesmen as Daniel Webster and the young Abraham Lincoln, condemned the activities as taking hostile advantage of a troubled neighboring country and an attempt to extend slavery.

A term originally used to describe West Indian pirates who preyed on South American shipping came to be used to describe these adventurers, especially the Americans, who became embroiled in the political quarrels in Central and South American countries, and used the unsettled conditions to their own advantage. These soldiers of fortune were called filibusters, from the Dutch *vrijbuiter,* or plunderer. Of course, one man's plundering and adventuring is another man's revolution, and many of the *Norteamericanos* who were involved in various uprisings in Texas called themselves anti-imperialist revolutionaries, while their enemies and critics called them filibusters.

One of the most fascinating aspects of Texas history before *the* Revolution is how many other revolutions there were, and how frequently Americans had been involved. Around the turn of the nineteenth century, Spanish authorities in Texas were outraged by the adventures of an American soldier of fortune who had basically been a horse thief until he met a grisly fate at the hands of the Spanish army. The thief was shot and his ears were cut off and presented to the governor of Texas. Now the American outlaw became, at least to some, a symbol of American virtue gone astray. So Philip Nolan became the inspiration, at least in part, for Edward Everett Hale's *The Man Without A Country.*

In 1813, and again in 1818, there were attempts to liberate Texas from Spanish rule that included Americans. Both revolts included participants who would later figure prominently in the story of the Alamo. In 1813 one of the junior officers of the Spanish Royalist Army was Santa Anna, and for a short time one of the Americans involved in the 1818 adventure was a young man from Louisiana named Jim Bowie.

The area of South Central Texas that included San Antonio de Bexar and Goliad seemed to attract the attention of those trying to bring about social change for better or for worse. The distance from other centers of military or political power gave the citizens of these places a sense of independence and self-reliance not all that different from the attitudes of the freedom-loving Americans, and the attraction of so much land so sparsely settled was a great draw to many from the ever more populous United States.

Although both these earlier rebellions ended in disaster for the rebels, they helped set the stage for the final battle over Texas. In the mix of Anglos and Hispanics they showed that, at least to some, there were considerations more important than race. And in their violence and eventual defeat of the rebels, they convinced more peace-loving or conservative Hispanics of the danger of opposing the existing government.

return revived it. After a failure in the first year, crops flourished, and families began to migrate to the growing colony. Soon Austin had the 300 families required by his contract, meeting his standards of diligence and morality. These families are still known in Texas as "The Old Three Hundred."

Life on the Texas frontier demanded constant work from almost everyone. For field animals and homemakers, this was tremendously taxing. But for those "bringing home the bacon," there was a unique benefit. Much of the diet was filled by wild game, and hunting was a frequent occupation. This led one woman to observe that Texas was "Hell for women and oxen, Heaven for men and dogs."

There were frequent raids by Indian tribes angered by what they saw as squatters on their lands. This led to the establishment of hard-riding "ranging companies" of mounted settlers, forerunners of the Texas Rangers. Yet, despite the hard work and the dangers, many pioneers felt they had found the Promised Land.

PART 2: CHANGE, CRISIS, CONFLICT

In 1825 changes meant to improve conditions led to crisis and, finally, conflict. New laws passed by the Federalists intended to give new power to the states, combined the adjoining states of Coahuila and Texas, and allowed the states to set their own immigration policies. The establishment of the state of Coahuila y Texas moved the capital to Saltillo, about 500 miles from San Felipe de Austin, and Texas was given only one seat in the state legislature. The change in immigration policies led to a massive influx of new immigrants and *empresarios,* the establishment of new colonies, and a drastic change in the demographics of Texas. By 1830, there were 16,000 Americans in Texas, about four times the Mexican population.

As often happens, there was bad along with the good. Although many of the immigrants to Texas were hardworking, industrious people looking for a fresh start, the type desired by the Austins, a number of them were only a few steps ahead of the law. "G.T.T." — Gone to Texas — was left on many a household door by those looking for a better life, but it was also used to note the flight of those with legal problems. It must be noted that most of the immigrants to Texas were not lawbreakers. They were hardworking, ambitious, and family-oriented people. But they were also strong-willed, independent, and took a dim view of any authority, especially that imposed by a "foreign" or "despotic" government.

The American settlers in Texas began to break into factions. One group, led by Austin, took their obligations to their adopted country seriously, and tended to be patient with the shifting policies and inefficiency of the young Mexican republic. Others were much less tolerant — of the Catholic church, of the frequent changes in government policy, and also of their more tolerant fellow colonists.

The increasing development and prosperity in the American colonies in Texas contrasted sharply with ongoing turmoil in Mexican political affairs. The Centralists and Federalists were constantly fighting for control, and each change in government meant a change in the laws for Texas.

In 1830 the Centralist government headed by Anastasio Bustamante ordered the military occupation of Texas, put an end to immigration from the United States, and imposed strict economic tariffs. While many Texians began contemplating violence, Austin continued negotiating with the authorities and gained some concessions. Meanwhile, in Mexico, Federalist opposition to Bustamente found a new champion in a military hero of incredible ambition — Antonio López de Santa Anna.

Santa Anna, who since the 1813 Arredondo Expedition had made a career serving as an officer in whatever army had the upper hand at any given moment, became a Mexican hero in 1829, when he drove off an attempted Spanish invasion. Spaniards had hoped to retake their New World colony, still wracked by the confusion and turmoil that frequently follow revolutions. Santa Anna's victory turned this somewhat known career officer into the self-proclaimed "Napoleon of the West."

The tensions between the new Texas settlements and the central government grew into open conflict in 1832. Ironically, the Mexican government official who caused this early crisis was a former American citizen who had been born in Virginia. Juan, or John, Davis Bradburn, had moved to Mexico years before as a filibuster and had become a career soldier in the Mexican army after the victory over Spain. As an officer of the Centralist government, Bradburn established a fort and customs house in the town of Anahuac, which served as the main port of entry for many vessels headed into the Texas colonies. He also imposed a number of new regulations, which he claimed were in keeping with his position and new laws from the Bustamente government. Opposition to Bradburn's decrees led to the arrest of two activist lawyers, the declaration of martial law, and eventually, gunfire. The Texians, inspired by one of the jailed lawyers, William Barret Travis, proclaimed themselves allies of the Federalist hero Santa Anna. A group of colonists en route to Anahuac to support the rebels there drove off a larger Mexican force, while crying *Viva Santa Anna!* In the end, Bradburn was recalled and peace was restored.

The jubilant Texians called a convention. Confident that Santa Anna would soon lead the Federalists to victory, the convention delegates requested statehood independent of Coahuila. They also asked that immigration from the United States once more be allowed.

Their requests never reached Mexico City. In January 1833, the Texians learned that Santa Anna —the hero of Tampico, the hope of the Federalists,

WHO WERE THE TEXIANS? WHO WERE THE TEJANOS? WAS IT TEJAS OR TEXAS?

A major source of concern for the Spanish government in Mexico was the unwillingness of their people to make the effort to move north across the desert and settle in the vast northern province of Tejas. One solution to this problem was the introduction of settlers from the Canary Islands, who were offered an opportunity to move up in the all important class structure in exchange for their willingness to move to the Texas frontier. Thus, the Hispanic settlers in Tejas were, in one sense, not really Mejicanos, but a breed apart, "Tejanos." Of course, as with all colonists, they spoke of their desire to be loyal citizens of both Tejas and Nuevo España. Their distance from Mexico City, and the general indifference of the central government to their needs, led many of the Tejanos to support their Anglo neighbors in the movement for an independent Tejas.

The Anglo settlers in what they called Texas were known both as "Texicans" and "Texians." Although some have claimed that as tensions between Texas and Mexico increased, there was a reluctance among Anglos to be called Texican because it sounded too much like Mexican, in fact the term continued in popular usage until around the time of the American Civil War. However, both earlier terms were replaced in popularity by the word "Texan" during the years of the Texas Republic.

the Napoleon of the West—had ousted Bustamente and was now president of Mexico. It seemed that, at last, the problems between Texas and Mexico would be resolved. In reality, they would soon explode into all-out war.

Following another convention, in April of 1833, Austin set off for Mexico City to meet Santa Anna and present the colonists' requests. He also carried a draft of a constitution for the new state. It was very closely patterned after the United States Constitution, as well as several state constitutions. It had been heavily influenced by a recent immigrant, Sam Houston. He had been one of the most promising young leaders in the United States, but had come to Texas seeking a new beginning following a failed marriage and political setbacks.

Treated coldly by the Mexican bureaucrats he first encountered, Austin eventually met with Santa Anna. Although the request for independent statehood was rejected, Santa Anna agreed to reopen Texas to immigration, and to several other smaller concessions. Believing once again that diplomacy had won out over violence, Austin headed back to San Felipe. He didn't make it.

During the period while he was being treated with contempt by the Mexican bureaucrats, and before his successful meeting with Santa Anna, Austin had written a controversial letter to the city council of San Antonio. Apparently composed in a fit of frustration, the letter instructed the colonists to go ahead and plan on separate statehood, no matter what happened with the negotiations in Mexico City. Conservative elements in the council saw to it that the letter was forwarded to Santa Anna.

The letter reached the president after Austin had already left Mexico City. Outraged, Santa Anna ordered Austin's arrest. The order was sent to Saltillo, capital of the state of Coahuila y Texas. Ever the diplomat, Austin stopped in Saltillo on his way home to pay his respects to the governor. He was immediately arrested.

PART 3: "WAR IS OUR ONLY RECOURSE . . ."

Austin was returned to Mexico City and placed in solitary confinement for three months. Moved into somewhat better quarters and allowed reading and writing supplies, he wrote to Texas and counseled caution. Still hoping for a peaceful settlement with Santa Anna, Austin advised his settlers and the other Texians to ignore the hotheads and hold no more conventions. He hoped that his imprisonment would prove to those who questioned his loyalty the sincerity of his commitment to Texas.

It was not difficult for the Texians to heed Austin's advice regarding slowing down their political activism. They had been battling a devastating cholera epidemic which had swept the colony. Those not inflicted with the deadly sickness were involved with tending those who had, or simply maintaining their livelihoods.

Jim Bowie, who had returned to Texas in 1828 and married into the Mexican aristocracy, had sent his wife to Monclova, where her parents had a summer home. The epidemic followed, and Ursula Veramendi Bowie and her parents all succumbed. According to many sources, the Bowies had two children who also died, but there is little firsthand documentation to support this story. In any case, Bowie found the only solace he could in a bottle.

Following the epidemic, it seemed as if problems might work out amiably. The relatively liberal government of Coahuila y Texas increased Texian representation in the legislature from one seat to three, eased immigration policies, made land ownership easier to achieve, and discussed other reforms.

Santa Anna, however, had other ideas. He was steadily enacting laws overturning the Constitution of 1824, and concentrating power in his own hands. To explain his change of heart from Federalist to Centralist, he would later write: ". . . I threw up my cap for liberty with great ardor, and perfect sincerity, but soon found the folly of it. A hundred years to come my people will not be fit for liberty. They do not know what it is, unenlightened as they are, and under the influence of a Catholic clergy, a despotism is the proper government for them, but there is no reason why it should not be a wise and virtuous one." (Huneycutt, 8)

Obviously, Santa Anna considered himself virtuous enough for the task. He must never have heard the cautionary words regarding absolute power. He also made plans to bring his most troublesome states under control. He ordered the Zacatecas militia disarmed and disbanded, and sent in the regular army to enforce his rule. When the state legislature objected, he ordered the capital sacked. Another army was sent to Coahuila y Texas under the command of Santa Anna's brother-in-law, Martín Perfecto de Cos.

The Federalist governor at Saltillo, and many of his supporters, tried to escape Cos but were arrested. In Texas, settlers divided into a Peace Party and a War Party, called the "War Dogs" by their opponents.

In late June 1835, settlers in San Felipe de Austin intercepted dispatches from Cos that solidified the War Party's influence among the Texians. Anahuac, newly garrisoned and with a hard-headed Centralist commander, was to be reinforced. The state government of Coahuila y Texas was to be replaced by martial law, with Cos in charge. And in case anyone objected to these changes, once Zacatecas was subjugated, Santa Anna planned to personally lead an expeditionary force into Texas to put down the opposition once and for all.

One of the most vocal War Party members, the former Santanista William Barret Travis, gathered a force of about twenty-five men and a small cannon and moved against Anahuac, hoping to take it before reinforcements arrived. Short of ammunition and with no artillery of any kind, the forty-five-man garrison surrendered. In keeping with European and American military tradition, the Mexican soldiers were given their parole. Agreeing not to fight again in Texas, the Mexicans were allowed to return home.

Instead of a hero's welcome, Travis returned home to censure in San Felipe de Austin. Both the governing council and Travis himself wrote apologies to Cos and sought to reestablish good relations. Cos demanded that the Texians turn over Travis as a rebel. Knowing this would almost ensure his execution, the Texians refused.

In August 1835, William Wharton called for another convention to be held in October. As a result of a general amnesty issued by the Mexican government, Stephen Austin was released and returned to Texas in early September. The *empresario* who had proudly called himself Don Esteban, and who had for so long advised negotiations and conciliation with the Mexican government, now proclaimed: "War is our only recourse. . . ." It was not long in coming.

BAKED-OVER DESERT OR GARDEN OF EDEN?

During the era of the *conquistadores,* the area north of the Rio Grande was regarded as a baked-over desert. When the northern deserts failed to be a source of gold and silver, serious colonization efforts came to a halt. By the beginning of the eighteenth century, the only communities of any size at all in Texas were San Antonio de Bexar, La Bahía del Espiritu Santo (later Goliad), and Nacogdoches.

With the heavy immigration that followed the establishment of the Austin colony, the Mexican government became curious about the attraction of the area it had written off for so long. In 1828 an expedition was sent into Texas to investigate. Commanded by Gen. Manuel de Mier y Teran, this expedition found that Anglos greatly outnumbered Tejanos, but that for the most part they had stayed close to the Gulf where they could raise sugar and cotton. Very few of them had ventured westward toward San Antonio de Bexar at that point.

Mier y Teran found cause for both optimism and fear in his report. On the one hand, the former wasteland had begun to flower, raising the possibility of increased prosperity for the home government. On the other hand, the tensions that would eventually lead to war were already appearing. In all, his report gave the Mexican government much to think about.

Six years later, on the eve of the Revolution, another Mexican officer made an exploratory visit of a different kind to Texas. Juan Almonte was sent to Texas in 1834, purportedly as a goodwill ambassador to hear the colonists' complaints and to return with their concerns to the central government. In fact, Almonte was analyzing the situation to prepare for a possible invasion, or at least further government intervention.

In his report to Santa Anna, Almonte, who hoped to be made governor of the state, recommended that the government begin a massive effort to increase Mexican settlements in Texas. He did not openly condemn the Anglo settlers, and in fact his report is full of evidence of their work and industry, but it is obvious that he did not believe that Mexico would keep Texas if it continued its policy of neglect.

In the end, neither report caused serious action on the part of the government. Tragically, following the loss of Texas and the internal strife caused by Santa Anna, Mier y Teran took his own life in despair. Following San Jacinto, Col. Juan Almonte was especially criticized by his captors because, remembering his 1834 visit, they had thought of him as a friend.

The fort at Anahuac, where William Barret Travis became the most celebrated member of the War Party and outraged both the Peace Party and the Centralists by his battle with Col. Juan Bradburn, the American-born Mexican officer.

Attempting to consolidate his resources, as well as keep the Texians in line, the commandant at San Antonio sent a force of dragoons to Gonzales to take back a cannon which had been given to the townspeople to keep the Indians away. The small bored gun, good for little more than starting horse races, mounted on a makeshift carriage with large wooden wheels, was guarded by 150 or so Texians. They flew a homemade flag imprinted with a picture of the cannon and the words *COME AND TAKE IT!* When the dragoons tried, the Texians opened fire. One soldier was killed, and the rest returned to San Antonio. It was October 2, 1835, the date of the Texas Revolution's "Battle of Lexington."

Soon Cos arrived in San Antonio, taking command of the 1,400 Mexican troops now gathered there. He also had a small garrison at Goliad. A week after driving the dragoons off from Gonzales, a small Texian force stole into Goliad during the night and captured the presidio and its garrison. Now more Mexican troops were headed home, agreeing never again to make war in Texas.

Goliad became the rallying point for Texians gathering under arms to oppose Santa Anna's rule. Despite his lack of military experience, Stephen Austin was elected commander of the all-volunteer Texian army. Without any real plan or immediate challenge, Texian volunteers came and went basically at will. Finally, it was decided to press the issue of Texas autonomy, and the army elected to march on San Antonio de Bexar.

CHAPTER TWO

The History of the Mission San Antonio de Valero

"In the southern part of Texas, in the town of San Antone,
There's a fortress all in ruins that the weeds have overgrown.
You may look in vain for crosses and you'll never find a one,
But sometimes between the setting and the rising of the sun,
You can hear a ghostly bugle as the men go marching by,
You can hear 'em as they answer to that roll call in the sky. . . ."

From "The Ballad of the Alamo"
A song in the John Wayne movie *The Alamo*
Lyrics by Paul Francis Webster

THE MISSION SAN ANTONIO de Valero was the first of five missions built along the San Antonio River to help secure Spain's claim to Texas and to Christianize the local Indians.

On April 13, 1709, on the feast of Saint Anthony, an expedition of Franciscan missionaries under Father Antonio de Olivares encamped near the banks of a shallow river. After celebrating a Mass on the site, they named the river the San Antonio de Padua. Impressed with the potential of this area, Father Olivares petitioned the viceroy of Mexico, the Marques de Valero, for permission to establish a mission there.

This petition was not only approved but was also expanded upon. Actual settlement, however, was not begun until 1718. The mission, named San Antonio de Valero, was founded on May 1. It consolidated several earlier missions in the region. A town and a military garrison, or presidio, were also established nearby, and they became known as San Antonio de Bexar.

These three settlements (the mission, the town, and the presidio) together were known as San Antonio de las Llanos, or San Antonio of the Plains. The settlement was a cooperative venture of the Spanish government and the Catholic church. The mission, run by Franciscan priests under Father Olivares, was originally located on the west side of the river but was moved to the east side and a little farther south in the summer of 1719. The mission San Antonio de Valero was named in honor of the Marques de Valero, the viceroy of Mexico, and the village was named after the viceroy's brother, the duke of Bexar.

In 1724 a hurricane destroyed much of the mission complex, and before being rebuilt, it was moved a short distance to its present location. By 1727, the mission was serving 273 resident Indians. Quarters for the Indians, an irrigation system, and a two-story *convento* were completed. The second story of the *convento* served as quarters for the missionaries, while the ground level contained a kitchen and dining room, offices, and a guest house. This *convento* eventually became the "long barracks" where much of the fiercest fighting took place during the final Battle of the Alamo.

On March 9, 1731, sixteen families from the Canary Islands came to settle in Bexar. These settlers were Spanish citizens, and had all the rights and privileges of Spanish landowners. They and their descendants became some of the most influential citizens in Bexar's history.

A stone church was begun at the mission in the spring of 1744. Unfortunately, the skills of the workmen and the quality of the materials were not adequate, and part of the structure collapsed before the church was completed.

The current chapel building dates from 1758,

and is a very formidable structure. The walls are forty-three to forty-eight inches thick. The *convento* has similar walls thirty-two to thirty-eight inches thick. The construction was carried out by the mission Indians, under the direction of Spanish army engineers. The chapel was never fully completed, however. In 1793 hard times and the lack of success of the mission program forced the abandonment of San Antonio de Valero. The mission was secularized on April 12, and shortly thereafter most of the surrounding farmlands were given over to the resident Indians.

On December 29, 1802, a presidial cavalry unit arrived at the old mission. It was called the Segunda Compania Volante de San Carlos de Parras, or the Second Flying Company of San Carlos de Parras. The company was raised in the village of Alamo de Parras, west of Saltillo, the capital of Coahuila. The mission eventually became known as Pueblo del Alamo, in honor of this unit that was stationed there. In 1805 a military hospital was established, possibly in the southern part of the *convento,* and the presidial cavalry continued to garrison the Alamo until 1825.

In 1829 more than 300 people were living on the east side of the river, in and around the Alamo. That year, José Juan Sanchez Estrada, chief engineer of the Mexican army, drew an interesting sketch of the Alamo. His sketch shows the chapel in far better condition than it would be seven years later, during the Siege of 1836. The chapel has a much higher front wall, and one bell tower is still intact. The sketch also shows a wooden peaked roof over a portion of the west wall, and the famous pecan tree that survived the siege is near the northwest corner. Estrada's sketch is very interesting, but may not be completely accurate. It is possible that he used a bit of "artistic license" in his composition of the scene.

The Alamo gained its greatest fame during the Texas Revolution of 1835-36. By that time, San Antonio de Bexar had become the largest city in Texas, with a population of 2,500 people. In the fall of 1835, Gen. Martín Perfecto de Cos improved the Alamo's fortifications prior to the Battle of Bexar. Cos' men built the artillery ramps up to the rear wall of the chapel, and also built the wooden palisade between the chapel and the low barracks that has become known as "Crockett's Wall." When Cos surrendered in December, the Alamo was taken over by the Texians, whose occupation continued until the famous siege of February and March 1836. Under the direction of Engineer Green B. Jameson, the defenders continued to strengthen the fortifications. After the Alamo's fall, the Mexicans destroyed nearly all that remained of these efforts.

In 1842, when Texas was a sovereign republic, the Catholic church petitioned for the return of the Alamo property. The petition was granted, but the church could not raise the money to repair the mission.

After the Mexican War, the U.S. Army leased the chapel from the Catholic church for use as a quartermaster depot. Under the army's supervision, the chapel was repaired, and the two second-story windows and the famous hump were added.

With the outbreak of the Civil War in 1861, the chapel became the armory for a local militia unit called the Alamo City Guards. At one point during the war, Confederate Gen. James Longstreet used the chapel as his headquarters. In 1865 the chapel reverted back to the U.S. government, and it again served as a quartermaster depot until the facilities were moved to the new Quadrangle at Fort Sam Houston in 1876.

That year, a French-born San Antonio businessman, Honore Grenet, purchased the *convento,* or long barracks, from the Catholic church, and turned it into a massive dry goods store. The chapel was purchased from the church by the State of Texas in 1883 for $20,000, and was temporarily turned over to the city pending legislation on how to handle it.

The long barracks were sold to the Hugo Schmeltzer Company after Grenet's death, and they retained title until the early 1900s. Fearing another private sale, a patriotic group known as the Daughters of the Republic of Texas (DRT) started a fundraising campaign to purchase the long barracks. When the fund drive fell far short of the $75,000 asking price, Clara Driscoll, the twenty-two-year-old daughter of a wealthy rancher, put in more than $65,000 of her own money to insure that the deal would not fall through. After successfully purchasing the building, Driscoll and the DRT deeded the long barracks building to the State of Texas. The State eventually reimbursed Driscoll.

The second floor of the long barracks building was removed in the early 1900s. In 1905 the State of Texas named the Daughters of the Republic of Texas as custodians of what remained of the Alamo, the chapel, and the long barracks. The "Daughters" were to manage and maintain these buildings without cost to the State. That arrangement is still in effect today. The Daughters have been able to successfully meet their obligations without ever having to charge visitors an admission fee to the Alamo!

The Alamo today consists of the two remaining original buildings, the chapel and the long barracks. The grounds consist of about 4.2 beautifully landscaped acres, which also contain a fine gift shop (1936) and the Daughters of the Republic of Texas Research Library (1950). The long barracks building was restored in 1968, and now serves as a museum.

By the 1870s, the area in front of the chapel that originally made up most of the Alamo compound had become a city plaza, which it remains to this day. In 1939 a large "cenotaph" monument, by noted sculptor Pompeo Coppini, was dedicated on the plaza.

Currently, a number of proposals to restore and preserve the Alamo are being considered. Proposals range from merely restoring the existing structures to reconstructing the entire Alamo compound. As of this writing, a specific plan has not been adopted. Museum exhibits are to be updated and expanded as a part of this renovation, and artist/historian Gary Zaboly has been commissioned to paint several large scenes depicting the history of the Alamo.

The Alamo during the battle

San Antonio de Valero mission. The Alamo

Above: *THE CHAPEL IN 1836. During the Siege of 1836, we know that the roofline of the chapel was nearly level, and that the roof itself had collapsed. Cos' men used the roofing material as fill when they built an earthen artillery ramp up to the rear wall of the chapel during the Mexican occupation of the Alamo.*

The treatment of the main entrance to the chapel in this view is speculative. It is very possible that the ornate wooden doors were removed by scavengers long before 1836. We do know that the chapel and the barracks buildings were to be the Texians' last line of defense. Therefore, it is also possible that the main chapel entrance was filled wlth rubble, sandbags, or perhaps a crude barricade fashioned from stretched cowhides filled with earth in order to make the position more defensible.

Left: *A THEORETICAL VIEW OF THE FINISHED CHAPEL. A view of what the front of the chapel might have looked like if it had been completed, based on typical Spanish mission design. While we do not know for sure how far the construction progressed, an 1829 drawing by Mexican Army Engineer José Juan Sanchez Estrada clearly shows a bell tower on the right side of the front of the church.*

The Alamo Today
ie: Post U.S. Army Use.

THE MODERN CHAPEL

When the U.S. Army leased the chapel for a supply depot in the 1840s, their repairs included the addition of the two upper windows, and also the unique "hump" across the front. Not everyone appreciated these improvements. Sgt. Edward Everett was an English-born member of the Quincy Riflemen, a volunteer American unit that was federalized for the war with Mexico. An accomplished artist, Everett was ordered to make sketches of buildings and places of interest. He made several sketches of the ruins of the Alamo, and also participated in the repair work there in the spring of 1847. Of the hump, he later wrote, "I regret to see by a late engraving of this ruin, tasteless hands have evened off the rough walls . . . surmounting them with a ridiculous scroll, giving the building the appearance of the headboard of a bedstead." (Sandweiss, 134) This is essentially the look of the Alamo chapel today.

CHAPTER THREE

The Army of the Provisional Government of Texas

AS WITH MANY REVOLUTIONARY armies, the Army of the Provisional Government of Texas is a little difficult to categorize. Anyone with the money or charisma to recruit a unit could become an officer of volunteers. Adding to the confusion in Texas was the large influx of units and individual volunteers from the United States.

The very names of the units coming into Texas show the influence of the Old South. Among these volunteer companies were the Kentucky Mustangs, the Alabama Red Rovers, the Tennessee Mounted Volunteers, the Mobile Greys, and two companies of New Orleans Greys. It would be a mistake to see the Texian army as being exclusively made up of former U.S. southerners, however. The volunteer units from the United States, especially the New Orleans Greys, included a number of immigrants and international adventure seekers. Also, a fair number of Texians had emigrated from places other than the American South. And during the "Runaway Scrape," Houston's army was augmented by deserters from the U.S. Army, many of whom also were immigrants.

In addition, many Tejanos were opposed to Santa Anna's Centralist policies. In fact, recent demographic studies suggest that as many as one in three adult male Tejanos may have joined the Texian army. Considering that other studies show that the Anglo/Texian settlers joined the army at a rate of one in seven, statistically a case can be made that the Tejanos were more actively opposed to Santa Anna than the Texians. Demographics have to be used cautiously, however. The last census before the Revolution was in 1830, and there were many immigrants after that time. Of course, many of these also became part of the Revolutionary Army, but the contributions of the Tejanos to Texas independence cannot be ignored or slighted.

There was no uniform as such for the Texas Army, regular or volunteer. A few officers had privately produced uniforms, but it is even questionable how much these were used. Travis had ordered a uniform from a tailor before he left for San Antonio de Bexar, but there is little chance it reached him before the siege.

Travis thought the infantry should be armed as in a regular army, with muskets. Then again, for a volunteer force, he decided rifles would be better, especially the flank companies. Travis was more specific about his corps of choice—the cavalry. He felt that a cavalry force was essential for their scouting and harassment abilities. He felt they should be armed with broadswords, pistols, and double-barreled shotguns or jaeger rifles.

One Texian volunteer, Noah Smithwick, wrote this classic description of the Volunteer Army en route from Goliad to San Antonio in the fall of 1835:

> Words are inadequate to convey an impression of the appearance of the first Texas army as it formed in marching order. Nothing short of ocular demonstration could do it justice. . . . Buckskin breeches were the nearest approach to uniform and there was wide diversity even there, some of them being new and soft and yellow, while others, from long familiarity with rain and grease and dirt, had become hard and black and shiny . . . shins (were) as guiltless of socks as a Kansas Senator's. Boots being an unknown quantity, some wore shoes and some moccasins. Here a broad brimmed sombrero overshadowed the military cap at its side; there, a tall "beegum" rode familiarly beside a coonskin cap, with the tail hanging down behind, as all well regulated tails should do . . . here a bulky roll of bed quilts jostled a pair of "store" blankets; there the shaggy brown buffalo robe contrasted with a gaily colored checkered counterpane on which the manufacturer had lavished all the skill of dye and weave known to art . . . in lieu of a canteen, each man carried a Spanish gourd. . . . Here a big American horse loomed above the nimble Spanish pony, there a half-broke mustang pranced beside a sober methodical mule. A fantastic military array to a casual observer, but the one great purpose animating every heart clothed us in a uniform more perfect in our eyes than was ever donned by regulars on dress parade.

As the Siege of Bexar progressed, the volunteer units from the United States began to arrive, and at least some of the units had a somewhat uniform appearance. The Alabama Red Rovers, who became part of the garrison of Fort Defiance at Goliad, were "uniformed" in matching red hunting shirts.

It has long been thought that the New Orleans and Mobile Greys took their name from U.S. Army fatigue uniforms obtained, along with much of their gear, from arsenals and armories in their respective cities of origin. However, recent research indicates this may not be the case. New translations of the classic account *Texas Und Seine Revolution* by German adventurer and New Orleans Grey Herman Ehrenberg suggest that the New Orleans Greys wore matching, but not military, suits of clothing suited for hard use on the Texas plains. According to reenactor and historian Ed Miller, who has undertaken one of the recent translations, and whose research has been published in *Military Collector and Historian*, the New Orleans Greys most likely wore matching gray roundabout jackets of a durable cloth popularly called "fustian" in the 1830s. Matching gray trousers were also worn. This new research will almost certainly be challenged, but for now offers an intriguing new angle on this famous unit.

As far as is now known, the Mobile Greys did obtain fatigue uniforms from U.S. arsenals. These were most likely supplemented with equipment from private sources, as well as militia stores. Except for some of the Greys, there were probably no uniformed soldiers on the Texian side at the Alamo. By the time of the siege, the Greys' uniforms were most likely very worn, and much of their gear had probably been replaced.

The Army of the Provisional Government of Texas was basically divided into three divisions: the Regular Army, the Permanent Volunteers, and the Volunteer Auxiliary Corps.

The Regular Army was made up of those willing to make a commitment beyond the War for Independence and be subject to regular army discipline and chain of command. The period of enlistment was two years.

The Permanent Volunteers were enlisted for the duration of the war. They were allowed to elect their own officers, which occasionally led to problems. Many of them were citizens of Texas before hostilities began, both Tejano and Texian, although some were recent emigrants from the United States.

Finally, there was the Volunteer Auxiliary Corps, who were enlisted for six months, and were almost entirely made up of recent emigrants and units from the United States. On occasion, soldiers were originally enlisted in the Volunteer Auxiliary Corps and then transferred to the Permanent Volunteers. This was the case with the New Orleans Greys.

In addition to the formally established branches of the army, there were hastily formed militia units drawn from established settlers, such as the Gonzales Ranging Company of Mounted Volunteers, which had no official status but which served with distinction nonetheless.

Although they played no part in the defense of the Alamo, there was one other major military force in Texas—the famous Texas Rangers. From the earliest days of the Anglo-American colonies in Texas, Austin had encouraged the establishment of ranger companies to combat the threat from the Comanches and other hostile Indian tribes. With the coming of the revolution, this informal idea began to take more formal shape.

In the fall of 1835 the Provisional Government passed a resolution to raise a Ranging Company of Riflemen. A law passed on November 24, 1835, authorized the raising of three companies of fifty-six men each. Every company would be led by a captain, a first lieutenant, and a second lieutenant. The corps would be commanded by a major. Robert "Three-Legged Willie" Williamson was named to that position. The Rangers were to be paid $1.25 per day, and were expected to be ready to ride as needed with full field gear and a hundred rounds of ammunition.

At the Alamo there were two companies of regular cavalry, plus the senior officer of the cavalry branch, Lieutenant Colonel Travis. There was also a regular officer of artillery, Capt. Almeron Dickinson. The Permanent Volunteers were represented by Bowie's Company, Carey's Artillery Company, and the San Antonio Greys, members of the New Orleans Greys who did not go on the ill-fated Matamoros expedition. The Tennessee Mounted Volunteers were part of the Volunteer Auxiliary Corps, and the Gonzales Ranging Company was part of the militia.

Houston's plan for the organization and pay of the army was as follows:

Platoon
28 Rank & File @ $8.00/mo.
2 Sergeants @ $11.00/mo.
2 Corporals @ $10.00/mo.

Company
2 Platoons
1 Captain
1 First Lieutenant
1 Second Lieutenant
2 Musicians

Battalion
5 Companies

Regiment
2 Battalions
1 Colonel
1 Lieutenant Colonel
1 Major

Officers and Staff Noncoms to be the same as in the U.S. Regular Army. (Chariton, *100 Days*, 71)

Noah Smithwick writes of sombreros and "bee-gums" (top hats) going side by side with military hats and coonskin caps. Here a Texian with a sombrero and plains rifle stands beside a Scottish immigrant with a top hat. Note the Scot's dirk and powder flask with the Cross of St. Andrew. There was an entire colony of Irish immigrants in Texas, and the Irish, Scots, and Scots-Irish were one of the largest ethnic groups in the American South and Texas.

Top left: *Smithwick's sombreros and coonskin caps again appear in this group of Texian volunteers. All are armed with rifles, knives and hunting gear, and two are wearing moccasins — another item mentioned by Smithwick. Note the patched trousers two of the men are wearing. After several months of service on the Texas frontier many of the volunteers from the United States were suffering from no blankets and clothing that was thin and worn.*

Top right: *Several of the "Tennessee Mounted Volunteers" take a respite by their posts at "Crockett's Palisade." The figure in the foreground wears a civilian-style military cap, and is armed with a shotgun. Note the tomahawks stuck in the palisade for later use as hand-to-hand weapons.*

Bottom right: *Following the departure of many of the New Orleans Greys for Matamoros, those who stayed behind renamed themselves the "San Antonio Greys." Recent research suggests that the clothing and equipment of the Greys may not have been as "military" as this figure suggests. However, this is an accurate depiction of what many historians believed for a long time the Greys looked like. This is just one of the many mysteries of the Alamo, some of which are solved by new discoveries, and some of which, as in this case, are created.*

Many people do not realize the great contribution made by the Tejanos to the cause of Texas' independence. In opposing Santa Anna's tyranny, they turned against their mother country, and their efforts were often ignored by later settlers in Texas. These Tejano defenders, most likely members of Seguin's scouting company, are shown at the south gate. The lunette can be seen in the background.

James Butler Bonham came to Texas with the Mobile Greys. Although he became a commissioned officer in the Texas Regular Army, he may have had a Greys' uniform, and been the most military looking officer in the Alamo. One of the most famous couriers in history, he learned that there would be no reinforcements for the garrison, and returned to share their fate anyway.

CHAPTER FOUR

The Mexican Army of 1836

Information about the Mexican army of the early nineteenth century is often incomplete, and at times, contradictory. As Joseph Hefter, one of the leading historians of the Mexican army, notes in his classic work *El Soldado Mexicano:*

> *"Troops frequently had to be raised by arbitrary methods, organized and equipped in a hurry without funds, under trying conditions of procurement and supply. Systematic records were seldom kept and repeatedly lost or destroyed. As late as 1851, the Army General Staff noted that '. . . the premises of the General Headquarters Secretariat being occupied by U.S. forces, its archives suffered general confusion . . . all files were found mixed up and mutilated; as a result there are mistakes in the decrees . . .' Solid documentary and pictorial evidence is still too scarce and fragmentary for this period."*
>
> (Hefter: *El Soldado Mexicano,* 50)

IN THIS OVERVIEW, WE shall attempt to describe the structure and character of the Mexican army based on the most reliable information available, with full acknowledgement that there is still much to be learned.

The Mexican army of 1836 was fashioned on European models, especially on the armies of Spain and Napoleonic France. In many respects, however, the Mexican army was more impressive on paper than it was in reality. It had undergone reorganization almost as often as the Mexican government changed. Uniform and equipment regulations underwent frequent revision, but in reality things were usually used until worn out. Several different versions of the same item could be in use in the same unit at any given time.

Besides being understrength, the Mexican army suffered from problems of organization, leadership, and supply. The Military Health Corps, or medical department, was practically nonexistent. Skilled personnel such as chaplains and gunsmiths were also in short supply.

While some battalions were made up of well-trained, experienced veterans, others consisted of raw recruits, often drawn from the lowest elements of society, or from the country's jails. The Yucatan Battalion was made up of Mayan Indians who had never been away from their home province, and most of them could not even speak the Spanish language.

In 1835 the Mexican army probably consisted of less than 2,000 effective troops. There was no standardization of weapons, and training was based primarily on outmoded Spanish manuals. Discipline was often very lax.

Volunteers in the Mexican army served for eight years, while conscripts were forced to serve for ten. Pay for a private in 1835 was nineteen pesos, four reals, and nine granos per month, which amounted to about twelve and a half cents per day. Most of the soldiers were from five foot to five foot six inches in height. By these standards, Santa Anna was quite tall at five feet ten inches.

Native Mexicans made up less than one-third of the field grade officers. There were many European mercenaries in the officer corps, possessing varying degrees of talent and dedication. Native officers with Indian blood were frequently discriminated against.

When Santa Anna came into power, he created a national standing army modeled after Napoleon's Grand Army. Its main purpose was to protect him from opposition from within Mexico. Santa Anna also took steps to dissolve the local militia, whose loyalty was sometimes less than certain.

Santa Anna fancied himself as "The Napoleon of the West," or as some contemporary accounts noted, "The Napoleon of the South." Gen. Vicente Filisola, an Italian who served as second-in-command of the Army of Operations in Texas, remarked that Santa Anna would not even listen to any ideas that were contrary to Napoleonic thinking. Other officers voiced similar sentiments.

In 1835 there was a massive buildup of the Mexican army in preparation for the campaign against Texas. Over 6,000 recruits were raised, but much of the "recruiting" was actually conscription. Military training was also updated during this period. Techniques were based largely on Napoleonic tactics.

After twenty-five years of civil wars, the treasury of the Mexican War Ministry was broke. Money had to be borrowed, and interest on the loans for Santa Anna's campaign ran as high as 48%. Corruption was rampant within the Mexican government, and many of the supplies destined for the army never reached it. The poor common soldiers were often left to fend for themselves on their meager wages. Ramon Caro, Santa Anna's secretary, wrote that the general ordered "that the troops should be placed on half rations of hard-tack and that each man be allowed one real a day. The officers were to provide themselves with their necessary supplies out of their regular pay, without receiving an extra campaign allowance." (Castaneda, 102)

The army consisted of both regular units *(permanente)* and active militia *(activo* or national guard). Due to their long service on active duty, many of the militia units were as experienced as the regulars.

INFANTRY UNITS

In December 1835, Mexican infantry units were reorganized into *"tercios,"* or battalions, named after leaders of the 1810-1821 War of Independence. The terms battalion and regiment were interchangeable.

The ten active infantry battalions were:

1. Hidalgo; formed from the old 1st and 2nd Battalions
2. Allende (Allendez); from the old 3rd Battalion
3. Morelos (Morelas); from the old 4th Battalion
4. Guerrero; from the old 5th Battalion
5. Aldama; from the old 6th Battalion
6. Jiminez; from the old 7th and 12th Battalions
7. Landero; from the old 8th and 9th Battalions
8. Matamoros; from the old 10th Battalion
9. Abasolo; from the old 11th Battalion
10. Galeana; from the old 13th Battalion

Each infantry battalion consisted of eight companies. There were six companies of fusiliers, which were the line companies. There were also two elite or "preference" companies per battalion. Enjoying higher pay and status than the line companies, these were the grenadier *(grenaderos)* and the light infantry (*chasseurs* or *cazadores*) companies. During the Texas Campaign, the light infantry companies were armed with British Baker Rifles rather than the smoothbore India Pattern Brown Bess Muskets used by most other troops.

In addition to the ten active infantry battalions, there were also eight "standing companies":

1. Acapulco
2. San Blas
3. Tampico
4. 1st Bacalar
5. 2nd Bacalar
6. Carmen Island
7. 1st Tabasco
8. 2nd Tabasco

There was also one sharpshooter company, which was issued better weapons and received grenadiers' pay.

When the Army of Operations in Texas mustered at San Luis Potosi, the average battalion strength was 344 men. Company strength was supposed to be four officers, twelve NCOs, three other ranks, and eighty privates. During the Texas Campaign, there were often considerably fewer men, perhaps as low as thirty-two to forty-two per company. (Young: "Understanding the Mexican Army," 1)

CAVALRY UNITS

The cavalry was also made up of regular *(permanente)* and militia *(activo)* regiments. It was reorganized in December 1835, and the regular units were named after battlefields of the Revolution.

The regular cavalry regiments were:

1. Dolores; from the old 3rd and 6th Regiments
2. Igula (Iguala); from the old 4th and 10th Regiments
3. Palmar (Palamar); from the old 2nd, 7th, and Mexico Regiments
4. Cuautla
5. Veracruz
6. Tampico

There were also two "independent" regular cavalry units:

1. Yucatan
2. Tabasco

Each cavalry regiment was made up of four squadrons of two companies each.

OTHER UNITS

A squad of pioneers was attached to each regimental headquarters. Pioneers were essentially combat engineers. They cleared roads, prepared campsites, and built fortifications and siegeworks.

The Zapadores were an elite, highly trained engineering unit, but only 185 strong.

Artillerymen were also considered specialists, but they were deployed throughout the army rather than concentrated in large units.

"Presidial companies" were mounted units that garrisoned frontier posts. During the Texas Revolution, most stayed loyal to Mexico, but some sided with the Texians.

SPANIARDS AND MEXICANS: RACE AND CLASS IN MEXICO

Critics of the Texas Revolution point to the Texians' reliance on slavery, but frequently ignore the class system in Mexico and its all too similar effect on human rights.

During the colonial period, the highest place in society was held by those who were born in Spain, called *peninsulares.* Regardless of ability or talent, the *peninsulares* held the top positions in society, in the military, and in the church. The power of this class is shown by the fact that many women set sail for Spain when they found out they were pregnant, so that their children could be born in Spain and be part of this class. Imagine combining the trials of pregnancy with those of eighteenth- and nineteenth-century ocean travel!

Next in line were the *criollos,* those of pure Spanish blood but who had been born in Mexico. They held lesser posts. Many of them were well-to-do ranchers, farmers, and businessmen, but as long as Mexico was a part of Spain's empire, they were second-class citizens. After independence, however, many of them joined with the former *peninsulares* to protect the status quo.

The *mestizos* were of mixed European and Indian ancestry, and mostly made up the trades and working middle class. A few amassed decent fortunes, and some found a home in the lower echelons of the church and state.

The lowest rung of the social ladder was occupied by the Indios, the Indians who made up the majority of the Mexican population. They were basically field hands for the large farms, laborers in the silver mines, and cannon fodder for the army. The fact that slavery was outlawed in Mexico would have been news to the Indios who were serving out legal ninety-nine-year indentures, or who had been forced into military service.

Those in the ranks of the army who were not Indios were mostly peon conscripts and convicts. Very few enlisted men entered the army voluntarily. As one army recruiter wrote: "Here are 300 volunteers. I will send you 300 more if you return the chains." (Nofi, 194)

Interestingly, the first Anglo settlers had little trouble fitting in with Mexican society, at least as it existed in Texas. "Ample evidence points to an early accommodation between old and new elites. Although initially outside this Spanish-Mexican structure, the Anglo-Saxon pioneers were accepted—depending on their class, of course—as equals by the 'Spanish' elite. By 1842, however, only six years after independence, the peaceful accommodation that had characterized Mexican-Anglo relations collapsed. The loss of land, the flight of the Mexican elite, and the Mexican War a few years later quickly eroded the influence of Mexicans." (Montejano, 35)

Top left: *TYPICAL MEXICAN INFANTRYMEN. Mexican army uniforms were influenced by European styles, especially French and Spanish. A mixture of surplus English and French weapons and equipment was used. The uniforms, weapons, and equipment of both sides will be covered in more detail in Chapter Fifteen.*

Top right: *When on the march, Mexican soldiers commonly wore less expensive and more comfortable white fatigue uniforms, such as the soldier on the left is wearing. The canvas gaiters are somewhat speculative, but they were common issue in European armies for both dress and field use. It is known that the Mexicans wore them for parade, and it is possible they were worn on campaign as well.*

When on the march in fatigue dress, a white canvas cover was often used to protect the cowhide shako. Mexican soldiers also were issued cloth fatigue caps, such as the one on the figure on the left.

Lower left: *A TYPICAL MEXICAN CAVALRYMAN. Mexicans were known as fine horsemen, and their cavalry was a formidable foe. They were armed with swords, eight foot lances, and British Paget Carbines.*

A MEXICAN ARTILLERYMAN. As in other armies, the Mexican artillery was a specialized service. Artillerymen had to be more skilled than common foot soldiers, and thus enjoyed a more elite status.

RECRUIT, YUCATAN BATTALION. The Yucatan Battalion was one of the least experienced of the Mexican units that participated in the Texas Campaign. Composed mainly of Mayan Indians, many of its members could not even speak the Spanish language. Used to the warm climate of the Yucatan Peninsula, the battalion suffered terribly in the cold winter weather encountered on the march to San Antonio de Bexar.

This recruit wears a white fatigue uniform that shows the effects of the march. His shako is strapped to his pack, and he wears a non-issue straw hat. He is armed with an India Pattern Brown Bess Musket with bayonet, and a personally owned machete.

CHAPTER FIVE

Prelude to the Alamo

PART 1: THE SIEGE OF BEXAR

"'All has been lost save honor!' I do not remember . . . what French king said this. . . . Bexar, and perhaps Texas has been lost. . . . We were surrounded by some gross, proud, and victorious men. . . ."

Lt. Col. José Juan Sanchez Navarro
(Chariton: *100 Days*, 22)

CONFIDENT OF AN EASY victory, the Texian army made its way toward San Antonio. Approximately 300 men, flying the Gonzales flag, and led by their newly elected general, Stephen Austin, marched toward the state capital. Among the leadership were William Wharton, Ben Milam, William Barret Travis, and James Bowie.

On October 27 a reconnaissance force of about ninety men was sent out by Austin to find a base of operations for the Texian army. Led by Bowie and James Fannin, the detachment scouted several of the missions along the San Antonio River. After scouting the abandoned missions of San Juan and San José, the Texians set up camp for the night at Mission Concepción, about two miles from San Antonio. The area outside the mission offered a natural defensive position in the form of a gully that dropped between six and ten feet to the river. The following morning a sentry was surprised by a Mexican cavalryman riding out of a fog that was so thick it had hidden the advance of a force of between 250 and 400 Mexican infantry and cavalry, supported by a four-pound cannon. As the fog cleared, the infantry began a steady advance across the open ground to the Texians' front, maintaining an almost constant fire. Using the gully for cover, firing from the edge and then falling back to reload, Bowie's men withstood several charges. Finally, the Mexican troops began to withdraw, leaving the four-pounder to the Texians. The Mexicans lost approximately sixty men killed; the Texians lost one. A little over an hour later, the main body of the Texas Army arrived. In their shared official report on the battle, Bowie and Fannin only regretted that the army could not have arrived sooner, cutting off the Mexican retreat and making the capture of Bexar much easier.

Following the victory at Mission Concepción, the Texian army established a position just outside of San Antonio de Bexar and a council of war was held. Faced with a choice of trying to storm the city and the Alamo, or just laying siege, the leaders of the army chose to try to starve out the Mexican garrison. This decision was prompted by the Texians' lack of artillery, coupled with the Mexicans' strategy of fortifying the several plazas in San Antonio de Bexar.

While the military activities of the conflict slowed, the political action heated up. Prior to leaving for San Antonio de Bexar, Austin had called for a Consultation to convene at San Felipe de Austin in early November. Now the time approached for the Convention, and many of the Texian leaders were with the army near San Antonio de Bexar.

Shortly after the start of the siege, Sam Houston arrived. Austin offered him command of the volunteer army, but Houston declined. He was more interested in convincing those members of the Consultation who were serving with the army that they must join the other delegates in San Felipe de Austin. Although some thought that the delegates should stay with the siege, a compromise was reached that allowed rank and file delegates and line officers to attend the Consultation while staff officers stayed with the army. Houston and Bowie were among those who left. Austin, Wharton, and Travis all stayed behind.

The Consultation, which convened on November 3, 1835, called for three delegates from every municipality in Texas. Since he could not personally take part in the Consultation, Austin sent along a statement that called upon the Convention to strictly adhere to the dictates of the Constitution of 1824, and asking the Consultation to issue a declaration explaining that the Texians were taking up arms not to gain independence from Mexico, or union with the United States, but rather to defend their rights as Mexican citizens under the Constitution of 1824 which Santa Anna had revoked. Many of the delegates were committed to independence, however. The main question to be decided at the Consultation was whether Texas should remain united with Mexico and continue to support the Constitution of 1824, or if independence should be declared. Not surprisingly, the War Party called for independence, while the Peace Party stood for continued adherence to the Mexican Constitution, yet seeking independent statehood for Texas. Perhaps the most significant speech was given by Houston, believed by many to be part of the War Party. Houston called for remaining in the Mexican Republic, reasoning that to declare independence would alienate Federalists in other parts of Mexico and throughout Texas who might otherwise support the rebels in their conflict with Santa Anna.

Following Houston's lead, the Consultation issued a declaration on November 7 that stated: "The people of Texas, availing themselves of their natural rights, solemnly declare that they have taken up arms in defense of their rights and liberties which were threatened by the encroachments of military despots and in defense of the Republican principles of the federal constitution of Mexico of 1824." (Boyd, 30) The Consultation also set up a provisional state government consisting of a president and a general council, which would include one representative from each municipality in Texas. Henry Smith, a member of the War Party from Velasco, was elected president.

Houston, who had spent much of his political career dealing with the Cherokees and other Indian nations, was made part of the Select Committee on Indian Affairs. The Texians knew that if the tribes were to join the Mexicans against the Texians, there was virtually no hope for victory. The Consultation also appointed Houston commander-in-chief of the Provisional Army of Texas. This appointment gave Houston no authority over the volunteer forces already in the field, however. He was to raise an army of 2,500 from scratch. These regulars were to serve for two years and be paid in land grants.

Knowing how important support from the United States was, the Consultation commissioned Stephen Austin to go there to seek money, volunteers, and supplies. Back with the army near San Antonio de Bexar, Col. Edward Burleson was elected commander of the volunteers, with Francis Johnson his second-in-command.

Unfortunately, the Consultation adjourned without defining the separation of powers and responsibilities of the president and council. This oversight would lead to several crises in the next several months, and would be a contributing factor to the loss of life at Goliad and the Alamo.

On November 6 the Mexicans received a morale boost when Colonel Ugartechea arrived with reinforcements, although most of them were conscripts. Cos' force now numbered about 1,500 men. There were occasional sorties by the Mexicans for food, firewood, and general harassment of the besiegers, but few casualties were suffered on either side.

On one occasion, a patrol led by Travis captured a 300-head Mexican horse herd, ten mules, five prisoners, six muskets, and two swords. Another time a party of New Orleans Greys drove in some Mexican pickets and found themselves actually in the town of San Antonio. While they celebrated their "conquest," Mexican artillery began firing on them, and they were almost overrun by a counterattack. Fortunately for the overly enthusiastic Greys, Texian scout "Deaf" Smith organized a rescue party and covered their retreat.

On the morning of November 26, "Deaf" Smith rode into the Texian camp with exciting news. A Mexican pack train was making its way toward San Antonio! Rumors had been circulating for several days that there was a shipment of silver and/or gold headed for San Antonio de Bexar to pay the Mexican troops and purchase supplies from the Bexar merchants. Inspired by an opportunity for action to break the boredom of the siege, as well as by a chance for plunder, Jim Bowie quickly organized a force of volunteers to go after the pack train. In a running battle called the Grass Fight, Bowie and his volunteers inflicted over seventy casualties on the Mexicans, while only losing one man. But the intercepted packs contained only fodder for Cos' horses. The train was not a new arrival from Mexico but rather a foraging party that had slipped through the Texians' blockade only a couple of days earlier.

So the siege continued. As time dragged on, Texian volunteers voted with their feet to leave for home. By early December, conditions reached a crisis point. At the height of the siege, there had been over a thousand volunteers ringing the town. Now there were just over 500, including over a hundred of the New Orleans Greys, who owned no property in Texas. Provisions had always been low, but were now reaching the nonexistent stage. Munitions were so low that the artillery only had roundshot to fire when they picked up what had been sent their way by the Mexican batteries. And with winter coming, few of the soldiers had any warm clothing or more than one blanket. Some began to say the only responsible option was to move into winter quarters closer to the colonies, in Gonzales and Goliad. Others pointed out that if things were so tough for the besiegers, they must be even worse for the besieged. The easy entry of the Greys into the town just a few days before seemed to support this view.

Then several Mexican deserters and some Anglo Texians who had been held prisoner confirmed that things were swiftly deteriorating in the Mexican camp. Burleson announced plans to assault San Antonio de Bexar. However, fearing the plans had been betrayed, he reversed his orders and announced a move to winter quarters. One of the most active members of the War Party, Ben Milam, had had enough. Grabbing a musket, he drew a line in the dirt with the butt and called out: "Who will follow old Ben Milam into San Antonio? Cross over the line!" About 300 of the remaining soldiers crossed over. Burleson then asked those who did not cross over to at least stay in camp as reserves while the attack took place.

Plans were made for the assault to begin during the night of December 4-5. It was decided to divide the strike force into three divisions. The first, consisting of a six-pounder crew, would be commanded by Capt. James Neill, and would create a diversion by opening up an artillery barrage on the Alamo. The other two divisions would actually assault the town. The first of these would be commanded by the overall commander of the attack, Ben Milam. The third division, consisting mostly of Greys, would be commanded by Col. Frank Johnson. The Texians settled in to try to get some sleep before the predawn attack began. During the night the weather turned bitterly cold, and more of the army disappeared. When the order to fall out came at approximately 3:00 A.M., less than 250 of the assault force were left. Undaunted, they moved into position.

When Neill's artillery opened fire on the Alamo, Cos' guns returned fire and the Mexicans prepared for an assault on the Alamo, just as Milam and the others hoped they would. While the artillery hammered back and forth and a small force of men kept the troops in the Alamo busy with small-arms fire, Milam's two divisions moved against the far side of San Antonio de Bexar, driving in the pickets and taking possession of some houses on the edge of town. As the morning sun dawned, a fierce firefight began between houses occupied by the Texians and those held by Cos' forces. Both sides also used artillery, but the Mexicans had an advantage in that they were holding the better built stone houses of the upper-class residents near the town's plazas, while the Texians occupied the smaller and more vulnerable adobe huts further out. For about two days a bitter stalemate took place, made worse for the Texians when one division mistakenly opened fire on a house held by the other division, and at least one Texian was killed before the friendly fire ceased.

On the morning of December 7, the Texians found that during the night the Mexicans had dug a new trench on the Alamo side of the river, which made the Texian left vulnerable to more effective small-arms fire. At about noon, the tide turned. Ironically it was a common tool, not a weapon, that brought the beginning of the end for the Mexicans. Wielding a crowbar, a Tennessee scout, Henry Karnes, yelled: "Damn the Mexicans and their *escopetas*!" (muskets) and raced for a Mexican held building. Helped by covering fire from the more accurate Texian rifles, Karnes made it to the door of the house, which was less substantial than the stone walls. Directly below the soldiers on the roof, he was now safe from *escopeta* fire. As he used the crowbar to force the door open, a group of Texians joined him and fought their way into the house. Most of the Mexicans ran out a back door, but a few surrendered. Unable to keep prisoners securely but not wanting to execute them, the Texians called upon the *soldados'* religion to ensure their parole agreement. Crosses were drawn on a house wall, and the prisoners were made to swear they would not fight in Texas again while putting their right hands on the cross and their left hands on their hearts.

Inspired by Karnes' example, the Texians began a steady advance through the town. Many of the houses had adjoining walls, and the attackers began avoiding the open streets and courtyards and smashing their way from house to house. Civilians and prisoners were also kept out of harm's way as they moved to the rear.

At midafternoon, during a break in the fighting, Milam held a council of war in the front yard of the Veramendi house, or "palace," as it was called. He and other Texian leaders, including Johnson, Karnes, and Creed Taylor, were planning an assault on the Military Plaza. Suddenly, a shot rang out and Ben Milam fell over backwards, a ball piercing his head. According to Taylor, a Mexican soldier fired from the branches of a large cypress tree near the banks of the San Antonio River. Unlike most of Cos' troops, who were armed with short-range *escopetas,* the *soldado* was armed with a Baker Rifle. Several Texian rifles replied, and the sharpshooter's body fell from the tree and rolled into the river.

Following a Masonic funeral for Milam, the Texians resumed their house-to-house assault. That night the Texians' officers held an election and chose Frank Johnson as their new commander.

One of the main centers of Mexican resistance was the tower of the San Fernando Cathedral. From this tower, Mexican sharpshooters and two small guns kept the Texians at a distance. In response, the Texians dragged a twelve-pounder from house to house until they had a clear shot at the tower. Firing several rounds, they collapsed part of the roof and forced the Mexicans to give up the tower.

Soon after abandoning this strategic position, Cos lost another strong point when the Texians overran the redoubt on the Military Plaza. While this was all happening, Ugartechea showed up with several hundred "reinforcements," about a hundred regular infantry, some regular cavalry, a handful of officers, a motley band of camp followers, and the rest recruits. It was the recruits that drove Cos to the edge of despair. Almost all of them were conscripts, many of them convicts in chains. None of them had been trained; all were hungry and tired.

"In such critical circumstances," Cos would write in his official report to Santa Anna, "there was no other measure than to advance and occupy the Alamo which, due to its small size and military position, was easier to hold. In doing so, I took with me the artillery, packs and the rest of the utensils I was able to transport." (Chariton: *100 Days,* 75) While this was going on, more than 175 of his best troops, the presidial cavalry, deserted along with some infantry.

Writing years later, Capt. Sanchez Navarro, who came in with Ugartechea, would claim that the presidial troops did not desert but misunderstood the order to withdraw and headed for the Rio Grande; that Cos never intended to abandon the town, but only to move the wounded into the Alamo; and that a diehard contingent of the Morelos Battalion held the Main Plaza with a howitzer and a handful of muskets until Cos gave the order to surrender. This last may be true, because F. W. Johnson, in his account of the battle, states that "the enemy opened a furious cannonade from all their batteries, accompanied by incessant volleys of small arms, against every house in our possession . . . which continued unceasingly until half-past six o'clock, A.M. of the 9th, when they sent a flag of truce, with an invitation that they desired to capitulate. . . ." (Chariton: *100 Days,* 17)

It took almost a full day for the two sides to come to terms, but at last an agreement was reached. The Mexicans had six days to remain in the Alamo and prepare for their trip back to Mexico. In the interim, no member of either army was to approach the other side under arms. The recently arrived convicts had to return to Mexico, but any regular Mexican soldier who wished to remain in Texas could do so. Personal property would be respected, and no one would be molested because of political opinions expressed before or during the conflict. Most of the military stores would be left with the Texians, but each Mexican soldier would be allowed his musket and ten rounds of ammunition for defense from Indians on the journey home. The column would also be allowed to take a four-pound cannon and ten rounds of powder and shot. Considering that during the height of the battle Cos had run up the blood red flag that proclaimed no quarter for Texians if they lost, the terms could be considered quite generous.

While the Siege and Battle of Bexar had been taking place, colonists to the east had taken the presidio at Goliad and Fort Lipantitlan, so that with Cos' withdrawal there were no more Mexican troops in Texas. According to their surrender terms, the defeated *soldados* were not to be used to "in any way oppose the re-establishment of the Federal Constitution of 1824." But few Texians had any delusions that the war was over. What few of them understood was that the greatest threat to their just-won freedom would not come from Santa Anna, but from their own leaders.

MASONS IN MEXICO

One of the least examined aspects of the frequent upheaval in Mexico and the conflicts between Mexicans and Americans, and between Centralists and Federalists, is the role played by the Masonic lodges in Mexico. The role of the Masons in history since the eighteenth century has provided conspiracy buffs with an enormous amount of material for speculation. This has led most mainstream historians to downplay or ignore Masonic influences almost entirely. Such is a significant oversight. Although the Masons are almost certainly not guilty of everything they have been accused of, or, for that matter, responsible for everything they'd like to take credit for, their impact on society and politics during the eighteenth and nineteenth centuries has been generally underestimated.

In Mexico during the revolutionary era, the Royalist (later Centralist) faction dominated the Scottish Rite lodges. Recognizing the advantage to American interests of there being a place for the liberals to gather and talk in private, Ambassador Joel Poinsett helped establish the first York Rite Lodge in Mexico. As time went on, conservatives were sometimes identified as "Escoses" and liberals as "Yorkinos," based on their allegiance to the Scottish Rite or York Rite lodges. And although belonging to the Masonic brotherhood did not prevent the Texians and Mexicans from going to war with each other, Masonic traditions did have some influence.

Following his death during the Siege of Bexar, Ben Milam was buried in full Masonic regalia with all accompanying rites. According to some sources, Almeron Dickinson wrapped his Mason's apron around Susannah before the final Mexican assault, trusting that this would ensure that the Mexican officers would protect her from harm. There are also stories that Sam Houston spared Santa Anna after San Jacinto because the Mexican dictator flashed the Masonic distress sign which obliged Houston, a fellow Mason, to do all in his power short of endangering his own life to save Santa Anna.

While these last stories may only be folklore, the abundance of lodges in both the United States and Mexico in the early nineteenth century can only lead one to conclude that there must be more to the Masonic influence than is currently known.

PART 2: A WINTER OF DISCONTENT

"The farmers and substantial men of Texas can yet save themselves, but to do so they must act in union and as one man. I fear it is impossible."

Stephen F. Austin
(Chariton: *100 Days,* 57)

With the Mexican military threat out of the way for a time, the Texian leadership had several other problems to solve. They had to develop a more stable and well-defined system of government. A regular army had to be raised to confront Santa Anna when he returned, and, in the meantime, there had to be some way to keep the volunteers who had flooded Texas in the last few months busy until the war started again.

To many in the government, a controversial proposal by several Mexican Federalist leaders seemed like a good way to solve the last problem. The plan was to invade northeastern Mexico and take over the rich city of Matamoros. It was hoped that the Mexican Federalists would then rise against Santa Anna and join the Texian army in restoring the constitution. This plan was supported by liberal politician Lorenzo de Zavala, Brig. Gen. José Antonio Mexia, former governor of Coahuila y Texas Augustin Viesca, and former acting president of the Republic of Mexico Valentin Gomez Farias, among others. Also heavily promoting the expedition was Dr. James Grant, a lively and popular Scot with extensive holdings in the Matamoros area.

This plan drew strong support in spite of an earlier expedition which set out from New Orleans and ended in disaster. In November, Mexia led about 200 volunteers, a combined force of Texians, Americans, and exiled Mexicans, in a raid on the port city of Tampico. The idea was to secure Tampico, wait for Federalist reinforcements, and then move north to Matamoros. Although the fort and customs house were taken, the hoped for Federalist support never came. When Santa Anna's troops were reinforced, it became necessary for the rebels to withdraw. In retreating back to their ship, more than thirty men were taken prisoner, twenty-seven of them Americans. This was in addition to the sixty who had been killed or wounded earlier in the fighting. Despite U.S. diplomatic intervention, all of the prisoners were executed.

Unaffected by this tragedy, the council voted to support the plan. Governor Smith promptly vetoed the proposal. Still unaffected, the council overrode the veto. They instructed Mexia to go to San Antonio de Bexar to gather troops and supplies.

Governor Smith, choosing to go along with the plan but not the leadership, and also realizing that defense of the Texas borders had to be the first priority, wrote to Sam Houston: "You will adopt such measures as you deem best, for the reduction of Matamoros—and the occupation of such posts as you may deem necessary for the protection of the frontier—Keeping up a constant system of vigilance necessary for the protection of the country." (Chariton: *100 Days,* 42) Houston responded by ordering Jim Bowie to proceed to Matamoros if he could raise a sufficient number of men for the purpose. The city was to be occupied and held until further orders. If this could not be done, Bowie was to harass Santa Anna's troops as much as possible, using the tactics that typified Bowie's hit and run kind of warfare, but also following the rules of civilized warfare. Leaving no room for question of who should be in charge, Houston stated: "You will conduct the campaign." (Chariton: *100 Days,* 43)

In late December, angered that the Texian government had not formally responded to his proposal, Mexia wrote to Governor Smith that he was moving his base of operations to New Orleans, where he would continue recruiting American volunteers and exiled Federalists for his cause.

The council still clung to the idea of invading Mexico, but Stephen Austin, en route to the United States, wrote to Frank Johnson that the Texians must be very careful not to let the Centralists turn the conflict into a national war. The Texians must encourage all the Mexican Federalists to begin their own campaigns against Santa Anna, and then only support them in an auxiliary capacity. Austin felt it was a mistake to not allow Mexia to command the Matamoros expedition. If Texas were to send an expedition of foreign troops against Matamoros, or declare independence from Mexico, it would turn all of the parties in Mexico against Texas. Still holding to his dream, Austin wrote that the Texians should call a convention, amend the declarations of the Consultation, declare Texas a state of the Mexican confederacy, form a constitution, and organize a permanent government.

Also trying to infuse some order into the chaos, on December 12 Sam Houston issued a proclamation establishing the Regular Texas Army. With the backing of Governor Smith, Houston offered those who would accept service in the army a cash bonus of $24, as well as 800 acres of land and instant Texas citizenship under the regulations of the Constitution of 1824. Enlistment was for two years or the duration of the war. A Volunteer Auxiliary Corps was also established. Volunteers would receive 640 acres if they served for two years or the duration of the war, 320 acres if they served at least one year. Although they could elect officers, the volunteers were still ultimately under Houston's command. Washington-on-the-Brazos was named headquarters because it was more centrally located than San Felipe de Austin. Calling for 5,000 volunteers, Houston ended with the cry: "Let the brave rally to our standard!" (Chariton: *100 Days,* 30)

Unfortunately for Houston, many of those arriving in Texas already belonged to military units, and rather than submit to a new command structure they moved to places where their independent status would be respected. Goliad became a popular rallying point. Among these new groups were the Kentucky Mustangs, the Alabama Red Rovers, the Georgia Battalion, and the Mobile Greys.

Perhaps it was the influx of newcomers that led the garrison at Goliad to take the step so long anticipated, debated, and feared. On December 20, 1835, a proclamation signed by the entire garrison declared "that the former province and department of Texas is, and of right ought to be, a free, sovereign and independent state."

Heavily promoted by the Congress, the Matamoros expedition steadily grew in momentum. Despite having appointed Houston commander-in-chief of the Army of Texas, the council issued secret orders to Fannin, Johnson, Grant, and others to prepare for the assault on Matamoros. Trying to hold back the tide, Houston made a speech to Fannin's troops in Goliad, beseeching them to stay and guard the Texas frontier from the almost certain invasion coming, and not go off adventuring in Mexico. According to an eyewitness, Houston praised and admonished the troops at the same time: "I praise your courage, but I will frankly confess to you, my friends, that I do not approve of your plans." (Williams: *Sam Houston,* 130)

In late December, Houston assigned James C. Neill to command the post at San Antonio de Bexar, and ordered Green B. Jameson to make a survey of articles necessary for Neill's command. Neill was also ordered to detail a capable officer to oversee fortifying the post in the best manner possible. Houston ordered Travis to send some junior officers to the United States and other points useful for raising troops. They were to report with their new recruits to San Felipe de Austin by March 1, 1836.

Disturbed by rumors that Mexican agents were stirring up trouble among the Indians in the north, the Texas government appointed Houston, along with John Fortes and John Cameron, as commissioners to treat with the Cherokees and their twelve associated bands. This responsibility was a natural for Houston, who had lived with the Cherokees, and had at least two Indian names, "The Raven" and "Big Drunk."

The loose discipline of troops not used to regular service and bored with inactivity became a source of concern to the government. At San Antonio de Bexar, captains of the volunteer companies of the garrison informed the commander, F. W. Johnson, that a recent order from the convention placing the volunteer companies under the authority of the commander of the regular army was in direct opposition to the understanding of a prior decree that the volunteers were to be free to elect their own officers, and be subject only to the commander-in-chief, if they so chose. This disagreement over who should command volunteers would eventually become a source of contention between Travis and Bowie.

Meanwhile, Johnson wrote to J.W. Robinson that an expedition against Matamoros could be easily undertaken. Every man in the garrison would willingly volunteer to move against Mexico, so the real concern was waiting for sufficient reinforcements to leave a proper garrison in San Antonio de Bexar when the expedition set off.

On December 30, Horatio Alsbury wrote to Houston from San Antonio de Bexar and informed him that 300 men were leaving that evening for Matamoros. Of the troops gathered in Bexar, all but 100 set out on what they believed would be a great adventure. Johnson left Neill in command, with orders to collect all the guns in the town and move them into the Alamo, and to destroy the fortifications that General Cos had built in the town. Ironically, Johnson himself believed that at least fifty more men were needed to properly defend San Antonio de Bexar, but he refused to leave that many extra behind.

As the year that began Texas' fight for freedom drew to a close, a proposal was made to the General Council that no free Negroes or mulattoes be allowed into Texas, and that any found there would be arrested and sold into slavery. A third of the sale price would go to the arresting person and the balance to the treasury. Early in the new year, the ordinance passed. The irony, or hypocrisy, of the Texians claiming to fight for liberty while promoting slavery was the source of much criticism from some quarters at the time, and continues to this day.

On January 6, 1836, Neill wrote from San Antonio de Bexar to the governor and General Council:

> .... We have 104 men and two distinct fortresses to garrison, and about twenty four pieces of artillery. . . . we have no provisions or clothing since Johnson and Grant left. If there has ever been a dollar here I have no knowledge of it. The clothing sent here by the aid and patriotic exertions of the honorable Council, was taken from us by arbitrary measures of Johnson and Grant, taken from men who endured all the hardships of winter and who were not even sufficiently clad for summer, many of them having but one blanket and one shirt, and what was intended for them given away to men some of whom had not been in the army more than four days, and many not exceeding two weeks. If a divide had been made of them, the most needy of my men could have been made comfortable by the stock of clothing and provisions taken from here.
>
> About 200 of the men who had volunteered to garrison this place for 4 months left my command contrary to my orders. . . . I want here for this garrison at all times 200 men and I think 300 until the repairs and improvements of the fortifications is completed, a chart and index of which has been sent to headquarters at Washington, with the present condition of the fort, and such improvements suggested by Mr. Jameson as has met my approbation. . . .
>
> .... The men have not even money to pay for their washing, the hospital is in want of stores and even the necessary provisions for well men was not left the wounded by Grant and Johnson.

Neill asked for money in haste, because some of the men had not had so much as a dollar in over three months. He did not know when the enemy "of 1,000 in number" might be coming, and as there were no supplies or provisions, the garrison could be starved out in four days "by anything like a close siege." To make matters worse, the impressment of cattle and horses by Grant and Johnson deprived many of the local Mexicans of the means of cultivating their crops for the coming season. (Chariton: *100 Days,* 105-106)

As if this was not trouble enough, Houston also wrote to Governor Smith, echoing Neill's concerns regarding the garrison at San Antonio de Bexar. He begged the governor and council to meet and plan a course of action that would "redeem our country from a state of deplorable anarchy." He asked that the government rush supplies to "the wounded, the sick, the naked, and the hungry, for God's sake!" He ended with the plea, "What will the world think of the authorities of Texas. Prompt, decided, and honest independence, is all that can . . . redeem our country." (Chariton: *100 Days,* 107)

The following day, Johnson, upset because the commissions he recommended for volunteer officers were not approved by the council, and because Houston's new plan for the army put the volunteers under the ultimate authority of the commander-in-chief, declined any participation in the Matamoros expedition. The council then appointed Fannin as its agent in carrying out the campaign. Johnson reconsidered, and then wrote that he would "proceed on the expedition as I first contemplated." (Chariton: *100 Days,* 110)

The same day, in a letter from New Orleans to R. R. Royall and S. Rhoads Fisher, Stephen Austin wrote: "The universal wish and expectation in this quarter is that Texas ought to declare herself independent at once." (Chariton: *100 Days,* 113)

Acting on his orders from the council, Fannin ordered all volunteers for the Matamoros expedition to assemble at San Patricio January 24-27. The fleet convoy would then sail from Velasco on or about February 18, to "cripple the enemy . . . at home." Fannin said ". . . all who feel disposed to join . . . are invited to join the ranks forthwith." (Chariton: *100 Days,* 114)

On January 9 the town of San Augustine welcomed an American folk hero to Texas. Former Congressman David Crockett of Tennessee, who like so many others had come to Texas to start a new life following failure at home, wrote to his family that he had received a hero's welcome in Texas, that he expected to be elected to the upcoming convention, and that he wished every friend he had would settle in Texas, for he believed it was the garden spot of the world and it would mean good fortune for them all. But first, he enrolled as a volunteer in the army for six months. (Chariton: *100 Days,* 118)

In mid-February, the most famous Alamo defender of all arrived. Former United States Congressman David Crockett of Tennessee came to aid the Texians in any way he could—and to build a new future for himself and his family.

The next day, not to be outdone by Fannin, Johnson issued a call to arms for the Federal Volunteer Army of Texas. Claiming to march under the flag of 1824, committed to the principles of that constitution and to wiping out despotism throughout Mexico, he called for Americans and native Mexicans to join together to drive tyranny from Matamoros and wherever else it might raise its "malignant form." (Chariton: *100 Days,* 123)

On the same day, in a letter from New Orleans, Austin at last acknowledged the death of his dream. "The information from Mexico recd. here is that the leading men of the federal party have united with Santana to invade Texas; consequently, the position taken by the declaration of 7 November in favor of the republican principles of the Constitution of 1824 can no longer do any good, the object of that declaration having been to extend light and liberty over Mexico, and thus secure the cooperation of the liberal party. On the other hand, mentioning the federal constitution in that declaration has done us an injury in this country and would ruin us if it were not confidently expected and believed that a new convention would soon meet and make an absolute declaration." (Chariton: *100 Days,* 125)

Ignoring the threat posed by the possible return of Mexican troops and the already desperate state of the army, the Texas government tore itself apart trying to assign blame for, among other things, the awful conditions at San Antonio de Bexar. On January 11 the Congress impeached Governor Smith, calling upon him to answer charges and specifications preferred against him based on the Mexican Constitution of 1824 and the organic law of the Provisional Government of Texas. Smith responded, "Well, you have adopted your course and I will pursue mine!" (Chariton: *100 Days,* 127) James Robinson, the lieutenant governor, was sworn in as acting governor.

The Congress next published articles of impeachment against Governor Smith. Smith was condemned for refusing to back the Congress' chosen commander for the Matamoros expedition, Fannin, and appointing his own favorite, James Bowie, "not known to the government as an officer of any rank whatever." The Congress also denied any responsibility for Grant's raiding the stores in San Antonio de Bexar to help the expedition, denying "having ever recognized in Dr. Grant any authority whatever." (Chariton: *100 Days,* 130)

In the midst of this legislative chaos, some local officials continued to do their duty. One such local official had an unexpected brush with celebrity while carrying out his responsibilities. John Forbes of Nacogdoches wrote to James W. Robinson: "I have been very busily engaged in attending to numerous Volunteers from the States fifty two of whom will leave here tomorrow for the frontier almost all are Gentlemen of the best respectability and mostly hailing from Tennessee. . . . I have had the honor of administrating the oath of allegiance to them the Celebrated David Crockett is of the number. . . ." (Chariton: *100 Days,* 140) In a similar vein, Micajah Autry, in a letter to his wife, wrote, "P.S. Col. Crockett has joined our company." (Chariton: *100 Days,* 143)

On January 14 Neill wrote to Houston, complaining again of lack of supplies, clothing, rifle powder, and no pay. At least twenty men were planning to leave the following day, so the garrison would shrink to about eighty effective men. Several of the locals, both Anglo and Mexican, had offered support. Neill wrote to the governor and council that he was convinced that Santa Anna was closer than generally believed, but he did not have the horses necessary for sending out scouting patrols.

For his part, Houston was trying to consolidate what strength the Texians had before he left on his diplomatic mission to the Cherokees. He sent one of the men he trusted most, Jim Bowie, to San Antonio de Bexar with thirty to fifty men, to assist in hauling away what supplies and arms they could and destroying the rest. He issued various orders to the regulars and as many of the volunteers as would listen to rally in a few places to await the anticipated Mexican invasion. How precise Houston's orders were and how well they were followed have served as fuel for controversy for more than a hundred years. His supporters claim that if his orders had been obeyed, the slaughters at the Alamo and Goliad would have been prevented. Detractors say the orders were vague, and Houston's later claims to have tried to prevent the Texian losses were self-serving fiction.

Regardless of the clarity of Houston's orders, shortly after his arrival at San Antonio de Bexar, Bowie, along with Neill, Jameson, and most of the garrison, decided that if Santa Anna were to be stopped, it would have to be there. For one thing, the artillery and munitions couldn't be moved. There simply were not enough animals and carts, but to destroy the supplies would be unthinkable. Jameson submitted a map showing current and planned improvements to the Alamo designed to make it a more respectable fortification. Finally there was the question of honor, of not abandoning a major post in the face of an advancing enemy. Bowie spoke for the entire garrison when he wrote to Governor Smith on February 2: "The salvation of Texas depends in great measure in keeping Bejar out of the hands of the enemy. It serves as the frontier picquet guard and if it were in the possession of Santa Anna there is no strong hold from which to repel him in his march towards the Sabine. . . . It does, however, seem certain that an attack is shortly to be made on this place. . . . The citizens of Bexar have behaved well. . . . These citizens deserve our protection and the public safety demands our lives rather than to evacuate this post to the enemy. . . ." The same letter includes one of the immortal quotes connected with the Alamo story: "Colonel Neill and myself have come to the solemn resolution that we will rather die in these ditches than give up this post to the enemy. . . ." (Chariton: *100 Days,* 203)

The following day, Travis arrived with a company of regular cavalry. An incurable romantic who loved tales of adventure and gallantry, he had been unhappy as a footslogging infantryman. He almost certainly saw himself as a knight errant, or at least a cavalier bold, and was determined to be a cavalryman. Smith had obliged him, and Travis set out enthusiastically to raise and equip a regular cavalry regiment. His efforts bore little fruit, but his sense of drama and honor remained intact. Shortly after his arrival, Travis would echo Bowie's declaration in a letter to the governor: "We would consider death preferable to disgrace, which would be the result of giving up a Post which has been so dearly won . . . should Bejar fall, your friend will be buried beneath its ruins. . . ." (Time Life: *The Texans,* 90)

A few days after Travis' arrival, the third member of the legendary Alamo triumvirate rode into San Antonio de Bexar. Davy Crockett, recently enlisted in the volunteer forces of the Texian army, came in with the Tennessee Mounted Volunteers, commanded by William B. Harrison. Popular stories and Hollywood have frequently portrayed Crockett leading a group of "Tennessee Mountain Boys," including such colorful characters as the Preacher, Thimblerig the Gambler, and a Comanche they had picked up on the Texas prairie. One or more of these apparently fictional characters have found their way into most Alamo novels and movies. They have their origin, at least in part, in an account supposedly written by Crockett himself.

In truth, Crockett came to Texas alone and joined Harrison's group en route to San Antonio de Bexar. Just what authority he held within the unit, and later within the garrison, is hard to determine. Crockett claimed he was just a "high private," but his post at the Alamo has become known as "Crockett's Palisade," and his leadership of the men at that wall is rarely questioned. It seems likely, whatever his formal status, his charisma and national reputation made him a de-facto leader of the Texians.

With Bowie, Travis, and Crockett available to provide leadership for the garrison, Neill asked for and received permission to go on leave. This event has also caused occasional and sometimes heated debate. Considering that Neill, along with many of the troops in Bexar, believed that the Mexican army was drawing near, some have accused him of cowardice. Many sources claim that he left to spend time with family members who were suffering illness. Although not considered a coward for going to them, some have questioned Neill's judgment. However, in recent years, research has indicated that the most likely reason Neill left his post at Bexar was to gather supplies and pay for his men. Given the tone of his letters to the government and Houston, this seems very likely.

In any event, on February 11 Neill departed San Antonio de Bexar, leaving behind orders that Travis was to be in command. The volunteers immediately reacted, again claiming their right to choose whether or not to be commanded by a regular army officer, and demanding to elect their own officer. Apparently to prevent open mutiny and/or abandonment, Travis agreed. The volunteers chose Bowie. This decision, coupled with some of Bowie's behavior, nearly drove Travis away. Bowie was frequently drunk. He let some prisoners go from the jail. He was turning everything "topsy turvy." After a few days, however, the two agreed on a joint command. Strictly speaking, Bowie would command the volunteers, Travis the few regulars. Practically, military decisions would be made jointly, and they would both sign orders.

For the next ten days, the Bexar garrison settled into a sort of routine. Sympathetic townspeople and occasional patrols brought regular reports of Santa Anna's approach. The garrison kept improving the fortifications of the Alamo, guided by Green Jameson's plans. As part of these improvements, the lunette outside the main gate, begun by Cos, was strengthened. Also, a palisade and dirt wall were erected in the open area between the south wall and the chapel.

On most evenings, the garrison and the townspeople held *fandangos,* festive parties that lasted well into the night. On the night of February 21, one of these *fandangos* was held in honor of George Washington's birthday. It almost ended the Siege of the Alamo before it ever began. While the Texians were celebrating, Santa Anna's advance guard was only twenty-five miles away, camped on the south banks of the Medina River. Receiving word from spies about the party, Santa Anna ordered a force of dragoons to push ahead, cut off the town from the Alamo, and subdue the rebels while they were most vulnerable. Only a sudden storm and a rapid rise in the height of the river prevented this bold scheme from being successful.

Unaware of their good fortune, the Texians danced and drank the night away, then went to their beds. When they woke up the next morning, February 22, 1836, they didn't know that this would be the last hangover for many of them. They didn't know that many of them had celebrated their last *fandango.* They didn't know that in a little over twenty-four hours, Santa Anna's army would occupy San Antonio de Bexar, and the Siege of the Alamo would begin.

Texas' winter of discontent was over. A glorious but bloody spring was about to begin.

Left: *At one point during the Siege of Bexar, a party of the Greys drove in some Mexican pickets, then found themselves in the city itself. They were almost cut off when Deaf Smith led a relief force to their aid. After that, Smith called the Greys "his boys."*

Right: *Erastus "Deaf" Smith led the rescue party for the New Orleans Greys during the Siege of Bexar, carried a message from the Alamo, burned Gonzales during the Runaway Scrape, and cut down Vince's Bridge to prevent Santa Anna being reinforced at San Jacinto. In all, he was one of the most remarkable men of the Revolution. He dressed mostly as an Anglo but wore Mexican* botas *on his lower legs — definitely practical on the Texas prairie.*

CHAPTER SIX

Santa Anna's March Into Texas

INCENSED WITH THE SITUATION in Texas, and particularly humiliated by the capture of San Antonio de Bexar, Santa Anna began to assemble an "Army of Operations in Texas" with the express purpose of putting down the rebellious Texians. Santa Anna began assembling his force at San Luis Potosi in December of 1835, about 365 miles from Bexar. Eventually the army numbered about 4,000 men.

General Ramirez y Sesma had already started north with the First Division, with orders to reinforce General Cos in San Antonio de Bexar. He did not arrive in time, and Bexar fell to the Texians in early December.

The rest of the Mexican army arrived at Saltillo on January 7, 1836. For the next several weeks, the troops, many of them new recruits or conscripts, underwent training while supplies for the campaign were gathered. Upon his arrival at Saltillo, Santa Anna was stricken with a stomach ailment that kept him out of commission for two weeks. Since the army had no medical department to speak of, Santa Anna was forced to hire Dr. Reyes, a local doctor, as his personal physician. Other critical professionals were equally lacking in the Army of Operations.

Santa Anna's illness slowed the process of training and equipping the entire army. He was what we today call a "micromanager," who insisted on handling many of the smallest details himself.

THE MEXICAN ARMY CHAIN OF COMMAND

The chain of command of the Army of Operations in Texas was as follows:

Commander-in-Chief: Antonio López de Santa Anna
Aide-de-Camp to Santa Anna: Gen. Manuel Fernandez Castrillon
Personal Secretary to Santa Anna: Ramon Martínez Caro
Second-in-Command: Gen. Vicente Filisola
Major Brigade General (third-in-command): Juan Arago
Quartermaster: Brig. Gen. Adrian Woll
Purveyor (Commissary) General: Col. Ricardo Dromundo
Commander of the First Infantry Brigade: Brig. Gen. Antonio Gaona
Commander of the Second Infantry Brigade: Gen. Eugenio Tolsa
Commander of the Cavalry Brigade: Brig. Gen. Juan José de Andrade
Commander of the Artillery: Lt. Col. Pedro Ampudia
Commander of the Zapadores Battalion: Col. Augustin Amat
Commander of the Vanguard of the Advance: Gen. Joaquin Ramirez y Sesma

In what most Texians considered an act of extreme treachery, Santa Anna ordered Gen. Martín Perfecto de Cos and his men, paroled after the capture of Bexar, to rejoin the Mexican army. Parole of a captured army, in return for a promise not to fight

DEGUELLO VS. PAROLE

Gen. Vicente Filisola stated that, "The massacres of the Alamo convinced the rebels that no peaceable settlement could be expected, and that they must conquer or die." (Time-Life: *The Spanish West,* 108)

One of the most controversial elements of the conflicts between the Anglo-Texians and the Mexican army had its roots in medieval Spain. During the wars of the *reconquista,* as Spanish knights fought to drive the Moors from their country, a bloody tradition was born. Driven by devotion to God as well as to country, both sides learned to shun mercy and fight to the death. Prisoners were executed or enslaved. The Spanish brought this military tradition to the New World, and it became part of the Mexican military culture.

The Texians, on the other hand, had come from the Anglo American tradition of parole, or releasing military prisoners after obtaining a promise not to bear arms again for the duration of the war, or whatever other terms were mutually agreed to. This was similar to removing chess pieces from a board. It was more humane, honorable, and less costly than establishing prison camps, or carrying out the wholesale execution of captured prisoners.

This difference in military culture was an integral part of the wars in Texas. During the Magee expedition, the Mexican members of Magee's army slaughtered the commander of the garrison at Bexar and several of his officers, after promising them safe passage to Mexico. Execution of prisoners by the Mexican army occurred during both the Magee and Long expeditions. Several accounts of the fall of the Alamo tell of the execution of Texians taken alive, and the slaughter of Fannin's unarmed men at Goliad outraged the Texians.

In time, the lack of mercy shown by the Mexicans was met by a fierceness in the Texians that embarrassed many of their fellow countrymen. At San Jacinto, during the following violent years of the Republic, and especially during the Mexican War, the Texas Rangers and other volunteers developed a reputation for cruelty

again, was a long established tradition among civilized nations. Much of the bitterness of the Texians against the Mexican government can be traced to actions such as this. While the Texians paroled vanquished foes, only to see them fight again, the Mexicans adopted a "no quarter" policy, killing their opponents to the last man.

On January 25, Santa Anna paraded his men in a grand review. The army consisted of two infantry brigades, one cavalry brigade, and the small corps of crack combat engineers, the Zapadores. As discussed in Chapter Four, most of the units were considerably understrength.

The first columns of the Mexican army resumed the march north from Saltillo on January 26. One segment, under Brig. Gen. José Urrea, headed for the Gulf Coast, while the main force, 4,000 men and 12 cannon, headed directly north under the command of Santa Anna himself.

The main column was spread out for miles. In addition to the soldiers, it consisted of 1,800 pack mules, 33 four-wheeled wagons, 200 two-wheeled carts, plus several hundred carts owned by the civilian sutlers.

Rations and supplies were always in short supply. The purveyor general, Col. Ricardo Dromundo, Santa Anna's brother-in-law, had been given funds enough to provision 6,000 men for two months, but suspiciously little of this ever reached the troops.

An important faction accompanying the army was the "*soldaderas,*" the women who followed the army with their children. Although they consumed valuable supplies and were a distraction to discipline, they were necessary. One Mexican officer, José Enrique de La Pena, estimated that, "At least three fifths or one half of the number of our soldiers were squadrons composed of women, muledrivers, wagon-train drivers, boys, and sutlers. . . ." (De La Pena, 22).

Had Santa Anna tried to ban the *soldaderas,* the negative effect on morale would have been far greater than the trouble that they caused by their presence. While this tolerance might be surprising by modern standards, it was common in nearly every army in the early nineteenth century. The *soldaderas* were not totally without value, for they performed services for the army as laundresses, nurses, and cooks.

The march was expected to be difficult, but Santa Anna was determined to engage the rebels as quickly as possible, so he drove his men on. Gen. Vicente Filisola, the second-in-command, wrote in his memoirs that, "All of this country, in all directions is a wilderness difficult to cross during half the year because of the lack of water, and during the other half because of too much of it." (Filisola: Vol. II:81) The soldiers suffered immensely as the weather grew worse. On February 13 a winter storm known as a "blue norther" blinded the men and covered the road knee deep with snow. Many soldiers actually froze to death along the line of march. If the weather was not enough torment for the soldiers, the columns were frequently attacked by hostile Comanches along the way. A Mexican newspaper, *El Mosquito Mexicano,* reported that, "There have been sufferings, but surprisingly small. These sufferings only spur them to greater efforts." (Lord: *A Time to Stand,* 71).

On half-rations, the soldiers only received one-half pound of hardtack per day. They were allowed one real per day to augment their rations, but the officers got only their regular salary. This action led to excessive foraging along the line of march, which in turn resulted in bitter feeling from the local population toward the army.

Even once the snow was gone, there was little forage for the horses. Sickness was rampant—dysentery, spotted itch, and exhaustion all took their toll. General Ampudia's artillerymen did their best to find room for the sick in their gun and ammunition wagons. Santa Anna himself traveled in style, riding in an elegant coach by day, and sleeping in a comfortable red-and-white striped marquee at night.

The reporters for *El Mosquito Mexicano* were beginning to get a clearer picture of what was really going on. In contrast to their early, optimistic stories, the paper now reported that "we learn that desertions are increasing daily and becoming scandalous. That hunger and nudity have the troops in despair; the troops are not getting their pay nor the officers their salaries." (Lord: *A Time to Stand,* 72-73).

The troops arrived at Monclova on February 1. On February 12 they reached the Rio Grande, where they rested for four days. On February 16, Santa Anna and the army crossed the Rio Grande into Texas. They were joined by General Ramirez y Sesma's First Brigade, which numbered 1,541 men. On that same date, Santa Anna wrote to officials in Mexico City that he hoped to reach San Antonio de Bexar by March 2.

Crucial events in history often hinge on seemingly insignificant twists of fate, and such was certainly the case at the Alamo. On February 21, Santa Anna reached the Medina River, only twenty-five miles from Bexar. Not realizing that the Mexicans were anywhere near this close, the Texians had planned a large *fandango* for the night of February 21.

Friendly Mexicans reported the party plans to Santa Anna. He in turn ordered General Ramirez y Sesma to mount a hand-picked force of cavalry on the more rested horses of the infantry officers, and make a surprise strike during the party. Such a blow most certainly would have crippled the small garrison, and made the later, heroic defense of the Alamo impossible. Fate, however, smiled upon the Texians. Sudden heavy rains made the Medina too treacherous for Sesma's cavalry to cross, and the raid had to be canceled.

Thus, Santa Anna had no choice but to continue his march into San Antonio. Surprising both himself, and especially the Texians, the first elements of Santa Anna's army entered Bexar on February 23. They had covered the 365 miles from San Luis Potosi to San Antonio de Bexar in twenty-nine days, a truly remarkable achievement. This was a full month before they were expected. The Texians thought that Santa Anna surely would wait for the spring grass for the horses to feed on.

The surprised Texians quickly scurried for the protection of the old mission of San Antonio de Valero, popularly known as the Alamo. No sooner did Santa Anna take possession of the city than he ordered a blood red flag, symbolizing "no quarter," raised from the spire of the San Fernando Cathedral. The garrison answered with a cannon shot, and the Siege of the Alamo was on!

Above*: At Saltillo, Santa Anna paused to organize and supply his army before continuing the march northward. Here he is shown in campaign dress, accompanied by one of his staff officers in full uniform.*

Top right: *Even though the Army of Operations suffered from a shortage of many critical supplies, transporting what was available was a massive undertaking. The harsh weather encountered was equally hard on men, animals, and equipment.*

This sketch shows a typical Mexican two-wheeled cart. The slashes on the sleeves of the soldier indicate that he holds the rank of corporal.

Left: *The Blizzard of February 13—the already difficult march of the Mexicans turned into a nightmare when a "blue norther" dumped fifteen to sixteen inches of snow on the miserable* soldados.

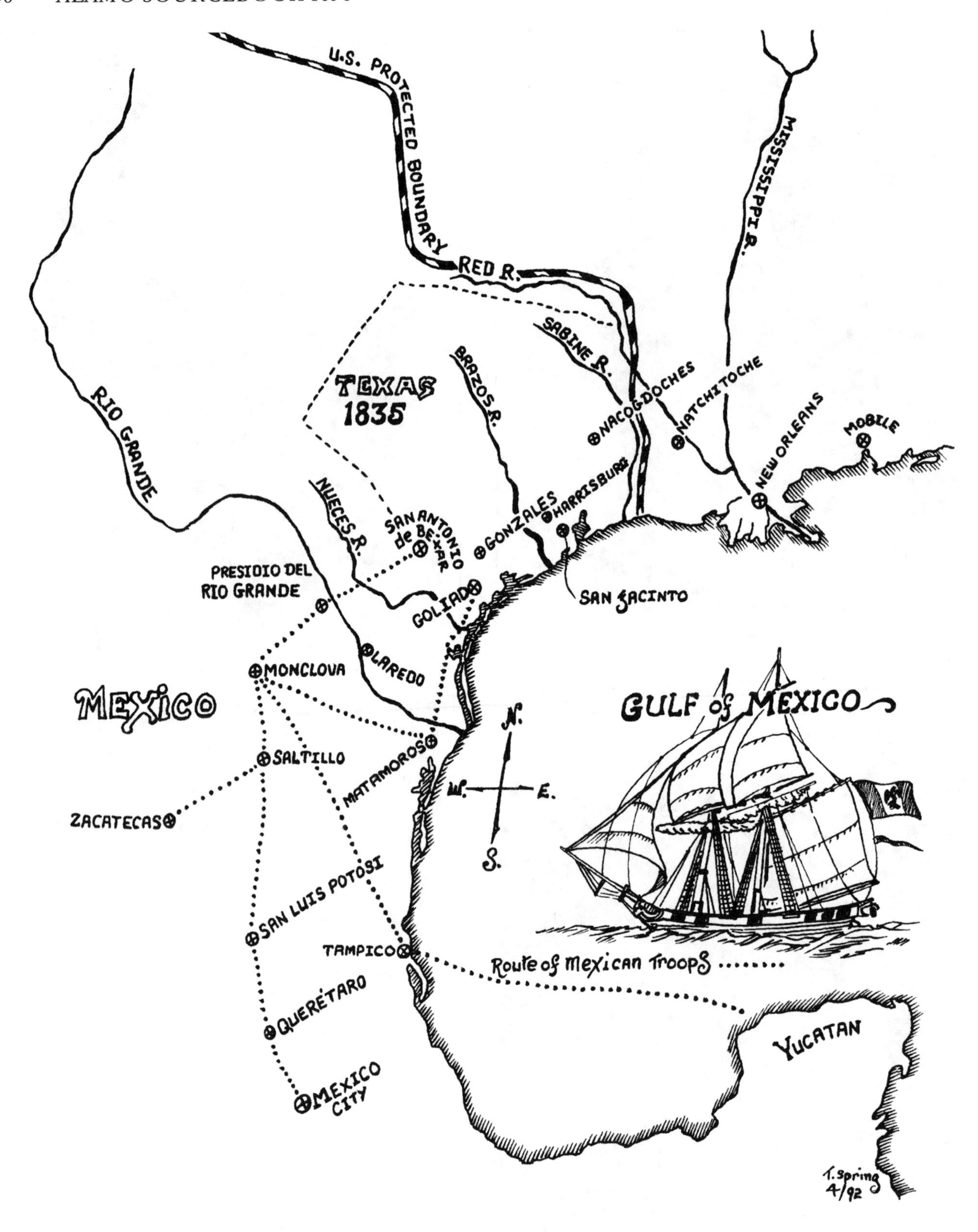

RENDEZVOUS WITH DESTINY

This map shows northern Mexico and Texas in 1835, detailing the line of march of Santa Anna's army.

CHAPTER SEVEN

The Siege and Final Battle of the Alamo

A Day-by-Day Account

Authors' Note: As explained elsewhere in this book, in some cases there is confusion over the exact time that certain events took place. In such instances, we have chosen the most logical dates and times for use in our text.

TUESDAY, FEBRUARY 23

With the failure of General Sesma's surprise attack, the Texians were given a second chance for immortality. Had Sesma succeeded with his surprise attack while the Texians were celebrating George Washington's birthday, the Alamo defenders would probably be remembered only as a band of patriots whose carelessness led to their own downfall. There never would have been a Siege of the Alamo. Also, Santa Anna might have been able to attack and destroy Houston's army before it became a formidable fighting force, thus almost certainly guaranteeing the end of the rebellion.

As dawn broke on February 23, San Antonio de Bexar was alive with activity. Large numbers of the local Tejanos were hurriedly preparing to flee the town. Friendly Mexicans advised Travis that Santa Anna's forces were less than a day's march away. Although reports had been arriving almost daily about the approach of the Mexican army, Travis had been fairly certain that they could not arrive until later in the spring, when they had sufficient forage for their horses. Now it appeared that he had been wrong.

The lookout posted in the bell tower of the San Fernando Cathedral was ordered to be extra vigilant. At about 1:00 P.M., the lookout rang the alarm bell, saying that he saw hordes of Mexican soldiers in the distance. More likely, he had seen the sun reflecting off shiny lanceheads and dragoon helmets, a sight which disappeared when the riders went into an arroyo. This would also explain why, when others went to look, they saw nothing.

Still suspicious, Travis had Dr. John Sutherland and the scout Erastus "Deaf" Smith ride out on a reconnaissance. A signal was arranged: If the scouts returned with their horses at anything faster than a walk, it meant that they had spotted the Mexicans. About a mile and a half out of town, Sutherland and Smith spotted a large force of Mexican cavalry. They turned around and headed back to Bexar at full speed. Along the way, Sutherland's horse tripped and fell on the doctor's leg. Although in pain, he managed to remount and continue his dash toward the town. When the sentry in the cathedral tower saw them coming, he again frantically rang the church bell. This time there was no doubt what it meant.

The soldiers, their families, and other townspeople who had decided to cast their lot with the Texians raced for the safety of the Alamo. Artillery officer Almeron Dickinson, who like many of the

Alamo garrison had been living in the town, had his twenty-two-year-old wife Susannah and fifteen-month-old daughter Angelina get up on his horse and ride with him to the fortress. Jim Bowie's two sisters-in-law, Juanita Alsbury, who was married to a local Anglo settler, and her younger sister Gertrudis, both went to the old mission with him. Mrs. Alsbury's husband, Dr. Horace Alsbury, formerly of Kentucky, was off recruiting reinforcements for the Alamo garrison.

Realizing how precarious his position now was, Travis sent out two urgent pleas for help. One was to Colonel Fannin at Goliad, and the other was to the *alcalde* and citizens of Gonzales. Before sending the message out, Travis replaced his original address with "To any of the inhabitants of Texas." (Lord: *A Time to Stand,* 97) Dr. Sutherland, who was in great pain from his fall from his horse, was selected to carry the messages. A short distance from the Alamo, he was joined by Deaf Smith, who had elected to head for Gonzales himself to gather up more volunteers. As they looked back at San Antonio one last time, they could see the lead elements of the Mexican army pouring into the town.

Sutherland and Smith traveled carefully, being watchful for Mexican patrols. They met up with a San Antonio storekeeper, Nat Lewis, who was traveling on foot with all he could carry crammed into his saddlebags. They also ran into James Butler Bonham, who was just returning to the Alamo after an unsuccessful attempt to get help from Fannin. After exchanging a few words, Sutherland and Smith rode east with their dispatches, while young Bonham rode west toward the Alamo. They could hear cannon fire in the distance.

As Santa Anna's forces approached San Antonio de Bexar, they spotted a Mexican tricolor flying on the outskirts of town. In the center section there were two stars, signifying the Mexican states of Coahuila and Texas. This flag was probably raised by some of Juan Seguin's cavalrymen as a symbol of their loyalty to the constitutional government.

By the time that the first Mexican troops entered the town, the flag was gone, and all of the rebels were inside the Alamo. By 3:00 P.M., Bexar's Military Plaza was full of Mexican troops. General Santa Anna was at their head, and the Siege of the Alamo was about to begin.

When the Vanguard of the Army of Operations entered the Military Plaza, they did so with a ceremonial flair that was designed to impress both the Alamo defenders and the local Tejanos whose loyalty might be wavering. The army's band and the massed battle flags of the various regiments stood formation in the plaza. At this point, the following units, about 1,500 men in all, were in San Antonio de Bexar: the Permanent Matamoros Battalion; the Permanent Jiminez Battalion; the Active Battalion of San Luis Potosi; the Dolores Cavalry Regiment; and eight pieces of artillery.

While Santa Anna began the initial deployment of his troops, Travis wrestled with the problem of how to best distribute his 150 or so men around a fortified mission that required many times that number to properly defend it. He established his own post at an artillery battery along the north wall. Almeron Dickinson was assigned to the guns at the rear of the chapel. According to tradition, Davy Crockett and "his" Tennesseans (who by now very well could have been his) were assigned perhaps the most vulnerable position—the wooden palisade between the south wall and the chapel. In military protocol, this was the post of the highest honor.

In addition to his show of force in the plaza, Santa Anna took one additional step to insure that the Texians knew he meant business. He ordered that a blood red flag be raised from the San Fernando Cathedral tower. This was the traditional symbol of deguello—signifying that the enemy could expect to receive no quarter.

The Texians responded to this Mexican show of force with a shower of cannon fire from the Alamo. Santa Anna reported that a corporal and a chasseur were killed and eight men were wounded. In return, the Mexicans fired four grenades from two howitzers, without inflicting any Texian casualties.

During this exchange, Bowie somehow came to believe that the Mexicans had tried to signal for a parley before the firing began. He sent Maj. Green B. Jameson to the Mexican lines to meet with Santa Anna. The general refused to receive him, but Jameson did meet with two of his aides, Colonels Juan Almonte and José Bartres. Almonte reported that Jameson stated that conditions inside the Alamo were not good, and asked about the possibility of an honorable surrender. Colonel Bartres sent a reply back to Bowie that stated, "I reply to you, according to the order of His Excellency, that the Mexican army cannot come to terms under any conditions with rebellious foreigners to whom there is no recourse left, if they wish to save their lives, than to place themselves immediately at the disposal of the Supreme Government from whom alone they may expect clemency after some considerations." (Chariton: *100 Days*, 263)

Shortly after Jameson took this reply back to the Alamo, Capt. Albert Martin went to the Mexican lines representing Colonel Travis. It is not really clear why a second envoy went out, unless it was because Travis was upset because Bowie had sent Jameson out without his knowledge and consent. Martin met with Colonel Almonte and received essentially the same reply. He told Almonte that if Travis was interested in pursuing the offer, they would both return together later, which never happened.

Sometime during the day, James Bonham safely made his way back into the fort. By the time the parleys were over, nightfall was approaching, and there was no further fighting that day. During the night, the Mexicans erected an artillery battery near the Veramendi house.

Santa Anna was now faced with a dilemma. He wrote to his second-in-command, Gen. Vicente Filisola, that, "Up to now, they [the Texians] still act stubborn, counting on the strong position which they hold, and hoping for much aid from their colonies and from the United States, but they shall soon find out their mistake." (Chariton: *100 Days*, 280) Santa Anna had made up his mind that he was not going to bypass the Alamo; he considered it to be too much of a threat to his rear to do that. The Texians, on the other hand, had resolved to dig in and fight.

Santa Anna was now committed to a siege of the Alamo. Many people believe that the defenders were always bound to a fight to the death, but a look at the military thinking of the day shows that there could have been some other honorable options. However, the preliminary negotiations had ruled out an early resolution, and Santa Anna's insistence on unconditional surrender definitely strengthened the Texians' resolve not to give up under such uncertain terms.

The precepts of French military strategist Sabastien Le Preste de Vauban (1633-1707) affected the thinking of the leaders on both sides during the Siege of the Alamo. Vauban was especially noted for his tactics on how to both defend and besiege fortresses, and his theories were still very much in use by all civilized countries in the 1830s. Many of the complaints that Chief Engineer Green B. Jameson had about the Alamo's defenses were based on Vauban's principles of fortification.

According to Vauban, there was no such thing as an impregnable fortress. By applying Vauban's slow and deliberate techniques, any fortress could eventually be reduced when besieged by a properly led and equipped army.

The strategy for the besieged garrison was to hold out as long as possible, consuming the enemy's time and resources so that they could not be used elsewhere. Wholesale loss of life on either side was not supposed to be part of the plan. While casualties during the siege were inevitable, an all-out assault, with its accompanying bloodbath, was to be avoided if at all possible. If the garrison could hold out long enough, the weather, supply problems, or some other factor would eventually force the enemy to withdraw. That was considered victory for the defenders.

The attackers, on the other hand, were expected to carry out a methodical plan designed to reduce the fortress' ability to resist. Sealed off from reinforcements and supplies, those within the fort would eventually have to give up. A series of steadily advancing trenches were dug, generally under cover of darkness, allowing the besieger's artillery to move ever closer to the walls of the fort. Eventually, the guns would reach a distance where they could batter the fort into submission.

If necessary, the fort could then be carried by infantry assault, but that was rarely the case. Protocol demanded that once this stage was reached, the besiegers offer the besieged honorable terms of surrender. In order to save both armies the heavy losses that would result from an assault, the offer was generally accepted. There was no disgrace in this; it was considered an honorable end to a courageous defense.

It is easy to see how much of this thinking was applied at the Alamo. The Texians' goal was to bide time so that Houston could organize and train his army, and the Texian government could organize itself into some kind of a stable body. To do this, the defenders had to hold Santa Anna at bay for as long as possible. The Mexicans, in turn, had to dispose of the Alamo as quickly as possible and continue their advance.

Santa Anna, to a certain extent, followed Vauban's plan. The discussion of surrender at the beginning of the siege was an expected courtesy. It was just as expected for surrender to be declined. There was an inherent conflict here that made the situation unique, however. The Moorish/Spanish/ Mexican tradition of unconditional surrender, as offered by Santa Anna, was not in keeping with the European/American expectation of honorable terms. Santa Anna's stance undoubtedly strengthened the Texians' resolve to fight to the death.

Although Santa Anna began his siege using Vauban's tactics, by starting siege lines and using his cavalry to seal off the Alamo garrison, he lacked the patience to see it through to its proper conclusion. He did not want to await the arrival of his heavy siege guns that could have reduced the Alamo's walls to rubble. Instead, and against the advice of a number of his own officers, Santa Anna ordered a premature infantry assault that resulted in heavy losses to his army. Convinced that they had no other viable options, the Alamo defenders sold their lives as dearly as possible.

WEDNESDAY, FEBRUARY 24

On the first full day of the siege, the Mexican army reconnoitered the Alamo's defenses and scouted the surrounding terrain and river crossings. At 11:00 A.M., Santa Anna went out with a cavalry patrol, and according to Colonel Almonte, at one point passed within a musket shot of the Alamo. As further testimony to his tendency to see to the smallest details himself, earlier in the day Santa Anna personally had presided over the distribution of shoes to the preference companies, the grenadiers and the light infantry.

Early in the afternoon, an artillery battery consisting of two eight-pounders and a mortar was completed and began to fire on the Alamo, at about 350 yards distance. Colonel Almonte reported, probably erroneously, that two of the fort's guns, including the eighteen-pounder, were dismounted in the barrage. If it was damaged, the eighteen-pounder was not out of service for long. The Mexicans also gained possession of several *jacales*, or huts, in the nearby village of La Villita, but suffered several casualties in the process.

On Wednesday, Colonel Bowie, who had been ill for some time, totally collapsed. There is no consensus regarding just what Bowie's illness was. Some accounts have said typhus, others pneumonia, still others TB. Those who refuse to believe one as strong as Bowie could have been felled by anything as inconsequential as a mere illness have theorized that Bowie was injured by a falling cannon, or by a fall from the wall.

Current research seems to eliminate any type of injury, in favor of illness, with typhoid pneumonia being a good possibility. Whatever the reason, as of the second day of the siege, any question of authority at the Alamo was solved. Bowie turned total command of the garrison over to Travis, and had to be helped to a small room in the low barracks. He is said to have entrusted his sisters-in-law to the care of Travis and Crockett.

No doubt encouraged by the heroic stories he loved to read, Travis composed what has become his most famous dispatch — his "Victory or Death" letter — and sent it out with courier Capt. Albert Martin. (See Chapter Thirteen for the full text of the letter.) The letter would be published and read throughout Texas, then North America, and finally most of Europe, and its message of heroism and defiance has become an essential part of the Alamo story.

During the day, Gregorio Esparza, a member of Juan Seguin's regular cavalry company, and his family made it safely into the Alamo. Gregorio's brother, Francisco Esparza, belonged to the local Presidial Cavalry Company, and would serve under Santa Anna during the siege.

In the evening, Col. Juan Bringas led a small scouting party across a footbridge over the river. Texian sharpshooters opened up on the party, killing one Mexican soldier. Bringas himself either fell or was pushed into the river in the confusion, and barely made it back to safety. And, in a strange irony, amid the cannon bombardment, Santa Anna ordered his military band to serenade the Texian defenders.

THURSDAY, FEBRUARY 25

At dawn on February 25, two more Mexican batteries that had been established during the night commenced firing. The Alamo's guns returned the fire.

General Santa Anna once again personally scouted the enemy's works, along with chasseurs from the Jiminez and Matamoros battalions. According to Gen. Vicente Filisola, Santa Anna "took up a position in the houses and the huts to the south of the Alamo about half a rifle shot's distance from the enemy parapets." (Filisola: Vol. II:170) Whatever else might be said about the dictator, Santa Anna's personal courage could not be disputed.

According to Colonel Travis, at about 10:00 A.M., two to three hundred Mexicans crossed the San Antonio River and took cover in the houses of the small settlement of La Villita, only about 90 to 100 yards from the walls of the Alamo. The Texians opened fire with canister and grapeshot from their artillery, as well as with small-arms fire. The fighting lasted about two hours, during which time the enemy replied with grape and canister from their own batteries. David Crockett and several other defenders distinguished themselves with their courage. Travis noted in a letter to Houston, "The Hon. David Crockett was seen at all points, animating the men to do their duty. . . ." (Chariton: *100 Days*, 271) Charles Despallier, Robert Brown, James Rose, and a few others valiantly sallied out of the Alamo and set fire to some of the huts and some hay that was affording cover to the Mexicans.

One corporal and a chasseur from the Matamoros Battalion were killed, and four more Mexicans were wounded in the fighting. The Jiminez Battalion reported two men wounded. The Texians had a few men scratched by pieces of flying rock, but none of the defenders were hurt seriously.

Later in the day, the Mexicans attempted to tighten their noose around the Alamo by posting men to the east, along the road to Gonzales. That night, there was another sortie out of the fort. This time the Texians gathered up some wood for firewood, and burned some additional huts that were giving cover to the enemy's new works.

The Mexicans were also busy that night. Under the brave and competent Col. Juan Morales, they were working to complete two more trenches. When these were finished about 11:30 P.M., they were occupied by men of the Matamoros Battalion. There were also two more artillery batteries established, one about 300 yards south of the Alamo, and the other near the old Powderhouse about 1,000 yards to the southeast. The Alamo was now under fire from three sides, with only the north still being open.

The weather got rather nasty about 9:00 P.M., when a norther blew in. Travis took advantage of the bad weather and the Mexican activity to send out another plea for help. This time he sent his trusted Tejano officer, Juan Seguin, and Seguin's orderly, Antonio Cruz. Although Seguin was an excellent choice for courier service, with his ability to speak fluent Spanish and his knowledge of the local terrain, there is some evidence that Travis resisted sending out one of his best officers. Seguin's choice may have been made by the proverbial drawing of straws. However, the selection was a fortunate one, for Seguin did encounter a Mexican patrol outside the walls, and had to employ both his knowledge of Spanish and the local terrain to escape.

Another factor in his escape was probably that he was riding what was believed to be the fastest horse in the Alamo, which had belonged to Jim Bowie. The desperately ill Bowie had loaned Seguin his horse for this mission. It is not known how alert Bowie was when he agreed to the loan. What is certain is that when Seguin asked Bowie for the horse, he saw his old friend for the last time.

Meanwhile, at Goliad, Fannin had begun preparations to go to the aid of the Alamo. There was some question of how effective the reinforcement effort would be, as one of the force referred to the expedition as a "forlorn hope." (Chariton: *100 Days*, 273) But it seemed, at least for the moment, that Travis' pleas would not fall on deaf ears.

FRIDAY, FEBRUARY 26

The norther that started up the previous evening continued to blow. Colonel Almonte noted that at one point during the day, the thermometer read only 39 degrees. At dawn, the Texians noticed that some of Ramirez y Sesma's cavalry were sweeping around to the east. A party of defenders sallied out of the north postern gate and engaged them. After a brief skirmish, the cavalry were driven back.

The Mexicans now had a total of eight guns in place to the west, south, and southeast of the Alamo. They kept up a steady bombardment during the day. The Texians occasionally returned fire, but kept it at a minimum to conserve ammunition.

Inside the Alamo, under the direction of Engineer Green B. Jameson, the Texians continued to work at strengthening their defenses. Small parties also ventured out of the fort throughout the day. According to General Filisola and Colonel Almonte, they were after water and firewood. There is no evidence, however, that the Alamo was ever seriously short of water. In fact, not long before the Mexican army arrived, a new well was begun inside the Alamo in anticipation of a siege.

The Texian sorties were quickly driven back by Mexican sharpshooters, but they did not suffer any casualties. The Texians were guardedly optimistic at this point. They had fought several skirmishes with the Mexicans and not lost a man. Their long-range accuracy with their long rifles had inflicted some troublesome casualties among the Mexican officer corps. And surely, they thought, Fannin and others must be coming to their aid.

In fact, during the afternoon of this day, Fannin had actually begun a relief effort. Leaving a token garrison at Fort Defiance, he set out with 320 men, four pieces of artillery, and some supplies. There were problems, however. Fannin's supplies were limited, his men poorly clothed and underfed. Goliad, too, had suffered in supplying the Matamoros expedition. Perhaps worst of all, Fannin had no horses to draw his supply wagons and artillery, so he had to rely on difficult and slow moving oxen. Still, he was determined to go to the aid of his besieged comrades.

During the night of February 26, the Texians burned some more huts that were affording cover to the enemy, this time near the position of the San Luis Potosi Battalion.

SATURDAY, FEBRUARY 27

The cold north wind continued, making things uncomfortable for the besiegers and the besieged alike. Colonel Almonte again noted that the temperature was only 39 degrees. There was not much firing done by either side.

Lt. Manuel Menacho of the presidial cavalry was sent to forage the ranches of the Seguin and Flores families, in an attempt to procure corn, hogs, and cattle.

The Mexicans also made an unsuccessful effort to cut off the Alamo's water supply by sealing off the irrigation ditch that ran into the fort. This effort caused the Texians to complete the partially finished well at the south end of the compound. They struck water, but they also damaged an earthen parapet near the low barracks that limited their ability to fire to the south.

While these activities were taking place in and around the Alamo, the rest of the Army of Operations was making its way to San Antonio de Bexar as quickly as it could. By February 25, the First Infantry Brigade had reached San Ambrosio, a day's march north of Rio Bravo. Lieutenant de la Pena reported that there was no water, but that there was "such an abundance of rabbits that the soldiers could catch them by hand as easily as chickens from a hen." (De la Pena, 32-33) He also stated that due to careless handling, the powder supply of the Aldama Battalion caught fire, causing "considerable alarm" in camp. (De la Pena, 33)

The march of the army had been hampered by bad weather, and also by the poor condition of the oxen and the desertion of their drivers. Santa Anna criticized General Gaona for his slow progress, but Lieutenant de la Pena reported that Gaona did everything he could considering the circumstances. De la Pena reported of Gaona, "On several occasions we saw him driving the carts and helping them to yoke the oxen," and that he "had done everything in his power to overcome the obstacles on the way." (De la Pena, 33)

Nonetheless, on the 27th, Gaona received a dispatch from Santa Anna ordering him to send the sappers of the Aldama and Toluca battalions ahead on a forced march under the command of Col. Francisco Duque. Realizing that the twelve-pound artillery pieces would be very helpful in the siege, Lieutenant de la Pena suggested that these also be sent on ahead. Gaona felt that since they had not been specifically requested, and since they might impede the forced march, they should remain with the main column. De la Pena himself was given command of the rear guard of Duque's column, and advanced with them.

Gaona wasn't the only one having trouble with travel. Fannin had only gone a short distance from Goliad when one of his wagons broke down. He then had to remount his gun carriages, because it took two yoke of oxen to get each gun across the San Antonio River but only one team to haul the gun on the road. By the time Fannin had gotten his four guns across, it was almost dark. His men, who had been struggling all day in the face of a norther, were exhausted, so they stopped for the night. The next morning, the oxen were gone. It took several hours, but finally they were retrieved and hitched up.

Then an officers' council was held, and it was decided to let discretion be the better part of valor. Fannin's army would return to Goliad. Just two days before, Fannin had written that Travis' and Bowie's pleas could not pass unnoticed. Now he wrote to acting Governor Robinson that returning to Goliad was the "expedient" thing to do.

Not everyone, though, was turning a deaf ear to the Alamo's plight. From the small town of Gonzales, a brave band that called themselves the "Gonzales Ranging Company of Mounted Volunteers" was riding west to assist the besieged garrison. After picking up a few additional volunteers, they numbered a grand total of thirty-two men, but they were willing to do what they could to help. Even today in Texas they are known as "The Immortal 32."

Unaware of these developments, inside the

Alamo Lt. Col. William Barret Travis penned another passionate plea to Fannin for help. He selected James Butler Bonham, who had just returned to the Alamo from a similar mission, to carry this message to Goliad.

This day Santa Anna also sent off a number of couriers of his own. One was dispatched to Mexico City to bring the government word of his reoccupation of San Antonio de Bexar. Similar messages were sent to the commanders of the other sections of his Army of Operations.

SUNDAY, FEBRUARY 28

At last, the weather finally began to moderate. The Mexicans continued to shell the Alamo, and they also made another attempt to cut off the fort's water supply.

Rumors circulated in the Mexican camp that 200 Texian reinforcements were coming from Goliad. Although this eventually proved to be untrue, it was based on fact. The informal Mexican intelligence network correctly reported that Fannin had started out to assist the beleaguered garrison; they just were not yet aware that it had been a false start.

By this time, Capt. Juan Seguin had delivered the messages that Travis had given him. He had rounded up twenty-five men who were willing to go back to the Alamo with him, and on February 28 he was waiting at the Cibolo River to join forces with Fannin's relief column. He had been joined by another courier, Dr. John Sutherland, and twelve more volunteers, but Fannin never showed.

Things were a little different on the Mexican side, however. As Colonel Duque's column hurried to San Antonio de Bexar, they were joined by Gen. Martín Perfecto de Cos and his men. These were the same men who had been paroled by the Texians after the Battle of Bexar in December, and now, in clear violation of their parole, they were heading back into Texas to fight again.

MONDAY, FEBRUARY 29

On Monday, the weather continued to moderate. The temperature reached 55 degrees, but there was still a brisk west wind.

The Allende Infantry Battalion was posted to the east side of the Alamo, while the Jiminez Battalion was positioned to the left of the Gonzales Road in order to more effectively seal off the fort.

Santa Anna again personally scouted the enemy's defenses during the course of the day. At about 7:30 P.M. that evening, Secundino Alvarez, a first-class private of the San Luis Battalion, was ordered to get in close to the Alamo and reconnoiter the works. As he did so, he was shot and killed by a Texian sharpshooter.

February 29 marked the end of the first week of the Siege of the Alamo. Although there were Mexicans all around the fortress, there were still enough gaps in the lines that several couriers had safely come and gone. It is also probable that there was enough contact between the Tejanos inside the Alamo and those in Bexar that both sides had a fairly good idea what the other was doing.

Supplies and ammunition, while not abundant, were adequate. Jim Bowie was seriously ill, and William Barret Travis had assumed full command of the garrison. Davy Crockett of Tennessee, although technically just a private—or a "high private," as he called it—had become one of the informal leaders of the garrison. Susannah Dickinson remembered that he raised the spirits of the men by playing his fiddle. He would engage in musical duels with Scotsman John McGregor—Crockett on the fiddle and McGregor on the bagpipes, each trying to outdo the other.

Still, things within the Alamo were grim. Everyone knew what their chances were unless help came, help that really should have been there already. Some, Crockett included, were having second thoughts about the wisdom of trying to hold the old mission. Henry Warnell summed it up when he said, "I'd much rather be out on that open prairie. . . . I don't like to be penned up like this." (Hardin: *Texian Iliad,* 132)

The past week of almost constant artillery bombardment had taken its toll. The men were tired. The weather had been bad. The food could be better. These were the age old complaints of soldiers under siege. It was a predicable part of the game. Vauban knew; Santa Anna knew; Travis knew. Deep down inside, the men themselves knew. If they chose to run, under cover of darkness, many of them probably would make it. To leave, though, would violate their trust, would leave the rest of Texas exposed to Santa Anna's butchery. No, the choice was clear. They had to stay—to stand and fight, to buy time, for as long as they could, with or without help. In spite of the odds, this was the choice that they made.

TUESDAY, MARCH 1

The night was again very cold, only 36 degrees at morning, according to Col. Juan Almonte. Outside the walls of the Alamo, the thirty-two volunteers from Gonzales carefully worked their way through the Mexican lines. Fortunately, they chose to approach from the northeast. Most of the Mexican patrols had been concentrating on the road to Goliad, off to the southeast, and the volunteers were able to make it through undetected. However, about 3:00 A.M., just as they thought that they had reached the fort safely, a nervous Texian sentry fired on them and wounded one of the men in the foot. The indignant outburst that followed left no doubt that the shadows in the dark were friends, and the "Immortal 32" were welcomed into the Alamo without further incident. According to some sources, they brought with them the first flag of the Texas Revolution—the "Come and Take It" flag that had flown above the cannon at the engagement at Gonzales.

Later in the day, General Ramirez y Sesma decided that he was not going to encounter any reinforcements from Goliad, so he brought his men back to their former positions encircling the Alamo. It will never be known for sure, but it is possible that if Sesma's men had not been drawn off by the false alarm from Fannin, the Gonzales men might not have been able to make their way into the fort safely.

The effect of the Gonzales Volunteers on the morale of the Alamo garrison was way out of proportion to their numbers. The beleaguered garrison now knew that the rest of Texas understood their plight. If these men had come, surely others would soon follow.

Even if it was only temporary, spirits soared. Ammunition had been running low, so firing, especially by the artillery, had been restricted. Now Colonel Travis authorized two shots from a twelve-pounder in celebration. One round crashed into the Military Plaza and did no harm. The second scored a direct hit on one of the adjacent houses. The Texians did not know it, but it was the house that Santa Anna was using as his headquarters. Unfortunately, he was not there at the time; he was out on another one of his scouting trips. About noon, he had left to reconnoiter the site of an old mill about half a mile northwest of the Alamo.

It is possible that in addition to the Gonzales 32, other reinforcements might have also gotten through. Research currently being conducted by Tom Lindley, of Austin, Texas, suggests that the garrison may have consisted of about 257 men on the day of the final battle. Although much more work must be done before anything definite can be said in this regard, one thing is certain. Those who did come knew full well what odds they faced, and they came to the Alamo anyway. They all died there, but in doing so, they gained a glorious place in Texas history.

Throughout the day, Lt. Col. Pedro Ampudia, acting general of artillery, was busy supervising work on the siege lines—lines that were advancing ever closer to the Alamo.

WEDNESDAY, MARCH 2

March 2 was another day of bitterly cold weather. Along its line of march, the First Infantry Brigade buried a soldier of the Toluca Battalion who expired from "the excessive cold and severe pain," and a captain of the grenadier company of the Aldama Battalion also died. (De la Pena, 36) Lieutenant de la Pena reported that it was so cold that written messages could not be sent because the ink froze in the inkwells. The column crossed the Medina River and marched to within a short distance of Bexar before stopping for the night. They rested and prepared for a grand entrance into the town the next day.

From Santa Anna's camp, Lieutenant Menacho was again sent to the Seguin ranch to forage corn. A chasseur from the San Luis Potosi Battalion, Trinidad Delgado, accidentally drowned. During the afternoon, Santa Anna went on another reconnaissance. He discovered a covered road within a pistol shot of the Alamo, and ordered the Jiminez Battalion posted there.

Inside the Alamo, the men waited and worried. The confidence they had felt when the men from Gonzales arrived began to wane. When was Fannin coming? He certainly should be there soon—Goliad was only ninety-five miles away.

Although the men inside the walls never knew it, March 2 was one of the most important dates in the history of Texas. This was the day that the convention at Washington-on-the-Brazos declared that "the people of Texas do now constitute a FREE, SOVEREIGN, and INDEPENDENT REPUBLIC. . . ." (Chariton: *100 Days,* 297) (See Chapter Thirteen for the complete text of the Texas Declaration of Independence).

Independence! No longer was Texas fighting for the Mexican Constitution of 1824. It was all or nothing now, especially for the Tejanos who had rebelled against Santa Anna's tyranny. The Anglos could always go back "home" if things got bad, but to the Tejanos, Texas was home. They had to win or they would perish—they could expect no mercy from Santa Anna. Still, they and the rest of the Texians saw independence as the best hope for their futures, and for that of their families. The men in the Alamo would most certainly have agreed, if only they had known.

THURSDAY, MARCH 3

Thursday, March 3, the tenth day of the Siege of the Alamo, dawned calm and clear with a temperature of 40 degrees. Despite the shortage of ammunition, throughout the day the Texians fired sporadic artillery rounds and small-arms fire at the Mexicans.

As had become his custom, Santa Anna went on a reconnaissance of the Mexican siegeworks and the Texians' defenses. A new Mexican battery was erected on the north side of the Alamo, which, according to Colonel Almonte, was within a musket shot of its walls.

At about 11:00 A.M., one of the bravest of the brave returned to the Alamo after his second mission seeking help for the besieged garrison. James Butler Bonham made it through the enemy lines without a scratch, passing between the powder house and the upper Mexican camp. He brought the sad news that there would be no help coming from Fannin and his men. Bonham had arrived at Goliad on February 29, and there he was informed that it would be impossible for Fannin to march his army to the Alamo's relief. He told Fannin that if he would not help the Alamo's garrison, then he would ride to Gonzales to seek volunteers there.

Bonham reached Gonzales on March 1, only to learn that all of the volunteers had already departed for the Alamo. Determined to see his duty through, Bonham then rode back to the Alamo alone, knowing that by doing so he faced almost certain death.

Although the news that Fannin was not coming was devastating to the garrison's morale, there is reason to believe that Bonham's return did not leave them completely without hope. He carried a letter addressed to William Travis from his friend, Maj. R. M. "Three-Legged Willie" Williamson, who had recently been appointed commander of the Texas Rangers. The letter, written in Gonzales on March 1, advised Travis that more than 300 reinforcements were on the way, and pleaded for the garrison to hold out until they arrived. The orignal letter, which has been lost, was reportedly found on or near Travis' body after the final battle. A Spanish translation of it was published as a Mexican broadside on March 31, 1836. Unless the broadside was a total fabrication, the garrison did still have some hope left. This in no way diminishes their courage, for by the time Bonham returned, every man had to be well aware of the tremendous odds that they were facing. And they surely knew that with the arrival of Santa Anna's siege guns, even 300 more men may not have been enough.

South and east of the Alamo, the Matamoros expedition had come to a final, bloody and tragic end. Ever since the expedition had left San Antonio, its leadership had been split by the kind of infighting that had plagued the Texas Legislature. Johnson, Grant, and Fannin, each believing himself to be the primary leader, had argued over almost everything. Fannin had abandoned the expedition shortly after it left Goliad, taking about half the force with him back to Fort Defiance. On the same day that he gave up his attempt to reinforce the Alamo, Fannin learned of the first disaster to befall his former comrades.

Johnson and Grant had advanced as far as the town of San Patricio, about 100 miles north of Matamoros. There they fought over how best to continue—whether they should push on rapidly, or wait for reinforcements. By this time, it was known that there was a Mexican force advancing toward them. Finally, Grant took about half of the remaining hundred or so men, including a number of New Orleans Greys, and set out west looking for horses. While they were gone, on February 27, about a hundred Mexican cavalry took Johnson's men by surprise in San Patricio. Sixteen of them were killed, thirty-four were taken prisoner, and the rest escaped in the confusion. They headed back north and joined Fannin at Goliad. Grant's men were caught by Mexican lancers on the third, and all but three were killed. The ambitious Texian dream of carrying the war into Mexico had ended on the banks of Agua Dulce Creek.

In the Mexican camp, there was much cause for jubilation. About 4:00 P.M., the soldiers were busy celebrating the news of General Urrea's victory at San Patricio, when Colonel Duque's reinforcements arrived. They came marching into the Military Plaza, flags flying and resplendent in their full dress uniforms. As the Texians watched from the walls of the Alamo, the men of the Aldama, Toluca, and Zapadores battalions finally arrived in Bexar, after their long and difficult march up from Mexico. Colonel Travis estimated their strength at 1,000 men. This was a fairly accurate guess, as Lieutenant de la Pena reported that the column consisted of 846 combatants, which, combined with officers, staff, and drivers, equaled approximately Travis' number. (Chariton: *100 Days,* 304-305; De la Pena, 37)

Late that evening, a party of the Texians sallied out of the fort and attacked the Mexicans encamped by the sugar mill, but they met heavy resistance and were forced to retire.

At midnight, scout Deaf Smith rode out of the Alamo carrying more dispatches and letters from the garrison. Among the papers was a letter from Travis to the president of the convention, in which he stated,

> I have so fortified this place, that the walls are generally proof against cannon-balls; and I shall continue to entrench on the inside, and strengthen the walls by throwing up dirt. At least two hundred shells have fallen inside our works without having injured a single man; indeed, we have been so fortunate as not to lose a man from any cause, and we have killed many of the enemy . . . I look to the colonies alone for aid; unless it arrives soon, I shall have to fight the enemy on his own terms. I will, however, do the best I can under the circumstances, and I feel confident that the determined valour and desperate courage, heretofore evinced by my men, will not fail them in the last struggle, and although they may be sacrificed to the vengeance of a Gothic enemy, the victory will cost the enemy so dear, that it will be worse for him than a defeat. (Chariton: *100 Days,* 304-305)

Travis also wrote to his friend Jesse Grimes that, "They [the Mexicans] are now encamped in entrenchments on all sides of us." The net was drawing ever tighter around the Texians. In the same letter, Travis offered his opinion on the question of complete independence for Texas, unaware that such a resolution had been passed the previous day: "Let the Convention go on and make a declaration of independence. . . . If independence is not declared, I shall lay down my arms, and so shall the men under my command. But under the flag of independence, we are ready to peril our lives a hundred times a day. . . ." (Chariton: *100 Days,* 306)

To his friend David Ayers, Travis wrote perhaps the most poignant Alamo letter of all. "Take care of my little boy," the Alamo commander wrote, ". . . If the country should be saved, I may make for him a splendid fortune; but if the country be lost and I should perish, he will have nothing but the proud recollection that he is the son of a man who died for his country." (Chariton, *100 Days,* 307)

So that people would know that the Alamo still held out, Travis also included in his dispatches that the garrison would fire the eighteen-pounder morning, noon, and night for as long as they were able.

FRIDAY, MARCH 4

Friday, the fourth of March, was a fair, windy day. The Mexicans began their bombardment early, but the Texian guns remained silent except for one or two rounds in the afternoon.

Santa Anna called a special meeting of his senior officers to discuss plans for an attack on the Alamo. He was growing impatient with the siege, and clearly was in favor of an all-out assault. Although the different accounts do not always agree which officers were on what sides of the issue, enthusiasm for the attack was definitely not universally shared by Santa Anna's staff. A number of them felt that such an attack would be far too costly. They wanted to wait for the arrival of the heavy artillery that could breach the walls first, which was the proper procedure according to the tactician Vauban. Colonel Almonte wrote that a pair of twelve-pounders were expected on Monday, March 7, so the wait would not have been all that long.

According to Lieutenant de la Pena, the question of what to do with any captured prisoners also came up at the meeting. De la Pena stated that General Castrillon and Colonel Almonte argued against the no-quarter policy ordered by Santa Anna. The meeting eventually broke up without a firm decision having been made on this issue.

The Mexican staff was operating with fairly accurate information about the conditions inside the Alamo. General Cos had firsthand knowledge of many of the defenses, because the work had been performed by his own troops during the Siege of Bexar. Additional information came from wounded officers that had been left behind to recuperate after the Mexican withdrawal, and also from some of the citizens of Bexar who were sympathetic to the Mexican army, yet still in contact with the Tejanos inside the fortress.

Another interesting story, although not supported by any other known source, is told by Enrique Esparza, Gregorio's young son. Years later, Enrique recalled that on the first night of the siege, his father was among a party of defenders that sortied out of the Alamo and captured a Mexican soldier. Brought back as a prisoner, throughout the siege he interpreted the Mexican bugle calls, which helped to keep the defenders apprised of the enemy troop movements. (Esparza: *The San Antonio Express,* March 7, 1905)

There were also several Mexican officers trained in engineering skills who were constantly assessing the enemy's defenses as well as directing the Mexican siege operations. Capt. (Acting Colonel) Ignacio Labastida drew an excellent sketch of both the Alamo and the town of San Antonio de Bexar that is often referred to as the "Mexican Engineer's Map." Lieutenants Ignacio Berrospe and Juan Ordones also performed valuable engineering services.

Rumors were circulating that the Texians were considering surrender. In his interview with *The San Antonio Express,* Enrique Esparza claimed that "Santa Ana had offered to let the Americans go with their lives if they would surrender, but the Mexicans would be treated as rebels." (Esparza: *The San Antonio Express,* March 7, 1905)

It does not seem likely, however, that Santa Anna was inclined to let any of the defenders off lightly at this point. On the evening of March 4, a Mexican woman from Bexar reportedly told Santa Anna that Travis had promised his men that they would either try to escape under cover of darkness or surrender if help did not come very soon. More than one historian, and even some of Santa Anna's own officers, have speculated that this information is what prompted him to push for an immediate assault rather than wait for his heavy siege guns. There would have been little glory in a bloodless victory, and glory is what Santa Anna craved above all else!

While we do not have any concrete proof that the Texians were actually seriously considering giving up, we do know that the constant bombardment and the discouragement of not receiving reinforcements was taking its toll. A letter possibly written by an Alamo defender on March 3 gives insight into Travis' mental state. Although the authenticity of Isaac Millsaps' letter to his family is questioned by many historians, its picture of the young commander rings true: "I have not seen Travis but two times since here he told us all this morning that Fanning was going to be here early with many men and there would be a good fight. He stays on the wall some but mostly to his room. . . ." (Chariton: *100 Days,* 303) Even the heroic Davy Crockett showed that he was having doubts when he said, "I think we had better march out and die in the open air. I don't like to be hemmed up." (Lord: *A Time to Stand,* 144)

As the exhausted defenders reflected on their fate, under the cover of darkness the Mexicans once again inched their trenches closer to the walls of the Alamo.

SATURDAY, MARCH 5

The fifth of March was a clear pleasant day, with temperatures starting out around 50 degrees and rising to 68. The Mexican artillery kept up a brisk fire from their north battery, which was answered only occasionally by the Texians.

Santa Anna held another staff meeting, during which he announced that a major assault would be made on the Alamo on the morning of March 6. Lieutenant de la Pena reported that although a number of officers spoke against an assault when it was still in the planning stages, once the orders were given, all stood ready to carry them out. According to General Filisola, the leaders of the four attack columns were selected for their unquestioned loyalty.

The battle orders, drawn up by Gen. Juan Valentín Amador, show the great attention that Santa Anna paid to small details. They also show that the troops that were employed in the actual assault were the seasoned veterans. The green recruits, which made up a good portion of the army, were ordered to remain in camp.

Although it was not stated directly in the orders, Santa Anna also saw to it that the presidial troops from Bexar did not take an active part in the actual fighting. In spite of whatever else he may have been, Santa Anna did not want to have relatives, friends, and neighbors fighting one another. Francisco Esparza, brother of Alamo defender Gregorio Esparza, was a member of the Presidial Cavalry troop from Bexar. Although some sources cite this as an example of brother fighting against brother, Francisco and his unit did not actually take an active part in the assault.

The complete text of the Mexican battle orders makes interesting reading, and is reprinted here in its entirety:

General Order of March 5th, 1836, 2:00 P.M.
To the Generals, Chiefs of Sections and
Corps Commanders:

Being necessary to act decisively upon the enemy defending The Alamo, the Most Excellent General-in-Chief has ordered that tomorrow at four o'clock the attacking columns, placed at short distance from the first trenches, undertake the assault to begin with a signal given by the General by means of the sounding of a bugle from the North battery.

General D. Martin Perfecto de Cos will command the First Column. If he cannot, I will. The Permanent Battalion, Aldama, with the exception of the Grenadier Company and the first three Active Companies of San Luis, will form the First Column.

The Second Column will be commanded by Colonel D. Francisco Duque. If he cannot, by General D. Manuel Fernandez Castrillon. The Active Battalion, Toluca, and the three Active Rifle Companies, San Luis, with the exception of the Grenadier Company, will form this Second Column.

Colonel D. Jose Maria Romero will command the Third. If he cannot, Colonel D. Mariano de Salas. The Rifle Companies from the Permanent Battalions, Matamoros and Jiminez, will form this column.

The Fourth will be commanded by D. Juan Morales. If he cannot, by Colonel D. Jose Minon. It will be formed by the Scouting Companies from the Permanent Battalions, Matamoros and Jiminez, and the Active Battalion, San Luis.

The points from which these columns will mount their attacks will be designated by the General-in-Chief at the opportune time, and then the Column Commanders will receive their orders.

The reserves will be formed by the Sapper Battalion and the five Grenadier Companies from the Permanent Battalions, Matamoros, Jiminez and Aldama, plus the Active Battalions, Toluca and San Luis. The reserve force will be commanded by the General-in-Chief at the moment of attack, but the gathering of this force will be carried out by Colonel D. Augustin Amat, under whose orders the reserves will remain from this afternoon until they are placed in positions to be designated.

The First Column will carry ten scaling ladders, two crowbars and two axes; the same number by the second; six ladders by the third, and two by the fourth.

The men carrying the ladders will sling their rifles on their backs until the ladders are properly placed.

The Companies of Grenadiers and Scouts will carry ammunition at six rounds per man and at four for the riflemen, and two flints in reserve. These men will not wear cloaks, carry blankets, or anything else which will inhibit them to maneuver quickly. During the day all shako chin-straps will be correctly worn — these the Commanders will watch closely. The troops will wear shoes or sandals. The attacking troops will turn in after the night's prayers as they will form their columns at midnight.

The untrained recruits will remain in the camps. All armaments will be in good shape—especially the bayonets.

As soon as the moon rises, the riflemen of the Active Battalion, San Luis, will move back to their quarters to get their equipment ready; this will be done by leaving their stations in the line.

The Cavalry, under the command of General D. Joaquin Ramirez y Sesma, will occupy the Alameda and will saddle up at three o'clock in the morning. Their duty will be to guard the camp and keep anyone from deserting.

Take this into consideration: Against the daring foreigners opposing us, the Honor of our Nation and Army is at stake. His Supreme Excellency, the General-in-Chief, expects each man to fulfill his duties and to exert himself to give his country a day of glory and satisfaction. He well knows how to reward those brave men who form The Army of Operations.

Juan Valentín Amador.

(Lamego, 32-34)

Throughout the rest of the afternoon, the senior Mexican officers studied the Alamo's defenses in preparation for the attack. Junior officers saw to the many details necessary so that their men would be prepared for the coming battle.

Legend has it that before the final battle, probably on the evening of the fifth, Colonel Travis called all of his men together and told them that there was no longer any hope of reinforcements arriving in time. To stay and defend the Alamo any longer meant only one thing—certain death. He planned to stay and continue to fight for Texas, but any who wished to do so were free to leave. Travis then drew his sword and scratched a line in the sand. Any man who was willing to stay and fight was asked to cross over the line and join Travis. The entire garrison, save one man, did so. That one man was Louis Rose, an old veteran of Napoleon's Grand Army. Rose simply said that it was not his time to die, and disappeared silently over the wall.

This is an inspiring story, but there is no conclusive proof that it really happened. Neither can it be disproved. It was well known that Ben Milam had made a similar challenge before the assault on Bexar, and given Travis' flair for the dramatic, he very well might have done just such a thing. Invoking the fallen hero's memory, in words or actions, would have inspired many in the garrison. Whether Travis actually did so or not, by this time in the siege, nearly every defender must have made a very similar choice in his own mind.

Something that we do know for certain is that the Mexican artillery kept up their bombardment throughout the afternoon and on into the evening of March 5. Then, about 10:00 P.M., the guns fell silent. Santa Anna wanted the defenders to fall into a much needed sleep as his men prepared for their predawn attack.

That night, the Alamo's last courier, sixteen-year-old James Allen, rode out through the Mexican lines, carrying a final desperate plea for help from Lt. Col. William Barret Travis.

SUNDAY, MARCH 6

Around midnight, sleeping Mexican soldiers were aroused by their noncommissioned officers, and began moving into their preassigned positions for the upcoming assault. By 5:00 A.M., they were all in place. According to one account, some were within 300 feet of the Alamo, and had to lie on their stomachs on the cold ground from 3:00 A.M. to 5:30 A.M. (Chariton: *100 Days,* 327)

At 5:30 A.M., Santa Anna finally gave the order for the advance to begin. Here we again run into the confusion that surrounds so much of the Alamo story. Some sources claim that the plan was to advance quietly on the exhausted Texians, getting as close as possible without discovery. Others state that the advance was signaled by trumpeter José María Gonzalez of the Zapadores Battalion, and then picked up by the massed bands of all of the units, stationed with the reserves. Santa Anna's written orders state that the start of the attack would be signaled by a bugle call. At any rate, it is known that enthusiastic *soldados,* unable to contain their nervous energy, soon began to shout, *"Viva Santa Anna, viva la republica,"* and whatever element of surprise the Mexicans had was quickly lost.

As previously decreed, the Mexican forces advanced in column, rather than in line, formation:

General Cos' men moved toward the northwest corner of the Alamo.

Colonel Duque's column headed directly for the north wall.

Colonel Romero brought his men in from the east.

Colonel Morales led his light companies toward what was structurally the Alamo's weakest point — the wooden palisade stretching between the chapel and the low barracks along the south wall.

Actually, the apparent structural weakness of this position was deceptive. Although the exterior was only wooden palisade, it was in fact a double wall about six feet wide, filled with earth in between. Fortifications of this type had been proof against artillery fire for hundreds of years. The combination of artillery at the rear of the chapel and in the lunette would catch any attacking force in a deadly crossfire. Just in front of the palisade was a ditch that would break up any attacking infantry formation, and the wall was wide enough that it could not be jumped by cavalry horses. Information recently discovered by Gary Zaboly indicates that fallen trees were stacked in front of the ditch. (Hardin: *Texian Iliad,* xviii) There was also at least one cannon mounted behind the palisade. Finally, this section was defended by the Tennessee Mounted Volunteers, including David Crockett, whose accuracy with their long rifles had already been proven several times during the siege. Most likely, Morales' main mission was to keep the riflemen pinned down so they could not help out at the main points of the assault, rather than to actually take the palisade.

Other Mexican light infantrymen, skilled in the use of their Baker Rifles, moved as a screen ahead of the advancing columns, ready to pick off any defenders who dared to show themselves. Texian pickets stationed outside the walls, who were supposed to give the alarm, were surprised and quickly dispatched.

The Alamo's adjutant, Capt. John Baugh, is believed to have been the first to notice the advancing Mexican columns. He quickly raised the alarm, and sleepy Texians rushed to their posts. Colonel Travis, followed by his loyal slave Joe, grabbed his shotgun and sword and ran to the battery on the north wall. As he ran past some of the Tejano defenders, Travis shouted *"¡No rendirse, muchachos!,"* a call for no surrender.

The opening fire from the Texians was devastating. While there were nowhere near enough defenders to properly cover the large expanse of the walls, this was partially made up for by the fact that each man had four or five loaded guns ready to go. (Lord: *A Time to Stand,* 156) Also, Santa Anna's love of Napoleonic tactics may have worked against his troops. Unlike the Anglo-American tactic of advancing in a long line, the Mexican army advanced in a French column formation, two companies wide, with the remainder of the assault force stretched out behind. Only the front two ranks could safely fire during the advance, and the tightly packed columns were perfect targets for both artillery and small-arms fire. The concentration of the Mexican forces allowed the Texians to also consolidate their much smaller force at the actual points of attack.

The Texian artillery opened fire as well, with terrible results at such close range. A single salvo took out half of the light infantry company of the Toluca Battalion, including its captain, José María Herrera. (De la Pena, 47) The Mexican gunners, on the other hand, had to remain silent throughout the battle, for fear of inflicting casualties on their own soldiers.

The front ranks of the Mexican columns wavered but were forced to press on by the ranks behind. Some made it right up to the walls, where they were safe from artillery fire but exposed to riflemen willing to risk leaning over the wall to fire down into them. Colonel Travis took such a chance from the north wall. He emptied both barrels of his shotgun into the Mexicans huddled below. As he did so, an enemy ball struck him in the head. He spun around and fell down the artillery ramp. The Alamo commander was among the very first to fall. With his master shot, Joe left the fighting and went back to one of the barracks rooms. He later testified that he continued firing from a window in the room. He also said that his mortally wounded master revived when the Mexicans began coming over the wall, managing to stab a Mexican officer with his sword before he was finally killed. Although Joe's account does seem to contain some heroic exaggerations, it also has the ring of truth. Travis' body was found where Joe said he had fallen, and Joe himself was eventually found in a barracks room near the north wall by Mexican soldiers after the battle.

With the intensity of the fighting, other Texians also inevitably became casualties. Galba Fuqua, a sixteen-year-old volunteer from Gonzales, ran into the sacristy of the chapel where Susannah Dickinson was hiding with her daughter Angelina. Fuqua frantically tried to say something to Susannah, but was unable to speak because his jaw was shattered. After several unsuccessful attempts to get his message out, he bravely turned and ran back to the fighting.

Unable to gain entry into the fort at the northern end, the Mexican columns started to falter and then withdraw. At the south end, raked by fire from the chapel, the lunette, the top of the low barracks, and the palisade, Colonel Morales' light infantrymen sought shelter in some of the *jacales,* or huts, near the southwest corner of the compound that had not been burned by the Texians.

After a brief respite, the *soldados* regrouped and attacked once more. They were again met by withering fire, and were still unable to break their way into the fortress.

The Mexican officers and noncommissioned officers bravely re-formed their men for a third charge. Off they started to the piercing notes of the *"Deguello,"* the haunting bugle call of no quarter. The attacking columns had more than Texian sharpshooters and artillery fire to contend with. Because of the crowded conditions in their long column formations, and the inexperience of many of the Mexican troops, some of the *soldados* fired into the backs of those in front of them, causing a significant number of casualties by "friendly fire."

Some writers have claimed that many of the *soldados* fired from the hip because they feared the recoil of their muskets, causing them to fire low and strike their own comrades. As reenactors experienced in the use of the weapons of the day, the authors feel that this is unlikely. The kick of a black powder musket is rarely even uncomfortable to the shoulder, and is certainly nothing to be seriously afraid of. Mexican gunpowder was often of such poor quality that there are reports of shots bouncing off the Texians. (Hardin: *Texian Iliad,* 81) Such powder certainly did not develop much recoil when it was fired. It must also be remembered that the Mexican troops involved in the actual assault were the tested veterans, not the raw recruits. The officers and NCOs would not allow these experienced *soldados* to exercise the awkward, inefficient, and dangerous practice of firing a single-shot musket from the hip. However, there was another very real threat to the *soldados* from their friends. Colonel Duque, and probably many others, fell wounded, and were trampled in the confusion by their own men.

Still, in the face of what must have looked to be almost certain death, the Mexicans bravely pushed on. The fact that the cavalry patrolling the rear had orders to ride down any deserters might have helped their motivation. Still, the courage of the common Mexican soldier in this frontal assault without the support of artillery deserves recognition, just as does the valiant resistance by the Texian defenders.

On and on came the Mexican columns, torn by musket and rifle fire, as well as by artillery rounds often made up of whatever deadly scrap the gunners could find to ram down their muzzles. When they did finally reach the walls, the Mexicans found that most of their scaling ladders did not end up in the right places, and those that did were poorly made.

This time, however, something different happened when the attacks reached the walls of the Alamo. As Colonel Romero's column, attacking from the east, ran into heavy fire, it began shifting to its right, joining forces with the Toluca Battalion that was assaulting the north wall.

Meanwhile, General Cos' column, also meeting heavy resistance as it attacked from the northwest, made an unplanned shift to its left. This resulted in three of the attack columns being concentrated against the north wall. When Santa Anna observed this unexpected event, he decided that it was time to commit the reserves, and they also came charging into the thick of the fight for the north wall.

Deliberately or otherwise, Cos' column began to move back to the right a bit, bringing it to bear on its original objective, the northwest bastion. This point marks the beginning of the end for the Texians. Little by little, the Mexicans now began to fight their way into the Alamo. The soldiers massed against the north wall found that they could claw their way up the timber reinforcements built by the Texians to strengthen the weakened section. Tradition holds that the first Mexican to reach the top of the Alamo's wall was Gen. Juan Amador. One Mexican account claims that suddenly *soldados* appeared on top of the wall as if by magic. Another states that the troops began pouring over the wall like sheep.

At the same time, some of Cos' men, using axes and crowbars, were able to break through the northern postern gate, and also climb through the open gun ports. Colonel Romero's men used similar tactics as they shifted their attack to the corrals on the northeast side.

The fighting at the south end of the Alamo was equally fierce. Colonel Morales' men, who had sought shelter in the *jacales,* moved their assault away from the lunette and the gate, and concentrated on the southeast bastion, the location of the eighteen-pounder. In a brutal, hand-to-hand struggle, they soon seized the battery.

Before long, Mexican troops were pouring into the Alamo courtyard from nearly every direction. This was more than the valiant Texians could withstand, so, following their prearranged plan, they fell back into fortified positions inside the rooms of the barracks and the chapel. Lieutenant de la Pena described one Texian, whom he mistook for Travis, calmly loading and firing as he led the withdrawal from the north wall. This person may have been the adjutant, Capt. John Baugh, or one of the officers of the Greys.

Some of the Texian guns, which had not been spiked before they were abandoned, were put to use by the Mexicans, adding to the carnage. Ramón Caro, Santa Anna's secretary, recorded that "The enemy immediately took refuge inside the rooms of the fortress, the walls of which had been previously bored to enable them to fire through the holes. Generals Amador and Ampudia trained the guns upon the interior of the fort to demolish it as the only means of putting an end to the strife." (Castaneda, 105)

Capt. Almeron Dickinson came running into the sacristy of the chapel, where his wife Susannah and daughter Angelina were hiding. "Great God, Sue, the Mexicans are inside our walls! If they spare you, save my child," he cried. (Lord: *A Time to Stand,* 160) He embraced his wife a final time, and then raced back to his station on a ramp at the back wall of the chapel. Dickinson had his men turn their gun and fire down into the mass of Mexicans now swarming in the courtyard.

Davy Crockett and the Tennesseans, who had driven Morales' elite troops away from the palisaded wall between the chapel and the low barracks, now turned to defend the interior *campo santo* wall between the low barracks and the *convento.* In their "little fort," the Tennesseans met the enemy in vicious hand-to-hand combat. Although heavily outnumbered, they sold their lives dearly.

The Alamo's quartermaster, Eliel Melton, and an unknown number of men, perhaps as many as twenty, decided to try to break through the Mexican charge. They leapt over the wall and made a mad dash for safety. This is exactly what the cavalry was waiting for, and one by one the Texians were cut down by Mexican sabers and lances. Several escaped immediate death, and some may have escaped entirely. One man tried to hide under a bush, but was quickly discovered and shot. Another hid under a bridge over the river, but was found by a Mexican woman doing her wash. He, too, was quickly killed when she summoned the soldiers. A ten-year-old girl reportedly witnessed the deaths of seven Texians cut down on the banks of the San Antonio River while trying to escape. A man named Henry Warnell died in his parents' house three months later of wounds he claimed to have received at the Alamo battle. And two men, one of whom was badly wounded, showed up in Nacogdoches in late March, claiming to have survived the San Antonio "massacre," as they called it. Their story was reported in the *Arkansas Gazette* a week before Houston's official first report of the fall of the Alamo.

Inside the walls, both sides fought with a combination of bravery and fanaticism. At a distance, the Texians' rifles and superior marksmanship were a distinct advantage, but up close this edge evaporated. The bayonet, which many Texians lacked, was a better weapon than the knife and the tomahawk. In fact, Lieutenant de la Pena complained that the seven cartridges issued to most of the soldiers was too much; they would be better served by their bayonets. (De la Pena, 50) One step at a time, one room at a time, the defenders were overrun by superior numbers.

Jim Bowie's sisters-in-law, Juana Alsbury and Gertrudis Navarro, had taken refuge in one of the rooms along the west wall, near the eighteen-pounder in the southwest bastion. They opened the door to their room, hoping to be spared because they were women, and Gertrudis had a baby at her breast. When discovered, they were threatened by the *soldados,* and a member of the garrison named Mitchell (it is unknown if it was Edwin Mitchell or Napoleon Mitchell) was bayonetted while trying to defend them. An unknown young Tejano was also bayonetted in their presence. Although their personal possessions were stolen, they were not harmed physically. Interestingly, at one point during the battle, they were approached by a Mexican officer who was looking for the main gate. Apparently he was part of Morales' column, trying to help his comrades find their way into the Alamo.

In the midst of the fighting near the long barracks, a young Lt. José María Torres of the Zapadores Battalion spotted a Texian flag flying on a staff over the building. He climbed up on the roof, determined to tear it down. Lt. Damasio Martínez bravely followed him. The bodies of three sergeants of the Jiminez Battalion already lay near the base of the flagpole. They had all been killed trying to do the same thing.

Lieutenant Martínez was shot dead before ever reaching the flag pole. Torres made it through the hail of bullets, tore down the Texian flag, and raised the Mexican tricolor. Just as he did so, the gallant Lieutenant Torres also fell, mortally wounded. He died shortly after the battle, and was buried in the *campo santo* in San Antonio de Bexar.

Once all of the defenders were driven from the courtyard, they had to be dislodged from the various rooms in the barracks and the chapel where they had taken refuge. This was the scene of some of the fiercest of the fighting. Jim Bowie died on his sickbed in his room in the low barracks. Legend has it that he went down fighting, surrounded by a pile of dead Mexicans. Mexican Lt. Col. Juan José Sanchez Navarro claims that Bowie died like a coward. Given his past history, this is hard to believe, but he may well have been too sick to offer any resistance, or he could even have already died from his illness before the Mexicans burst into his room. We will never know for sure.

One person that we are more certain about how he died is Maj. Robert Evans, the ordnance officer. Susannah Dickinson related that Evans died as the chapel was being overrun, while carrying a torch and trying to blow up the powder magazine. His final act is reminiscent of the death of John Wayne as Davy Crockett in the 1960 motion picture *The Alamo.*

One by one, the rooms fell, until only a few men were left in the chapel. Almeron Dickinson, James Bonham, and Gregorio Esparza all died defending their post at the gun deck at the rear of the chapel. They were probably among the last to die.

There is a lot of controversy over just how Davy Crockett met his fate. (See the special essay on the Crockett death controversy by Dr. Todd Harburn in Chapter Ten.) After the battle, Susannah Dickinson recalled seeing Crockett's body, and his "peculiar cap," in the area in front of the chapel. This is near the palisade that he and the Tennesseans so gallantly defended, and it is possible that he went down fighting there just as actor Fess Parker did in the Walt Disney series.

There is also a possibility that Crockett was one of about a half dozen captured prisoners who were brought before Santa Anna after the battle. Supposedly, they had been promised quarter by General Castrillon. Santa Anna, however, was furious that they had been spared, and ordered them executed on the spot. Whether or not Crockett was part of this group is widely debated, and it is the authors' position that there is not enough proof to resolve the issue one way or the other. What is important is that he and the others remained true to their cause, and stood and fought, when early in the siege they almost certainly could have safely escaped.

By 6:30 A.M. the battle was over. Besides Joe (Travis' slave), only one Texian soldier remained alive. Brigido Guerrero had formerly served in the Mexican army, but joined the rebel cause. He convinced the Mexicans that he was being held prisoner, and they believed him and spared his life. Joe and most, but not all, of the women and children were also spared. Anthony Wolfe's two young sons, aged about eleven and twelve years, were both killed during the battle. There are also reports of one or more women being slain in the fighting. Susannah Dickinson was shot in the calf, but the wound was not serious.

Santa Anna ordered the *alcalde* of San Antonio, Francisco Ruiz, to show him the bodies of Bowie, Crockett, and Travis. He then ordered Ruiz to gather up all of the rebels' bodies and burn them. There was but one exception. Presidial Cavalryman Francisco Esparza was allowed to claim his brother Gregorio's body and give it a Christian burial.

The next day, the self-styled Napoleon of the West called for the survivors. Charmed by the baby Angelina Dickinson, and perhaps by her young mother, Santa Anna offered to adopt the now fatherless child and pay for a fine education in Mexico City. Understandably, Susannah refused. No such offer was made to Mrs. Alsbury for her child. The Tejanos were allowed to return to Bexar, or go where they wished. Travis' slave Joe and the Dickinsons, escorted by Ben, Colonel Almonte's black cook, were sent east to the Anglo settlements with a warning: submit or die.

The Battle of the Alamo was over. Speaking to Capt. Fernando Urizza, Santa Anna remarked, "It was but a small affair." (Lord: *A Time to Stand*, 167) Lt. Col. José Juan Sanchez Navarro had a different view. He remarked that "with another such victory as this, we'll go to the devil." (Sanchez Navarro, 63)

Santa Anna had his victory, but the cost had been high. Estimates of the Mexicans killed in the assault vary widely, and range from 60 to 2,000. There were probably another 250-300 wounded, many of whom died later of their wounds due to inadequate medical care. A reasonable estimate of Mexican casualties is probably 400 to 600 killed and seriously wounded. This was approximately one-third of those actually involved in the assault, a tremendous casualty rate by any standards. For Lieutenant Colonel Sanchez Navarro and many other Mexicans, it was difficult to dismiss the Battle of the Alamo as just "a small affair."

Artist's Note: *In keeping with our "sketchbook" philosophy, and wanting to show as much detail as clearly as possible, the sketches of the final battle (which follow) were drawn as if it occurred in the daylight. The reader is reminded, however, that the final assault actually took place in the predawn darkness.*

TOWER OF THE SAN FERNANDO CATHEDRAL. When the Mexicans occupied San Antonio de Bexar, Santa Anna immediately ordered that the red flag of "no quarter" be raised from the bell tower of the San Fernando Cathedral. The Texians answered the Mexican surrender demand with a cannon shot, and the Siege of the Alamo was on.

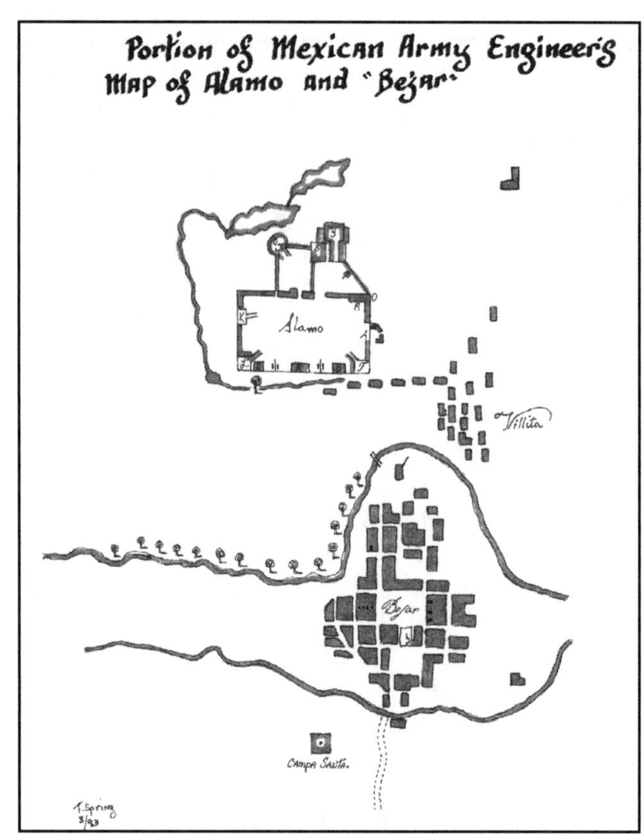

Above:
This map, based closely on one made by Col. Ignacio de Labastida, a Mexican army engineer officer, shows the relative positions of the Alamo, La Villita, the town of San Antonio de Bexar, and the San Antonio River. The original of this excellent map is now in the University of Texas Archives in Austin.

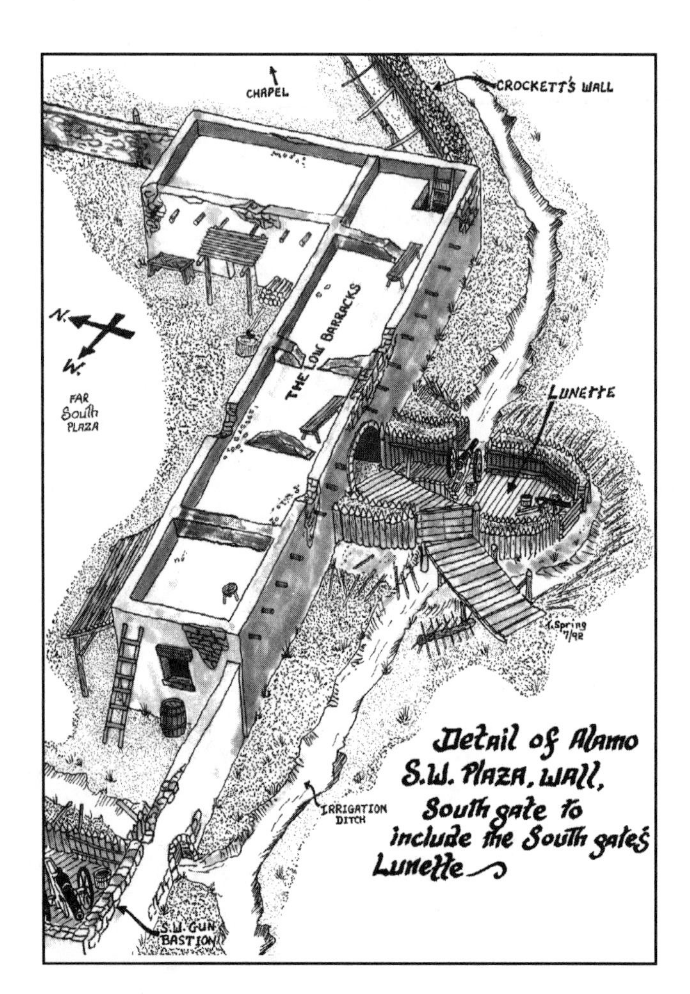

Left:
THE SOUTH WALL AND THE LUNETTE. This sketch shows the defenses along the south wall of the Alamo at the time of the siege. The lunette, designed to protect the vulnerable main gate, was begun by Cos' men when the Mexicans held the Alamo, and strengthened by the Texians under the direction of their chief engineer, Green B. Jameson.

ALAMO CHAPEL DETAIL, FEBRUARY 1836. The chapel walls are shown in very good condition; however, these walls were in disrepair at various areas during the time of the siege. The scaffolding and artillery piece in the front of the chapel is a fixture in most Alamo movies, but it is doubtful that it really existed.

THE LONG BARRACKS. The long barracks served as the garrison hospital. A low adobe wall stretched from the long barracks south across in front of the chapel. The courtyard created by this wall has been called the "little fort." This is the area where Susannah Dickinson recalled seeing Crockett's body after the battle. This view is the more correct of the "little fort" area.

THE NORTHEAST CORNER OF THE NORTH WALL. The north wall had been weakened by Texian cannon fire during the Siege of Bexar, and Alamo engineer Green B. Jameson strengthened the weak spot with a timber reinforcement. In spite of the legend perpetuated by Hollywood and many writers, the wall was never fully breached, even during the final Mexican assault on March 6.

COL. JAMES BOWIE. Col. James Bowie shared command of the Alamo with Lt. Col. William Barret Travis until he fell ill on February 24. Here Bowie is shown in the artillery emplacement in the main compound.

CAPT. JUAN SEGUIN. On February 25, Capt. Juan Seguin of the Regular Texas Cavalry borrowed Jim Bowie's horse and rode to Houston with a desperate plea for help from the Alamo. After delivering his dispatches, Seguin was returning to the Alamo with reinforcements when he learned of its fall. One of the most loyal and active of the Tejanos who supported the Revolution, Seguin presided over a burial service for the remains of the Alamo defenders one year later, on February 25, 1837. (See Chapter Thirteen for the complete text of his burial speech.)

THE SOUTHWEST BASTION. The Alamo's heaviest gun, the eighteen-pounder, was placed in a bastion in the southwest corner of the Alamo compound, so that it could be brought to bear on the town of San Antonio de Bexar. An earthen mound, shown here under construction, was built and then covered with a wooden platform to absorb the recoil of the gun.

A MEXICAN ARTILLERYMAN. The Mexicans started an artillery bombardment of the Alamo almost immediately, and slowly moved their guns closer and closer to the Alamo to increase the damage that they could do to the fort's walls. Once they got within rifle range, the artillery positions would have to be dug in and protected, or the Texians' marksmanship would have quickly dispatched the gun crews.

ALAMO DEFENDERS IN THE SOUTH PLAZA. Despite almost continuous fire from the Mexican artillery, the Texians were well protected by the Alamo's walls and did not suffer any serious casualties until the final assault. Here two Alamo defenders are shown in the main compound in front of the chapel. The man on the right is one of the officers of the garrison, as indicated by the sash worn around his waist.

INFANTRYMAN, MATAMOROS BATTALION. This battalion was part of Col. José María Romero's column that attacked the east wall of the Alamo.

TRAVIS IN HIS CAPOTE. Alamo Commander Lt. Col. William Barret Travis wearing a blanket coat or "capote." In his journal, Travis mentions purchasing material for a capote, a garment that was easily made and both warm and practical.

Left:
DAVID CROCKETT AT THE ALAMO, March 6, 1836. This sketch shows the way Davy Crockett was probably really dressed on the early morning of March 6. He wears a woolen civilian overcoat over a cloth shirt and broadfall trousers, rather than the frontier "buckskins" popularized by Hollywood. On his head he wears the "peculiar" cap that Susannah Dickinson later recalled seeing by his body near the front of the chapel.

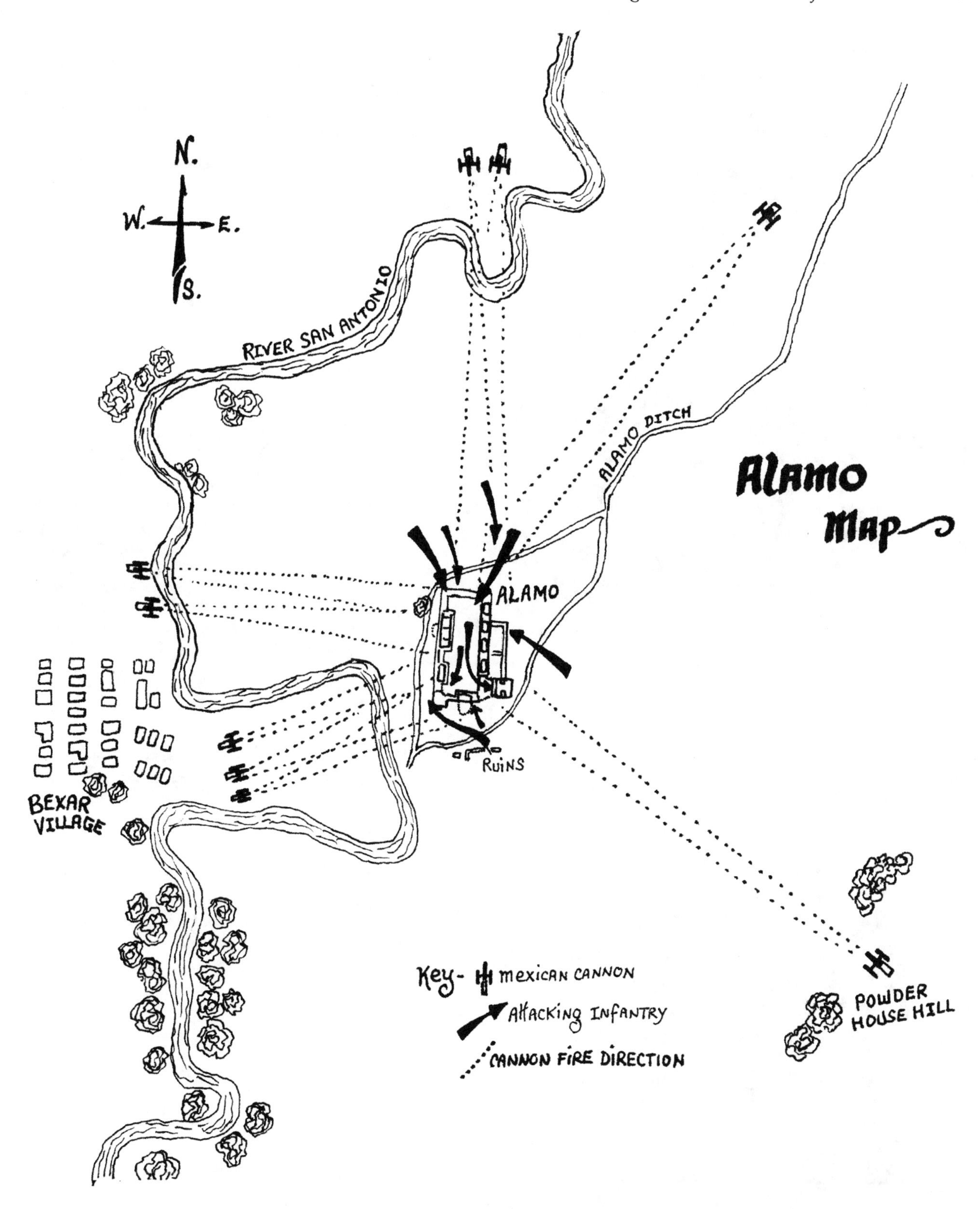

ALAMO SIEGE MAP. This map, based on a number of sources, shows the Alamo in relation to the town of Bexar and the San Antonio River. Also shown are Mexican artillery positions, and the paths of the final assault columns.

Top left:
GREGORIO ESPARZA. Gregorio Esparza was another Tejano who fought for the cause of Texas' liberty. A native of San Antonio de Bexar, he brought his entire family to the Alamo with him. Gregorio died manning the artillery at the rear of the chapel, and was the only Alamo defender to receive a Christian burial.

Above:
THE FINAL BATTLE. Once the Mexicans were over the walls, the fighting was furious, and the outnumbered Texians were forced to withdraw to prepared strongholds within the chapel and barracks buildings.

Bottom left:
PREPARING FOR THE ATTACK. In the cold predawn darkness, Mexican soldiers mass with their weapons, scaling ladders, and crowbars. Before the attack begins, packs and overcoats will be removed and bayonets will be fixed.

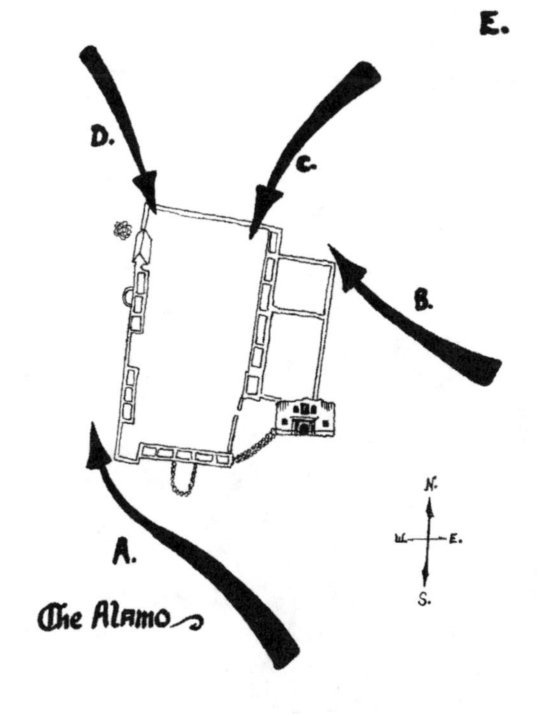

THE MEXICAN ATTACK. This map shows the paths of the four Mexican assault columns:

A. *Approximately 100 men under the command of Col. Juan Morales attacked the wooden palisade from the south. Heavy fire drove them to the left, where, after finding temporary cover in the remains of the* jacales, *they eventually captured the southwest bastion and the eighteen-pounder. The column consisted of the light infantry companies of the Matamoros, Jiminez, and San Luis battalions. They were equipped with two ladders.*

B. *Approximately 300 men under the command of Col. José María Romero. They attacked the east wall and the corrals. This column consisted of the regular companies of the Matamoros and Jiminez battalions, and carried six ladders.*

C. *This column attacked the north wall, and after being repulsed initially, it eventually joined with Cos' column and the reserves to fight its way into the Alamo compound. Col. Francisco Duque commanded this column, and after he was seriously wounded, Gen. Manuel Fernandez Castrillon took over. The column consisted of approximately 300 men of the regular and light infantry companies of the Toluca Battalion, and 100 men of the regular companies of the San Luis Battalion. They were equipped with ten ladders, two crowbars, and two axes.*

D. *Gen. Martín Perfecto de Cos commanded this column, which also attacked the north wall. It, too, was driven off at first, but then joined Duque/Castrillon's column and the reserves to carry the north wall. It consisted of 200 men of the Aldama Battalion and 100 men of the San Luis Battalion. They were equipped with ten ladders, two crowbars, and two axes.*

E. *The reserve force was made up of approximately 400 men of the elite Zapadores Battalion and the grenadier companies of the Matamoros, Jiminez, Aldama, Toluca, and San Luis battalions. It was sent to join Duque/Castrillon's and Cos' columns in their assault on the north wall.*

THE DEATH OF CAPTAIN DICKINSON. As the Mexicans swarmed over the Alamo's walls, Capt. Almeron Dickinson ran into the chapel and told his wife that the enemy was inside the walls. He told her to take care of their daughter Angelina if the Mexicans spared her, and then ran back to his battle station with the artillery on the ramp at the rear of the chapel. A short time later he died there, defending his guns to the last.

Top left:
A MEXICAN OFFICER. Junior Mexican officers such as the one depicted here deserve much credit for the bravery they displayed in leading their men against the fearsome Texian rifle and artillery fire.

Top right:
THE DEATH OF COLONEL TRAVIS. Lt. Col. William Barret Travis was killed early in the fighting. He had just discharged his shotgun from his position on the north wall when he was struck in the head with a lead ball, probably killing him instantly.

Bottom left:
CROCKETT'S FINAL MOMENTS. Perhaps no other detail about the final assault on the Alamo is as controversial as just how Davy Crockett met his death. Did he surrender? Was he captured and executed? Did he go down fighting? The real truth may never be known, but we do know that he died in the area in front of the chapel, for Susannah Dickinson saw his body there right after the battle.

Rather than take sides in the Crockett death controversy, this illustration shows him in the final moments—tattered, dirty, exhausted, and probably somewhat dazed, but definitely having put up a good fight. How did it finally end? You be the judge . . .

BROTHERS. Alamo defender Gregorio Esparza believed in the cause of Texas' liberty, and in the end he gave his life for it while manning the artillery at the rear of the chapel. Gregorio's brother, Francisco, was a member of the Presidial Cavalry Company from San Antonio de Bexar.

Santa Anna did not allow the Presidial Company to take part in the actual fighting at the Alamo, but rather used them as couriers and for other noncombatant duties. When the order was given to gather and burn all of the bodies of the Alamo defenders, Francisco went to General Cos and asked permission to claim his brother's body so that it could be given a Christian burial. Permission was granted, and therefore Gregorio Esparza was the only defender whose body was not burned on the funeral pyre.

THE DEATH OF LT. JOSÉ MARÍA TORRES. Lieutenant Torres was a young officer of the elite Zapadores Battalion. During the battle, several soldiers were shot trying to take down the Texian flag that flew over the long barracks hospital. Torres bravely rushed forward and was himself shot dead just after he tore down the Texian flag and replaced it with the Mexican colors. The courageous young officer was certainly one of the heroes of the battle for the Mexican side.

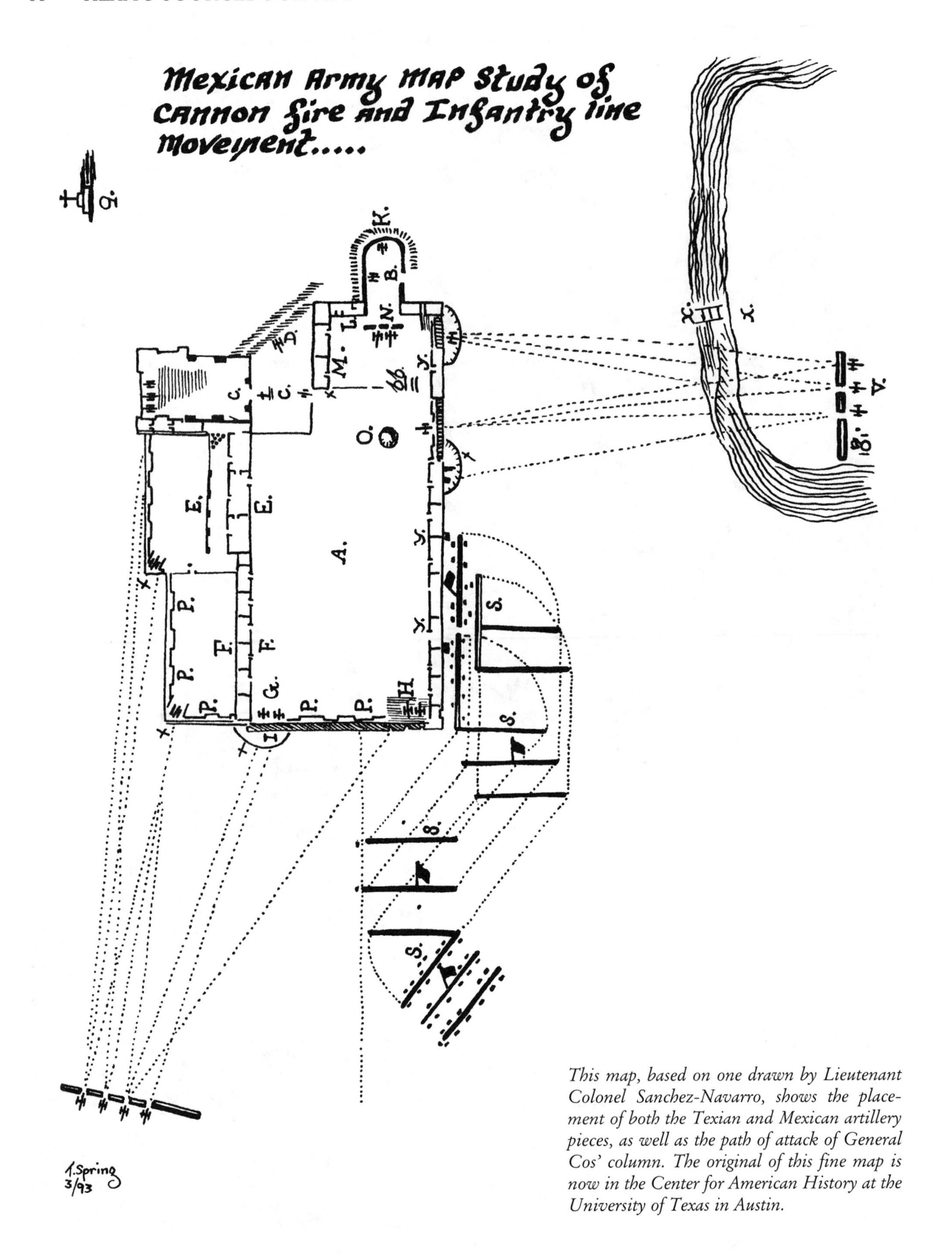

This map, based on one drawn by Lieutenant Colonel Sanchez-Navarro, shows the placement of both the Texian and Mexican artillery pieces, as well as the path of attack of General Cos' column. The original of this fine map is now in the Center for American History at the University of Texas in Austin.

CHAPTER EIGHT

The Aftermath

"Texas will take honor to herself for the defense of the Alamo and call it a second Thermopylae, but it will be an everlasting monument of national disgrace."

William Fairfax Gray
(Lord: *A Time to Stand,* 191)

"There was not a man in the Alamo but what, in his death, honored the proud name of an American. Let the men of Texas avenge their deaths."

Gen. Sam Houston
(Chariton: *100 Days,* 378)

FOLLOWING THE REDUCTION OF the Alamo, Santa Anna planned his strategy for completing the crushing of this rebellion. General Urrea would move on Goliad from the south with a 1,400-man column. General Gaona and 700 men would march on the rebel government at Washington-on-the-Brazos to the northeast. General Ramirez y Sesma, with 700 *soldados,* would drive across the central part of Texas, threatening the settlements at Gonzales, San Felipe de Austin, and Harrisburg.

With the Alamo lost, the hope of an independent Texas rested largely with two men: Fannin at Goliad, and Houston trying to raise a fighting-strength army. Arriving in Gonzales on March 11, Houston found just under 400 men waiting for him. Late that day, he heard the first rumors of the fall of the Alamo. He quickly jailed the Tejanos responsible for the reports as Mexican spies, although he most likely suspected they were telling the truth. Then, two days later, Deaf Smith returned from a scout with Susannah and Angelina Dickinson and Travis' slave Joe, who confirmed the news. Houston gathered what there was of his army, advised the civilians to evacuate, and headed east. He burned the town of Gonzales behind him.

On March 17, word reached the Texas Legislature at Washington-on-the-Brazos that Gaona's northern column was at Bastrop, sixty miles away. The newly elected president, David Burnet, and the rest of the government set off for Harrisburg, on Buffalo Bayou, seventy miles to the southeast.

The same day, Houston's troops and the accompanying refugees reached the Colorado River, where Houston called a halt. Determined not to let Fort Defiance become another Alamo, Houston ordered Fannin to abandon Goliad and move northeast to Victoria, then to protect Matagorda Bay on the Gulf Coast. If this was deemed too dangerous, then Fannin was to join the rest of the army at the Colorado River.

Once again, Fannin hesitated. He tarried at Fort Defiance, waiting for local settlers to join him. According to Herman Ehrenberg of the New Orleans Greys, the commander seemed confused and hindered by the many plans competing in his mind. When a company led by Captain King that had been sent to Refugio to help evacuate settlers failed to return, Fannin sent the Georgia Battalion to investigate. Both units were cut to pieces by Urrea's column, and most of those who surrendered were executed.

Finally, Urrea's advance guard appeared outside the Fort Defiance walls. They were driven back by a troop of volunteer cavalry. The next morning, under the cover of a heavy fog, the garrison set out across the open prairie.

Not far from the heavily wooded banks of Coleto Creek, about ten miles from Goliad, Fannin's force was stopped by Mexican troops.

Forming a hollow square, with artillery in the corners, the Texians fought the Mexicans to a stalemate. The next morning Fannin's men found themselves ringed by the main Mexican force, now equipped with artillery. Faced with the choices of surrender, fighting to the death, or trying to fight his way to the nearby woods leaving his wounded behind, Fannin surrendered.

Approximately 350 men were marched back to Goliad, where they spent a miserable week held in the chapel. It was so crowded that only about a quarter of them could sit at any time. Had the walls not been so high, the prisoners might have died of asphyxiation. Unknown to the Texians, a controversy was raging among the Mexican high command regarding the treatment of the prisoners. On Palm Sunday, March 27, most of Fannin's command was marched a short distance from Fort Defiance, and were shot down in cold blood. Those who were not immediately killed were bayonetted. A very few escaped. Most of the wounded in the makeshift hospital were dragged from their beds and killed in the yard. Fannin, too badly wounded to march out, was helped from his room by a Texan medical "assistant" who was spared. The ill-fated commander offered money and a watch to a Mexican officer in exchange for a promise that he would be shot in the body, not the head, and that he would be properly buried. The officer accepted the items, agreed to Fannin's requests, then stood by as the blindfolded Fannin was shot in the head and his body burned.

The Mexicans did spare some of the rebels. These included eighty newly arrived volunteers from the United States, who were taken without weapons and had never fired a shot. About thirty others were also allowed to live. These included the American surgeons who had been impressed into service doctoring the Mexican wounded, as well as some medical assistants and skilled laborers. Also, several lives were saved by the wife of a Mexican officer, Señora Francisca Alvarez, and a handful of sympathetic Mexican officers and enlisted men. Shortly after the executions, the doctors were sent to San Antonio de Bexar to care for the Mexican soldiers who had been wounded in the assault on the Alamo and had not yet received any medical attention.

Back on the Colorado River, Houston had finally seen the enemy. Encamped on the east bank, the Texians had spent five nervous days two miles and a swollen river away from Ramirez y Sesma's force. During the week, Ramirez y Sesma had been reinforced, and his army now numbered about 1,200 men. Houston also had been joined by more volunteers, and he now commanded approximately 700 men. On March 25, Houston learned how uncertain the future of the Revolution had become. He received a letter from President Burnet informing him of the government's flight and ordering him to Harrisburg to protect the Legislature. About the same time, a refugee from Fannin's debacle at Coleto Creek brought news of the surrender. Houston grimly told his aide that they would never again see Fannin or his men. Angering the men of his command who wanted to cross the river and avenge Travis and Fannin, Houston gave orders to abandon the camp on the Colorado and march east.

In what has become known as "the Runaway Scrape," the remains of the Texas Army retreated before the Mexicans' seemingly unstoppable advance. Criticized by almost everyone at the time, Houston's tactics today are seen as a classic "strategic withdrawal." Houston fell back to Austin's town of San Felipe, left a small defensive force there and sent another south along the Brazos to Fort Bend, then took the main army north to Groce's Ferry in the Brazos bottomlands. Houston told his grumbling troops there was corn there, and they could whip an enemy force ten times their size. Once there, Houston finally had a chance to organize his army into companies and regiments, and begin some rudimentary drills.

Meanwhile, the Mexican army advanced virtually unopposed across the Texas colonies. In early April, Santa Anna joined Ramirez y Sesma, who had been ordered to wait for him at the Colorado River. Reaching San Felipe de Austin, the Mexicans found it burned and abandoned. While Ramirez y Sesma's men were caught up in a firefight with the rearguard of the Texian force that had fled San Felipe de Austin, Santa Anna issued orders for the three columns to rendezvous at Fort Bend, which the Texians had already abandoned. He then set off with 750 infantry and about 50 cavalry to try to surprise the government at Harrisburg. On April 15 the dictator led a cavalry patrol into the town, only to find that the government had fled to New Washington, about twenty miles away. Interviewing the editors of *The Telegraph and Texas Register,* Santa Anna also learned that Houston was leaving Groce's Ferry and heading for Lynchburg. Santa Anna was certain that the end was near.

At Groce's Ferry, Houston and his men learned of Fannin's fate. Several times Houston had to outwit potential coups and/or mutinies by those who wanted revenge immediately—whether the time was right or not. Many in the Texian army had been raised on stories of knighthood and valor, and felt they had failed Travis and Fannin. They sought to redeem their honor through trial by combat.

Just after the middle of April, Houston learned about Santa Anna's personal detachment and his plan to take the Texian government prisoner. The Texian commander called together his army of about 800 men and told them the time had come to march again. If they could get between Santa Anna's strike force and the rest of his army, they could end the war. And so, the Texian army set off for Harrisburg.

Reaching New Washington, Santa Anna again found the Texian government had just barely escaped, but he was only mildly upset. He rested his men for a few days near New Washington, according to some stories dallying at the Morgan plantation with the mulatto Emily Morgan, the "Yellow Rose of Texas." The dictator planned to be reinforced and then confront Houston in or near Lynchburg. He sent for General Cos, who was at Fort Bend with Ramirez y Sesma's army, to bring 500 reinforcements and meet him near Lynchburg, between the Buffalo Bayou and the river of Saint Hyacinth—*San Jacinto* in Spanish.

During the night of April 19, Houston's army crossed Vince's Bridge, one of the two fords between New Washington and the rest of Texas. On the morning of April 20, Houston moved his men into a wooded area near the Lynchburg Ferry, the other crossing point. Later that day, Santa Anna arrived. Following an unsuccessful attempt to lure the Texians into a pitched battle in the open, the Mexicans withdrew a short distance and made camp.

The next morning the Texians had expected to strike the Mexican camp the first thing, but Houston had other plans. He had left orders not to be disturbed, and he slept until 8:00 A.M., the first good night's sleep he had had in weeks. At about 9:00 A.M., General Cos arrived with his reinforcements. They had just made a forced march from Fort Bend, and since there was no movement in the Texian camp, they rested. Houston ordered Deaf Smith to go and burn Vince's Bridge, ensuring that Santa Anna would receive no more aid. He told his men to fix their dinners and then get ready for battle. At about noon, during an officers' call, Houston's subordinates advised against attacking the Mexican encampment across open ground. Houston laughed and dismissed them. At 3:30 P.M., Houston gave the order his men had been waiting for. They were finally going to attack Santa Anna's army!

As the Texians formed up, lookouts in the tall trees sent word that the Mexican camp was quiet. Both the recently arrived troops and Santa Anna's strike force were resting in the midday heat. According to some accounts, Santa Anna was in his tent with Emily Morgan. More likely, he was resting under a tree.

At 4:30 the Texians moved out, walking forward silently until they were just 200 yards from the Mexican camp. Then, at a signal from Houston, the two Texian cannon, the "Twin Sisters," opened up. The cavalry under Mirabeau Buonaparte Lamar, future president of the Texas Republic, spurred toward the Mexican camp. The Texians ignored Houston's orders to fire and advance and just began running pell mell toward the enemy, firing and reloading at will, shouting "Remember the Alamo! Remember Goliad!" Suddenly, Deaf Smith appeared, riding across the Texian front and yelling that Vince's Bridge was down. For the Mexicans, any hope of escape or reinforcement was gone.

According to Houston, who had three horses shot from under him and was wounded by a musket ball in the ankle, the battle lasted only eighteen minutes from the first firing of the "Twin Sisters." That may be, but it is almost certain the killing went on much longer. The Texians, flushed with victory and determined to avenge the massacres at the Alamo and Goliad, slaughtered the Mexicans with little regard to age or condition.

General Castrillon, who allegedly had tried to save some captured Alamo defenders, was shot down unarmed after an unsuccessful attempt to rally a defense at a field piece. Drummer boys and wounded *soldados* were brutally cut down, many of them crying "Me no Alamo!" One Texan volunteer, ordered to stop killing by an officer, replied, "Colonel Wharton, if Jesus Christ were to come down and order me to quit shooting Santanistas, I wouldn't do it, sir!" (Time Life: *The Texans,* 140) Of the wanton killing, Houston reportedly proclaimed in disgust, "Gentlemen, I applaud your bravery, but damn your manners!" and left the field to rest his shattered ankle. (Hardin: *Texian Iliad,* 214)

At the end of the killing, about half the Mexican force was dead, the other half held as prisoners. Among the missing was Santa Anna, who had mounted a horse and fled at the start of the battle. The next morning he was found by a Texan patrol, dressed, it was said, in a private's uniform, or in a combination of his own clothing and some civilian attire found in an abandoned farmhouse near the destroyed Vince's Bridge. Taken into the Texian camp, his identity was revealed when his loyal troops began shouting, "*El Presidente!*" Led to Houston, with his courage bolstered by a dose of opium from his captured medicine box, the dictator declared, "That man may consider himself born to no common destiny who has conquered the Napoleon of the West. And now it remains for him to be generous to the vanquished."

"You should have remembered that at the Alamo," was Houston's reply. (Time Life: *The Texans,* 141)

By sparing Santa Anna, Houston ensured the survival of the Republic of Texas, at least for the time being. Ordered back to Mexico by their president, the remaining Mexican forces in Texas, who still greatly outnumbered the Texian army, reluctantly obeyed.

The political instability in Mexico that had led to the Texas Revolution continued. Army officers and politicians blamed each other for the debacle. Santa Anna fell from power, then returned.

There were unsuccessful Mexican attempts to retake the lost state, and ill-fated Texan invasions of Mexican territory. The Nueces Strip, between the Nueces and the Rio Grande, became a virtual no-man's land, a battleground fought over by Mexican outlaws and Texas Rangers. Many of the outlaws were displaced Tejanos, driven from their homes by recent immigrants or Texians who had forgotten, or chose to ignore, the contributions of the Tejanos to Texas' independence.

Texas' political unrest improved little with the coming of peace. Some factions favored ongoing independence, combined with the gaining of further territory to be taken from Mexico. Others, led by Houston, believed Texas' destiny was to become part of the United States. In 1845, Houston and his allies saw their dreams fulfilled as Texas became the twenty-eighth state of the Union. This led to the Mexican War, and to the expansion of the United States to the Pacific Ocean.

Eventually, both Houston and his Tejano allies would see their dreams die. In his old age, Houston saw the United States torn apart by the secessionist movement, and finally, the Civil War. Houston never took the Oath of Allegiance to the Confederacy, yet he was also critical of the North's attempts to compel the South to end slavery and return to the Union by force of arms. On July 26, 1863, Houston died. According to his family, his last words were "Texas . . . Texas . . . ."

For the Tejanos, the years after San Jacinto were tragic and enraging. The attitude of many in Texas toward the Tejanos was summed up by Frederick Law Olmstead: "Mexicans were regarded in a somewhat unchristian tone, not as heretics or heathen to be converted with flannel and tracts, but rather as vermin to be exterminated. . . . White folks and Mexicans were never made to live together, anyhow, and the Mexicans had no business here. They were getting so impertinent, and were so well protected by the laws, that the Americans would just have to get together and drive them out of the country." (Montejano: *Anglos and Mexicans in the Making of Texas,* 29)

In many cases, that is exactly what happened. Old Spanish land grants were ignored or overturned by Anglo courts. In what Texas historian J. Frank Dobie called "rocky times in Texas," many Tejanos were driven out or killed. The dream of Austin, Houston, de Zavala, Seguin, Bowie, and many others who fought and died at Bexar, Goliad, and San Jacinto, or who labored to make Texas a home for all who preferred freedom over tyranny, regardless of race, seems to some to have truly been impossible.

But, despite all the trials, challenges and injustices, some Tejanos held on. And, over the years, many more Mexicans have made the journey north that their eighteenth- and nineteenth-century ancestors were unwilling to make. Their presence has added immeasurably to the cultural richness of modern-day Texas. As artist, author, and historian Jack "Jaxon" Jackson stated in his graphic novel, *Los Tejanos: The True Story of Juan N. Seguin and the Texas-Mexicans During the Rising of the Lone Star:*

> But the story was not all as ugly and grim as I may have led the reader to suspect. Like any other clash of cultures, the human spirit soared as well as staggered during the experience. Then, as now, many people maintained their respect for each other; they lived together, worked together, and sought to make Texas a better place for all its citizens. Their courageous example should not be overlooked amidst all the blood and thunder, for in the end, it will triumph.
> (Jackson, 126)

Left:
James Walker Fannin is one of the least sympathetic of the heroes of the Texas Revolution. He was a West Point dropout and early leader of the War Party. However, when the war actually started, Fannin seemed to lose all resolve, according to New Orleans Grey Herman Ehrenberg. He failed to reinforce the Alamo, held off obeying Houston's order to abandon Fort Defiance at Goliad (seen in the background) until it was too late, and then surrendered his troops at Coleto Creek. He was killed in cold blood, along with most of his men, by the Mexicans on Palm Sunday, 1836.

Right:
The Alabama Red Rovers were raised by Dr. James Shackleford, and traveled part of the way to Texas on locomotive trains. They were quite possibly the first military unit in history to have used a "troop train." The Rovers wore matching red hunting shirts, made and dyed by women back home. They fought with distinction at Coleto Creek, and, along with the members of the New Orleans Greys present, argued against surrender. Because he was a doctor, Shackleford was spared from the mass executions at Goliad. His son and most of the others were not so fortunate.

Right:
When Houston received word of Fannin's surrender at Coleto Creek, he told his aide that they would never see those men again. Houston knew that the future of Texas depended on his leadership, and his army's success.

Left:
A typical Texas militiaman, based on a sketch by Texas historian and artist Peter Stines. With all of his gear brought from home, most likely with a homemade quilt for a blanket, he left his family to defend Texas against Santa Anna. Many members of the garrisons at the Alamo and Goliad were volunteers from the United States and elsewhere, but at San Jacinto, it was these colonists who cried "Remember the Alamo" and "Remember Goliad" and avenged their ill-fated garrisons.

CHAPTER NINE

Heroes of the Alamo

"When visitors to the Alamo stand in reverent silence before the names of the defenders of the Alamo, they are acknowledging their own kind. They are honoring people of different nationalities, religions, and races, from every walk of life, who made up the garrison of the Alamo for two short weeks in 1836."

(Bill Groneman: *Alamo Defenders,* xii)

PART 1: INTRODUCTION

THERE IS NO SUCH thing as a complete and accurate list of all of the valiant defenders of the Alamo. This chapter attempts to present as accurate a list as possible at this time, with a caution that research currently under way will probably significantly alter it in the future. The list is divided into three sections: those killed, those who survived, and the known noncombatants. Basic biographical information is included on each person listed. Although there is reasonable supposition for everything that we list, much of the information will be presented as "maybe" or "could have been," simply because absolute proof is lacking.

The first attempt to document the names of the defenders of the Alamo was in 1837, when the Texas Adjutant General's Office began compiling muster rolls of all those who served in the Texas Revolution. These rolls were later copied by the General Land Office. Today, only the Land Office transcripts survive, as the Adjutant General's copies were destroyed by fire in 1855.

In the early 1930s, Amelia Williams compiled information for her doctoral dissertation entitled "A Critical Study of the Siege of the Alamo and the Personnel of Its Defenders." Although dated, and in some respects inaccurate, Williams' study has served as the basis for most Alamo defender lists since then.

In the 1980s, two Alamo historians, Bill Groneman and Phil Rosenthal, began publishing the results of their own extensive research on the Alamo defenders. They coauthored the limited edition *Roll Call at the Alamo,* which was published in 1985. Each author has since published a text on their own continuing research.

Bill Groneman remains very active in Alamo research. He has written a number of periodical articles, and has recently published a book on the controversial narrative of Mexican officer José Enrique de la Pena. Bill worked closely with us in assembling the information presented in this chapter.

The generally accepted number of defenders killed at the Alamo now stands at 189. In addition, there are the noncombatants, as well as the soldiers who survived, primarily because they left as couriers before the final battle.

It is probable that research currently being conducted by Texas historian Thomas Ricks Lindley, when made public, will drastically change the list of defenders killed at the Alamo. While Lindley's efforts may result in the removal of some names from the current list, he expects that the final total will be about 257 defenders killed, rather than 189. A recently discovered document, the Alamo garrison's February 1 ballot for the Texas Constitutional Convention, may add approximately thirty more verified names to the list. Lindley also has information suggesting that in addition to the "Gonzales 32," the Alamo received a second reinforcement of about fifty men on March 4, only two days before the final battle.

Is it possible that after all these years, this many more names can legitimately be added to the Alamo Roll Call? We believe so. Not only do Lindley's preliminary findings seem plausible, but they are supported by two eyewitness accounts of Mexican officers. Col. Juan Almonte said that 250 Texians were killed, and Lt. Col. José Sanchez Navarro claimed that there were 257:

> Almonte Diary, Sunday, March 6: *On the part of the enemy the result was 250 killed, and 17 pieces of artillery—a flag, muskets and firearms taken.* (Chariton: *100 Days,* 317)
>
> Sanchez-Navarro Diary, Sunday, March 6: *The enemy have suffered a heavy loss; twenty-one field pieces of different caliber, many arms and munitions. Two hundred fifty seven of their men were killed; I have seen and counted their bodies.* (Sanchez Navarro: University of Texas Library Chronicle, 63)

This large increase is not to be verified yet, though. Caution must still be exercised, for other eyewitness evidence is contradictory. Francisco Ruiz, the *alcalde* (mayor) of San Antonio de Bexar, wrote:

> *"The men burnt numbered one hundred and eighty two. I was an eyewitness . . ."* (Chariton: *100 Days,* 327)

Only time will tell whether an increased number will be properly verified, but one thing is certain—those who gave up their lives at the Alamo did so knowingly, for the cause of freedom, and they deserve the respect and thanks of free people everywhere.

THE FORMAT OF THE LISTS

It is not an easy task to assign all of the defenders of the Alamo to a specific military unit at the time of the siege. As with most revolutionary armies, the Army of the Republic of Texas was in a constant state of flux. Individuals came and went, and whole units were absorbed into other units or just disappeared from the table of organization. Many defenders had served in several units by the time they reached the Alamo. Even so, we thought it desirable to give military unit designations when it could be done with reasonable accuracy.

The Texas Army had four main classifications that remained fairly stable throughout the Revolution, and we use these for our lists of defenders. The following abbreviations reflect the soldier's "Military Status" as of March 1836:

RTA: Regular Texas Army
PV: Permanent Volunteers
VAC: Voluntary Auxiliary Corps
MIL: Militia

Where known, a defender's specific unit is given in the "Comments" section.

THE REGULAR TEXAS ARMY

Members of the Regular Army of the Provisional Government of Texas (RTA) enlisted for either two years or the duration of the war. There were three individual officers and two companies of Texas Regulars at the Alamo:

Individuals with regular commissions:

—William Barret Travis, lieutenant colonel of Texas Cavalry
—Almeron Dickinson, captain of Texas Artillery
—James Butler Bonham, second lieutenant of Texas Cavalry

Companies of the Regular Texas Army:

—Capt. Juan Seguin's company of Texas Cavalry
—Capt. John Forsyth's company of Texas Cavalry

THE PERMANENT VOLUNTEERS

Members of the Permanent Volunteers (PV) enlisted for the duration for the war. The following Permanent Volunteer companies are known to have taken part in the Battle of the Alamo:

—Capt. William Blazeby's infantry company, which evolved from what once was the New Orleans Greys and the San Antonio Greys (some members of other companies were also absorbed into Blazeby's company by the time of the Alamo siege)
—Capt. William Carey's artillery company
—Col. James Bowie's volunteer company

Some records suggest that another infantry

company, commanded by Capt. Robert White (and earlier by G. A. Passett), retained its individual identity as part of the Alamo garrison.

—Capt. William Harrison's company of Tennessee Mounted Volunteers

THE VOLUNTEER AUXILIARY CORPS

The Volunteer Auxiliary Corps (VAC) was made up primarily of soldiers who had recently arrived in Texas. Enlistment was generally for six months. There was one unit of the Voluntary Auxiliary Corps at the Alamo:

THE MILITIA

Texas Militia Companies (MIL) were organized in each municipality, with the original purpose of defending the colonists against Indian attack. There was one militia company at the Alamo:

—The Gonzales Ranging Company of Mounted Volunteers

SUSANNAH DICKINSON

Susannah Dickinson, the twenty-two-year-old wife of Capt. Almeron Dickinson, was present in the Alamo throughout the entire siege. During the final assault, she took refuge in the chapel with her young daughter, Angelina. They were both freed by Santa Anna, and brought word of the fall of the Alamo to General Houston.

JOE

Joe was the young slave of Lt. Col. William Barret Travis. He served throughout the siege, and during the final assault he was on the north wall with Travis. After Travis' death, he went to the chapel. Because he was a slave, he was spared by the Mexicans, but he received both a bullet and a bayonet wound during the fighting. Joe escorted Susannah and Angelina Dickinson on their journey to join Houston's army.

PART 2: KILLED AT THE ALAMO

NAME: **Abamillo, Juan**
AGE ?
BIRTHPLACE: Possibly San Antonio de Bexar, Texas
RANK/MILITARY STATUS: Sergeant; RTA
MILITARY SPECIALTY:
CIVILIAN PROFESSION:
COMMENTS: Member of Seguin's cavalry company

NAME: **Allen, Robert**
AGE: ?
BIRTHPLACE: Virginia
RANK/MILITARY STATUS: Private; RTA
MILITARY SPECIALTY:
CIVILIAN PROFESSION:
COMMENTS: Member of Forsyth's cavalry company

NAME: **Andross, Miles De Forest** (Also shown as **Mills Andross**)
AGE: 27
BIRTHPLACE: Bradford, Vermont
RANK/MILITARY STATUS: Private; PV
MILITARY SPECIALTY:
CIVILIAN PROFESSION:
COMMENTS:

NAME: **Autry, Micajah**
AGE: 42
BIRTHPLACE: Sampson County, North Carolina
RANK/MILITARY STATUS: Private; VAC
MILITARY SPECIALTY:
CIVILIAN PROFESSION: Teacher, lawyer, businessman, amateur poet and writer
COMMENTS: Member of the Tennessee Mounted volunteers

NAME: **Badillo, Juan Antonio** (Also shown as **Antonio Padillo**)
AGE: ?
BIRTHPLACE: Texas
RANK/MILITARY STATUS: Sergeant; RTA
MILITARY SPECIALTY:
CIVILIAN PROFESSION:
COMMENTS: Member of Seguin's cavalry company

NAME: **Bailey, Peter James III**
AGE: 24
BIRTHPLACE: Springfield, Logan County, Kentucky
RANK/MILITARY STATUS: Private; VAC
MILITARY SPECIALTY:
CIVILIAN PROFESSION: Lawyer
COMMENTS: Member of the Tennessee Mounted Volunteers; law degree from Transylvania University (1834) is on display at the Alamo

NAME: **Baker, Isaac G.**
AGE: 32
BIRTHPLACE: Arkansas
RANK/MILITARY STATUS: Private; MIL
MILITARY SPECIALTY:
CIVILIAN PROFESSION:
COMMENTS: Member of the Gonzales Ranging Company

NAME: **Baker, William Charles M.**
AGE: ?
BIRTHPLACE: Missouri
RANK/MILITARY STATUS: Captain; PV
MILITARY SPECIALTY:
CIVILIAN PROFESSION:
COMMENTS: Member of Bowie's company; probably took over command when Bowie was felled by illness.

NAME: **Ballentine, John J.** (Also shown as **"Voluntine"**)
AGE: ?
BIRTHPLACE: Pennsylvania
RANK/MILITARY STATUS: Private; PV
MILITARY SPECIALTY:
CIVILIAN PROFESSION:
COMMENTS: Member of Carey's artillery company

NAME: **Ballentine, Richard W.** (Also shown as **"Robert W."** and **"Vallentine"**)
AGE: 22
BIRTHPLACE: Scotland
RANK/MILITARY STATUS: Private; PV?
MILITARY SPECIALTY:
CIVILIAN PROFESSION:
COMMENTS:

NAME: **Baugh, John J.**
AGE: 33
BIRTHPLACE: Virginia
RANK/MILITARY STATUS: Captain; PV
MILITARY SPECIALTY: Adjutant and nominal second in command of the Alamo garrison
CIVILIAN PROFESSION:
COMMENTS: Originally an officer in Breece's 2nd Company of New Orleans Greys

NAME: **Bayliss, Joseph**
AGE: 28
BIRTHPLACE: Tennessee
RANK/MILITARY STATUS: Private; VAC
MILITARY SPECIALTY:
CIVILIAN PROFESSION:
COMMENTS: Member of the Tennessee Mounted Volunteers

NAME: **Blair, John**
AGE: 33
BIRTHPLACE: Tennessee
RANK/MILITARY STATUS: Private; PV
MILITARY SPECIALTY:
CIVILIAN PROFESSION:
COMMENTS: May have been a member of Bowie's company

NAME: **Blair, Samuel**
AGE: 29
BIRTHPLACE: Tennessee
RANK/MILITARY STATUS: Captain; PV
MILITARY SPECIALTY: Assistant ordnance officer of the Alamo garrison
CIVILIAN PROFESSION:
COMMENTS:

NAME: **Blazeby, William**
AGE: 41
BIRTHPLACE: England
RANK/MILITARY STATUS: Captain; PV
MILITARY SPECIALTY: Commander of an infantry company consisting primarily of former members of the New Orleans Greys
CIVILIAN PROFESSION:
COMMENTS: Originally an officer in Breece's 2nd Company of New Orleans Greys

NAME: **Bonham, James Butler**
AGE: 29
BIRTHPLACE: Edgefield County, South Carolina
RANK/MILITARY STATUS: 2nd lieutenant; RTA

MILITARY SPECIALTY:
CIVILIAN PROFESSION: Attorney
COMMENTS: Helped to organize the Mobile Greys, but did not serve with them. Commissioned in the Texas Cavalry, but not assigned to a specific unit. Probably came to the Alamo with Bowie's company. Left the Alamo as a courier on or about February 16, and returned on March 3. May have been Travis' second cousin.

NAME: **Bourne, Daniel**
AGE: 26
BIRTHPLACE: England
RANK/MILITARY STATUS: Private; PV
MILITARY SPECIALTY:
CIVILIAN PROFESSION:
COMMENTS: Member of Carey's artillery company

NAME: **Bowie, James**
AGE: 40
BIRTHPLACE: Terrapin Creek, Logan County, Kentucky
RANK/MILITARY STATUS: Colonel; PV
MILITARY SPECIALTY: Co-commander of the Alamo garrison
CIVILIAN PROFESSION: Sugar planter, land speculator, slave trader
COMMENTS: Came to Bexar with orders from Houston to blow up and abandon the town and the Alamo. Decided, with Colonel Neill, to defend it instead. Elected commander of volunteers on or about February 12. Shared command of the garrison with Travis from February 14 until felled by illness on February 24.

NAME: **Bowman, Jesse B.**
AGE: 51
BIRTHPLACE: Tennessee
RANK/MILITARY STATUS: Private; PV?
MILITARY SPECIALTY:
CIVILIAN PROFESSION: Hunter, trapper
COMMENTS:

NAME: **Brown, George**
AGE: 35
BIRTHPLACE: England
RANK/MILITARY STATUS: Private; ?
MILITARY SPECIALTY:
CIVILIAN PROFESSION:
COMMENTS:

NAME: **Brown, James**
AGE: 36
BIRTHPLACE: Pennsylvania
RANK/MILITARY STATUS: Private; PV?
MILITARY SPECIALTY:
CIVILIAN PROFESSION:
COMMENTS: Possibly a member of Blazeby's infantry company

NAME: **Buchanan, James**
AGE: 23
BIRTHPLACE: Alabama
RANK/MILITARY STATUS: Private; ?
MILITARY SPECIALTY:
CIVILIAN PROFESSION:
COMMENTS:

NAME: **Burns, Samuel E.**
AGE: 26
BIRTHPLACE: Ireland
RANK/MILITARY STATUS: Private; PV
MILITARY SPECIALTY:
CIVILIAN PROFESSION:
COMMENTS: Member of Carey's artillery company

NAME: **Butler, George D.**
AGE: 23
BIRTHPLACE: Missouri
RANK/MILITARY STATUS: Private; ?
MILITARY SPECIALTY:
CIVILIAN PROFESSION:
COMMENTS:

NAME: **Cain, John** (Also shown as **"Cane"**)
AGE: 34
BIRTHPLACE: Pennsylvania
RANK/MILITARY STATUS: Private; PV
MILITARY SPECIALTY:
CIVILIAN PROFESSION:
COMMENTS: Member of Carey's artillery company. Left the Alamo prior to the siege and returned home to Gonzales. Returned on March 1 with the Gonzales relief force.

NAME: **Campbell, Robert**
AGE: 26
BIRTHPLACE: Tennessee
RANK/MILITARY STATUS: 1st lieutenant; VAC
MILITARY SPECIALTY:
CIVILIAN PROFESSION:
COMMENTS: Member of the Tennessee Mounted Volunteers

NAME: **Carey, William R.**
AGE: 30
BIRTHPLACE: Virginia
RANK/MILITARY STATUS: Captain; PV
MILITARY SPECIALTY: Commanded the Alamo's artillery company, called "The Invincibles"
CIVILIAN PROFESSION:
COMMENTS: Before the siege, commanded the Alamo while Colonel Neill commanded Bexar; may have had a slave with him who was also killed in the battle

NAME: **Clark, Charles Henry**
AGE: ?
BIRTHPLACE: Missouri
RANK/MILITARY STATUS: Private; PV
MILITARY SPECIALTY:
CIVILIAN PROFESSION:
COMMENTS: Previously a member of Breece's 2nd Company of New Orleans Greys

NAME: **Clark, M. B.**
AGE: ?
BIRTHPLACE: Mississippi
RANK/MILITARY STATUS: Private; PV
MILITARY SPECIALTY:
CIVILIAN PROFESSION:
COMMENTS: Probably a member of Bowie's company

NAME: **Cloud, Daniel W.**
AGE: 24
BIRTHPLACE: Lexington, Kentucky
RANK/MILITARY STATUS: Private; VAC
MILITARY SPECIALTY:
CIVILIAN PROFESSION: Lawyer
COMMENTS: Member of the Tennessee Mounted Volunteers

NAME: **Cochran, Robert E.**
AGE: 26
BIRTHPLACE: New Jersey
RANK/MILITARY STATUS: Private; PV
MILITARY SPECIALTY:
CIVILIAN PROFESSION:
COMMENTS: Member of Carey's artillery company; Cochran County, Texas, is named for him

NAME: **Cottle, George Washington**
AGE: 25
BIRTHPLACE: Hurricane Township, Lincoln County, Missouri
RANK/MILITARY STATUS: Private; MIL
MILITARY SPECIALTY:
CIVILIAN PROFESSION:

COMMENTS: Member of the Gonzales Ranging Company; brother-in-law of defender Thomas J. Jackson.

NAME: **Courtman, Henry**
AGE: 28
BIRTHPLACE: Germany
RANK/MILITARY STATUS: Private; PV
MILITARY SPECIALTY:
CIVILIAN PROFESSION:
COMMENTS: Member of Blazeby's infantry company. Previously a member of Breece's 2nd Company of New Orleans Greys. His brother George was killed in the Goliad Massacre.

NAME: **Crawford, Lemuel**
AGE: 22
BIRTHPLACE: South Carolina
RANK/MILITARY STATUS: Private; PV
MILITARY SPECIALTY:
CIVILIAN PROFESSION:
COMMENTS: Member of Carey's artillery company

NAME: **Crockett, David**
AGE: 49
BIRTHPLACE: Franklin (an independent state under the Articles of Confederation; later became part of Green County, Tennessee, when the Constitution was ratified)
RANK/MILITARY STATUS: Private; VAC (called Colonel because he had once held that rank in an American militia unit)
MILITARY SPECIALTY:
CIVILIAN PROFESSION: Hunter, frontiersman, former U.S. congressman
COMMENTS: Member of the Tennessee Mounted Volunteers. Because of his reputation and his charisma, he became the unit's nominal leader, although it was officially commanded by Capt. William Harrison. His cousin John Harris was also killed at the Alamo.

NAME: **Crossman, Robert** (Also shown as **"Crosson"** or **"Crasson"**)
AGE: 26
BIRTHPLACE: Pennsylvania
RANK/MILITARY STATUS: Private; PV
MILITARY SPECIALTY:
CIVILIAN PROFESSION:
COMMENTS: Member of Blazeby's infantry company; previously a member of Breece's 2nd Company of New Orleans Greys

NAME: **Cummings, David P.**
AGE: 27
BIRTHPLACE: Pennsylvania
RANK/MILITARY STATUS: Private; PV
MILITARY SPECIALTY:
CIVILIAN PROFESSION: Surveyor
COMMENTS: Member of Blazeby's infantry company. Left Bexar sometime after February 14, and then returned with the Gonzales Relief Force. Cousin by marriage to defender John Purdy Reynolds.

NAME: **Cunningham, Robert**
AGE: 31
BIRTHPLACE: Ontario County, New York
RANK/MILITARY STATUS: Private; PV
MILITARY SPECIALTY:
CIVILIAN PROFESSION: Flatboatman
COMMENTS: Member of Carey's artillery company; former sergeant in Parrott's artillery company

NAME: **Darst, Jacob** (Also shown as **"Durst"** or **"Dust"**)
AGE: 42
BIRTHPLACE: Woodford County, Kentucky
RANK/MILITARY STATUS: Private; MIL
MILITARY SPECIALTY:
CIVILIAN PROFESSION: Farmer
COMMENTS: Member of the Gonzales Ranging Company

NAME: **Davis, John**
AGE: 25
BIRTHPLACE: Kentucky
RANK/MILITARY STATUS: Private; MIL
MILITARY SPECIALTY:
CIVILIAN PROFESSION:
COMMENTS: Member of the Gonzales Ranging Company

NAME: **Day, Freeman H. K.**
AGE: 30
BIRTHPLACE: Scotland
RANK/MILITARY STATUS: Private; PV
MILITARY SPECIALTY:
CIVILIAN PROFESSION:
COMMENTS: Possibly a member of Blazeby's infantry company. Previously a member of White's infantry company and the Bexar Guards. Some evidence suggests that White's company retained its individual identity at the Alamo.

NAME: **Day, Jerry C.**
AGE: 20
BIRTHPLACE: Missouri
RANK/MILITARY STATUS: Private; RTA
MILITARY SPECIALTY:
CIVILIAN PROFESSION:
COMMENTS: Member of Forsyth's cavalry company

NAME: **Daymon, Squire**
AGE: 28
BIRTHPLACE: Tennessee
RANK/MILITARY STATUS: Private; PV
MILITARY SPECIALTY:
CIVILIAN PROFESSION:
COMMENTS: Member of Carey's artillery company. Left Bexar to return home to Gonzales sometime after February 2. Returned to the Alamo with the Gonzales Relief Force.

NAME: **Dearduff, William**
AGE: ?
BIRTHPLACE: Tennessee
RANK/MILITARY STATUS: Private; MIL
MILITARY SPECIALTY:
CIVILIAN PROFESSION:
COMMENTS: Member of the Gonzales Ranging Company; brother-in-law to defender James George

NAME: **Dennison, Stephen**
AGE: 24
BIRTHPLACE: England or Ireland
RANK/MILITARY STATUS:
MILITARY SPECIALTY:
CIVILIAN PROFESSION: Glazier, painter
COMMENTS: Member of Blazeby's infantry company; previously a member of Breece's 2nd Company of New Orleans Greys

NAME: **Despallier, Charles**
AGE: 24
BIRTHPLACE: Louisiana
RANK/MILITARY STATUS: Private; ?
MILITARY SPECIALTY:
CIVILIAN PROFESSION:
COMMENTS: Took part in the raid on La Villita. Left the Alamo as a courier sometime after February 25, and then returned with the Gonzales Relief Force.

NAME: **Dewall, Louis** (Also shown as **"Duel"** or **"Dewell"**)
AGE: 24

BIRTHPLACE: Manhattan, New York
RANK/MILITARY STATUS: Private; PV
MILITARY SPECIALTY:
CIVILIAN PROFESSION: Plasterer, mason, blacksmith, boatman
COMMENTS: Member of Blazeby's infantry company; former member of the Bexar Guards.

NAME: **Dickinson, Almeron** (Also shown as **"Dickerson"** & **"Almaron"**)
AGE: 26
BIRTHPLACE: Tennessee
RANK/MILITARY STATUS: Captain; RTA
MILITARY SPECIALTY: Artillery officer
CIVILIAN PROFESSION: Blacksmith
COMMENTS: Commanded the chapel battery during the siege. His wife Susannah and young daughter Angelina survived the battle.

NAME: **Dillard, John Henry**
AGE: 31
BIRTHPLACE: Smith County, Tennessee
RANK/MILITARY STATUS: Private; ?
MILITARY SPECIALTY:
CIVILIAN PROFESSION:
COMMENTS:

NAME: **Dimpkins, James R.** (Also shown as **"Dimkins," "Dickens," "Dinkin,"** or **"Dockon"**)
AGE: ?
BIRTHPLACE: England
RANK/MILITARY STATUS: Sergeant; PV
MILITARY SPECIALTY:
CIVILIAN PROFESSION:
COMMENTS: Member of Blazeby's infantry company; previously a member of Breece's 2nd Company of New Orleans Greys

NAME: **Duvalt, Andrew** (Also shown as **"Devault"**)
AGE: 32
BIRTHPLACE: Ireland
RANK/MILITARY STATUS: Private; MIL
MILITARY SPECIALTY:
CIVILIAN PROFESSION: Plasterer
COMMENTS: Previously a member of the Bexar Guards. Joined the Gonzales Ranging Company on February 23, 1836, and is believed to have returned to the Alamo with the Gonzales Relief Force.

NAME: **Espalier, Carlos**
AGE: 17
BIRTHPLACE: San Antonio de Bexar, Texas
RANK/MILITARY STATUS: Private; RTA?
MILITARY SPECIALTY:
CIVILIAN PROFESSION:
COMMENTS: May have been a member of Seguin's cavalry company

NAME: **Esparza, José Gregorio**
AGE: 27
BIRTHPLACE: San Antonio de Bexar, Texas
RANK/MILITARY STATUS: Private; RTA
MILITARY SPECIALTY:
CIVILIAN PROFESSION:
COMMENTS: Member of Seguin's cavalry company. Served on one of the chapel cannon crews. His brother Francisco was a member of one of the local Mexican army units who fought in the Battle of Bexar, but was held in reserve during the assault on the Alamo. General Cos, Francisco's commander, granted him permission to recover Gregorio's body for burial. Gregorio was the only defender who was given a Christian burial.

NAME: **Evans, Robert**
AGE: 36
BIRTHPLACE: Ireland
RANK/MILITARY STATUS: Major; PV
MILITARY SPECIALTY: Chief Ordnance officer of the Alamo garrison
CIVILIAN PROFESSION:
COMMENTS: According to Susannah Dickinson, Evans was killed while trying to blow up the powder magazine in the chapel with a torch.

NAME: **Evans, Samuel B.**
AGE: 24
BIRTHPLACE: Jefferson County, New York
RANK/MILITARY STATUS: Private; ?
MILITARY SPECIALTY:
CIVILIAN PROFESSION:
COMMENTS:

NAME: **Ewing, James L.**
AGE: 24
BIRTHPLACE: Tennessee
RANK/MILITARY STATUS: Private; PV
MILITARY SPECIALTY: Served as secretary to Colonel Neill, Captain Carey, and possibly to Lieutenant Colonel Travis
CIVILIAN PROFESSION:
COMMENTS: Member of Carey's artillery company

NAME: **Fishbaugh, William** (Also shown as **"Fishback"**)
AGE: ?
BIRTHPLACE: Possibly Alabama
RANK/MILITARY STATUS: Private; MIL
MILITARY SPECIALTY:
CIVILIAN PROFESSION:
COMMENTS: Member of the Gonzales Ranging Company

NAME: **Flanders, John**
AGE: 36
BIRTHPLACE: New Hampshire
RANK/MILITARY STATUS: Private; MIL
MILITARY SPECIALTY:
CIVILIAN PROFESSION:
COMMENTS: Member of the Gonzales Ranging Company

NAME: **Floyd, Dolphin Ward** (Also shown as just **"Dolphin Ward"**)
AGE: 32
BIRTHPLACE: Nash County, North Carolina
RANK/MILITARY STATUS: Private; MIL
MILITARY SPECIALTY:
CIVILIAN PROFESSION: Farmer
COMMENTS: Member of the Gonzales Ranging Company. He was killed on his 32nd birthday. Floyd County, Texas, is named after him

NAME: **Fontleroy, William Keener** (Also shown as **"Furtleroy," "Fautleroy,"** and **"Fauntleroy"**)
AGE: 22
BIRTHPLACE: Logan County, Kentucky
RANK/MILITARY STATUS: Private; VAC
MILITARY SPECIALTY:
CIVILIAN PROFESSION:
COMMENTS: Member of the Tennessee Mounted Volunteers

NAME: **Forsyth, John Hubbard**
AGE: 38
BIRTHPLACE: Avon, Livingston County, New York
RANK/MILITARY STATUS: Captain, RTA
MILITARY SPECIALTY: Commanded one of the Alamo's two regular cavalry companies

CIVILIAN PROFESSION: Farmer; non-practicing physician
COMMENTS:

NAME: **Fuentes, Antonio**
AGE: 23
BIRTHPLACE: San Antonio de Bexar, Texas
RANK/MILITARY STATUS: Corporal, RTA
MILITARY SPECIALTY:
CIVILIAN PROFESSION:
COMMENTS: Member of Seguin's cavalry company

NAME: **Fuqua, Galba**
AGE: 16
BIRTHPLACE: Alabama
RANK/MILITARY STATUS: Private; MIL
MILITARY SPECIALTY:
CIVILIAN PROFESSION:
COMMENTS: Member of the Gonzales Ranging Company

NAME: **Garnett, William**
AGE: 24
BIRTHPLACE: Virginia
RANK/MILITARY STATUS: Private; RTA
MILITARY SPECIALTY:
CIVILIAN PROFESSION: Baptist preacher
COMMENTS: Probably a member of Forsyth's cavalry company

NAME: **Garrand, James W.**
AGE: 23
BIRTHPLACE: Louisiana
RANK/MILITARY STATUS: Private; PV
MILITARY SPECIALTY:
CIVILIAN PROFESSION:
COMMENTS: Member of Blazeby's infantry company

NAME: **Garrett, James Girard**
AGE: 30
BIRTHPLACE: Tennessee
RANK/MILITARY STATUS: Private; PV
MILITARY SPECIALTY:
CIVILIAN PROFESSION:
COMMENTS: Member of Blazeby's infantry company; previously a member of Breece's 2nd Company of New Orleans Greys

NAME: **Garvin, John E.**
AGE: 27
BIRTHPLACE: Possibly Missouri
RANK/MILITARY STATUS: Private; PV
MILITARY SPECIALTY:
CIVILIAN PROFESSION:
COMMENTS: Member of Carey's infantry company. Went home to Gonzales after the Battle of Bexar, then returned to the Alamo with the Gonzales Relief Force.

NAME: **Gaston, John E.**
AGE: 17
BIRTHPLACE: Possibly Kentucky
RANK/MILITARY STATUS: Private; MIL
MILITARY SPECIALTY:
CIVILIAN PROFESSION:
COMMENTS: Member of the Gonzales Ranging Company

NAME: **George, James**
AGE: 34
BIRTHPLACE: Possibly Tennessee
RANK/MILITARY STATUS: Private; MIL
MILITARY SPECIALTY:
CIVILIAN PROFESSION:
COMMENTS: Member of the Gonzales Ranging Company. Married to Elizabeth Dearduff, sister of defender William Dearduff.

NAME: **Goodrich, John C.**
AGE: 27
BIRTHPLACE: Virginia
RANK/MILITARY STATUS: Cornet; RTA (a cornet was the lowest commissioned rank in a cavalry unit, equal to an ensign; the cornet's duty was to carry the troop's flag)
MILITARY SPECIALTY:
CIVILIAN PROFESSION:
COMMENTS: Some confusion exists here. Goodrich was probably a member of Forsyth's cavalry company, but may have belonged to Blazeby's infantry company. In that case, the rank of cornet would have been very unusual. His brother Benjamin was a signer of the Texas Declaration of Independence.

NAME: **Grimes, Albert Calvin**
AGE: 18
BIRTHPLACE: Georgia
RANK/MILITARY STATUS: Private; RTA
MILITARY SPECIALTY:
CIVILIAN PROFESSION:
COMMENTS: Probably belonged to Forsyth's cavalry company. His father Jessie was a signer of the Texas Declaration of Independence.

NAME: **Gwynne, James C.** (Also shown as **"Gwin," "Groya,"** and **"Groyn"**)
AGE: 32
BIRTHPLACE: England
RANK/MILITARY STATUS: Private; PV
MILITARY SPECIALTY:
CIVILIAN PROFESSION:
COMMENTS: Member of Carey's artillery company

NAME: **Hannum, James** (Also shown as **"Hannan"** or **"Hanuam"**)
AGE: 20
BIRTHPLACE: Pennsylvania
RANK/MILITARY STATUS: Private; PV
MILITARY SPECIALTY:
CIVILIAN PROFESSION:
COMMENTS: May have been a member of Blazeby's infantry company. Hannum's death at the Alamo is not a certainty, but he is included here to give him the benefit of the doubt. There is also evidence that he may have died of natural causes at La Bahía, and is buried outside the wall there.

NAME: **Harris, John**
AGE: 23
BIRTHPLACE: Kentucky
RANK/MILITARY STATUS: Private; MIL
MILITARY SPECIALTY:
CIVILIAN PROFESSION:
COMMENTS: Member of the Gonzales Ranging Company. Formerly a member of the Bexar Guards. Cousin of Davy Crockett.

NAME: **Harrison, Andrew Jackson**
AGE: 27
BIRTHPLACE: Tennessee
RANK/MILITARY STATUS: Private; ?
MILITARY SPECIALTY:
CIVILIAN PROFESSION:
COMMENTS:

NAME: **Harrison, William B.**
AGE: 25
BIRTHPLACE: Ohio
RANK/MILITARY STATUS: Captain; VAC
MILITARY SPECIALTY: Commander of the Tennessee Mounted Volunteers
CIVILIAN PROFESSION:
COMMENTS: Was in charge of the defense of the wooden paliside between the chapel and the low barracks. Davy Crockett was a member of his unit.

NAME: **Hawkins, Joseph M.** (Sometimes shown as **"M. Hawkins"**)
AGE: 37
BIRTHPLACE: Ireland
RANK/MILITARY STATUS: Private; PV
MILITARY SPECIALTY:
CIVILIAN PROFESSION:
COMMENTS: May have been a member of Bowie's company, and may previously have served in Baker's company

NAME: **Hays, John M.**
AGE: 22
BIRTHPLACE: Nashville, Tennessee
RANK/MILITARY STATUS: Private; PV
MILITARY SPECIALTY:
CIVILIAN PROFESSION: Possibly a lawyer
COMMENTS: May have been a member of Bowie's company; previously served in Chenoweth's company of the New Orleans Greys, and also possibly in Baker's company

NAME: **Heiskell, Charles M.** (Also shown as **"Haskell"** & **"Huskill"**)
AGE: 23
BIRTHPLACE: Possibly Tennessee
RANK/MILITARY STATUS: Private; PV
MILITARY SPECIALTY:
CIVILIAN PROFESSION:
COMMENTS: Member of Bowie's company. Previously served in Carey's artillery company, but left the Alamo to take part in the Matamoros expedition. Returned with Bowie's volunteers.

NAME: **Herndon, Patrick Henry**
AGE: 34
BIRTHPLACE: Virginia
RANK/MILITARY STATUS: Private; PV
MILITARY SPECIALTY:
CIVILIAN PROFESSION:
COMMENTS: May have been a member of Bowie's company. Previously served in Chenoweth's company of the New Orleans Greys, and also possibly in Baker's company.

NAME: **Hersee, William Daniel**
AGE: 31
BIRTHPLACE: England
RANK/MILITARY STATUS: Sergeant; PV
MILITARY SPECIALTY:
CIVILIAN PROFESSION:
COMMENTS: Member of Carey's artillery company. Wounded in the Siege of Bexar. It is not known if he recovered enough to fight during the battle for the Alamo, but he was killed during the final assault.

NAME: **Holland, Tapley**
AGE: 26
BIRTHPLACE: Ohio
RANK/MILITARY STATUS: Private; PV
MILITARY SPECIALTY:
CIVILIAN PROFESSION:
COMMENTS: Member of Carey's artillery company

NAME: **Holloway, Samuel**
AGE: 28
BIRTHPLACE: Philadelphia, Pennsylvania
RANK/MILITARY STATUS: Private; PV
MILITARY SPECIALTY:
CIVILIAN PROFESSION:
COMMENTS: Member of Blazeby's infantry company; previously served in Breece's 2nd Company of New Orleans Greys

NAME: **Howell, William D.** (Also shown as **"Homrell"**)
AGE: 45
BIRTHPLACE: Massachusetts
RANK/MILITARY STATUS: Surgeon or private soldier; PV
MILITARY SPECIALTY: Possibly served as a surgeon
CIVILIAN PROFESSION: Physician
COMMENTS: Member of Blazeby's infantry company; previously served in Breece's 2nd Company of New Orleans Greys

NAME: **Jackson, Thomas**
AGE: ?
BIRTHPLACE: Ireland
RANK/MILITARY STATUS: Private; MIL
MILITARY SPECIALTY:
CIVILIAN PROFESSION:
COMMENTS: Member of the Gonzales Ranging Company. His wife Louise was the sister of defender George W. Cottle.

NAME: **Jackson, William Daniel**
AGE: 29
BIRTHPLACE: Possibly Ireland
RANK/MILITARY STATUS: Private; PV
MILITARY SPECIALTY:
CIVILIAN PROFESSION: Sailor
COMMENTS: Member of Carey's artillery company

NAME: **Jameson, Green B.**
AGE: 27
BIRTHPLACE: Kentucky
RANK/MILITARY STATUS: Major; PV
MILITARY SPECIALTY: Chief engineer of the Alamo garrison
CIVILIAN PROFESSION: Lawyer
COMMENTS: Designed and coördinated the work on the improvements in the Alamo's defenses. Acted as a messenger to the Mexicans on the first day of the siege.

NAME: **Jennings, Gordon C.**
AGE: 56
BIRTHPLACE: Pennsylvania
RANK/MILITARY STATUS: Corporal; PV
MILITARY SPECIALTY:
CIVILIAN PROFESSION: Farmer
COMMENTS: Member of Carey's artillery company. He was the oldest Alamo defender. His brother Charles was executed at Goliad.

NAME: **Jiminez, Damacio** (Also shown as **"Ximines"** and **"Jimines"**)
AGE: ?
BIRTHPLACE: Probably San Antonio de Bexar, Texas
RANK/MILITARY STATUS: Private; RTA?
MILITARY SPECIALTY:
CIVILIAN PROFESSION:
COMMENTS: Possibly a member of Seguin's cavalry company. Helped bring the eighteen-pounder to the Alamo from San Felipe de Austin. Fought at Anahuac and in the Siege of San Antonio de Bexar. One of the most recently identified Alamo defenders, being formally recognized on March 6, 1987. His presence at the Alamo was verified by newly discovered affidavits filed in 1861 by Juan Seguin and Cornelio Delgado, a citizen of Bexar who was forced to dig graves for some of the Mexicans killed in the assault.

NAME: **John**
AGE: ?
BIRTHPLACE: Louisiana
RANK/MILITARY STATUS: Civilian
MILITARY SPECIALTY:
CIVILIAN PROFESSION: Store clerk and possibly a Negro slave
COMMENTS: Early Alamo lists show a "John" with no last name who was a

clerk in DeSauque's store. The first known mention of his being Negro or a slave is from the 1930's. This is possible, however, because Travis' slave Joe mentions that he was not the only Negro in the Alamo. Although a civilian, it is probable that John took an active part in the fight. He stayed at the Alamo when DeSauque left with dispatches for Fannin. John died at the Alamo, and DeSauque was executed with Fannin's men at Goliad.

NAME: **Johnson, Lewis**
AGE: 25
BIRTHPLACE: Possibly Illinois Territory
RANK/MILITARY STATUS: Private; PV
MILITARY SPECIALTY:
CIVILIAN PROFESSION:
COMMENTS: Possibly a member of either Carey's artillery company or Blazeby's infantry company

NAME: **Johnson, William**
AGE: ?
BIRTHPLACE: Philadelphia, Pennsylvania
RANK/MILITARY STATUS: Private; PV
MILITARY SPECIALTY:
CIVILIAN PROFESSION:
COMMENTS: Possibly a member of either Carey's artillery company or Blazeby's infantry company

NAME: **Jones, John**
AGE: 26
BIRTHPLACE: New York
RANK/MILITARY STATUS: 1st lieutenant; PV
MILITARY SPECIALTY:
CIVILIAN PROFESSION:
COMMENTS: Member of Blazeby's infantry company; previously served in Breece's 2nd Company of New Orleans Greys

NAME: **Kellogg, John Benjamin**
AGE: 19
BIRTHPLACE: Kentucky
RANK/MILITARY STATUS: Private; MIL
MILITARY SPECIALTY:
CIVILIAN PROFESSION:
COMMENTS: Member of the Gonzales Ranging Company. His wife Sidney was formerly married to defender Thomas R. Miller.

NAME: **Kenny, James**
AGE: 22
BIRTHPLACE: Virginia
RANK/MILITARY STATUS: Private; ?
MILITARY SPECIALTY:
CIVILIAN PROFESSION:
COMMENTS: His riding whip is on display at the Alamo.

NAME: **Kent, Andrew**
AGE: 34-38
BIRTHPLACE: Kentucky
RANK/MILITARY STATUS: Private; MIL
MILITARY SPECIALTY:
CIVILIAN PROFESSION: Farmer and possibly a carpenter
COMMENTS: Member of the Gonzales Ranging Company

NAME: **Kerr, Joseph**
AGE: 22
BIRTHPLACE: Lake Providence, Louisiana
RANK/MILITARY STATUS: Private; ?
MILITARY SPECIALTY:
CIVILIAN PROFESSION:
COMMENTS: Previously served with Capt. S. L. Chamblis' Company of Louisiana Volunteers for Texas Independence, but was honorably discharged when his horse went lame. His brother Nathan, who served with him, died of illness on February 19, 1836.

NAME: **Kimball, George** (Also shown as **"Kimbell"** & **"Kimble"**)
AGE: 33
BIRTHPLACE: Pennsylvania
RANK/MILITARY STATUS: Lieutenant; MIL
MILITARY SPECIALTY: Commander of the Gonzales Ranging Company
CIVILIAN PROFESSION: Hatter; business partner with Almeron Dickinson
COMMENTS: Led the "Gonzales 32" into the Alamo. Kimble County, Texas, is named for him.

NAME: **King, William Philip**
AGE: 15
BIRTHPLACE: Texas
RANK/MILITARY STATUS: Private; MIL
MILITARY SPECIALTY:
CIVILIAN PROFESSION:
COMMENTS: Member of the Gonzales Ranging Company. The youngest Alamo defender to die.

NAME: **Lewis, William Irvine**
AGE: 23
BIRTHPLACE: Virginia
RANK/MILITARY STATUS: Private; VAC
MILITARY SPECIALTY:
CIVILIAN PROFESSION:
COMMENTS: Member of the Tennessee Mounted Volunteers

NAME: **Lightfoot, William** (Also shown as **"John W. Lightfoot"**)
AGE: 25
BIRTHPLACE: Virginia
RANK/MILITARY STATUS: Corporal; PV
MILITARY SPECIALTY:
CIVILIAN PROFESSION:
COMMENTS: Member of Carey's artillery company

NAME: **Lindley, Jonathan L.**
AGE: 22
BIRTHPLACE: Sangamon County, Illinois Territory
RANK/MILITARY STATUS: Private; PV
MILITARY SPECIALTY:
CIVILIAN PROFESSION: Surveyor
COMMENTS: Member of Carey's artillery company. Went home to Gonzales after the Battle of Bexar, then possibly returned to the Alamo with the Gonzales Relief Force. New evidence indicates that he possibly did not die at the Alamo, but he is included here to give him the benefit of the doubt.

NAME: **Linn, William**
AGE: ?
BIRTHPLACE: Boston, Massachusetts
RANK/MILITARY STATUS: Private; PV
MILITARY SPECIALTY:
CIVILIAN PROFESSION:
COMMENTS: Member of Blazeby's infantry company; previously served in Breece's 2nd Company of New Orleans Greys

NAME: **Losoya, Toribio Domingo**
AGE: 28
BIRTHPLACE: San Antonio de Bexar, Texas
RANK/MILITARY STATUS: Private; RTA?
MILITARY SPECIALTY:
CIVILIAN PROFESSION:
COMMENTS: Possibly a member of Seguin's cavalry company.

NAME: **Main, George Washington**

AGE: 29
BIRTHPLACE: Virginia
RANK/MILITARY STATUS: 2nd lieutenant; PV
MILITARY SPECIALTY:
CIVILIAN PROFESSION:
COMMENTS: Was a member of White's infantry company. Badly wounded in the Battle for Bexar, and probably did not actively participate in the Siege of the Alamo.

NAME: **Malone, William Thomas**
AGE: 18
BIRTHPLACE: Athens, Georgia
RANK/MILITARY STATUS: Private; PV
MILITARY SPECIALTY:
CIVILIAN PROFESSION:
COMMENTS: Member of Carey's artillery company; previously served in Parrott's artillery company

NAME: **Marshall, William**
AGE: 28
BIRTHPLACE: Tennessee
RANK/MILITARY STATUS: Private; PV
MILITARY SPECIALTY:
CIVILIAN PROFESSION:
COMMENTS: Member of Blazeby's infantry company; previously served in Breece's 2nd Company of New Orleans Greys

NAME: **Martin, Albert**
AGE: 28
BIRTHPLACE: Providence, Rhode Island
RANK/MILITARY STATUS: Captain; PV
MILITARY SPECIALTY:
CIVILIAN PROFESSION: General store owner
COMMENTS: Acted as Travis' emissary in a meeting with Col. Juan Almonte on February 23. On February 24 he carried a message from Travis to Gonzales, where he turned it over to Launcelot Smither. Martin then returned to the Alamo with the Gonzales Relief Force.

NAME: **McCafferty, Edward**
AGE: ?
BIRTHPLACE: ?
RANK/MILITARY STATUS: Lieutenant, PV
MILITARY SPECIALTY:
CIVILIAN PROFESSION:
COMMENTS: May have been a member of Bowie's company

NAME: **McCoy, Jesse**
AGE: 32
BIRTHPLACE: Gyrosburg, Tennessee
RANK/MILITARY STATUS: Private; MIL
MILITARY SPECIALTY:
CIVILIAN PROFESSION: Sheriff of Gonzales
COMMENTS: Member of the Gonzales Ranging Company

NAME: **McDowell, William** (Also shown as **"McDowelly"**)
AGE: 42
BIRTHPLACE: Mifflin County, Pennsylvania
RANK/MILITARY STATUS: Private; VAC
MILITARY SPECIALTY:
CIVILIAN PROFESSION:
COMMENTS: Member of the Tennessee Mounted Volunteers

NAME: **McGee, James**
AGE: ?
BIRTHPLACE: Ireland
RANK/MILITARY STATUS: Private; PV
MILITARY SPECIALTY:
CIVILIAN PROFESSION:
COMMENTS: Member of Blazeby's infantry company. Previously served in Breece's 2nd Company of New Orleans Greys. Wounded in the Battle for Bexar, and may not have been an active participant in the Alamo fighting.

NAME: **McGregor, John**
AGE: 28
BIRTHPLACE: Scotland
RANK/MILITARY STATUS: Sergeant; PV
MILITARY SPECIALTY:
CIVILIAN PROFESSION:
COMMENTS: Member of Carey's artillery company. Tradition holds that during the siege, he entertained the Alamo garrison by playing his bagpipes, accompanied by Davy Crockett on the fiddle.

NAME: **McKinney, Robert**
AGE: 27
BIRTHPLACE: Tennessee
RANK/MILITARY STATUS: Private; PV
MILITARY SPECIALTY:
CIVILIAN PROFESSION:
COMMENTS: May have been a member of Bowie's company

NAME: **Melton, Eliel**
AGE: 38
BIRTHPLACE: Georgia
RANK/MILITARY STATUS: Lieutenant; PV
MILITARY SPECIALTY: Quartermaster of the Alamo garrison
CIVILIAN PROFESSION: Merchant
COMMENTS:

NAME: **Miller, Thomas R.**
AGE: 41
BIRTHPLACE: Tennessee
RANK/MILITARY STATUS: Private; MIL
MILITARY SPECIALTY:
CIVILIAN PROFESSION: Farmer, shopkeeper, clerk of the Gonzales City Council
COMMENTS: Member of the Gonzales Ranging Company. His ex-wife Sidney was married to defender John Kellogg.

NAME: **Mills, William**
AGE: 20
BIRTHPLACE: Chattanooga, Tennessee
RANK/MILITARY STATUS: Private; PV
MILITARY SPECIALTY:
CIVILIAN PROFESSION:
COMMENTS: May have been a member of Bowie's company

NAME: **Millsaps, Isaac**
AGE: 41
BIRTHPLACE: Mississippi
RANK/MILITARY STATUS: Private; MIL
MILITARY SPECIALTY:
CIVILIAN PROFESSION:
COMMENTS: Member of the Gonzales Ranging Company. His wife Mary was blind, and they had seven children. Characters based on the Millsaps played an emotional scene in John Wanye's movie *The Alamo.* A famous "Alamo letter," long believed to have been written by Isaac, has recently been proven a forgery.

NAME: **Mitchasson, Edward** (Also shown as **"Mitcherson" & "Mitchson"**)
AGE: 29
BIRTHPLACE: Virginia
RANK/MILITARY STATUS: Possibly surgeon; PV
MILITARY SPECIALTY: May have served the garrison as a surgeon
CIVILIAN PROFESSION: Physician
COMMENTS: May have been a member of Bowie's company. Previously

served in Chenoweth's Company of the New Orleans Greys. Wounded in the Battle of Bexar, and may not have recovered in time to take part in the Alamo fighting.

NAME: **Mitchell, Edwin T.**
AGE: 30
BIRTHPLACE: Georgia
RANK/MILITARY STATUS: Private; PV
MILITARY SPECIALTY:
CIVILIAN PROFESSION:
COMMENTS: Possibly a member of Blazeby's infantry company. Previously served in White's infantry company and the Bexar Guards. Some evidence suggests that White's company retained its individual identity at the Alamo. Either he or Napoleon Mitchell was bayonetted while trying to protect Juana Alsbury in the chapel. His brother DeWarren was killed in the Goliad Massacre.

NAME: **Mitchell, Napoleon Bonaparte**
AGE: 32
BIRTHPLACE: Possibly Tennessee
RANK/MILITARY STATUS: Private; PV
MILITARY SPECIALTY:
CIVILIAN PROFESSION:
COMMENTS: Member of Carey's artillery company. Previously served in Breece's 2nd Company of New Orleans Greys. Either he or Edwin Mitchell was bayonetted while trying to protect Juana Alsbury in the chapel.

NAME: **Moore, Robert B.**
AGE: 55
BIRTHPLACE: Martinsburg, Virginia
RANK/MILITARY STATUS: Private; PV
MILITARY SPECIALTY:
CIVILIAN PROFESSION:
COMMENTS: Member of Blazeby's infantry company. Previously served in Breece's 2nd Company of New Orleans Greys. Cousin of defender Willis Moore.

NAME: **Moore, Willis A.**
AGE: 28
BIRTHPLACE: Raymond, Mississippi
RANK/MILITARY STATUS: Private; PV
MILITARY SPECIALTY:
CIVILIAN PROFESSION:
COMMENTS: May have been a member of Bowie's company. Previously served in Chenoweth's company of the New Orleans Greys. Cousin of defender Robert Moore.

NAME: **Musselman, Robert**
AGE: 31
BIRTHPLACE: Ohio
RANK/MILITARY STATUS: Sergeant; PV
MILITARY SPECIALTY:
CIVILIAN PROFESSION:
COMMENTS: Member of Blazeby's infantry company; previously served as a sergeant in Breece's 2nd Company of New Orleans Greys

NAME: **Nava, Andres**
AGE: 26
BIRTHPLACE: San Antonio de Bexar, Texas
RANK/MILITARY STATUS: Private; RTA?
MILITARY SPECIALTY:
CIVILIAN PROFESSION:
COMMENTS: Possibly a member of Seguin's cavalry company

NAME: **Neggan, George**
AGE: 28
BIRTHPLACE: South Carolina
RANK/MILITARY STATUS: Private; MIL
MILITARY SPECIALTY:
CIVILIAN PROFESSION:
COMMENTS: Member of the Gonzales Ranging Company

NAME: **Nelson, Andrew M.**
AGE: 27
BIRTHPLACE: Tennessee
RANK/MILITARY STATUS: Private; ?
MILITARY SPECIALTY:
CIVILIAN PROFESSION:
COMMENTS:

NAME: **Nelson, Edward**
AGE: 20
BIRTHPLACE: South Carolina
RANK/MILITARY STATUS: Private; PV
MILITARY SPECIALTY:
CIVILIAN PROFESSION:
COMMENTS: May have seen a member of Blazeby's company. Previously served in Parrott's artillery company and Chenoweth's company of the New Orleans Greys. Younger brother of defender George Nelson.

NAME: **Nelson, George** (Also shown as **"H.G." & "H.J." Nelson**)
AGE: 31
BIRTHPLACE: South Carolina
RANK/MILITARY STATUS: Private; PV
MILITARY SPECIALTY:
CIVILIAN PROFESSION:
COMMENTS: Member of Blazeby's infantry company. Previously served in Breece's 2nd Company of New Orleans Greys. Older brother of defender Edward Nelson.

NAME: **Northcross, James**
AGE: 32
BIRTHPLACE: Virginia
RANK/MILITARY STATUS: Private; PV
MILITARY SPECIALTY:
CIVILIAN PROFESSION: Methodist minister
COMMENTS: Member of Carey's artillery company

NAME: **Nowlan, James** (Also shown as **"Nolind"**)
AGE: 27
BIRTHPLACE: England
RANK/MILITARY STATUS: Private; ?
MILITARY SPECIALTY:
CIVILIAN PROFESSION:
COMMENTS: Previously served in Cooke's company of New Orleans Greys. Badly wounded in the Siege of Bexar, and it is unlikely that he was able to take an active part in the Alamo fighting.

NAME: **Pagan, George**
AGE: 26
BIRTHPLACE: Possibly Mississippi
RANK/MILITARY STATUS: Private; PV?
MILITARY SPECIALTY:
CIVILIAN PROFESSION:
COMMENTS: Alamo unit affiliation uncertain, but previously served under Colonel Neill.

NAME: **Parker, Christopher Adams**
AGE: 22
BIRTHPLACE: Possibly Mississippi
RANK/MILITARY STATUS: Private; PV?
MILITARY SPECIALTY:
CIVILIAN PROFESSION:
COMMENTS: Alamo unit affiliation uncertain, but previously may have served in Dimitt's company.

NAME: **Parks, William**
AGE: 31

BIRTHPLACE: Rowan County, North Carolina
RANK/MILITARY STATUS: Private; PV
MILITARY SPECIALTY:
CIVILIAN PROFESSION:
COMMENTS: Member of Blazeby's infantry company. Previously served in White's infantry company and the Bexar Guards. Some evidence suggests that White's company retained its individual identity at the Alamo.

NAME: **Perry, Richardson**
AGE: 19
BIRTHPLACE: Texas
RANK/MILITARY STATUS: Private; PV
MILITARY SPECIALTY:
CIVILIAN PROFESSION:
COMMENTS: Member of Carey's artillery company

NAME: **Pollard, Amos**
AGE: 32
BIRTHPLACE: Ashburnham, Massachusetts
RANK/MILITARY STATUS: Surgeon; PV
MILITARY SPECIALTY: Chief surgeon of the Alamo garrison
CIVILIAN PROFESSION: Physician; medical degree from Vermont Academy, Castletown, Vermont, Class of 1825
COMMENTS: Probably died defending the hospital

NAME: **Reynolds, John Purdy**
AGE: 29
BIRTHPLACE: Cedar Springs, Mifflin County, Pennsylvania
RANK/MILITARY STATUS: Private; VAC
MILITARY SPECIALTY: May have served the garrison as a surgeon
CIVILIAN PROFESSION: Physician; medical degree from Jefferson Medical College, Pennsylvania, Class of 1827
COMMENTS: Member of the Tennessee Mounted Volunteers; medical books on display at the Alamo

NAME: **Roberts, Thomas H.**
AGE: ?
BIRTHPLACE: Possibly England
RANK/MILITARY STATUS: Private; PV
MILITARY SPECIALTY:
CIVILIAN PROFESSION:
COMMENTS: May have been a member of Bowie's company; previously served in Chenoweth's company of the New Orleans Greys

NAME: **Robertson, James Waters**
AGE: 24
BIRTHPLACE: Tennessee
RANK/MILITARY STATUS: Private; ?
MILITARY SPECIALTY:
CIVILIAN PROFESSION:
COMMENTS:

NAME: **Robinson, Isaac**
AGE: 28
BIRTHPLACE: Scotland
RANK/MILITARY STATUS: Sergeant; PV
MILITARY SPECIALTY:
CIVILIAN PROFESSION:
COMMENTS: Member of Carey's artillery company. Traditionally listed as one of those killed at the Alamo, but a person named Isaac Robinson was still alive after the battle. He is listed here to give him the benefit of the doubt.

NAME: **Rose, James Madison**
AGE: 31
BIRTHPLACE: Ohio
RANK/MILITARY STATUS: Private; VAC
MILITARY SPECIALTY:
CIVILIAN PROFESSION:
COMMENTS: Member of the Tennessee Mounted Volunteers; nephew of President James Madison.

NAME: **Rusk, Jackson Jefferson**
AGE: ?
BIRTHPLACE: Ireland
RANK/MILITARY STATUS: Private; PV
MILITARY SPECIALTY:
CIVILIAN PROFESSION:
COMMENTS: Probably belonged either to Bowie's company or Blazeby's infantry company

NAME: **Rutherford, Joseph**
AGE: 38
BIRTHPLACE: Kentucky
RANK/MILITARY STATUS: Private; PV
MILITARY SPECIALTY:
CIVILIAN PROFESSION:
COMMENTS: Member of Carey's artillery company

NAME: **Ryan, Isaac**
AGE: 31
BIRTHPLACE: St. Landry Parish, Louisiana
RANK/MILITARY STATUS: Private; PV?
MILITARY SPECIALTY:
CIVILIAN PROFESSION:
COMMENTS: May have been a member of Blazeby's infantry company. Previously served in White's infantry company and the Bexar Guards. Some evidence suggests that White's company retained its individual identity at the Alamo.

NAME: **Scurlock, Mial**
AGE: 27
BIRTHPLACE: Chatham County, North Carolina
RANK/MILITARY STATUS: Private; PV?
MILITARY SPECIALTY:
CIVILIAN PROFESSION:
COMMENTS: May have been a member of Bowie's company

NAME: **Sewell, Marcus L.**
AGE: 31
BIRTHPLACE: England
RANK/MILITARY STATUS:
MILITARY SPECIALTY: Private; MIL
CIVILIAN PROFESSION: Shoemaker
COMMENTS: Member of the Gonzales Ranging Company

NAME: **Shied, Manson** (Also shown as **"Shudd"**)
AGE: 25
BIRTHPLACE: Georgia
RANK/MILITARY STATUS: Private; PV
MILITARY SPECIALTY:
CIVILIAN PROFESSION: Carpenter
COMMENTS: Member of Carey's artillery company

NAME: **Simmons, Cleveland Kinloch** (First name also shown as **"Clelland"**)
AGE: 20
BIRTHPLACE: Charleston, South Carolina
RANK/MILITARY STATUS: 1st lieutenant; RTA
MILITARY SPECIALTY:
CIVILIAN PROFESSION:
COMMENTS: Member of Forsyth's cavalry company

NAME: **Smith, Andrew H.**
AGE: 21
BIRTHPLACE: Tennessee
RANK/MILITARY STATUS: Private; RTA

MILITARY SPECIALTY:
CIVILIAN PROFESSION:
COMMENTS: Member of Forsyth's cavalry company. The record is unclear as to whether Smith was actually present with his unit at the Alamo. His name appears on many Alamo defender lists, but it is possible that he did not actually die there. There is an Andrew Smith who is listed as a deserter from Forsyth's company on January 28, 1836.

NAME: **Smith, Charles Sommerset**
AGE: 30
BIRTHPLACE: Maryland
RANK/MILITARY STATUS: Private; PV
MILITARY SPECIALTY:
CIVILIAN PROFESSION:
COMMENTS: Member of Carey's artillery company; previously served in Parrott's artillery company

NAME: **Smith, Joshua G.**
AGE: 28
BIRTHPLACE: North Carolina
RANK/MILITARY STATUS: Sergeant; RTA
MILITARY SPECIALTY:
CIVILIAN PROFESSION:
COMMENTS: Member of Forsyth's cavalry company

NAME: **Smith, William H.**
AGE: 25
BIRTHPLACE: Possibly England
RANK/MILITARY STATUS: Private; PV
MILITARY SPECIALTY:
CIVILIAN PROFESSION:
COMMENTS: Member of Carey's artillery company; may have served previously in Chenoweth's company of the New Orleans Greys

NAME: **Starr, Richard**
AGE: 25
BIRTHPLACE: England
RANK/MILITARY STATUS: Private; PV
MILITARY SPECIALTY:
CIVILIAN PROFESSION:
COMMENTS: Member of Blazeby's infantry company; previously served in Breece's 2nd Company of New Orleans Greys

NAME: **Stewart, James E.** (Also shown as **"Stuart"**)
AGE: 28
BIRTHPLACE: England
RANK/MILITARY STATUS: Private; PV?
MILITARY SPECIALTY:
CIVILIAN PROFESSION:
COMMENTS: Possibly a member of Blazeby's infantry company

NAME: **Stockton, Richard L.**
AGE: 19
BIRTHPLACE: Essex County, New Jersey
RANK/MILITARY STATUS: Private, VAC
MILITARY SPECIALTY:
CIVILIAN PROFESSION:
COMMENTS: Member of the Tennessee Mounted Volunteers

NAME: **Summerlin, A. Spain**
AGE: 19
BIRTHPLACE: Tennessee
RANK/MILITARY STATUS: Private; PV
MILITARY SPECIALTY:
CIVILIAN PROFESSION:
COMMENTS: May have been a member of Blazeby's infantry company. Previously served in White's infantry company and the Bexar Guards. Some evidence suggests that White's company retained its individual identity at the Alamo.

NAME: **Summers, William E.**
AGE: 24
BIRTHPLACE: Tennessee
RANK/MILITARY STATUS: Private; MIL
MILITARY SPECIALTY:
CIVILIAN PROFESSION:
COMMENTS: Member of the Gonzales Ranging Company

NAME: **Sutherland, William DePriest**
AGE: 17
BIRTHPLACE: Alabama
RANK/MILITARY STATUS: Private; RTA
MILITARY SPECIALTY:
CIVILIAN PROFESSION: Physician; medical degree from LaGrange College, Tuscumbia, Alabama, Class of 1825
COMMENTS: May have come to the Alamo with Captain Patton. Also possibly was a member of Forsyth's cavalry company. Nephew of defender Dr. John Sutherland.

NAME: **Taylor, Edward**
AGE: 24
BIRTHPLACE: Tennessee
RANK/MILITARY STATUS: Private; PV?
MILITARY SPECIALTY:
CIVILIAN PROFESSION: Farm hand; worked on Captain Dorsett's farm
COMMENTS: May have been a member of Blazeby's infantry company. Older brother of defenders George and James Taylor. Taylor County, Texas, is named for them.

NAME: **Taylor, George**
AGE: 20
BIRTHPLACE: Tennessee
RANK/MILITARY STATUS: Private; PV?
MILITARY SPECIALTY:
CIVILIAN PROFESSION: Farm hand; worked on Captain Dorsett's farm
COMMENTS: May have belonged to Blazeby's infantry company. Younger brother of defenders Edward and James Taylor. Taylor County, Texas, is named for them.

NAME: **Taylor, James**
AGE: 22
BIRTHPLACE: Tennessee
RANK/MILITARY STATUS: Private; PV?
MILITARY SPECIALTY:
CIVILIAN PROFESSION: Farm hand; worked on Captain Dorsett's farm
COMMENTS: May have been a member of Blazeby's infantry company. Middle of the three Taylor brothers. Taylor County, Texas, is named for them.

NAME: **Taylor, William**
AGE: 37
BIRTHPLACE: Tennessee
RANK/MILITARY STATUS: Private; RTA
MILITARY SPECIALTY:
CIVILIAN PROFESSION:
COMMENTS: May have been a member of Forsyth's cavalry company

NAME: **Thomas, B. Archer M.**
AGE: 18
BIRTHPLACE: Kentucky
RANK/MILITARY STATUS: Private; VAC
MILITARY SPECIALTY:
CIVILIAN PROFESSION:
COMMENTS: Member of the Tennessee Mounted Volunteers

NAME: **Thomas, Henry**
AGE: 25
BIRTHPLACE: Germany
RANK/MILITARY STATUS: Private; PV
MILITARY SPECIALTY:

CIVILIAN PROFESSION:
COMMENTS: Member of Blazeby's infantry company; previously served in Breece's 2nd Company of New Orleans Greys

NAME: **Thompson, Jesse G.**
AGE: 38
BIRTHPLACE: Arkansas
RANK/MILITARY STATUS: Private; ?
MILITARY SPECIALTY:
CIVILIAN PROFESSION:
COMMENTS: Previously served in Seals' Ranger Company

NAME: **Thomson, John W.**
AGE: 29
BIRTHPLACE: North Carolina
RANK/MILITARY STATUS: Private; VAC
MILITARY SPECIALTY: Possibly served the garrison as a surgeon
CIVILIAN PROFESSION: Physician
COMMENTS: Member of the Tennessee Mounted Volunteers, but left the group and went ahead alone to the Alamo; previously served in Gilmer's company

NAME: **Thurston, John Mountjoy** (Also shown as **"Thruston"**)
AGE: 23
BIRTHPLACE: Pennsylvania
RANK/MILITARY STATUS: 2nd lieutenant; RTA
MILITARY SPECIALTY:
CIVILIAN PROFESSION:
COMMENTS: Member of Forsyth's cavalry company

NAME: **Trammel, Burke** (Also shown as **"Tommel"**)
AGE: 26
BIRTHPLACE: Ireland
RANK/MILITARY STATUS: Private; PV
MILITARY SPECIALTY:
CIVILIAN PROFESSION:
COMMENTS: Member of Carey's artillery company

NAME: **Travis, William Barret**
AGE: 26
BIRTHPLACE: Red Banks Church, South Carolina
RANK/MILITARY STATUS: Lieutenant colonel; RTA
MILITARY SPECIALTY: Alamo garrison commander (in Colonel Neill's absence)
CIVILIAN PROFESSION: Lawyer, newspaperman, schoolteacher
COMMENTS: Originally commissioned as a major of artillery; was the highest ranking officer in the Regular Texas Cavalry

NAME: **Tumlinson, George W.**
AGE: 22
BIRTHPLACE: Missouri
RANK/MILITARY STATUS: Private; PV
MILITARY SPECIALTY:
CIVILIAN PROFESSION:
COMMENTS: Member of Carey's artillery company. Returned home to Gonzales after the Siege of Bexar, then returned to the Alamo with the Gonzales Relief Force.

NAME: **Tylee, James**
AGE: 41
BIRTHPLACE: New York
RANK/MILITARY STATUS: Private; PV?
MILITARY SPECIALTY:
CIVILIAN PROFESSION:
COMMENTS: May have been a member of Blazeby's infantry company

NAME: **Walker, Asa**
AGE: 23
BIRTHPLACE: Tennessee
RANK/MILITARY STATUS: Private; PV?
MILITARY SPECIALTY:
CIVILIAN PROFESSION:
COMMENTS: May have been a member of Blazeby's infantry company. Previously served in White's infantry company and the Bexar Guards. Some evidence suggests that White's company retained its individual identity at the Alamo. Cousin of defender Jacob Walker.

NAME: **Walker, Jacob**
AGE: 37
BIRTHPLACE: Rockridge County, Tennessee
RANK/MILITARY STATUS: Private; PV
MILITARY SPECIALTY:
CIVILIAN PROFESSION:
COMMENTS: Member of Carey's artillery company. Shot and bayonetted to death in the chapel in front of Susannah Dickinson. Cousin of defender Asa Walker and brother of mountain man Joseph R. Walker.

NAME: **Ward, William B.**
AGE: 30
BIRTHPLACE: Ireland
RANK/MILITARY STATUS: Sergeant; PV?
MILITARY SPECIALTY:
CIVILIAN PROFESSION:
COMMENTS: May have been a member of Bowie's company

NAME: **Warnell, Henry** (Also shown as **"Wornell," "Warnal,"** & **"Wurnall"**)
AGE: 24
BIRTHPLACE: Possibly Arkansas
RANK/MILITARY STATUS: Private; PV
MILITARY SPECIALTY:
CIVILIAN PROFESSION: Jockey, hunter
COMMENTS: Member of Carey's artillery company. Although wounded, Warnell escaped, probably during the final battle, but then died of his wounds in Port La Vaca in June 1836.

NAME: **Washington, Joseph G.** (May also have gone by the name **"James Morgan"**)
AGE: 28
BIRTHPLACE: Logan County, Kentucky
RANK/MILITARY STATUS: Private; PV
MILITARY SPECIALTY:
CIVILIAN PROFESSION:
COMMENTS: Member of the Tennessee Mounted Volunteers

NAME: **Waters, Thomas**
AGE: 24
BIRTHPLACE: England
RANK/MILITARY STATUS: Private; PV
MILITARY SPECIALTY:
CIVILIAN PROFESSION:
COMMENTS: Member of Carey's artillery company; previously served in Breece's 2nd Company of New Orleans Greys

NAME: **Wells, William, Sr.**
AGE: 37
BIRTHPLACE: Hall County, Georgia
RANK/MILITARY STATUS: Private; PV?
MILITARY SPECIALTY:
CIVILIAN PROFESSION:
COMMENTS: May have been a member of Blazeby's infantry company; may have previously served in Patton's company

NAME: **White, Isaac**
AGE: ?
BIRTHPLACE: Possibly Kentucky

RANK/MILITARY STATUS: Sergeant; RTA?
MILITARY SPECIALTY:
CIVILIAN PROFESSION:
COMMENTS: May have been a member of Forsyth's cavalry company

NAME: **White, Robert**
AGE: 30
BIRTHPLACE: England
RANK/MILITARY STATUS: Captain; PV
MILITARY SPECIALTY: Commanded the Bexar Guards
CIVILIAN PROFESSION:
COMMENTS: May have returned home to Gonzales after the Siege of Bexar, then returned to the Alamo with the Gonzales Relief Force. It is possible that White's infantry company was absorbed into Blazeby's company, but other evidence suggests that it retained its individual identity at the Alamo.

NAME: **Williamson, Hiram James** (Also shown as **"H.S. Williamson"**)
AGE: 26
BIRTHPLACE: Philadelphia, Pennsylvania
RANK/MILITARY STATUS: Sergeant major; PV
MILITARY SPECIALTY: Ranking NCO of the Alamo garrison
CIVILIAN PROFESSION:
COMMENTS:

NAME: **Wills, William**
AGE: ?
BIRTHPLACE: Possibly Tennessee
RANK/MILITARY STATUS: Private; PV?
MILITARY SPECIALTY:
CIVILIAN PROFESSION: Farmer
COMMENTS: May have been a member of Blazeby's infantry company

NAME: **Wilson, David L.**
AGE: 29
BIRTHPLACE: Scotland
RANK/MILITARY STATUS: Private; PV?
MILITARY SPECIALTY:
CIVILIAN PROFESSION:
COMMENTS: May have been a member of Bowie's company; may have previously served in Dimitt's company

NAME: **Wilson, John**
AGE: 32
BIRTHPLACE: Pennsylvania
RANK/MILITARY STATUS: Private; PV?
MILITARY SPECIALTY:
CIVILIAN PROFESSION:
COMMENTS: May have been a member of Blazeby's infantry company.

NAME: **Wolf, Anthony** (Also shown as **"Wolfe," "Woolf," & "Wollf"**)
AGE: 54
BIRTHPLACE: Popular tradition holds that he was born in England, but there is no solid evidence of this.
RANK/MILITARY STATUS: Private; PV
MILITARY SPECIALTY:
CIVILIAN PROFESSION: Indian scout and interpreter
COMMENTS: Member of Carey's artillery company. His two young sons were also killed in the final assault. One of the most misunderstood of all Alamo defenders; much of what has previously been written about him is now suspect.

NAME: **Wright, Claiborne**
AGE: 26
BIRTHPLACE: North Carolina
RANK/MILITARY STATUS: Private; MIL
MILITARY SPECIALTY:
CIVILIAN PROFESSION:
COMMENTS: Member of the Gonzales Ranging Company

NAME: **Zanco, Charles** (Also shown as **"Zanor," "Lance," & "Danor"**)
AGE: 28
BIRTHPLACE: Denmark
RANK/MILITARY STATUS: Lieutenant; PV
MILITARY SPECIALTY: Assistant ordnance officer
CIVILIAN PROFESSION: Painter, farmer
COMMENTS: Believed to have painted one of the first "lone star" flags—the flag of his previous unit, the "First Volunteers at Lynchburg." The design included one lone star and the word "Independence."

This list of defenders killed at the Alamo numbers 187 names. The two young sons of defender Anthony Wolf, who were also killed and who are listed in the "Noncombatants" section, bring the total killed to 189, the currently accepted number.

PART 3: SURVIVORS OF THE ALAMO

NAME: **Allen, James L.**
AGE: 21
BIRTHPLACE: Kentucky
RANK/MILITARY STATUS: Private; PV
MILITARY SPECIALTY:
CIVILIAN PROFESSION: Student, Marion (Ohio) College
COMMENTS: The last courier to leave the Alamo—March 5, 1901

NAME: **Baylor, John Walker, Jr.**
AGE: 22
BIRTHPLACE: Bourbon County, Kentucky
RANK/MILITARY STATUS: Private; PV
MILITARY SPECIALTY:
CIVILIAN PROFESSION: Former West Point cadet; had medical training but was not a practicing physician
COMMENTS: Served in Captain Philip Dimitt's company; died on September 3, 1836, as a result of a wound received during the Battle of San Jacinto. Family tradition holds that he was at the Alamo but left as a courier. Although not substantiated by contemporary sources, we give him the benefit of the doubt and include him here.

NAME: **Brown, Robert**
AGE: 18
BIRTHPLACE: Texas
RANK/MILITARY STATUS: Private; ?
MILITARY SPECIALTY:
CIVILIAN PROFESSION:
COMMENTS: Participated in the raid on the huts at La Villita; left the Alamo as a courier on or after February 25

NAME: **Cruz y Arocha, Antonio**
AGE: ?
BIRTHPLACE: Texas

RANK/MILITARY STATUS: Private; RTA
MILITARY SPECIALTY: Capt. Juan Seguin's orderly
CIVILIAN PROFESSION:
COMMENTS: Member of Seguin's cavalry company; either left the Alamo with Seguin on February 25, or met up with him outside the walls. Accompanied Seguin on his mission to raise reinforcements.

NAME: **De la Garza, Alexandro**
AGE: ?
BIRTHPLACE: Texas
RANK/MILITARY STATUS: Private; RTA
MILITARY SPECIALTY:
CIVILIAN PROFESSION:
COMMENTS: Member of Seguin's cavalry company; left the Alamo as a courier, date unknown.

NAME: **Desauque, Francis L.**
AGE: ?
BIRTHPLACE: Philadelphia, Pennsylvania
RANK/MILITARY STATUS: Captain; PV
MILITARY SPECIALTY:
CIVILIAN PROFESSION:
COMMENTS: Probably belonged to Dimitt's company; left the Alamo with dispatches for Fannin on February 22; captured with Fannin's command and executed on March 27, 1836.

NAME: **Dimitt, Philip**
AGE: 35
BIRTHPLACE: Kentucky
RANK/MILITARY STATUS: Captain; PV
MILITARY SPECIALTY:
CIVILIAN PROFESSION: Merchant
COMMENTS: Left the Alamo on February 23, saying that he was going to get reinforcements. He served throughout the rest of the Texas Revolution. On July 4, 1841, he was captured by a Mexican raiding party while building a trading post on Corpus Christi Bay. He was imprisoned at Saltillo, where on July 8 he committed suicide rather than wait to be executed by the Mexicans.

NAME: **Guerrero, Brigido**
AGE: 26
BIRTHPLACE: Tallenango, Mexico
RANK/MILITARY STATUS: Private; PV
MILITARY SPECIALTY:
CIVILIAN PROFESSION:
COMMENTS: A former Mexican soldier who possibly served with Bowie. As the final battle ended he hid in the chapel, and was spared because he was able to convince the Mexicans that he had been held prisoner by the Texians.

NAME: **Highsmith, Benjamin Franklin**
AGE: 18
BIRTHPLACE: St. Charles District, Missouri Territory
RANK/MILITARY STATUS: Private; ?
MILITARY SPECIALTY:
CIVILIAN PROFESSION:
COMMENTS: Left the Alamo with messages for Fannin on or about February 18; attempted to return, but was chased off by Mexican cavalry; carried Houston's message to Fannin ordering him to abandon Goliad, and fought at San Jacinto; served with the Texas Rangers after the Revolution. He died on November 20, 1905.

NAME: **Joe**
AGE: Early twenties
BIRTHPLACE: Alabama
RANK/MILITARY STATUS: Civilian
MILITARY SPECIALTY:
CIVILIAN PROFESSION: Travis' slave
COMMENTS: Fought on the north wall with Travis; after Travis' death, took refuge in the chapel; was wounded by a musketball and a bayonet; was taken prisoner and spared by the Mexicans; escorted Susannah and Angelina Dickinson to Houston's camp.

NAME: **Johnson, William P.**
AGE: 19?
BIRTHPLACE: ?
RANK/MILITARY STATUS: Sergeant?; PV
MILITARY SPECIALTY:
CIVILIAN PROFESSION:
COMMENTS: Dr. Sutherland mentions that a man named Johnson left the Alamo with dispatches for Goliad when he and John W. Smith went to Gonzales. If this is true, then that person was probably Sgt. William P. Johnson. A person named William P. Johnson was executed at Goliad with Fannin's men.

NAME: **Lockhart, Byrd**
AGE: 54
BIRTHPLACE: Virginia or Missouri
RANK/MILITARY STATUS: Captain; PV
MILITARY SPECIALTY:
CIVILIAN PROFESSION: Surveyor
COMMENTS: Possibly a member of Bowie's company, or may have come in with the Gonzales reinforcements; left the Alamo with Andrew Sowell, date unknown, to attempt to obtain additional supplies for the garrison. He died in 1839.

NAME: **Oury, William Sanders**
AGE: 18
BIRTHPLACE: Abingdon, Virginia
RANK/MILITARY STATUS: Private; ?
MILITARY SPECIALTY:
CIVILIAN PROFESSION:
COMMENTS: Left the Alamo as a courier on or about February 29; fought at San Jacinto; served in the Mexican War with the Texas Rangers. He died on March 31, 1887.

NAME: **Patton, William Hester**
AGE: 28
BIRTHPLACE: Hopkinsville, Kentucky
RANK/MILITARY STATUS: Captain; PV
MILITARY SPECIALTY:
CIVILIAN PROFESSION: Merchant; surveyor
COMMENTS: Left the Alamo, probably as a courier, sometime after February 5. Served as an aide-de-camp to General Houston during the Battle of San Jacinto. Was part of Santa Anna's escort to Washington, and also served as quartermaster general of the Texas Army, and later as Bexar County's representative to the Texas Congress. He was murdered by a band of Mexicans on June 12, 1842.

NAME: **Rose, Louis "Moses"**
AGE: 50
BIRTHPLACE: Lafaree, Ardennes, France
RANK/MILITARY STATUS: Private; PV
MILITARY SPECIALTY:
CIVILIAN PROFESSION: Former soldier in Napoleon's army; sawmill worker; teamster
COMMENTS: Member of Bowie's company; left the Alamo sometime between March 3 and March 6, saying that he was not yet ready to die. He died in 1850.

NAME: **Seguin, Juan Nepomuceno**
AGE: 29

BIRTHPLACE: San Antonio de Bexar, Texas
RANK/MILITARY STATUS: Captain; RTA
MILITARY SPECIALTY: Commanded one of the two Regular Cavalry companies at the Alamo
CIVILIAN PROFESSION: Rancher; political chief of Bexar
COMMENTS: Left the Alamo with dispatches on February 25; was attempting to return with reinforcements when it fell; fought at San Jacinto; supervised the burial of the remains of the Alamo defenders in 1837. He died on August 27, 1890.

NAME: **Smith, John William**
AGE: 44
BIRTHPLACE: Virginia
RANK/MILITARY STATUS: PV
MILITARY SPECIALTY: Storekeeper
CIVILIAN PROFESSION: Civil engineer; carpenter; boardinghouse keeper
COMMENTS: Left the Alamo with dispatches on February 23; returned on March 1, guiding the Gonzales 32 into the Alamo; left again on March 3, and was returning from San Felipe with 25 volunteers when the Alamo fell. He died in 1845.

NAME: **Smither, Launcelot**
AGE: 36
BIRTHPLACE:
RANK/MILITARY STATUS: Private/ ?
MILITARY SPECIALTY:
CIVILIAN PROFESSION: Farmer; horse trader; medic to the Mexican garrison at San Antonio de Bexar prior to the Texas Revolution
COMMENTS: Left the Alamo on February 23 to notify the citizens of Gonzales of the arrival of the Mexican army. Killed on September 11, 1842, by Mexican soldiers who were part of General Woll's invasion of Texas.

NAME: **Sowell, Andrew Jackson**
AGE: 20
BIRTHPLACE: Davidson County, Tennessee
RANK/MILITARY STATUS: Private; ?
MILITARY SPECIALTY:
CIVILIAN PROFESSION: Farmer
COMMENTS: Left the Alamo, date unknown, with Capt. Byrd Lockhart to attempt to find additional supplies for the garrison; later served with the Texas Rangers, fought in the Mexican War, and served in the Confederate Army during the Civil War. He died on January 4, 1883.

NAME: **Sutherland, John**
AGE: 43
BIRTHPLACE: Danville, Virginia
RANK/MILITARY STATUS: Private; PV
MILITARY SPECIALTY: Physician; assistant to Dr. Amos Pollard
CIVILIAN PROFESSION. Physician; banker; businessman
COMMENTS: Member of Blazeby's company of the New Orleans Greys; left the Alamo as a courier on February 23; was attempting to return with a small group of volunteers when the Alamo fell. Later served as private secretary to President David G. Burnet. He died on April 11, 1867.
NOTE: Sutherland is traditionally credited with being a member of the Alamo garrison, but new evidence suggests that he might not have been anywhere around in spite of the stories about his activities. It is not possible to draw any definite conclusions yet, and he is included here to give him the benefit of the doubt.

The contributions of both the Mexican "soldaderas" *and the Tejano women who accompanied their families and friends into the Alamo should not be overlooked. The* soldaderas *endured the same hardships as the Mexican* soldados *on the march up from Mexico, many of them only to be widowed or orphaned during the siege. The Tejano women who chose to go to the Alamo also endured hardships, and were exposed to considerable danger during the siege and final battle.*

PART 4: THE NONCOMBATANTS

NAME: **Alsbury, Juana Navarro de**
AGE: ?
BIRTHPLACE: Texas
COMMENTS: Wife of Dr. Horace Alsbury, a Texian soldier who was away on a scouting mission during the Siege of the Alamo. Gertrudis Navarro was her sister, and both were nieces of Vice-Governor Juan Martín Veramendi, Jim Bowie's father-in-law. She died on July 25, 1888.

NAME: **Castro, María de Jesus (Esparza)**
AGE: About 10
BIRTHPLACE: San Antonio de Bexar, Texas
COMMENTS: Daughter of Ana Esparza by her first husband, Victor de Castro, who died in 1825. Stepdaughter of Gregorio Esparza. She died in San Antonio in 1899.

NAME: **Dickinson, Angelina Elizabeth** (Also shown as **"Dickerson"**)
AGE: 15 months
BIRTHPLACE: Gonzales, Texas
COMMENTS: Daughter of Almeron and Susannah Dickinson. The night before the final assault on the Alamo, Lieutenant Colonel Travis tied his ring around her neck for safekeeping. The ring is now on display in the Alamo Museum. After the battle, Santa Anna offered to adopt Angelina and have her sent to Mexico. She died of a uterine hemorrhage in 1871.

NAME: **Dickinson, Susannah Arabella** (Also shown as **"Dickerson"**)
AGE: 22
BIRTHPLACE: Tennessee
COMMENTS: Wife of Almeron Dickinson. Shot in the right calf after the battle while being led from the chapel by a Mexican officer. Released by Santa Anna, she brought word of the fall of the Alamo to Gen. Sam Houston. On April 27, 1881, she visited the Alamo and gave her recollections of the siege to a newspaper reporter. She died on October 7, 1883, and is buried in Oakwood Cemetery in Austin.

NAME: **Esparza, Ana Salazar**
AGE: ?
BIRTHPLACE: San Antonio de Bexar, Texas
COMMENTS: Wife of Alamo defender Gregorio Esparza. She died on December 12, 1847.

NAME: **Esparza, Enrique**
AGE: 7
BIRTHPLACE: San Antonio de Bexar, Texas
COMMENTS: Oldest son of Gregorio and Ana Esparza. Late in life gave his recollections of the Siege of the Alamo. He died on December 20, 1917.

NAME: **Esparza, Francisco**
AGE: 3
BIRTHPLACE: San Antonio de Bexar, Texas
COMMENTS: Youngest son of Gregorio and Ana Esparza. Served in the Confederate Army during the Civil War. He died in July 1887.

NAME: **Esparza, Manuel**
AGE: 5
BIRTHPLACE: San Antonio de Bexar, Texas
COMMENTS: Son of Gregorio and Ana Esparza. He died in 1886.

NAME: **Gonzales, Petra**
AGE: Elderly woman
COMMENTS: May have been a relative of Ana Esparza.

NAME: **Losoya, Concepcion**
AGE: ?
COMMENTS: Possibly the mother of defender Toribio Losoya.

NAME: **Losoya, Juan**
AGE: ?
COMMENTS: Possibly the brother of Toribio Losoya.

NAME: **Melton, Juana**
AGE: ?
COMMENTS: Possibly married to defender Eliel Melton and sister of defender Toribio Losoya.

NAME: **Navarro, Gertrudis**
AGE: 19
BIRTHPLACE: San Antonio de Bexar, Texas
COMMENTS: Sister of Juana Navarro de Alsbury and niece of Vice-Governor Juan Martín de Veramendi. She died in April 1895.

NAME: **Perez, Alejo, Jr.**
AGE: 11 months
BIRTHPLACE: San Antonio de Bexar, Texas
COMMENTS: Son of Juana Navarro de Alsbury by her first husband (deceased), Alejo Perez, Sr. He died on October 21, 1918.

NAME: **Saucedo, Trinidad**
AGE: About 17
COMMENTS: A former servant to the Veramendi family. She possibly left the Alamo prior to the final battle.

NAME: **Victoriana, Mrs.**
AGE: ?
COMMENTS: Very little known about her. Enrique Esparza recalled seeing her in the Alamo with her daughters.

NAME: **Wolf, First Name Unknown**
AGE: Less than 12
BIRTHPLACE: ?
COMMENTS: Killed; son of defender Anthony Wolf.

NAME: **Wolf, First Name Unknown**
AGE: Less than 1
BIRTHPLACE: ?
COMMENTS: Killed son of defender Anthony Wolf.

NAME: **Black slave woman— name unknown**
AGE: ?
COMMENTS: Killed; death reported by Travis' slave, Joe.

PART 5: THE MYSTERY OF EDWARD EDWARDS

On the Edwards family memorial at St. John's Church in Aderdare, Wales, an inscription proclaims that one Edward Edwards, late major general in the Honorable East India Company's service, ". . . lost his Life at San Antonio de Bexaz *(sic)* in *Texas North America,* on the 6th of March, 1836; in his 57th year."

Edward Edwards was born in Ystradyfodwg, Glamorgan, Wales, on January 4, 1779. He was commissioned an ensign in the army of the East India Company on August 11, 1797. Edwards rose through the ranks, and eventually was promoted to the rank of full colonel on May 30, 1833.

Edwards was known to have been in New Orleans while on furlough in 1834. He had relatives in Texas, and can be tracked to Brazoria, Texas, and Monterrey, Mexico. There is no direct evidence placing him at the Alamo in 1836, but neither can it be proven that he was not there.

If Edwards *was* at the Alamo, what was his status? Was he a defender whose death has not yet been documented, or was he possibly an observer with the Mexican army? With his military experience, he certainly would have been an asset to the Texian cause. It is also conceivable that he could have been an observer with the Mexicans, since Great Britain was on friendly terms with Mexico, one of its major creditors. Either option is possible, but it is strange that there is no mention of a man of Edwards' stature in the records of either side.

The words "lost his life" on the memorial certainly imply that his death was not natural. Since he was still an actively serving British officer, the lack of detailed documentation is all the more remarkable, if he had been acting in any official capacity when killed.

The only thing that we know for sure about the circumstances surrounding his death comes from an article that appeared first in the *New York Evening Post* and then was reprinted in the *London Times* on September 8, 1840. The article stated that a gold ring belonging to Edwards was found on a corpse along the road between Gonzales and Goliad, just after the Battle of the Alamo. The person who found the ring was attempting to locate Edwards' family so that it could be turned over to them.

There is no evidence that the body that the ring was taken from was actually that of Edward Edwards. It could, of course, have been him. On the other hand, the ring could have been found on the body of a Mexican soldier, or anyone else, who had obtained it from Edwards under who knows what circumstances. The main bodies of Mexican troops had not reached the Gonzales-Goliad road at the time the ring was reportedly found, so that possibility must be viewed with caution. On the other hand, if the ring was taken from Edwards' own body, then the distance between the Gonzales-Goliad road and the Alamo would pretty much preclude Edwards having taken part in the final battle. He could possibly have been there earlier, however.

Further complicating this mystery is the fact that on July 30, 1836, someone withdrew sixty pounds at a Brazoria bank from an account Edwards had established with Baring's North American Ledger. The details of the transaction are illegible, so it is impossible to determine exactly who made the withdrawal.

If the family received word of Edwards' death prior to the *London Times* article, no record has been found of it. The East India Company promoted him to major general on June 28, 1838, and did not strike him from their rolls until April 28, 1841, after the publication of the *London Times* article.

On November 10, 1857, Edward M. Edwards, a nephew of Major General Edwards, filed a claim for land owned by his uncle at Mill Creek in Austin County. The document simply states that his uncle was "murdered" but does not give the circumstances.

A number of people have been trying to unravel the mystery of Edward Edwards for several years. They include Bill Groneman, Kevin Young, and noted British historian Philip Haythornthwaite. Mr. Howard Shearring, of Kent, England, has probably compiled the most information about Edwards. He has covered Edwards' life and his career with the Army of the East India Company fairly well, but there are still many unanswered questions about his exploits in North America.

At least one source (Whitmarsh: "*A Welsh Mexican?*") claims that Edwards was a recipient of the prestigious British award, the Order of the Star of India. Bob Lancaster, a friend of the authors' and a knowledgeable collector of British medals, agreed to look into Edwards' career through the records of any medals he might have received.

Lancaster, working with the assistance of Howard Shearring, was able to conclude that Edwards was definitely not awarded the Order of the Star of India. Officially titled "The Most Exalted Order of the Star of India," this award was not even instituted until 1861. Unfortunately, a survey of available records did not reveal any other medals awarded to Edwards that would cast further light on his life.

However, there is hope that future research may reveal more details of the Edwards story. It does not appear that he came from a particularly well-connected family, and the fact that he rose to the rank of major general was no small achievement. His promotions must have been based at least as much on ability as on patronage, and he certainly must have earned some honors and recognition along the way. If that is true, then some as yet undiscovered records may well fill in further pieces of the puzzle.

At the present time, there is no way to tell just what part, if any, Edward Edwards, late major general of the Army of the East India Company, played in the battle for the Alamo. He must remain another one of its many interesting mysteries.

CHAPTER TEN

Davy Crockett: Fact vs. Legend

PART 1: A BRIEF BIOGRAPHY

WITHOUT A DOUBT, THE most famous defender killed at the Alamo was the Honorable David Crockett of Tennessee. Popularly known as "Davy," Crockett was a legend in his own time, and he remains one to this day. Although not everything written about him is true, enough of it is that he fully deserves his place in history.

Davy Crockett was born to John and Rebecca Hawkins Crockett on August 17, 1786. He was born in what was, under the Articles of Confederation, the independent state of Franklin. When the Constitution was ratified, Franklin became part of Green County, Tennessee. John Crockett, a veteran of the Revolutionary War, struggled hard to make ends meet, and the family moved several times in search of a better life.

Davy left home at twelve, taking a number of different jobs and learning the skills and self-reliance that would serve him so well in later life. Even though he had little formal schooling, Davy developed a reputation for being intelligent, humorous, generous, and polite, with refined manners. It would appear that the character played by Fess Parker in the 1950s Walt Disney television series was pretty close to the mark.

On August 6, 1806, Davy married Polly Finley, and together they had two sons and a daughter. Davy supported his family mainly by farming and hunting. In 1813 he fought in the Creek Indian War, serving two different enlistments. He participated in at least two significant engagements, Tallusahatchee and Talladega, and attained the rank of sergeant before his discharge. Perhaps the most important things to come out of Davy's military service were the sympathetic feelings that he developed for Indians, and his contempt for government waste.

Polly Crockett died in 1815, and Davy later married Elizabeth Patton, a widow whose husband had been killed in the Creek War. Elizabeth already had two children, and she and Davy had another son and a daughter. The family moved to western Tennessee, where Davy became active in local politics. He served as a magistrate, and was also elected colonel of the local militia. This accounts for the title "colonel" that followed him to the Alamo.

Davy engaged in a number of business ventures, without any notable success, but he fared better in his political career. He was elected to the Tennessee Legislature in 1821, and again in 1823. Davy then was elected to the United States Congress, in 1827. He served until 1831, when he was narrowly defeated by William Fitzgerald, a supporter of President Andrew Jackson. Crockett was a sincere but somewhat naive congressman who championed Indian rights and bitterly opposed the removal policies of the president. Davy knew that there would be political consequences for his stand on Indian rights, but he stood by his principles anyway—a character trait that helped him gain his honored place in American history.

In 1833 Crockett managed to defeat Fitzgerald and regain his seat in Congress, but he was beaten again in 1835 by Adam Huntsman, another Jackson supporter. It was then that Davy decided to seek new opportunities in the promised land of Texas. Before he left, he told a crowd at the Union Hotel Bar in Memphis: "Since you have chosen to elect a man with a timber toe [Huntsman had a wooden leg] to succeed me, you may all go to hell and I will go to Texas." (Foreman, 41)

Davy's youngest daughter, Matilda, recalled that when he left for Texas, he was "dressed in his hunting shirt, wearing a coon skin cap, and carried a fine rifle. . . ." (Foreman, 41) James Davis, a newspaperman who was present, also reported that Crockett was wearing a hunting shirt and coonskin cap. On January 29, 1836, the *New York Sun* reported that Crockett, "has gone to Texas, and he says that he will 'have Santa Anna's head, and will wear it for a watch-seal.'" (Zaboly: *Crockett Goes Into Texas*, 9)

Everywhere that he went in Texas, Davy was warmly received, and there is possibly some truth to the speculation that he hoped to run again for public office when the Revolution was over. Davy was sworn into the Voluntary Auxiliary Corps of the Texas Army on January 14, 1836, at Nacogdoches. He joined Capt. William Harrison's company, which was popularly known as the Tennessee Mounted Volunteers. Although Harrison was the official company commander, Davy was quickly recognized as one of the informal leaders of the group. For the time being, at least, he did not seek any official command; he said that he would be content just to serve as a "high private."

The Tennessee Mounted Volunteers, including Davy Crockett, arrived in San Antonio de Bexar on or about February 8, 1836. When the Mexicans arrived on February 23, Harrison's men were given the job of holding the town while the rest of the garrison moved into the Alamo. When stations were assigned for the coming battle, the Tennessee Mounted Volunteers were given one of the most difficult tasks—the defense of the wooden palisade between the chapel and the low barracks.

During the siege, Davy is reported to have entertained the Alamo defenders by playing his fiddle, accompanied by Scotsman John McGregor on the bagpipes. Davy was also commended in the official dispatches of garrison commander William Barret Travis, for his bravery and energy during the early fighting.

There is no doubt that Davy Crockett died

David Crockett in 1836. This portrait is based on paintings by William H. Huddle, Chester Harding, James Hamilton Shegogue, and Samuel S. Osgood.

during the final attack on the Alamo, but just how he was killed is uncertain and the subject of much controversy. Some reports suggest that he was captured and then executed along with several other defenders. There are also reports that he went down fighting fiercely to the very end. It is the opinion of the authors that there was not enough legitimate proof to substantiate either theory, and that, for the time being at least, Davy's death must remain one of the many mysteries of the Alamo. For a more detailed account of this controversy, see Dr. Todd Harburn's special essay in Part Three of this chapter.

Davy Crockett had a motto that he lived by: "Be always sure you're right—then go ahead." (Foreman, 40) When the time came, he also chose to die by this motto. Whether Davy went down swinging, or whether he was captured and executed, is really not important. What matters is that he chose to stay and fight, when he and any of the other defenders, early in the siege, could easily have made their way through the Mexican lines to safety. To stay, and most certainly die, for the cause of freedom was a conscious choice made by the Alamo garrison. That is how Davy and the rest should be judged.

Davy Crockett and his fiddle. Some accounts claim that Davy entertained members of the Alamo garrison by playing his fiddle, accompanied by Scotsman John McGregor on the bagpipes.

PART 2: DAVY CROCKETT: FRONTIERSMAN . . . CONGRESSMAN . . . POET?

NOTE: This section, by Tim J. Todish, is reprinted from The Alamo Journal, *Issue # 76, April 1991, with the permission of editor Bill Chemerka.*

* * * * *

Davy Crockett is one of the best known of all early American heroes. He is Walt Disney's *King of the Wild Frontier* and the hero of John Wayne's epic masterpiece *The Alamo.*

The real David Crockett was a product of the frontier spirit of the fledgling United States. He was also a leader of his times. Crockett fought both for and against the Indians. An accomplished woodsman, hunter, and trapper, he also served in the Congress of the United States.

Although lacking in formal education, Crockett was an intelligent and perceptive person who knew how to use his talents to accomplish his goals. In his life, he experienced defeat as well as victory. When he was voted out of his congressional seat by pro-Jackson forces, he told his constituents that they could go to hell, and that he was going to Texas.

Big enough in real life, he was made even bigger in legend. Even before his death at the Alamo, much had been written about him. Some of it was true, and some of it was not. In 1834 E. L. Carey and A. Hart of Philadelphia publishled an autobiography entitled, *A Narrative of the Life of David Crockett of the State of Tennessee, Written by Himself.*

In 1836, shortly after the Battle of the Alamo, Philadelphia publishers T. K. and P. G. Collins published *Col. Crockett's Exploits and Adventures in Texas,* which was supposedly also "written by himself." This book was purported to be a diary kept by Crockett during his travels in Texas. By some unexplained chain of events, it was reportedly recovered after the battle and delivered to the publishers. Understandably, its authenticity is suspect. It is conceivable, however, that the publishers did have some ongoing correspondence with Crockett about the eventual publication of a sequel to his earlier autobiography. If this is true, then the book, or at least portions of it, may have some legitimate historical value. It is not my purpose to speculate on that issue here, however.

The book contains a poem that allegedly was written by Crockett. It is this poem, set to music, that Fess Parker sings just before the final assault in the Walt Disney series. Since there are contemporary accounts of Crockett entertaining the Alamo defenders with his fiddle, it is at least possible that something similar did actually occur.

Even if it did not, or even if Crockett did not really write the poem himself—"Farewell to the Mountains" does capture the spirit of both the man and the times. Just as we say about the old John Ford movies, "If that's not the way it was, then that's the way it should have been!"

The following is the complete poem, as printed in an original copy of *Col. Crockett's Exploits and Adventures in Texas.* This book is now in the rare book collection of the William L. Clements Library at the University of Michigan in Ann Arbor. I gratefully acknowledge their courtesy in allowing me to reproduce it here.

Of his poem, Davy says: "It being my first, and no doubt last piece of poetry, I will print it in this place, as it will serve to express my feelings on leaving home, my neighbors, and friends and country, for a strange land . . ."

Farewell to the mountains whose mazes to me
Were more beautiful far than Eden could be;
No fruit was forbidden, but Nature had spread
Her bountiful board, and her children were fed.
The hills were our garners—our herds wildly grew,
And Nature was shepherd, and husbandman too.
I felt like a monarch, yet thought like a man,
As I thank'd the Great Giver, and worshipp'd his plan.

The home I forsake where my offspring arose:
The graves I forsake where my children repose.
The home I redeem'd from the savage and wild;
The home I have loved as a father his child;
The corn that I planted, the fields that I clear'd,
The flocks that I raised, and the cabin I rear'd;
The wife of my bosom—Farewell to ye all!
In the land of the stranger I rise—or I fall.

Farewell to my country!—I fought for thee well,
When the savage rush'd forth like the demons from hell.
In peace or in war I have stood by thy side—
My country, for thee I have lived—would have died!
But I am cast off— my career is now run,
And I wander abroad like the prodigal son
Where the wild savage roves, and the broad prairies spread,
The fallen—despised—will again go ahead!

PART 3: THE CONTROVERSY

NOTE: This essay is an updated revision of an article that was previously published in two versions: in The Bexar Dispatch, *the newsletter of the San Antonio Living History Association for April 1990, and in* The Alamo Journal, *Issue # 76, April 1991. It is reprinted here with the kind permission of the San Antonio Living History Association and The Alamo Society.*

* * * * *

THE CROCKETT DEATH CONTROVERSY

A Brief Commentary and
Opinion Regarding the Same
By Dr. Todd E. Harburn, D.O.

Among the numerous disputed events which occurred during the siege and fall of the Alamo, perhaps none has been more controversial than the death of David Crockett. Legend and some evidence suggest that the famous Tennessean died fighting valiantly to the end during the final assault on March 6, 1836, defending the wooden palisade in front of the Alamo chapel. In recent years, however, there have been several published accounts, including those of Carmen Perry, Dan Kilgore, Richard B. Hauck, Michael Lofaro, and James Burke, which present evidence asserting that Crockett was among five or six Alamo defenders who surrendered or were captured at the end of the final battle, and were subsequently executed.

As is well known to almost every Alamo enthusiast, the evidence on which the surrender theory is based is attributed to several accounts provided by Mexican officers, in particular José Enrique de la Pena, José Juan Sanchez Navarro, Juan Almonte, Ramon Caro, and Fernando Urriza. Opponents of the original "eyewitness accounts" have alluded to the various discrepancies and contradictions contained in each, and thus have credited them as unreliable.

Other Alamo authors and historians, including Wallace Chariton, Bill Groneman, and Thomas Ricks Lindley, have meticulously examined the evidence supporting both sides of the controversy, and offered reasonable conclusions. Their studies include examining theories as to whether or not the Mexicans would have known and/or recognized Crockett, the background and credibility of the Mexican officers who presented the "original" accounts, and even speculation that some Alamo defender may have claimed to be the famous congressman in hopes of being spared. Their work has been discussed both pro and con in numerous books and articles, not only by themselves but also by numerous other Alamo historians and authors. It is not my purpose to totally reexamine the evidence and conclusions reached by the aforementioned authors on either side of the controversy, but rather to briefly present several key aspects of their theories, and then offer my personal opinions for consideration regarding Crockett's final moments.

The surrender/execution theory is not a new discovery. Reports of Crockett's supposed demise in this manner were circulating within several days and weeks after the fall of the Alamo. This theory was acknowledged, although not necessarily endorsed, by various respected historians and authors in early publications concerning the Alamo and Crockett. The release of Carmen Perry's translation of the narrative of Mexican officer José Enrique de la Pena in 1975 rekindled the fire. The debate was further fueled, quite vehemently by supporters on both sides, with the publication in 1978 of Dan Kilgore's controversial book *How Did Davy Die?*

Some Alamo historians and authors who support the surrender theory view the de la Pena writings as the most reliable eyewitness account, and essentially as absolute fact. De la Pena's narrative is, in fact, suspect, if one truly examines the account. There are numerous discrepancies, contradictions, and/or outright erroneous descriptions concerning a variety of aspects of the Siege of the Alamo and Texas Campaign in general. These discrepancies include, for example, William Barret Travis' physical stature, the details of his death (de la Pena claims he was killed in the courtyard by the chapel, rather than on the north wall), and the failure to offer an explanation as to how de la Pena came to know Crockett's personal background and about his presence at the Alamo.

Another discrepancy is de la Pena's statement that, "Though tortured before they were killed, these unfortunates died without complaining and without humiliating themselves before their torturers." (De la Pena, 53) Yet at the conclusion of his Crockett segment, de la Pena states that he "can still hear the penetrating, doleful sound of the victims." (De la Pena, 54) There are other discrepancies as well, and the results of all of these raise a very important question: Why should de la Pena's account of Crockett's death be accepted as TOTAL fact, as Kilgore and others assert, when there are numerous discrepancies and known erroneous facts contained in this and other portions of his narrative?

In his book *Exploring the Alamo Legends,* Wallace Chariton discusses several shortcomings in Kilgore's acceptance of de la Pena's version as fact and valid documentation of Crockett's death. Chariton further suggests that it is very probable that de la Pena's entire account of the Alamo's carnage is "an embellished narrative based on brief and sketchy notes, hearsay, innuendos, undoubtedly some pure fiction, and perhaps some plain old self-serving lies." (Chariton: *Alamo Legends*, 49)

Bill Groneman, in his latest book *Defense of a Legend,* has meticulously reviewed and researched the de la Pena narrative. He presents some new evidence challenging the authenticity of the narrative, including the possibility that it may even be a forgery. Yet Groneman allows readers to reach their own conclusions on the entire controversy concerning Crockett's death. Groneman is a proponent for further evaluation and diagnostic testing of the narrative, in an effort to substantiate or refute its authenticity.

More recently, Thomas Ricks Lindley and Dr. James Crisp have written a series of extensive, opposing essays and engaged in academic debate concerning the de la Pena and other accounts. Lindley has made meticulous comparisons of the diverse and similar aspects in support of Crockett's fighting to the end, as well as portions of Groneman's theories. Crisp, on the other hand, has presented some new evidence and opinion in support of the de la Pena account and in opposition to Groneman's and Lindley's contentions. This further academic debate has stimulated even more fury concerning the entire controversy among those interested in this aspect of Alamo history.

Nevertheless, readers are referred to Carmen Perry's translation of de la Pena, as well as to the specific books and articles by Chariton, Groneman, Lindley, and Crisp for complete details of the above discussions. If one is to truly consider the entire de la Pena document in an unbiased manner, it just does not make sense to accept it as unadulterated fact. This is not to imply de la Pena's account is totally untrue, or that he was outright lying. Rather, it merely suggests that at least parts of the narrative are suspect, and that the account should not be accepted as pure fact.

A few additional important points should be mentioned concerning basic discrepancies in the other Mexican accounts of the siege and the death of Crockett. First, none of them agree on the exact number of those executed at the end of the battle. Navarro and Urriza relate one, Becerra relates two, Cos and Caro relate five, Almonte says six, and de la Pena states seven Alamo defenders were found hiding, or fighting in the barracks, or resting, or fighting in the open, or surrendered either in the barracks or in the open.

Supporters of the surrender/execution theory will undoubtedly refer to the generally accepted fact that no two eyewitnesses to an event will necessarily coincide exactly in their description of the same. However, it is legitimate to state, and cannot be easily dismissed, that there are just too many significant variations in the number of those executed among the several Mexican officers who presented these accounts. Although obviously not impossible, it is very suspect that these officers would not have a more closely corresponding count of those involved if they had truly witnessed the event.

Secondly, the person who discovered them is also in dispute. They were found by General Castrillon, or General Cos, or even Sergeant Jose Becerra, depending on the source. In addition, not all of them specifically mention Crockett, nor are the descriptions of Crockett or the "old venerable man" (which some researchers/authors claim is Crockett) similar. He was being led by the hand, was gray, was red-faced, stooped forward, of great stature, well- proportioned, bold as a lion, with arms folded, and so on. Again, Chariton and Groneman examine these issues in further detail in their respective books.

Another major discrepancy in these accounts is the MODE of executions. Some report that the five or six Texans, including Crockett, were shot by a firing squad (Urriza, Navarro, Almonte, Becerra). Others (de la Pena, Cos, and Caro) report that they were put to death and mutilated by swords or bayonets. It is reasonable to assume Crockett's mutilated body could have resulted from the latter mode of execution, but these wounds could also have been caused by sword blows or the piercing of bayonets as he was fighting to the end.

Again, it is extremely suspect that there is such an incredible variation in the accounts of these officers as to the mode of execution, since they supposedly were eyewitnesses. One can more readily accept that they could have been mistaken in the exact number of the victims in the confusion of the moment. However, the blatant and significant difference in the weapons utilized is preposterous. The discrepancy does exist, and it cannot be overlooked as an important aspect which further taints the Mexican accounts.

Equally perplexing, and this might be the most important aspect of all, is the question as to why Santa Anna would want to specifically identify or be shown the bodies of Travis, Bowie, AND CROCKETT, if he had witnessed the executions himself. This is known and documented as having occurred, per Francisco Ruiz, the *alcalde* (mayor) of San Antonio de Bexar at the time of the siege. Discrepancies exist as to whether Santa Anna merely ordered the executions, or actually witnessed them. Some of the Mexican accounts, including de la Pena, allude to the fact that the prisoners, including Crockett, were brought in front of the general, and that Santa Anna was thus present at the time of the executions. If this were true, there would be no need for him to be shown, and have identified, Crockett's body. Further discussion about Santa Anna's knowledge of whether Crockett survived and was included in the executions is offered by Chariton and Groneman in their books.

Taking all of the previous discussions into consideration, as Chariton, Groneman, Burke and others have stated, in effect, *the absolute truth regarding David Crockett's final moments may never be known.*

Chariton, Lindley, and Groneman in particular, when considering the opposing evidence supporting Crockett's fighting to the end, compared to the surrender/execution theories, suggest that the former seems to be "every bit as convincing as all the Mexican evidence, probably more so." (Chariton: *Alamo Legends,* 60)

Groneman is even more specific in a book that he co-authored with Phil Rosenthal:

> As long as some question exists, no single explanation can be taken as the final word as to Crockett's final moments. If selected accounts are taken at only face value, then it would appear that Crockett was captured and executed. . . .
>
> A deeper analysis of all the existing accounts reveal that there is still the strong possibility that the Alamo hero did go out in a blaze of glory, even without the assistance of myth and legend. (Rosenthal & Groneman: *Roll Call,* 37)

It is obvious that one could debate both theories indefinitely. Every Alamo enthusiast, researcher, and author, whether professional historian or not, will choose to believe what he or she wants to, based on the "facts" available to him or her. They are entitled to their opinion, and deserve the courtesy/respect thereof.

No one will dispute the fact that there were five, six, or possibly seven Alamo defenders who were executed at the end of the battle. However, to say UNEQUIVOCALLY that Crockett was among this group simply cannot be proven at this time. There is just as much collective evidence to support David Crockett living up to his legendary reputation and dying while fighting to the last. Until new evidence is discovered, and/or the de la Pena narrative is refuted or authenticated, the Crockett death controversy will most likely continue.

CHAPTER ELEVEN

Leaders of the Revolution

PART 1: THE TEXIANS

The following brief biographies are intended to familiarize readers with the contributions that these important people made to the cause of freedom during the Texas Revolution and the Siege of the Alamo.

MOSES AUSTIN
(October 4, 1761–June 10, 1821)

Moses Austin was the father of Stephen F. Austin. He grew up in Middleton, Connecticut. He was a dry goods importer and became involved in lead mining in southwest Virginia. In 1798 he moved his family to Missouri, which was then under the rule of Spain. He founded the town of Potosi, and again was involved in lead mining, as well as banking.

At one time financially well to do, Austin lost everything in the Panic of 1819. In December 1820 he traveled to San Antonio and obtained permission from the Spanish authorities to settle 300 Anglo families in Texas. Unfortunately, he died before he could carry out the plan. His dying wish was that his son Stephen carry on his dream.

STEPHEN FULLER AUSTIN
(November 3, 1793–December 27, 1836)

Stephen F. Austin was an *"empresario"* who settled over 1,500 Anglo families in Texas. He originally worked hard to ensure that his settlers were loyal to and obeyed the laws of Mexico, but once war was declared, he worked just as hard for the cause of independence. He is justly remembered as one of the "Fathers of Texas."

Stephen Austin was born in Wythe County, Virginia, the son of Moses Austin. After his father suffered financial disaster in the Panic of 1819, the family moved to Missouri, which was then under Spanish control. Austin was educated at Yale and at Transylvania University. He worked at a variety of jobs and held a number of public offices. At various times, he was a merchant, a land speculator, a militia officer, and a territorial legislator. He also served as a judge in Arkansas, and edited a newspaper in New Orleans.

Stephen's father secured permission from Spanish authorities to settle 300 Anglo families in Texas but died before he could implement the plan. Stephen promised that he would carry on his father's dream, and became the most successful of all of the Texas *empresarios.*

In January 1822, Austin settled his first 300 families between the Brazos and Colorado rivers, and these settlers became known as the "Old Three Hundred." He eventually obtained permission to expand his grants, and in time settled over 1,500 families in Texas.

"Estaban" Austin, as he liked to be called, worked hard to preserve harmony among the Mexicans, the Tejanos, and his Anglo settlers. He served in the legislature of the state of Coahuila y Texas. In 1830, when Mexico prohibited further immigration into Texas, Austin's colony was exempted from this act.

In July 1833, as relations with Mexico were deteriorating, Austin went to Mexico City with a petition advocating separate statehood for Texas. The Mexican government did make some concessions, but independent statehood was not granted. A discouraged Austin sent a letter back to San Antonio de Bexar advocating separation without government authority.

When Mexican authorities learned of this, they were incensed, and Austin was arrested and kept in solitary confinement for three months in Mexico City. He was then allowed somewhat better conditions, but was still confined for a total of eighteen months. He finally returned to Texas on September 1, 1835, his health much the worse for his ordeal.

Austin, long an advocate of peaceful relations with Mexico, declared in a famous speech on September 8 that "war is our only recourse." He was elected commander of the Texas Army, although he really did not want the job. Austin led his army to San Antonio de Bexar to capture it from General Cos, but when the Provisional Government was formed, he was recalled and sent to the United States to appeal for men and money. After Austin's departure, Col. Edward Burleson assumed command of the army at Bexar.

After the Revolution, Austin ran unsuccessfully against Sam Houston for the office of president of the Republic of Texas. Such was Houston's respect for Austin that he asked him to serve in the most important of his cabinet posts, that of secretary of state. Austin's tenure was short lived, however, for he died of pneumonia on December 27, 1836.

JAMES BOWIE
(1795?–March 6, 1836)

Famous knife fighter and adventurer Jim Bowie was born in Terrapin Creek, Logan County, Kentucky, probably in 1795. Although he never received a formal education, Bowie was a shrewd and energetic man. Before heading for Texas, he made his living by farming, logging, and smuggling slaves with famed pirate Jean Lafitte.

When he arrived in Texas in 1828, both Jim Bowie and his large knife were already famous. He became a Mexican citizen on October 5, 1830, and on April 25, 1831, Bowie married Ursula María de Veramendi, the daughter of Juan Martín de Veramendi, the governor of the Mexican state of

Col. James Bowie

Coahuila y Texas. Ursula's godfather was none other than Antonio López de Santa Anna. Bowie was very devoted to his family and well accepted into the Mexican society. One of his most notable endeavors was his search for the legendary San Saba silver mines.

In 1833, while Bowie was in Mississippi on a business trip, tragedy struck. A cholera epidemic was raging in Texas, and Bowie had sent his family to the Mexican town of Monclova where he thought they would be safe. Unfortunately, between the fifth and eighth of September, Ursula and her parents were all swiftly taken by the disease. Tradition holds that Bowie had two young sons who were also killed, but it has never been positively established that he and Ursula actually had any children. Bowie was deeply grieved by this loss.

He rallied to the cause of Texas' freedom, and commanded the Texian forces at the Battle of Concepción on October 28, 1835, and again during the Grass Fight on November 26. In December, he fought in the Siege of San Antonio de Bexar.

Bowie returned to San Antonio on January 19, 1836, with orders from Houston to evacuate and blow up the Alamo. However, these orders were vague enough to leave some discretion, and both Bowie and the garrison commander, Col. James Neill, decided that they would "rather die in these ditches" than give up the Alamo.

Bowie shared command of the garrison with William Barret Travis until a severe illness forced him to relinquish command. During the final battle, he was bedridden and reportedly near death. Juana Alsbury, Bowie's sister-in-law who nursed him during his illness, claimed that he had contracted typhoid pneumonia. Contrary to what some movies have portrayed, he was not incapacitated by a fall from a horse or from being crushed by a cannon.

Like Crockett, we do not know exactly how Jim Bowie met his death. According to popular tradition, when his time came, although bedridden, he took a number of the enemy with him. Other accounts imply that he was too sick to put up a fight, and may have even been unconscious when killed. Given the known courage and spirit of the man, his mother was probably right, when upon learning of his death she said, "So Jim is dead?. . . I'll wager they found no wounds in his back." (Daughters of the Republic of Texas: *The Alamo,* 28)

EDWARD BURLESON
(December 15, 1798–December 26, 1851)

Edward Burleson was born in Buncome County, North Carolina, but his family moved to Tennessee about 1812. Burleson moved to Howard County, Missouri, in 1816, where he became colonel of the local militia. He returned to Tennessee in 1823, where he again became colonel of the militia.

Burleson first visited Texas in 1830, and in 1831 he moved his family there. In 1832 he was elected lieutenant colonel of militia. He took over command of the Texas Army on November 24, 1835, after Stephen F. Austin was recalled to go to the United States to raise money and recruit men.

Burleson commanded during the Siege of Bexar in December 1835. He originally wanted to storm Bexar, but relented when outvoted by a council of his officers. On December 4 he announced that he was calling off the siege, which had gone on for about seven weeks. One of his officers, Col. Ben Milam, was unwilling to give up, and challenged his fellow Texians to follow him into the town. When it was clear that Milam had enough volunteers to make the assault, Burleson supported the effort.

After Cos' surrender, Burleson paroled the Mexican army on Cos' promise that he would retire south of the Rio Grande and not take any further part in the hostilities. This parole, of course, was broken when Cos and his men returned to fight in the Siege of the Alamo.

At the Battle of San Jacinto, Burleson commanded a regiment from Gonzales. Along with the famous scout Deaf Smith, he carried the news of Santa Anna's capture, and the orders to evacuate Texas, to the other Mexican army columns.

After the war, Burleson served in the first Senate of the Republic of Texas. He also was with the Texas Rangers, and fought in the wars against the Comanches and Cherokees. In 1841 he was elected vice-president of the Republic of Texas, and unsuccessfully ran for president in 1844. He supported annexation to the United States, and fought again in the Mexican-American War. After the war, he served in the state senate.

DAVID GOUVERNEUR BURNET
(April 14, 1788–August 5, 1870)

David Burnet was an accountant from Newark, New Jersey. In 1806 he joined an unsuccessful expedition under Miranda to free Venezuela from Spanish rule. He also lived among the Comanches in Texas for a while.

In 1826 Burnet was authorized, as an *empresario,* to establish a colony of settlers in Texas. He was not successful in his efforts, however, and eventually had to sell his rights.

In 1833 he was part of the convention at San Felipe de Austin that drew up the petition requesting separate statehood for Texas. He became active in the early revolutionary efforts, as a conservative at first, but eventually shifting to the side of complete independence. He was elected president of the Provisional Republic of Texas on March 16, 1836, at the convention at Washington-on-the-Brazos.

Burnet had to flee to Harrisburg the next day because of the approach of the Mexican army. On April 15, Burnet then had to abandon Harrisburg because of the continued Mexican advance. He fell back to New Washington, on Galveston Bay about ten miles south of San Jacinto, where he, his family, and some members of his cabinet narrowly missed capture by Mexican soldiers under Col. Juan Almonte. The Mexicans arrived just as Burnet's party was being rowed out to a steamship in the bay. Almonte declined to fire on the Texians because there were women aboard the small boat. This is a good example of the chivalry that the Mexican soldiers were capable of when not under the direct influence of Santa Anna.

Burnet did not get along well with Gen. Sam Houston. During the Runaway Scrape, he sent Secretary of War Rusk with orders instructing Houston to stop and fight the advancing Mexicans. He also gave Rusk the authority to relieve Houston and take command of the army himself if he thought it necessary. Rusk, however, became a strong supporter of Houston's plan, and stayed with the army to serve gallantly at San Jacinto.

Burnet resigned as provisional president on October 22, 1836, after Houston was elected to replace him. Later, he served as Mirabeau B. Lamar's vice-president. Burnet ran against Houston for president in 1841, but was soundly defeated. In 1846-47, after annexation, he served as Texas' secretary of state.

JAMES WALKER FANNIN

(January 1, 1804?–March 27, 1836)

James Walker Fannin is one of the most maligned soldiers that served Texas during its war for independence. After a period of over 150 years, it appears that much of this criticism is warranted, but some of it is not.

Fannin was born in Georgia, probably in 1804, the illegitimate son of Dr. Isham Fannin. He was raised as James Fannin Walker by his maternal grandfather, James W. Walker. He entered the United States Military Academy at West Point as Cadet James F. Walker in 1819, and left without graduating in November 1821. He stood sixtieth in a class of eighty-six at the time of his separation. Fannin is believed to have been the only officer in the Texas Army that had any West Point training.

In 1834 Fannin left Georgia with his wife and two children and settled in Velasco, Texas. He earned his living as a land speculator and slave trader, and was one of the early supporters of Texas independence.

At the Battle of Gonzales on October 20, 1835, Fannin commanded a volunteer unit known as the "Brazos Guards." He also served as a captain under Jim Bowie at the Battle of Concepción on October 28, and during the Siege of Bexar in December. On December 7, 1835, after being discharged from the volunteers, Fannin was commissioned as a colonel of artillery in the Regular Texas Army.

During the Siege of the Alamo, Fannin commanded the largest body of troops in the entire Texas Army, some 400 men, stationed at La Bahía, or Goliad. Many of these men were new, untrained recruits. Fannin has been severely criticized for not coming to the relief of the Alamo, and there is certainly justification for this feeling. Fannin is one of those who believed that San Antonio de Bexar should be defended rather than abandoned. However, he also believed that Goliad had to be defended, and he felt that his new recruits were not ready for battle and were ill equipped. One officer, Capt. John Brooks, reported that "most of the men were nearly naked and entirely destitute of shoes." (Boyd, 152)

On February 26, Fannin set out for the Alamo with about 300 men, but gave up when a wagon broke down after going only about 200 yards. After this, in spite of repeated pleas for help from the garrison, Fannin made no further attempt to assist them.

Even if Fannin had made an early and enthusiastic effort to relieve the Alamo, there is no guarantee that he would have gotten through. The Mexicans knew Fannin's position, and on February 29, General Ramirez y Sesma was sent to cut him off with the Dolores Cavalry and Allende Infantry Regiments. Still, there is little doubt that history would have been much kinder to Fannin's memory if he had made such an effort.

When Houston received word of the fall of the Alamo, he ordered Fannin to abandon Fort Defiance, as the fort at Goliad had been named. The Texians were ordered to retreat to Victoria, and eventually to link up with Houston's force. Fannin again hesitated before finally moving out on March 19. The Texians had gone only about ten miles when they were caught out in the open by General Urrea's column, near a place called Coleto Creek. On March 20, after brave resistance, the highly outnumbered Texians agreed to surrender.

Although many believe that the Texians were promised parole, the discovery of the original documents in Mexico show that it was an unconditional surrender. The terms state that, "All the detachment shall be treated as prisoners of war and placed at the disposal of the supreme government." (*Dictionary of American Biography,* Volume III: 263) While the surrender document does not specifically mention parole for the Texians, it does establish that they were to be recognized as legitimate prisoners of war, and not as "pirates," as Minister Tornel had decreed.

It is probable that Urrea did plan on dealing humanely with his captives until he received direct orders from Santa Anna ordering their execution.

Fannin's men were taken back to Goliad, where they were held for a week. Then, on Palm Sunday, March 27, they were told that they were going to be taken to boats for passage to New Orleans. Instead, they were divided into three groups and marched three separate directions away from the fort. When they had marched a short distance from the fort, the members of all three groups were shot down at point-blank range by their Mexican guards. A few managed to flee into the San Antonio River and lived to tell the story. Fannin and the wounded that were unable to walk were then executed back inside the fort. More than 400 Texians died in this deliberate massacre ordered by Santa Anna.

While Fannin was certainly no hero, many of his detractors fail to thoroughly consider all of the factors that influenced his decisions. Perhaps he understood himself best, for he wrote: "I am a better judge of my military abilities than others, and if I am qualified to command an Army, I have not found it out. I well know I am a better company officer than most men now in Texas, and might do well with Regulars, &c. for a Regiment. But this does not constitute me a commander." (Chariton: *Alamo Legends,* 140-141)

Gen. Sam Houston

SAM HOUSTON

(March 2, 1793–July 26, 1863)

Sam Houston is a giant in both the history of Texas and also in the history of the United States. He was born in Rockbridge County, Virginia, but moved to Tennessee with his remaining family after the death of his father in 1807. He lived among the Cherokees for three years, during which time they nicknamed him "The Raven."

Houston served with distinction as a U.S. Army officer under Andrew Jackson during the Creek Wars, and was wounded three times. Although a very effective Indian fighter, Houston also learned to respect them. In 1818 he gave up his promising army career rather than be a part of the Indian removal policies of the U.S. government.

After resigning his commission, Houston opened a successful law practice in Tennessee, and also began his long involvement with politics. In 1819 he was elected attorney general of Tennessee, and in 1823 and 1825 he was elected to the U.S. Congress. He was a friend of Andrew Jackson, whose influence helped Houston win the election as governor of Tennessee in 1827.

Houston was definitely a rising political star, but a tragedy in his personal life brought it all to a sudden halt. In January 1829, he married Eliza Allen, who came from an influential family in Gallatin, Tennessee. The marriage ended when Eliza left him after only three months. No one knows for sure what caused the breakup, and Houston never said anything negative about Eliza. He took the breakup hard, and on April 23, 1829, he resigned as governor. He again went to live among his old friends, the Cherokees, in Arkansas. Along the way, it is said that he met a man that he would cross paths again with—James Bowie.

While among the Cherokees, Houston took to heavy drinking, and this time the Indians began calling him "The Big Drunk." Eventually, he married a Cherokee woman by the name of Tiana Rogers, an ancestor of Will Rogers, who helped him to give up drinking and get his life back together. During this period, he made three trips to Washington to speak out for Indian rights. In 1832 he was the first private citizen ever tried in the House of Representatives, for an alleged assault on Representative Stanberry of Ohio.

In 1833 he was sent to Texas on a mission for President Andrew Jackson. His job was to try to convince the warlike Comanches to stop raiding on U.S. soil. Apparently, like so many others, Houston was taken by the vast opportunities that Texas offered, and he decided to try to rebuild his life there.

Houston opened a law office in Nacogdoches and soon became involved in local politics. At a convention in San Felipe on November 3, 1835, he came out in support of the Mexican Constitution of 1824, rather than complete independence. A provisional government was formed, and it appointed Houston commander of all Texas forces except those under Austin at San Antonio de Bexar. Houston did not take immediate command, but rather left for another visit with his Indian friends. Reportedly, he wanted to gain assurances that they would remain neutral during the coming hostilities with Mexico.

Shortly thereafter, Houston was named commander of the entire Texas Army, and he was in charge during the Siege of the Alamo and the difficult days that followed. Houston slowly molded the army into a credible fighting force during the retreat across Texas, known as the "Runaway Scrape." He eventually led the army to victory at San Jacinto six weeks after the Alamo's fall. Virtually the entire Mexican army under Santa Anna's immediate command was destroyed or captured, with a loss of only six Texians killed and twenty-five wounded. Houston himself was shot through the ankle. The wound became infected, requiring him to eventually leave the army and go to New Orleans for specialized treatment.

Gen. Sam Houston was elected as the first president of the Republic of Texas, and took the oath of office on October 22, 1836. By law he was limited to one two-year term, after which he returned to his law practice and engaged in several business ventures.

On May 9, 1840, he married twenty-year-old Margaret Lea, and they remained happily married for the rest of his life. Together they had eight children.

In 1841 Houston was again elected president of the Republic of Texas for what was now a three-year term. When Texas was annexed by the United States in 1845, he was elected to the U.S. Senate, where he served until 1859. When he returned from Washington, Houston served as governor of Texas. War clouds were again building, this time over the question of slavery. Bitterly opposed to secession, Houston resigned his governorship rather than take the oath of allegiance to the Confederacy. He died on July 26, 1863.

MIRABEAU BUONAPARTE LAMAR

(August 16, 1798–December 19, 1859)

Born in Warren County, Georgia, Mirabeau Lamar was a painter, a poet, and a publisher. He came to Texas in 1835 after an unsuccessful bid for the U.S. Congress.

Lamar served as a private with the mounted rifles during Houston's Runaway Scrape. His unit was involved in a skirmish on the day before the Battle of San Jacinto, during which he rescued Secretary of War Thomas Jefferson Rusk from almost certain capture or death. As a reward for his bravery, he was given command of the Texian cavalry during the next day's decisive battle.

After the fighting, Lamar was elected as the first vice-president of the Republic of Texas, serving under Sam Houston. When Houston's term was up in 1838, Lamar succeeded him and thus became the second president of the Republic of Texas.

Lamar's term as president was marked with controversy. He laid the foundation for free public education in Texas, and opposed annexation to the United States. He wanted Texas to remain free, and was involved in a scheme to entice New Mexico to become a part of the Republic. When Mexican authorities discovered this plot, it destroyed any chance for peaceful relations between Mexico and Texas.

In one of his most controversial actions, he used armed force to drive the Cherokees out of Texas. The campaign seriously depleted the new Republic's treasury, and Chief Bowles, an old friend of Houston's, was killed in the fighting. Houston became Lamar's bitter enemy for his actions against the Cherokees.

Lamar eventually changed his position from anti- to pro-annexation, and during the Mexican-American War he served at Monterey and at Laredo. In 1857 he was named the U.S. minister to Nicaragua. His performance was again controversial, and he was recalled in July 1859. He died later that same year.

BENJAMIN RUSH MILAM

(1788–December 7, 1835)

Ben Milam, hero of the Battle of Bexar, was born in Frankfort, Kentucky, in 1788. He was a veteran of the War of 1812, and an early immigrant to Texas. He became a Mexican citizen, and fought with the Mexican army against the Spanish in 1819.

Although he suffered from severe arthritis in his legs, Milam joined the Texan cause and fought in the capture of Goliad in October 1835. He commanded a company of scouts during the Siege of Bexar. Just when the Texian resolve seemed about to crumble, he challenged the troops by asking, "Who will follow old Ben Milam into San Antonio?" (Hardin: *Texian Iliad,* 78) He secured enough volunteers to make an attack feasible, but the Mexicans put up a valiant defense. On the third day of intense street fighting, in the courtyard of the Juan Veramendi house, Milam was shot through the head by Felix de la Garza, a Mexican sharpshooter armed with a Baker Rifle. He died instantly. After his death, his friend, the famous scout Erastus "Deaf" Smith, wrote a poem about him. It closed with the following lines:

"As bright as thy example, so bright shall be thy fame.
And generations yet unborn shall honor Milam's name."

(Daughters of the Republic of Texas: *The Alamo,* 21)

JOSÉ ANTONIO NAVARRO
(1795–1871)

Navarro was a close friend of Stephen F. Austin, and helped Austin obtain his *empresario* contracts. José was the son of Angel Navarro, an *alcalde* (mayor) of San Antonio de Bexar. José became a lawyer, and also managed a general store and his family's ranch. Prior to the Texas Revolution, he served as Bexar's representative in the Congress of Coahuila y Texas. He and Austin both worked for legislation that would benefit the citizens of Texas.

When Santa Anna came into power, José advocated independence for Texas. José and his uncle, Francísco Ruiz, were the only native-born Texans to sign the Texas Declaration of Independence. He was elected as one of Bexar's four delegates to the Constitutional Convention, and was then appointed to the committee charged with drafting the actual document.

In 1841 he took part in the Santa Fe expedition, for which he was imprisoned for three and one-half years in Acordada Prison in Mexico. In 1842, under pressure to renounce his loyalties to Texas, he said, "I have sworn to be a good Texan. . . . I will die for that which I firmly believe. . . . One life is a small price for a cause so great. As I fought, so shall I be willing to die. I will never forsake Texas and her cause. I am her son." (Daughters of the Republic of Texas: *The Alamo,* 12)

After escaping from prison, Navarro wrote the constitution for the State of Texas, and later served as one of Texas' first United States senators.

JAMES C. NEILL
(?–1845)

Little is known of James C. Neill's early life, but he reportedly came to Texas from Alabama. He was a lieutenant colonel of the Regular Texas Artillery, and on December 21, 1835, Gen. Sam Houston appointed him commander of the garrison at San Antonio de Bexar. When Jim Bowie reported to the Alamo, he was extremely impressed by Neill's efforts in maintaining the post, and by the way Neill had gained the loyalty of his men in spite of their difficult circumstances.

On February 11, apparently due to an illness in his family, Neill left the Alamo and went home. He left William Barret Travis in command of the garrison.

While on leave, Neill also worked to raise men and money for the Alamo. He was in San Felipe on February 28, where he received $600 for the garrison. On March 6 he purchased $90 worth of medical supplies in Gonzales. It appears that he left Gonzales with about fifty men on the seventh, and headed back to the Alamo. He was within about eighteen miles of the mission when he was turned back by a Mexican patrol. On March 10 Neill was back in Gonzales.

Neill commanded the Texian artillery at San Jacinto and was wounded in action by fire from the lone Mexican field piece. He died at his home in 1845.

JOSÉ FRANCISCO RUIZ
(1783–1840)

Members of the Ruiz family were among the founders of San Antonio de Bexar. José was born in Bexar in 1783 and educated in Spain. After returning in 1803, he became Bexar's first public schoolmaster. He joined the Mexican independence movement in 1810, and took part in the Battle of Medina in 1813. After the Royalist victory, he and other rebels fled to safety in the United States. He returned to Texas in 1822.

In 1836, José was serving as the *alcalde* (mayor)

of San Antonio de Bexar. He was elected as a representative to the convention at Washington-on-the-Brazos, where he was one of the signers of the Texas Declaration of Independence. While José was at the convention, his son Francisco filled in as the acting mayor in Bexar, and played an important part in the Siege of the Alamo.

FRANCISCO ANTONIO RUIZ
(1805–1876)

Francísco Ruiz was the son of José Francísco Ruiz. He was the *alcalde* (mayor) of San Antonio de Bexar during the Siege of the Alamo. When the Mexican army arrived, because of his pro-revolutionary sympathies, he was placed under house arrest by Santa Anna. After the final assault, he was ordered to identify the bodies of Travis, Bowie, and Crockett for Santa Anna. Ruiz also supervised the burial of the Mexican dead and the cremation of the Alamo defenders.

THOMAS JEFFERSON RUSK
(December 5, 1803–July 29, 1857)

Thomas Jefferson Rusk was born in Pendleton District, South Carolina. In 1835 he was an attorney in Clarksville, Georgia, and a partner in a gold mining venture whose managers embezzled the corporate funds. Rusk pursued them to Texas, and liked it there so well that he decided to stay.

Rusk became involved in the revolutionary efforts, and was a signer of the Texas Declaration of Independence. He became a conciliatory voice between extremists on both sides, in the Peace Party and the War Party.

Rusk served as a captain during the Siege of Bexar. He was a friend of Sam Houston's, and supported his tactics during the Runaway Scrape. As secretary of war for the Provisional Government, he was sent to join the army at Groce's Plantation, with the authority to relieve Houston and take over command himself if he did not think that Houston's avoidance of a fight was necessary and proper. After conferring with Houston, Rusk strongly supported his tactics, and stayed on with the army as a volunteer.

The day before the Battle of San Jacinto, Rusk was on a scouting mission with Col. Sidney Sherman's mounted Kentuckians. They were engaged by Mexican cavalry, and at one point Rusk was cut off by enemy horsemen. He most certainly would have been killed or captured if Pvt. Mirabeau Lamar had not bravely ridden to his aid and helped him to escape.

For his bravery, Lamar was made a colonel and given command of the cavalry during the next day's decisive battle. During the battle, Rusk is reported to have unsuccessfully tried to save the life of a Mexican general, Manuel Fernandez Castrillon, who was Santa Anna's aide-de-camp.

Rusk commanded the Texian army that followed the retreating Mexicans back to the Rio Grande. On his way through Goliad, he supervised the burial of the victims of the Palm Sunday massacre. He took over the command of the entire Texas Army on May 5, when the infection in the wound Houston received at San Jacinto forced him to leave the field and seek specialized treatment in New Orleans.

Rusk served as secretary of war in President Houston's first cabinet. He later served in the Texas House of Representatives, was a major general of militia, and, in 1838, became chief justice of the Texas Supreme Court. He favored annexation by the United States, and was president of the convention that confirmed it for Texas. He then served with Houston as one of Texas' U.S. senators. In 1857, despondent over the death of his wife a year earlier, Rusk committed suicide.

JOSÉ ERASMO SEGUIN
(1782–1857)

José Erasmo Seguin was the father of well-known revolutionary Juan Seguin. Born in San Antonio de Bexar in 1782, he became one of the town's political and intellectual leaders. Erasmo was highly supportive of the Anglo settlers in Texas. He and Juan Martín de Veramendi were close friends of Stephen Austin, and worked hard to help his colony succeed.

Erasmo became one of the leading citizens of San Antonio de Bexar, and served as *alcalde* (mayor) of Bexar, postmaster of all of Texas, and as a representative to the Mexican legislature. He supported the Anglo colonists in their fight for fair treatment by the Mexican government. Because of his pro-revolutionary sympathies, he was removed from the office of postmaster by General Cos in 1835.

JUAN NEPOMUCENO SEGUIN
(October 27, 1806–August 27, 1890)

Juan Seguin was born in San Antonio de Bexar in 1806, the son of Don Erasmo and María Seguin. The Seguins were an old and respected San Antonio family, and Don Erasmo tried to raise his children respectably. In an 1824 letter, while he was away on business, he urged Juan and his sister, in words that can be echoed by modern parents, to "read and write and not to be out on the streets." (De la Teja, 16)

Don Erasmo was the *alcalde* (mayor) of San Antonio de Bexar and a staunch friend of the Anglo settlers. Juan followed in his father's footsteps, both in politics and in his friendship for the Anglo settlers. In 1832 Juan organized a cultural society in San Antonio known as the "Society of Friends."

In 1829 he was elected to his first public office, that of alderman. In 1834 he was elected *alcalde* of Bexar, and subsequently was appointed the political chief of the San Antonio area. He also served as a peace emissary to the Comanches.

Juan opposed the oppressive policies of Santa Anna, and did his best to influence other Tejanos to fight with the Texians. He recruited a company of Tejano horsemen, and was commissioned a captain by General Austin in October 1835. Juan served as a scout during the Battle of Concepción. He also fought during the Siege of Bexar, and afterwards took part in raids on the Mexican horse herds with William Barret Travis. On January 2, 1836, he was formally commissioned a captain of the Regular Texas Cavalry, and was ordered to report to San Antonio de Bexar. Juan was chosen by Travis to ride to Gonzales with his plea for help, and left the Alamo on the night of February 25.

After the fall of the Alamo, Juan reorganized his company at Gonzales. They helped with the evacuation of settlers in the face of the Mexican advance, and also served as part of Houston's rear guard during the Runaway Scrape. Juan himself carried the news of the Alamo's fall to the convention at Washington-on-the-Brazos.

Juan fought again at San Jacinto, and then, on June 4, 1836, he led his company of twenty-two men back into his hometown of San Antonio de Bexar. He accepted the surrender of the small Mexican garrison under Lt. Francisco Castaneda, who, ironically, had commanded the Mexicans at the opening skirmish of the Revolution at Gonzales. Juan then organized and administered the military government of the San Antonio District.

Capt. Juan Seguin

On February 25, 1837, Juan, then a lieutenant colonel, delivered a moving eulogy and conducted a burial service for the remains of the Alamo defenders. (See Chapter Thirteen for the complete text of this speech.)

In 1838 Juan was elected as Bexar's senator to the Texas Congress. He was the only Tejano to serve in the Senate, and while in office he introduced a bill for the relief of the families of the Alamo defenders. He also was chairman of the Committee on Military Affairs.

In cooperation with Texas Representative José Antonio Navarro, Juan worked hard to establish educational opportunities for Tejanos, and also did his best to protect their rights in the face of the ever increasing, and sometimes hostile, population of Anglos.

Like most other Texians at the time, Juan engaged in numerous private ventures, including land speculation, to support himself and his family. The methods that he employed, while maybe not totally legitimate by today's standards, were no worse than what was being practiced by many other Texians at the time. Even so, he made enemies in the process.

In 1840 Juan resigned his congressional seat in order to join a Mexican military expedition against the Centralist government in Mexico City. While many Texians sympathized with this effort, it did not have the official support of the new Republic. To have done so could very well have provoked another war with Mexico, a war that Texas could ill afford at the time.

On his return, Juan was again elected mayor of San Antonio de Bexar, during which time he became involved in a number of political battles between the Tejanos and the Anglos, especially the newcomers. People began to question his loyalty, and on April 18, 1842, he resigned as mayor. Shortly thereafter, he fled to Mexico to escape the controversy, and also the possibility of physical harm to himself and his family.

In Mexico, his loyalty was also questioned, and he was forced to serve in the Mexican army to prove himself. The alternative was to be put in jail. Juan served in the Woll expedition that briefly recaptured San Antonio de Bexar on September 11, 1842. In 1845, during the United States–Mexican War, he led a unit known as the "Defensores de Bexar."

During this period, a number of Texians who felt that Juan had been unjustly treated loyally stood by him and defended his reputation. Perhaps the most notable person among these was Sam Houston himself. In 1848 he requested and was given permission to return to Texas with his family.

Once again Juan became involved in the political scene and acted as a mediator in Tejano, Anglo, and Mexican affairs. He wrote his memoirs in 1858, and fought relentlessly to convince the government to authorize benefits for veterans of the Texas Revolution.

Late in his life, Juan again pulled up stakes and moved to Nuevo Laredo, Mexico, where he died on August 27, 1890. In 1976 his remains were moved from Nuevo Laredo to Seguin, Texas, were a new grave and monument were dedicated on July 4, the 200th anniversary of our nation's independence.

Juan Seguin was certainly a man who personified the struggles faced by the early Tejanos, who were torn by loyalty to their native Mexico and their desire to be free of its oppressive Centralist government. While most Tejanos and the early Anglo settlers in Texas generally got along well, the tremendous influx of new settlers in the years following the Texas Revolution brought new difficulties. Few Tejanos played a more active roll during these formative years than Juan Seguin. His accomplishments are all the more noteworthy considering that during his long and busy life, he never became fluent in the English language.

ERASTUS "DEAF" SMITH
(1787-1837)

Erastus Smith was born in Dutchess County, New York, but grew up in Mississippi. He was partially deaf since childhood, thus accounting for his nickname "Deaf" Smith.

Smith came to Texas in 1817, and settled in San Antonio de Bexar in 1821. The climate improved his poor health, caused by what is believed to have been tuberculosis. He became fluent in Spanish, assimilated into the culture, and married Guadalupe Ruiz de Duran, a Mexican woman descended from the Canary Island settlers. His Mexican friends called him *"El Sordo,"* the "Deaf One."

Smith became known as an accomplished hunter and scout. He was a friend of Jim Bowie, and joined him in his search for the legendary San Saba silver mines. Smith was also present during Bowie's famous fight against 150 Caddo Indians.

When the Texas Revolution broke out, Smith at first attempted to remain neutral. However, when Mexican soldiers under General Cos attempted to capture him, and deny him the right to return to his home and family, he cast his lot with the rebels.

Smith and his son-in-law, a free black man named Hendrick Arnold, warned Bowie of the Mexicans' approach just before the Battle of Concepcion, in October of 1835. Smith served as a scout during the Siege of Bexar in December, and was wounded during the street fighting. He was with Ben Milam when he was killed, and wrote a poem about him after his death. (See Milam's biography in this section.)

During the Siege of the Alamo, Smith was serving as a scout for Houston. He discovered Susannah Dickinson and her party, and brought them to Houston, at Gonzales, on March 13. Susannah's arrival confirmed the rumors that the Alamo had fallen.

During the Runaway Scrape, Smith again acted as a scout for Houston. He captured a Mexican courier carrying dispatches in Travis' captured saddlebags. These documents confirmed that Santa Anna had allowed himself to become separated from the rest of his army, which in turn helped Houston to decide that the time was right to fight at San Jacinto.

Just before the battle, Smith convinced Houston to allow him to burn Vince's Bridge, which insured that no reinforcements could join Santa Anna, and also sealed off one of the Mexicans' avenues of retreat. Smith returned in time to take part in the battle, and is credited with personally capturing General Cos.

Afterwards, Smith carried Santa Anna's surrender orders to the other Mexican columns, and then accompanied the Texian forces that followed the retreating Mexican to insure that they did indeed leave Texas. Along the route, Smith participated in the burial of the victims of the massacre at Goliad.

After the Revolution, Smith commanded a company of Texas Rangers. He fought and defeated a detachment of Mexican soldiers at Laredo on February 17, 1837. Smith was not destined to long enjoy the fruits of the Revolution, however, for he died shortly afterwards. It is believed that his death was caused by the effects of the tuberculosis that plagued him throughout his life.

Lt. Col. William Barret Travis

WILLIAM BARRET TRAVIS
(August 9, 1809–March 6, 1836)

William Barret Travis was born in Red Banks Church, South Carolina, in 1809. In 1818 he moved with his family to Conecuh County, Alabama, where he worked as a schoolteacher and studied law.

On October 28, 1828, he married a seventeen-year-old student, Rosanna Cato, by whom he had two children. Their marriage was a troubled one, however, and in 1831 he left his family and moved to Texas. He and Rosanna were divorced in November 1835.

In 1831 Travis opened a legal practice in Anahuac, and a year later moved to San Felipe de Austin, continuing his law career there. He also became active in local politics. Travis became a member of the "War Party" and was involved in the political unrest in Texas almost from the beginning. In 1832 he was arrested for opposing the Mexican commander in Anahuac, Col. Juan Bradburn. In January 1835 he led the capture of the new Mexican garrison in Anahuac, which had been abandoned since 1832. This act caused much embarrassment to the more moderate Texian leaders. In 1834 Travis met and became engaged to Rebecca Cummings, planning to marry her when things settled down.

When the Revolution broke out, Travis was initially appointed lieutenant of cavalry, then captain of cavalry, then a major of artillery. He did not feel qualified for this technical arm, and requested a cavalry command instead. On December 24, 1835, he was commissioned a lieutenant colonel in the Regular Texas Cavalry, and was sent to join Col. James Neill at San Antonio de Bexar. Travis traveled to Bexar with Capt. John Forsyth's cavalry company, but did not initially have much enthusiasm for his assignment. He was the highest ranking officer in the Texas Cavalry, and apparently thought that he should have been assigned to a more important mission.

Travis arrived at Bexar about February 2, and when Colonel Neill left to care for his sick family, Travis became the commander of the garrison. He and James Bowie agreed to joint command on February 14, but he regained full command when Bowie became incapacitated by a serious illness.

Much of what we know about the Siege of the Alamo is due to the written records that Travis left behind. He was a complicated man with a flair for the dramatic, but no one can doubt his courage, or his dedication to his cause of Texas' freedom.

JUAN MARTÍN DE VERAMENDI
(1778–September 1833)

Juan de Veramendi was a native of San Antonio de Bexar and one of its most influential citizens. He served as *alcalde* (mayor) and as a government tax collector. In 1832-33, he also served as the governor of the state of Coahuila y Texas. He was a friend of Stephen Austin, and a firm supporter of the Anglo settlers.

Juan's daughter, Ursula de Veramendi, married Jim Bowie, and he and Bowie were partners in a cotton mill in Saltillo, Mexico. He and his family died at their summer home at Monclova, during a cholera epidemic in September 1833. The massive front doors of their home in San Antonio de Bexar are on display at the Alamo.

ROBERT McALPIN WILLIAMSON

Robert Williamson was known as "Three-Legged Willie" because of a leg that bent backwards, due to childhood polio, and had to be supplemented by a wooden leg.

Williamson was a Georgia native and an accomplished attorney. On November 28, 1835, he was appointed major and commander of the three companies of Texas Rangers that had just been authorized by the interim Texas government.

Williamson first came to Texas in 1826, and his passionate support for the cause of independence earned him the name of "The Patrick Henry of the Texas Revolution." He was a musician, a ladies' man, and in spite of his wooden leg, an enthusiastic dancer. Williamson was a close friend of the Alamo commander, William Barret Travis. After the Revolution he became justice of the Texas Supreme Court.

During the Siege of the Alamo, Williamson wrote a letter to Travis implying that help was on the way to the besieged garrison. This recently discovered letter raises the possibility that the defenders, rather than knowing they were doomed, may have had hope that they would be relieved, if only they could hold out just a little longer.

LORENZO de ZAVALA
(1789–1836)

Lorenzo de Zavala was the most prominent Tejano who opposed Santa Anna's Centralist government and cast his lot with the rebels.

De Zavala was born in Yucatan of a well-to-do Mestizo family. He entered the seminary, but left to study medicine. A political liberal, he was opposed to a strong central government. He was elected as the provincial representative from Yucatan, and went to Spain to serve in the legislature. When Mexico declared its independence, he returned home and helped draft the Constitution of 1824. De Zavala held a number of offices in the new Mexican government, including minister of finance.

In 1829 de Zavala received a grant to settle 500 families in Texas, but fled Mexico when the conservative Anastasio Bustamante gained control of the government. He spent the next three years in the United States and in Europe.

In 1833 the new liberal president, Antonio López de Santa Anna, appointed de Zavala as minister to France. He resigned his position in 1835, when Santa Anna began to show his true intentions.

De Zavala then went to Texas, where he became one of the most active of the revolutionaries. He was a signer of the Texas Declaration of Independence, and was elected as the first vice-president of the Provisional Government of Texas. Ill health soon forced him to resign his office, however.

Lorenzo's son, Capt. Lorenzo de Zavala, Jr., served as an officer in the Texas Army and as an aide-de-camp to General Houston. One of Lorenzo, Sr's. granddaughters, Adina de Zavala, was one of the leaders in the fight to preserve the Alamo as a Shrine of Texas Liberty.

PART 2: THE MEXICANS

NOTE: This section contains brief biographical information about figures on the Mexican side during the Texas Revolution and the Siege of the Alamo. While similar in format to Part 1, which covers "rebel" personalities, in this section we have included some individuals of admittedly lesser importance, simply because information on the Mexican participants is much harder to come by. We are especially indebted to Kevin Young for sharing the fruits of his intense study of the Mexican army with us.

* * * * *

AGUSTÍN ALCERRICA

Alcerrica was an acting colonel in command of the Active Battalion from "Tres Villas" during the early stages of the Texas Campaign. This battalion was raised in the towns of Jalapa, Cordoba, and Orizaba, and was part of the 2nd Infantry Brigade. On February 17, 1836, Col. Cayetano Montoya took over command of the Tres Villas Battalion.

Col. Juan Almonte

JUAN NEPOMUCENO ALMONTE
(1803–March 21, 1869)

Juan Almonte was the illegitimate son of Mexican revolutionary hero Father José Morelos. He was educated in Catholic schools in New Orleans, and was fluent in English. In 1834 he traveled through Texas assessing the political and military situation for the Mexican government.

During the Texas Campaign, Almonte was a colonel on Santa Anna's staff, and acted as his interpreter. Almonte presented Santa Anna's surrender demands to Alamo engineer Green B. Jameson on February 23, 1836.

After the fall of the Alamo, Almonte accompanied Santa Anna's army on its march eastward, and commanded a column of dragoons that nearly captured Provisional President David Burnet and members of his cabinet. He chivalrously declined to fire on the fleeing Texians' boat because there were family members on board.

Almonte was captured at San Jacinto, and some believe that he is the source of the information about the capture and execution of David Crockett that was printed in the famous letter by Sgt. George Dolson. He did keep a detailed diary throughout most of the Texas Campaign. Almonte accompanied Santa Anna to the United States after San Jacinto, and returned to Mexico with him in 1837.

When the Mexican-American War broke out, Almonte was the Mexican minister to the United States. After Benito Juarez was ousted, Almonte served as president of Mexico, from April until September 1862. He supported the French attempt to install Maximilian as emperor. When Maximilian was overthrown, Almonte fled to Paris, where he died in 1869.

JUAN VALENTÍN AMADOR
(1781–1851)

Amador was a Cuban-born officer who had previously served in the Spanish army. During the Texas Campaign he was a brigadier general. In the final assault on the Alamo, he led the troops over the north wall.

AGUSTÍN AMAT

Amat was the acting colonel of the elite Zapadores Regiment that was part of the 1st Infantry Brigade. He also was second-in-command of the reserve column during the final Alamo assault.

PEDRO AMPUDIA
(?–August 7, 1869)

Pedro Ampudia was another Cuban-born Mexican officer. During the Texas Campaign he was a lieutenant colonel who served as commanding general of artillery for the Army of Operations, and took part in the final battle for the Alamo.

Ampudia fought against the Texians at the Battle of Mier in 1842, and against the Americans at Monterey, Palo Alto, and Reseca de la Palma during the Mexican-American War. Later, he fought under Benito Juarez.

JUAN JOSÉ de ANDRADE
(1796–1843)

A native-born Mexican officer who was a veteran of the Spanish army, Andrade commanded the

Cavalry Brigade as a brigadier general during the Texas Campaign. He also commanded the garrison at San Antonio de Bexar from March 11 through May 30, 1836, and supervised the destruction of the Alamo's fortifications. After the Texas Revolution, he served as the commandant general of Puebla.

JUAN ARAGO
(1788–1836)

A native of France, Arago was a veteran of the Spanish artillery before joining the Mexican revolutionary forces. During the Texas Campaign, he was a major brigade general and the nominal third in command of the Army of Operations.

ESTEVAN BARBERO

Barbero was a lieutenant colonel who served as major general of artillery during the Texas Campaign.

JOSÉ BARTRES
(?–April 21, 1836)

As a colonel in the Army of Operations, Bartres presented the Mexican surrender demands to Albert Martin on February 23, 1836. He was killed in action at the Battle of San Jacinto.

FRANCISCO BECERRA
(1810–1876)

During the Texas Campaign, Becerra was a sergeant in the Matamoros Battalion. He fought at the Alamo, and was captured at San Jacinto.

After the Texas Revolution, Becerra settled in Texas. He fought in the Texas Army against hostile Indians, and on the side of the Americans during the Mexican-American War. During the Civil War, he served as an officer in the Confederate Army. Later, he was a police officer in Brownsville, Texas, and died from the effects of a bayonet wound suffered while trying to arrest a disorderly soldier.

In 1875 Becerra recorded his memories of the Texas Revolution for Col. John S. Ford, whom he had served with during the Civil War. At one time he also worked for Reuben Potter, one of the earliest Alamo historians, and no doubt passed his recollections on to him.

JUAN DAVIS BRADBURN

Bradburn was one of a number of native-born Americans in the service of Mexico. He fought under Mina in the Mexican War of Independence, and also with Agustin Iturbide. He was the commander at Anahuac in 1832, when William Barret Travis was arrested for revolutionary activities.

During the Texas Revolution, Bradburn was a colonel in charge of the port of Copano, but had an understanding with the Mexican government that he would not take the field in active combat against the Texians.

JUAN MARÍA BRINGAS

Bringas was a colonel serving as an aide-de-camp to General Santa Anna.

MANUEL CANEDO
(1782–1855)

Manuel Canedo was born in Guadalajara, and began his military career in the Spanish army. He fought for Mexican independence under Iturbide.

During the Texas Campaign, Canedo was an acting general, and commanded the Active Battalion from Guadalajara, part of the 2nd Infantry Brigade. He died at Jalisco in 1855.

RAMON MARTÍNEZ CARO

Ramon Caro was a civilian who served as Santa Anna's personal secretary during the Texas Campaign. He left a detailed written account of the campaign.

FRANCISCO CASTANEDA

Castaneda was captain of the Presidial Cavalry Company of Alamo de Parras. He commanded the Mexican force of 100 dragoons during the Battle of Gonzales, and was the last officer to leave San Antonio de Bexar when the Mexicans withdrew in June 1836.

MANUEL FERNANDEZ CASTRILLON
(?–April 21, 1836)

Manuel Castrillon was born in Havana, Cuba. He came to Mexico with the Spanish army, but changed sides and joined the Mexican revolutionaries. Castrillon was intelligent and well educated. During the Texas Campaign, he was a general and aide-de-camp to Santa Anna.

During the Siege of the Alamo, Castrillon opposed Santa Anna's plan for a direct assault, and wanted to wait for the arrival of the heavy siege guns. He took personal command of the column that attacked from the north after Colonel Duque was severely wounded. Castrillon is credited in several accounts with trying to save the lives of several Alamo defenders who were taken prisoner during the final battle.

During the Battle of San Jacinto, Castrillon refused to retreat and was killed while trying to rally the Mexican troops. "I have been in forty battles and never showed my back," he is reported to have said. "I am too old to do it now." (Hardin: *Texian Iliad,* 213) Castrillon is believed to have been in his late fifties at the time of his death.

Gen. Martín Perfecto de Cos

MANUEL CESPEDES

Cespedes was the colonel commanding the Permanent Guerrero Battalion of the 2nd Infantry Brigade. He was captured at San Jacinto.

NICOLAS CONDELLE
(1790?–1846?)

A Spanish officer who joined the revolutionaries under Iturbide, Condelle was second-in-command under General Cos during the Siege of San Antonio de Bexar, in December 1835.

During the Texas Campaign, Condelle was the colonel commanding the Permanent Morelos Battalion of the 2nd Infantry Brigade.

MARTÍN PERFECTO de COS
(1800–October 1, 1854)

Born in Tehuantepec, Mexico, of a Criollo family, Cos was another former Spanish officer who changed allegiance to fight with Iturbide. When the Texas Revolution broke out, Cos was a division general in command of the Internal Eastern Provinces. Although he possessed only modest talents, he was Santa Anna's brother-in-law, and, obviously, politically well connected.

Cos was sent into Texas in September 1835, with orders to expel all settlers who arrived after 1830, disarm the rest of the Texians, and arrest all those who opposed Santa Anna. His army of approximately 1,200 men and twenty-one pieces of artillery was defeated by about 300 Texians in the Battle of Bexar, which ended on December 10. After the surrender, the Mexicans were paroled and given arms, ammunition, and supplies enough to get them safely home, upon Cos' promise not to fight anymore. When Cos' army joined Santa Anna's Army of Operations, it was a clear violation of this generous parole.

During the final assault on the Alamo, Cos commanded the second column that assaulted the north wall. He was captured at San Jacinto, but later was released.

During the Mexican-American War, Cos commanded the defenses south of Santa Cruz. He died in Minatittan on October 1, 1854.

RICARDO DROMUNDO

Like General Cos, Ricardo Dromundo was Santa Anna's brother-in-law. He held the rank of colonel, and was the commissary general of the Army of Operations. In the opinion of Ramon Caro, Santa Anna's secretary, Dromundo's handling of the finances was suspicious, and not necessarily in the best interests of the army.

FRANCISCO DUQUE
(1792–1854)

Francisco Duque was born in Cocula, Jalisco, in 1792. He was the colonel and commander of the Active Toluca Battalion of the 1st Infantry Brigade during the Texas Campaign. During the final assault on the Alamo, Duque was in charge of the column that attacked from the northeast. He was badly wounded in the leg during the fighting, and General Castrillon took over command of his column. After the Texas Revolution, Duque was the commanding general in Sonara and Sinaloa.

FRANCISCO ESPARZA

Francisco Esparza was a native of San Antonio de Bexar, and a brother of Alamo defender Gregorio Esparza. He was a member of the Presidial Cavalry Company of Los Alamos de Parras, and fought during the Siege of Bexar in 1835. Santa Anna held his company out of actual combat during the Siege of the Alamo.

After the final battle, Francisco received permission from General Cos to claim his brother's body and give it a Christian burial. Gregorio Esparza was the only Alamo defender who was allowed that honor.

ANTONIO ESTRADA

During the Texas Campaign, Antonio Estrada was a lieutenant colonel and the "keeper of orders," or adjutant, of the Cavalry Brigade.

VICENTE FILISOLA
(1789–July 23, 1850)

Vicente Filisola was a native of Italy, having been born in Ravello in 1789. He enlisted in the

Gen. Vicente Filisola

Spanish army in 1804, became a lieutenant in 1810, and was sent to Mexico in 1811. Filisola rose through the ranks until, as a lieutenant colonel, he commanded the largest Royalist army in Mexico in 1821.

When Iturbide became emperor in 1821, Filisola was made a brigadier general, and was sent to conquer Central America for Mexico. After Iturbide's fall, Filisola advocated an independent union of Central American provinces. In 1829 he was promoted to major general, and in 1830 became the president of the Supreme War Council.

In 1833, while commander of the region that included Texas, ill health forced Filisola to retire from active service. He recovered his health and was able to return to the army in 1836. During the Texas Campaign, as a division general, Filisola served as Santa Anna's second-in-command. He handled most of the logistical details of the campaign, and did a reasonably competent job considering the difficulties that he faced. Filisola did not arrive at the Alamo until March 9, so he missed the siege and final battle.

After the Battle of San Jacinto, Filisola assumed command of the remaining Mexican forces, and obeyed Santa Anna's orders to evacuate Texas. He was subjected to much criticism for obeying this order, since it was issued while Santa Anna was a prisoner and under duress.

In 1837, Filisola opposed an anti-Centralist coup by Gen. José Urrea, and later fought against the French in the "Pastry War." In 1839 he was the commanding general of the Mexican army. In 1840 he was removed from his command and court-martialed for following Santa Anna's orders after San Jacinto. He was acquitted, and retired from the army in 1841.

During the Mexican-American War, Filisola was again recalled to the army, and served with distinction. In 1853 he was again serving as the head of the Supreme War Council when he died of cholera. Vicente Filisola may not have been a native-born Mexican, but he served his adopted country as an honest, dedicated, capable, and nonpolitical professional soldier.

ANTONIO GAONA
(1793–1848)

Antonio Gaona was a Cuban-born officer and Spanish army veteran in the Mexican service. During the Texas Campaign, he was an acting brigadier general in command of the 1st Infantry Brigade. Along the march into Texas, Gaona engaged in personal profiteering, buying up needed supplies and then reselling them to the army at a one hundred percent profit.

After the Siege of the Alamo, Gaona commanded the column of about 700 men that marched toward Bastrop. He also served during the Mexican-American War.

EULOGIO GONZALEZ

During the Texas Campaign, Gonzalez was a colonel serving as the "keeper of orders," or adjutant, of the Vanguard, under General Ramirez y Sesma.

JOSÉ MARÍA HERRERA

Herrera was the captain of the chasseur, or light infantry, company of the Toluca Battalion, and was killed in the final assault on the Alamo.

MIGUEL INFANSON

Infanson was an acting colonel and "keeper of orders," or adjutant, of the 1st Infantry Brigade under General Gaona.

JULIAN JUVERA

Julian Juvera was a colonel commanding the Permanent Guadalajara Cavalry Regiment, of the Cavalry Brigade, during the Texas Campaign.

IGNACIO LABASTIDA
(1806–1838)

During the Texas Campaign, Labastida was a brevet lieutenant colonel in the Zapadores Battalion of the 1st Infantry Brigade. He drew an excellent map of the Alamo and San Antonio de Bexar, commonly referred to as the "Mexican Engineer's Map." (See a rendition of his map in Chapter Seven.)

JOSÉ MARÍA MACOTELA
(?–March 1836)

Macotela was a captain of the Toluca Battalion who was badly wounded in the final assault on the Alamo. He died of his wounds shortly afterwards.

DAMASO MARTINEZ
(?–March 6, 1836)

Lieutenant Martinez was shot to death while attempting to help Lt. José María Torres take down the Alamo's colors.

JOSÉ VICENTE MINON
(1802–1878)

Minon was born in Cadiz, Spain, but once in Mexico he supported the independence movement. During the Texas Campaign, Minon was a colonel and second-in-command of the fourth column, led by Col. Juan Morales, that attacked the south wall during the final assault on the Alamo.

JOSÉ MIRAMON

During the Texas Campaign, Miramon was a lieutenant, and the artillery commander of the 2nd Infantry Brigade.

CAYETANO MONTOYA
(1791–1868)

During the Texas Campaign, Colonel Montoya commanded the Active Battalion from Queretaro, of the 1st Infantry Brigade. On February 17 he took over command of the Tres Villas Battalion of the 2nd Brigade.

Later in his career, Montoya served as the commanding general of the Departments of Queretaro, Guanajuato, and Zacatecas, and he also fought in the Mexican-American War.

ESTEBAN de la MORA
(?–April 21, 1836)

A colonel on Santa Anna's staff, de la Mora took part in the assault on the north wall during the final battle at the Alamo. He was killed at San Jacinto.

VENTURA MORA
(1796–1853)

A native of Tampico, Mora was a colonel, with the acting rank of general, during the Texas Campaign. He commanded the Permanent Dolores Cavalry Regiment, which was part of the Vanguard.

Mora also served in the Mexican-American War, and at the time of his death was the commandant general of Zacatecas.

JUAN MORALES
(1802–1847?)

Col. Juan Morales was born in Puebla, one of the few native-born officers in the Mexican army. During the Texas Campaign, he commanded the Active Battalion from San Luis Potosi, part of the Vanguard. During the Siege of the Alamo, Morales supervised the construction of the earthworks around La Villita. In the final attack, he led the assault on the south wall and the wooden palisade near the chapel that was defended by Davy Crockett and the Tennessee Mounted Volunteers.

After the fall of the Alamo, Morales was sent to join General Urrea's column. He took part in the attack on Fannin's men at La Coleto Creek, and was one of the Mexican officers who negotiated the surrender. Morales was captured at San Jacinto, and afterwards supported Urrea in his opposition to the retreat across the Rio Grande.

During the Mexican-American War, Morales commanded Vera Cruz when it was captured by Winfield Scott's army. Energetic and widely respected, he is often referred to as "the brave Morales" in Mexican journals and diaries.

JOSÉ MARÍA ORTEGA

Ortega was a lieutenant colonel who held the office of "commander of equipment" for the Army of Operations.

FRANCISCO PAVON

During the Texas Campaign, Pavon was a colonel in command of the Permanent Tampico Cavalry Regiment of the Cavalry Brigade.

JOSÉ ENRIQUE de la PENA
(1807–1841 or 1842)

José Enrique de la Pena is probably the most controversial Mexican officer, next to Santa Anna, to have participated in the Texas Campaign. His alleged narrative of the campaign, first published in Mexico in 1955, contains much interesting detail, but its accuracy has been debated, often passionately, by professional and amateur historians alike. De la Pena himself has been characterized as anything from a loyal and gifted officer, to a calculating, self-seeking, politically motivated opportunist.

José Enrique de la Pena was born in Jalisco, Mexico, in 1807. According to Carmen Perry, who translated de la Pena's narrative, he received a good education as a mining engineer. He joined the Mexican navy as a first-class cadet in 1825. In 1827 he was only a second lieutenant, but was very outspoken in his ideas about the management of the navy. That same year, he was on detached duty with the army engineers when he asked to be assigned to a Mexican legation in a European country.

In 1828 de la Pena published his first of several articles in the newspaper *El Sol,* under the pseudonym "Lover of the Navy." These were uncomplimentary articles about David Porter, an American who was serving as commander of the Mexican navy.

De la Pena met Santa Anna for the first time in 1828, while on his way to Vera Cruz for a tour of sea duty. Instead of going to sea, he wound up being assigned to serve with Santa Anna, and fought under him in the Battle of Tampico. In 1829 de la Pena became adjutant to Gen. Melchor Muzquiz, and in 1830 he was ill with smallpox for several months.

In 1831 de la Pena attended a mathematics course at the Mexican Military College, and then was ordered to Acapulco for sea duty and navigational study. He claimed illness and tried to get out of the assignment, but was eventually required to report for duty on the corvette *Morales.*

When Santa Anna came into power in 1833, de la Pena petitioned for a commission as a lieutenant colonel in the army. He was made a captain of cavalry, effective March 9, 1833. In December he was assigned to the "Federal Division of the President." In May 1834 he requested to be assigned to the Mexican Legation in the United States. When his orders finally came through, de la Pena was assigned to London instead. Unhappy with this, he requested that the assignment be changed to Paris.

When the Texas Revolution broke out, de la Pena was serving as a staff officer in the elite Zapadores Battalion, with the rank of lieutenant (and that is the rank we will use). It is unknown when or why he was demoted from captain. During the Texas Campaign, although still technically assigned to the Zapadores, de la Pena served as an aide to Col. Francisco Duque of the Toluca Battalion.

Carmen Perry claims that de la Pena held the rank of lieutenant colonel at this time, but this is not supported by army records. On the march into Texas, he may have been promoted back to captain. Gen. Miguel A. Sanchez Lamego implied this in his book on the history of the Zapadores Battalion. (This book is very rare, has never been translated into English, and the authors have not had the opportunity to examine it. This information was passed on to us by Alamo historians Bill Groneman and Thomas Ricks Lindley.)

De la Pena arrived in San Antonio de Bexar with the Toluca Battalion on March 4. He is known to have made several trips to and from the rear, carrying messages, during the Toluca Battalion's attack on the north wall in the final assault on the Alamo. Army records indicate that he received a bruise during the battle, but no further details are given. (Tom Lindley advises us that Sanchez Lamego states in his Zapadores history that de la Pena suffered a head wound in the fighting. However, Sanchez Lamego makes no mention of this in his other book, *The Siege and Taking of the Alamo.*)

De la Pena saw no further action after the Battle of the Alamo, although he received letters from several senior officers commending his service during the campaign. He was definitely a captain in the Zapadores Battalion in December 1836, when he testified at an inquiry into General Filisola's actions after San Jacinto. De la Pena also authored a series of newspaper articles that were critical of Filisola. In these articles, de la Pena mentions having kept a diary during the Texas Campaign, but makes no mention of any executions after the fall of the Alamo.

By April 1837, and perhaps earlier, de la Pena was brevetted to the rank of lieutenant colonel, while apparently still retaining the permanent rank of captain. At that time, he was ordered to Sonora to serve under General Urrea. He took part in Urrea's uprising in support of the Constitution of 1824, was captured by government troops, and was imprisoned at Guadalajara.

In 1839 de la Pena wrote an article from prison, which was never published, that contains his first known mention of the Alamo executions. He did not mention Davy Crockett by name, and did not claim to have been an eyewitness to these executions. (Unfortunately, no original copies of this article are known to exist, only reprints, so its authenticity cannot be clearly established.)

De la Pena is believed to have been dishonorably discharged from the Mexican army in 1839 or 1840, and he died poor and in obscurity in either 1841 or 1842.

AGUSTÍN PERALTA

During the Texas Campaign, Peralta was an acting colonel and the "keeper of orders," or adjutant, for General Tolsa, of the 2nd Infantry Brigade.

IGNACIO PRETULIA

Pretulia was a colonel in command of the Guanajuato Auxiliaries, of the 1st Infantry Brigade, during the Texas Campaign.

THE TROUBLESOME DE LA PENA NARRATIVE

It is not our intent to get into a full-blown discussion of the validity of the de la Pena narrative in this book. Those who are really interested can follow up on the sources listed in our bibliography for the pros and cons of the argument. However, so as not to leave the reader totally confused, we offer the following brief explanation.

The actual de la Pena manuscript is not bound in book form. It is a series of loose papers currently housed at the University of Texas in San Antonio. If the book was ever published in de la Pena's lifetime, or in the nineteenth century for that matter, no copies or legitimate references to it have been found.

The first known printed version was published in Spanish by J. Sanchez Garza, in Mexico City, in 1955. The book was entitled *La Rebelion de Texas—Manuscrito Inedito de 1836 por un Ofical de Santa Anna.* In Spanish, *inedito* is an adjective meaning "unpublished," implying that this is the first time that the book was appearing in print. The English translation, *With Santa Anna in Texas: A Personal Narrative of the Revolution,* was published by Texas A&M University in 1975. It was translated and edited by Carmen Perry.

The book is most certainly not a diary kept chronologically by de la Pena as the events transpired. If it is authentic, it is a "narrative," completed after the fact. Such a narrative could reasonably combine de la Pena's personal notes with other information that he was able to accumulate, such as the copy of Travis' "Victory or Death" letter that the manuscript contains. It is also possible that some of the work is authentically de la Pena's, while other parts were added by other, unknown individuals.

At any rate, the de la Pena document is an interesting account of the Texas Campaign, containing some very perceptive observations. If it is not original, then the person who wrote it or added to it had a pretty good feel for the subject. In using the narrative for this book, we have focused on the more generic sections, and have tried to stay away from the controversial portions that are not supported by other verifiable sources.

FRANCISCO QUINTERO
(1805–1872)

Quintero was a native Mexican officer born in Puebla. During the Texas Campaign, he was an acting colonel, commanding the Active Battalion from Mexico City, part of the 2nd Infantry Brigade. Later in his career, Quintero fought against the French Intervention.

JOSÉ RAMIREZ

José Ramirez was a captain who commanded the Permanent Tampico Cavalry Regiment, part of General Urrea's Column, during the Texas Campaign.

JOAQUIN RAMIREZ y SESMA

Joaquin Ramirez y Sesma was an acting brigadier general during the Texas Campaign. He was sent to reinforce General Cos during the Battle of Bexar in December 1835. He was unable to reach Cos before his surrender, however, so he took up station along the Rio Grande and awaited the arrival of the rest of Santa Anna's army.

Ramirez y Sesma commanded the Vanguard of the Army of Operations during its march into Texas. During the final assault on the Alamo, he commanded the cavalry, with instructions to intercept any of the defenders who tried to escape.

Ramirez y Sesma also commanded the first element of the Mexican army to march east out of San Antonio de Bexar, on March 11, after the fall of the Alamo. After San Jacinto, he was the second-in-command of the remaining Mexican forces, under General Filisola, on the retreat back to Mexico.

JOSÉ REYES y LOPEZ

Reyes y Lopez was the commissary general of the Army of Operations. He suffered from rheumatism, and had to ride in General Filisola's carriage during the campaign.

JOSÉ ROBELO

Robelo was the civilian treasurer/accountant of the Army of Operations.

JOSÉ MARÍA ROMERO
(1798?–?)

Romero was the colonel of the Permanent Matamoros Battalion, which was part of the Vanguard. He also commanded the column that attacked from the east during the final assault on the Alamo. Romero was captured after the Battle of San Jacinto.

ANTONIO LÓPEZ de SANTA ANNA PEREZ de LEBRON
(February 21, 1794–June 22, 1876)

Santa Anna was born in Jalapa, Vera Cruz, of middle-class Criollo parents. He was a vain, ambitious, and cruel man who was an opium addict and a womanizer. He tended to favor whichever side was in power at the time. Along with his vices, however, he had a number of gifts that he used to his full advantage.

Santa Anna was charismatic, and possessed an uncanny ability to regain power when he lost it. He held the presidency of Mexico four times: 1833–1835, 1841–1844, in 1847, and again in 1853–1855.

Santa Anna was appointed as a cadet in the Fio de Cruz infantry regiment in 1810. He first saw service against hostile Indians in the Mexican interior. In the Mexican Revolution of 1810–1821, he fought for the Royalists. In 1813 he went to Texas with Gen. Joaquin de Arredondo to fight against American and Tejano rebels, where he was cited for bravery at the Battle of Medina.

In 1821 Santa Anna was a lieutenant colonel, serving on the staff of Gen. Agustin Iturbide, commander of the Royalist armies. However, when Iturbide declared himself emperor in 1822, Santa Anna joined the Republicans, who eventually forced Iturbide into exile. Santa Anna's changing sides may have been personal as much as political, for he was angry with Iturbide for failing to support him in a quarrel with another officer.

Santa Anna was one of those who drafted the liberal Constitution of 1824. He served as the military governor of Yucatan, and then as the civil governor of Vera Cruz. In 1829 he became a national hero for his actions at Tampico, against a Spanish force that was trying to reconquer Mexico.

Santa Anna was elected president as a liberal in 1833. As was so typical of him, however, he soon changed from his liberal position, and began to concentrate power under the central government. He eventually established himself as dictator, and abolished the Constitution of 1824, which he had originally helped to write. In 1835 he put down a revolt in Zacatecas with extreme ruthlessness.

Gen. Antonio López de Santa Anna

Santa Anna next determined to do the same to the rebels in Texas. He assumed personal command of the Army of Operations during the Texas Campaign, and commanded the Mexican forces during the Siege of the Alamo. After the disastrous Mexican defeat at San Jacinto, Santa Anna was captured by the Texians. In exchange for his personal safety, he ordered his armies out of Texas and back south across the Rio Grande. After the Texas Revolution, he was taken to Washington, D.C., and then was allowed to return to Mexico in 1837.

In the 1838 "Pastry War" against France, Santa Anna lost a leg, and he used this injury to make himself a hero to the Mexican people. At the beginning of the Mexican-American War, he sent overtures to the United States, offering to arrange a quick end to the fighting in exchange for his own return to power.

In 1855 Santa Anna was forced from the presidency for the last time, and spent most of the rest of his life in exile. Late in his life, he was permitted to return to Vera Cruz to live out his remaining days.

MARIANO SALAS

Salas was an acting colonel and commander of the Permanent Jiminez Battalion, part of the Vanguard, during the Texas Campaign. He was second-in-command of the column that attacked the Alamo from the east during the final assault.

Salas lead the charge against Fannin's center during the Battle of La Coleto Creek, and was one of the Mexican officers who negotiated the Texians' surrender. On April 21 he was made military commandant at Columbia.

JOSÉ JUAN SANCHEZ-NAVARRO
(?–1849)

At the beginning of the Texas Campaign, Sanchez-Navarro was the assistant inspector of the provinces of Tamaulipas and Nuevo Leon. As a lieutenant colonel, and General Cos' adjutant, he fought in the Battle of Bexar in December 1835, and signed the surrender papers for the Mexicans.

Sanchez-Navarro also fought during the Siege of the Alamo, and made an excellent, detailed map that is one of the best sources of information about positions during the siege. (See Chapter Seven.) He died in Saltillo in 1849.

AGUSTÍN TERAN

Teran was a captain and commander of artillery for the 1st Infantry Brigade of the Army of Operations.

LUIS TOLA
(1802–1887)

Luis Tola was a lieutenant colonel and commander of engineers for the Army of Operations. Later in his career, he served as the director of the Mexican Military College.

EUGENIO TOLSA

Tolsa was an acting brigadier general in command of the 2nd Infantry Brigade during the Texas Campaign.

JOSÉ MARÍA TORNEL y MENDIVIL
(1789–1853)

Tornel y Mendivil fought with the rebels during the Mexican Revolution. He was captured and sentenced to death, but managed to escape. He was a staunch Centralist during the Texas Revolution, and as an acting brigadier general, served as minister of war and of the navy.

Tornel tended to underrate the fighting abilities of the Texians, while overestimating what the Mexican army was capable of. "The superiority of the Mexican soldier over the mountaineers of Kentucky and the hunters of Missouri is well known. . . . Veterans seasoned by twenty years of wars can't be intimidated by the presence of an army ignorant of the art of war, incapable of discipline, and renowned for insubordination," he boldly stated. (Hardin: *Texian Iliad,* 98)

Tornel was also a man of intellect, a great orator, and a strong force in Mexico's educational system. Above all, he was a staunch Mexican patriot who energetically opposed any threat to his country.

JOSÉ MARÍA TORRES
(?–March 6, 1836)

José María Torres was a young sublieutenant in the Zapadores Battalion. He entered the Mexican Military College in 1832 or 1833, and received his commission as a sublieutenant in July of 1834.

During the final assault on the Alamo, Torres was killed while valiantly trying to take down the Texians' colors—probably the flag of the New Orleans Greys. He is buried in the *campo santo* (Catholic cemetery) in San Antonio.

GREGORIO URUNUELA

Gregorio Urunuela was a lieutenant colonel, in command of the Aldama Battalion of the 1st Infantry Brigade, during the Texas Campaign.

DOMINGO de UGARTECHEA
(?–1839)

Domingo de Ugartechea served in the Spanish army during the Battle of Medina. In 1832 he commanded the Mexican forces at Velasco when they were forced to surrender to the Texians.

In 1835 de Ugartechea was a colonel, in command of San Antonio de Bexar. It was he who ordered Lt. Francisco Castaneda to Gonzales to recover a loaned cannon from the Texians. The resulting skirmish was the opening action of the Texas Revolution.

When Cos' army was besieged by the Texians, de Ugartechea led a relief column from Laredo to Bexar. He commanded the presidial cavalry during the Siege of Bexar, and also commanded the Mexican forces at the Battle of Concepción. De Ugartechea was killed during a rebellion in Saltillo in 1839.

JUAN JOSÉ URREA
(1795–1849)

Juan José Urrea, whom many believe was the most talented Mexican officer in the Army of Operations, was born in Tucson in 1795. He was the son of a presidial cavalry officer, and entered the army himself as a cadet at age twelve. He fought in a number of battles on the rebel side during the Mexican Revolution. After the Spanish were defeated, Urrea left the army with the rank of captain.

Urrea returned to active duty when the Spanish captured Tampico in 1829. He was promoted to lieutenant colonel in 1832, and to full colonel when Santa Anna became president. He served as the Mexican minister to Columbia, where he became friends with William Henry Harrison, who was the U.S. minister there. In 1834 Urrea helped to put down the rebellion in Zacatecas. In 1835 he was promoted to acting brigadier general and was sent to Durango to fight the Apaches.

During the Texas Campaign, Urrea commanded the southern wing of the Army of Operations, which came up along the Gulf Coast. He won victories at San Patricio, Refugio, and La Coleto Creek. the latter resulting in the capture of Fannin's army. Urrea opposed the subsequent massacre of Fannin's men, but complied after he received a direct order from Santa Anna.

After San Jacinto, Urrea urged Filisola to disregard Santa Anna's orders to evacuate Texas. He replaced Filisola as commander of the Army of Operations in June 1836.

Urrea was a strong anti-Centralist and joined the resistance against Santa Anna. He was defeated at Mazatlan in 1838, and was imprisoned and escaped several times. In 1840 he fought unsuccessfully against the Bustamante government.

In 1841 Urrea helped the newly proclaimed "Federalist" Santa Anna regain power. He served as governor of Sonora, and held other military and civil posts. During the Mexican-American War, he led a cavalry division. He died of cholera in Durango in 1849.

RAFAEL de la VARA

During the Texas Campaign, de la Vara was an acting colonel commanding the Permanent Cuautla Cavalry Regiment, part of General Urrea's column.

ROMULO DIAZ de la VEGA

De la Vega was "First Battalion Aide" to Colonel Duque. He was one of the first men to fight his way up and over the wall of the Alamo during the final battle. This brave accomplishment is noted in his official service record.

ADRIAN WOLL

A German by birth, Woll fought with Mina's forces during the Mexican Revolution. As an acting brigadier general, he served as quartermaster general of the Army of Operations. He commanded the Mexican Army of the North that invaded Texas in 1842, and supported the French occupation of Mexico. Woll died in France.

CHAPTER TWELVE

A Chronology

PART 1: A CHRONOLOGY OF THE TEXAS REVOLUTION

This chronology gives an overview of the important events of the Texas Revolution. A basic knowledge of these events is important for a clear understanding of the defense of the Alamo. In some cases there are slight discrepancies among various sources as to exactly when a particular event occurred. In these instances, we have used the most logical date in this chronology.

* * * * * 1833 * * * * *

September

Jim Bowie's wife Ursula, and according to some sources, his two children, die of cholera.

* * * * * 1835 * * * * *

Late June

William Barret Travis raises a company of twenty-five volunteers and captures Capt. Antonio Tenorio and the Mexican garrison at Anahuac, in East Texas.

October 2

The Stand at Gonzales

A Mexican cavalry detachment, the Second Flying Company of El Alamo de Parras, is sent to repossess a cannon that the government has given to the citizens of Gonzales for protection against hostile Indians. Under a flag defying the Mexicans to "Come and Take It," 150 Texians under Col. John Moore briefly exchange fire with 100 Mexicans under Capt. Francisco Castaneda. When the Texians advance, Castaneda withdraws his men rather than provoke a larger incident.

October 3

In Mexico City, the Mexican National Congress strips the state legislatures of their power, giving full control of the government to Santa Anna, and effectively abolishing the Constitution of 1824.

October 9

Gen. Martín Perfecto de Cos arrives in San Antonio de Bexar with reinforcements, and assumes personal command of the garrison.

In the evening, a force of forty-seven Texians under Capt. George M. Collinsworth take Goliad, also known as La Bahía. The presidio's twenty-eight-man garrison and a quantity of valuable supplies are captured in the surprise attack.

October 28

The Battle of Concepción

At Mission Concepción, about two miles south of San Antonio de Bexar, ninety Texians under Col. James Bowie are attacked by vastly superior numbers of Mexicans from the Morelos Battalion. Bowie's men dig in along the riverbank and withstand several assaults before the Mexicans withdraw. The Texians capture a six-pound cannon and kill an estimated fifty to sixty of the enemy. They also suffer their first combat death of the war, Richard Andrews, of La Vaca.

October 30

The Mexican National Congress authorizes war against the rebels in Texas.

November 1

Renowned frontiersman and former U.S. Congressman David Crockett starts down the Mississippi River for Texas.

Texian forces have General Cos' garrison in San Antonio de Bexar surrounded.

November 15

William Barret Travis, now a captain in the Regular Texas Cavalry, is leading a twelve-man patrol about seventy miles west of San Antonio. He encounters and captures a herd of 300 Mexican horses and ten mules, which will be put to good use by the Texian Army.

The Tampico Expedition

As the climax of an expedition marked by mishaps, Mexican Federalist José Antonio Mexia and American George Fisher lead an ill-advised attack on the Mexican city of Tampico, hoping that Mexican liberals would join them to help overthrow Santa Anna. The Mexican garrison easily defeats them; three of the invaders are killed in battle, and twenty-eight are executed by the Mexicans. Mexia himself escapes and flees back to Texas.

November 25

Governor Henry Smith signs a bill establishing the Texas Navy, consisting of two twelve-gun schooners and two six-gun schooners.

November 26

The Grass Fight

As the Texians besiege San Antonio de Bexar, Col. James Bowie takes a detachment to attack a thirty-mule Mexican pack train about a mile south of town along Alazan Creek. During the give and take battle, both sides are reinforced. The Mexicans are eventually driven from the field and the supply train is captured by the Texians. However, instead of carrying the expected payroll for the Mexican garrison, the mules are loaded with freshly cut grass to be used as forage for the Mexican horses. The somewhat embarrased Texians dub the incident "The Grass Fight."

November 28

Santa Anna leaves Mexico City to organize his army and put down the rebellion in Texas.

December 2

Two residents of San Antonio de Bexar, Samuel Maverick and John W. Smith, report to the Texian besiegers that Cos' men are hungry, demoralized, and low on ammunition as a result of the siege.

December 5

Tired of the boredom and lack of progress of the siege, Col. Ben Milam asks for volunteers to follow him in an attack on San Antonio de Bexar.

December 9

After a seven-week siege and several days of house to house, hand to hand fighting, General Cos asks for a truce.

December 10

San Antonio de Bexar is formally surrendered by General Cos, and the garrison is paroled after promising never to fight in Texas again.

December 12

The Mobile Greys, including James Butler Bonham, arrive in San Antonio.

December 20

The "first" Texian Declaration of Independence is ratified by the garrison at La Bahía, or Goliad. The rash, unauthorized act is quickly disavowed by other Texian leaders.

December 21

Gen. Sam Houston appoints Lt. Col. James Neill, of the Regular Texas Artillery, commander of the garrison at San Antonio de Bexar.

December 30

Colonels Frank Johnson and James Grant lead a controversial expedition from San Antonio de Bexar against the Mexican town of Matamoros.

December 31

Santa Anna begins assembling his army at San Luis Potosi, some 365 miles from Bexar. One segment, under General Ramirez y Sesma, is already waiting at the Rio Grande.

*** * * * * 1836 * * * * ***

January 7

Santa Anna's army arrives at Saltillo.

January 10-11

Reflecting the new Texas government's political

troubles, on January 10 Governor Henry Smith dissolves the General Council until a general convention meeting scheduled for March 1. In retaliation, on January 11, the General Council impeaches Governor Smith, and appoints Lieutenant Governor James Robinson as acting governor until the March 1 convention. Although there are many reasons for the disagreement, the controversy over the Matamoros expedition is a major cause of this crisis.

January 19

Col. James Bowie arrives at the Alamo. Most sources claim that Bowie had instructions from Sam Houston to destroy and abandon the mission, but there is controversy over just how much discretion, if any, he was given.

January 22

The Navarro family of San Antonio de Bexar reports to Bowie that Santa Anna is approaching with 4,600 men.

January 25

Prior to beginning his march into Texas, Santa Anna holds a grand review of his army at Saltillo.

January 27

José Cassiano comes into San Antonio de Bexar, bringing Bowie detailed information about the strength of Gen. Joaquin Ramirez y Sesma's division of the army. Sesma has about 2,000 soldiers, and is camped at the Rio Grande, awaiting the arrival of Santa Anna's main force.

January 31

The new Texas Navy now consists of four ships:

1. The *Invincible,* 125 tons, six carronades, and a nine-pound swivel gun. It is the flagship of the fleet.
2. The *Independence,* 125 tons, 11 guns.
3. The *Brutus,* 160 tons, seven guns, including one eighteen-pounder.
4. The *Liberty,* 60 tons, 6 six-pounders.

February 1

Santa Anna's army arrives at Monclova.

February 2

After careful consideration of the situation at the Alamo, Bowie writes Governor Smith that he and the garrison commander, Lt. Col. James Neill, have decided that the old mission must be defended. Scouts report that Santa Anna's main army, 5,000 strong, is marching to join Sesma's force.

On or About February 3

Lt. Col. William Barret Travis and about thirty men arrive at the Alamo.

On or About February 8

The "Tennessee Mounted Volunteers," including the famous David Crockett, arrive at the Alamo.

February 10

A *fandango* is held to celebrate the arrival of Crockett and his men. The combined Bexar/Alamo garrison now numbers approximately 142 men.

February 11

Lt. Col. William Barret Travis takes over command of the Bexar/Alamo garrison from Lt. Col. James Neill, who goes on leave because of an illness in his family.

February 12

Santa Anna's army reaches the Rio Grande and joins Ramirez y Sesma's division.

February 14

After some initial friction, James Bowie and William Barret Travis arrive at an agreement to share the command of the garrison.

February 16

A relative of the Ambrosio Rodriguez family arrives from Laredo to warn his relatives that Santa Anna is about to cross the Rio Grande into Texas. They share the warning with Travis.

Santa Anna's army, including Ramirez y Sesma's division, crosses the Rio Grande into Texas. Another division, under Gen. José Urrea, is moving up the Gulf Coast.

In an official dispatch to Mexico, Santa Anna writes that he hopes to take San Antonio de Bexar by March 2.

February 17

Santa Anna reaches the Nueces River, 119 miles from San Antonio de Bexar.

February 19
Santa Anna is at the Rio Frio, sixty-eight miles from San Antonio de Bexar.

February 20
Santa Anna is at the Hondo River, less than fifty miles from San Antonio de Bexar. Blas Herrera, a member of Juan Seguin's cavalry company, reports that he personally saw Santa Anna's army crossing the Rio Grande.

February 21
Santa Anna arrives at the Medina River, twenty-five miles from San Antonio de Bexar.

February 21-22
Upon receiving word of a *fandango* planned for that evening, Santa Anna orders General Ramirez y Sesma's cavalry to launch a surprise night attack on the garrison at San Antonio de Bexar. Heavy rains force the cancellation of the raid.

February 23
Reliable scouts report that the Mexicans have nearly reached San Antonio de Bexar, and the Texians and loyal Mexicans quickly make their final move into the Alamo. Travis sends another courier with a plea for help, "To any of the inhabitants of Texas . . ."

The first elements of the Mexican army arrive in San Antonio de Bexar. The Mexicans raise the red flag of "no quarter" from the tower of the San Fernando Cathedral, and the Texians defiantly respond with a cannon shot.

James Butler Bonham returns to the Alamo after his mission to get help from Col. James Walker Fannin, the commander at Goliad.

February 24
Early in the morning, a gravely ill Jim Bowie turns complete command of the Alamo garrison over to William Barret Travis.

In the early afternoon, the first Mexican guns open fire on the Alamo.

Travis writes his famous "I am besieged" letter. Courier Albert Martin carries it through the Mexican lines without incident. The letter reaches Gonzales on February 25, San Felipe de Austin on February 27, New Orleans on March 16, New York City on March 30, and Washington, D.C. and Boston on March 31.

During the evening, the Mexican army band serenades the Alamo garrison.

February 25
About 300 Mexican troops occupy La Villita. A party of Texians sortie out to burn some of the *jacales,* or huts, that offer the Mexicans cover only about 100 yards from the walls of the Alamo. By noon, the Mexicans withdraw, but later return to La Villita and dig in.

Juan Seguin borrows Bowie's horse and rides out of the Alamo carrying a desperate message from Travis to Houston.

Col. James Fannin's relief expedition leaves Goliad bound for the Alamo.

February 26
In the early morning, a party of Texians drive off Mexican cavalry that is trying to circle around to the rear of the Alamo. There is also more fighting around La Villita. Members of the Alamo garrison burn some *jacales* near the position of the San Luis Potosi Battalion.

Discouraged by wagon breakdowns and bad weather, Fannin gives up his relief effort and returns to Goliad.

February 27
The Mexicans attempt to seal off the irrigation ditch that supplies the Alamo garrison with water.

James Bonham carries another message from Travis to Fannin.

Santa Anna sends a courier to Mexico City, boasting of his capture of San Antonio de Bexar. He fails to mention the continuing resistance of the garrison defending the Alamo.

The Gonzales Ranging Company of Mounted Volunteers, the "Immortal 32," leave Gonzales to reinforce the Alamo.

The Battle of San Patricio
A Mexican cavalry force about 450 strong, under Gen. José Urrea, surprises part of the Matamoros expedition under Col. Frank Johnson, who had sought refuge from bad weather in the town of San

Patricio. Ten Texians are killed and eighteen captured in a three-hour battle. Mexican losses are four dead and six wounded. Six Texians, including Colonel Johnson, escape.

February 28

The Mexicans again try to cut off the Alamo's water supply, and establish an artillery battery at the Old Mill, 800 yards north of the mission.

February 29

Bonham reaches Goliad, where Fannin advises that he is unable to relieve the Alamo garrison. Determined to find help, Bonham rides on to Gonzales. Sam Houston joins the political convention at Washington-on-the-Brazos.

March 1

Bonham reaches Gonzales, only to find that all of those able to help have already left for the Alamo.

The Gonzales Volunteers, under Captains George Kimball and George Martin, ride into the Alamo at 3:00 A.M.

To celebrate the arrival of the reinforcements from Gonzales, Travis authorizes two artillery rounds. One shot strikes Santa Anna's headquarters, but His Excellency is off inspecting troop positions, and is unharmed.

March 2

The delegates to the convention at Washington-on-the-Brazos unanimously ratify the Texas Declaration of Independence.

Dr. James Grant and fifteen men are ambushed and killed by General Urrea's forces at Agua Dulce Creek, as they are returning from a horse hunting expedition along the Rio Grande.

March 3

Bonham rides into the Alamo for the final time. He brings a message from Maj. R. M. Williamson urging Travis to hold out, promising that help is on the way.

More Mexican reinforcements arrive at San Antonio de Bexar, giving Santa Anna a total of 2,400 men and ten pieces of artillery.

Scout Erastus "Deaf" Smith, who led the "Gonzales 32" into the Alamo, rides out at midnight for Washington-on-the-Brazos with another plea for help, as well as final personal letters from Travis.

March 4

Gen. Sam Houston is appointed commander-in-chief of all Texian forces, regular and volunteer alike, by the convention at Washington-on-the-Brazos.

A new Mexican battery, only 200 yards from the north wall, opens fire on the Alamo, causing severe damage but no deaths.

Santa Anna calls a meeting of his senior officers to discuss whether they should attempt to take the Alamo by storm.

During the evening, a Mexican woman slips out of the Alamo and into Santa Anna's camp, reporting on the desperate state of the defenders.

March 5

The Mexican battery bearing on the north wall of the Alamo is now only 200 yards away. The garrison still has not had a man killed.

Santa Anna decides that the time has come to storm the Alamo, and by midafternoon, has his battle plan formulated.

Mexican fire slows considerably in the late afternoon. Travis calls the garrison together and delivers a passionate speech, offering each man the choice between fighting to the death or trying to escape. If Travis really drew a line in the sand with his saber, this is most likely when it happened.

The Mexican units designated as the reserve force for the coming assault begin to move into position at 5:00 P.M.

The Alamo defenders take advantage of the lull in the bombardment to make repairs on the damaged walls, and then catch some much needed rest.

Twenty-one-year-old James Allen rides out of the Alamo with Travis' last plea for help.

Mexican officers and NCOs begin to awaken their sleeping men at midnight.

March 6

The four Mexican attack columns begin to move to their positions, 1:00 A.M.

All of the Mexican attack columns are now in position, 4:00 A.M.

As officer of the day, Capt. John Baugh begins making his rounds in the Alamo, 5:00 A.M.

The assault begins at 5:00 A.M., with the four Mexican columns rushing toward their assigned walls simultaneously.

After ninety minutes of fierce hand-to-hand fighting, the Alamo falls by 6:30 A.M. and all of the defenders are dead.

March 7

Santa Anna meets with the noncombatant survivors of the Alamo.

March 10

Mexican reinforcements continue arriving in San Antonio de Bexar. Gen. Vicente Filisola, second-in-command of the Army of Operations, is among them. Santa Anna issues the following orders for the continuation of his Texas Campaign:

1. A force under Gen. Juan Andrade is ordered to remain in San Antonio de Bexar to care for the men wounded in the assault on the Alamo.
2. Col. Juan Morales is ordered to take a column to reinforce General Urrea's men at La Bahía, or Goliad. After capturing Goliad, this force is to continue eastward, then up the coast to Brazoria, crushing any Texian resistance that it meets.
3. Gen. Antonio Gaona is instructed to march from San Antonio de Bexar to Bastrop, and then to Nacogdoches, also engaging any Texian forces they meet along the way. This column consists of 700 men.
4. Gen. Joaquin Ramirez y Sesma and 1,500 men are to go from Bexar to the Colorado River, cross to the east bank, and then march on San Felipe.

March 11

Susannah Dickinson and her daughter Angelina leave the Alamo for Gonzales, escorted by Col. Juan Almonte's chef, Ben, and Travis' slave, Joe.

Sam Houston arrives at Gonzales to organize his army.

The first elements of the Mexican army, under Gen. Ramirez y Sesma, march east from the Alamo headed for Gonzales and San Felipe de Austin.

March 13

A scouting party led by Deaf Smith runs into the Dickinson party twenty miles from Gonzales, and brings them to Houston. They confirm the fate of the Alamo's defenders.

March 14

Houston burns and abandons Gonzales then heads east, moving away from Santa Anna's army.

The Battle of Refugio

Refugio, an old mission twenty-seven miles southeast of Goliad, is occupied by twenty-nine men of the Kentucky Mustangs under Capt. Amon King, and 120 men of the Georgia Battalion under Maj. William Ward. They are attacked by 1,500 Mexicans under Gen. José Urrea. The Texians repel four Mexican assaults, and then slip away under cover of darkness. Before they leave, they insure the safe escape of friendly local families. The Texians lose about fifteen men, while the Mexican losses are estimated at eighty.

March 16

Thirty of the men who fled from the Mission Refugio, mostly from the Kentucky Mustangs and including Captain King, are overtaken by the Mexicans. After a twelve-hour battle, they surrender with the understanding that they will be treated as prisoners of war. They are taken back to the mission, and in keeping with Santa Anna's policy of no quarter, they are all executed.

The Convention at Washington-on-the Brazos ratifies the new constitution for the Republic of Texas, and elects the following interim officers until a regular election can be held:

President: David G. Burnet
Vice-President: Lorenzo de Zavala
Secretary of State: Samuel P. Carson
Secretary of War: Thomas J. Rusk
Secretary of the Navy: Robert Potter
Secretary of the Treasury: Bailey Hardeman
Attorney General: David Thomas

March 17

Houston halts his army at the Colorado River for a week, hoping to rendezvous with Fannin's men.

March 18

Complying with orders from General Houston, Col. James W. Fannin makes plans to abandon Goliad and head for Victoria, twenty-four miles to the southeast.

March 19

The Battle of La Coleto Creek

Near La Coleto Creek, about ten miles from Goliad, Fannin's men halt to repair an ammunition wagon and are overtaken by General Urrea's troops. In several hours of fighting, the Mexicans surround the Texians but suffer an estimated 250 casualties in the process. Texian losses are nine killed and about 60 wounded, including Fannin.

March 20

Surrounded by Urrea's 1,500 men, Fannin surrenders after being assured that the Texians will be treated as prisoners of war and that the wounded will receive medical treatment. The Texians are marched back to La Bahía and interned inside their former fort.

March 23

Maj. William Ward and the survivors of the Georgia Battalion who fled Refugio are discovered by some of Urrea's men as they try to hide near the banks of the Guadalupe River. Their ammunition almost gone, the Texians are forced to surrender after a brief exchange of shots. They are taken to La Bahia, where they join Fannin's men as prisoners.

March 26

Having learned of Fannin's surrender, Houston orders his army to resume its march eastward.

March 27

After being held prisoner for a week, Fannin's men are marched out into the open and executed. In spite of the terms of surrender, Santa Anna has ordered that the prisoners be killed. "As the supreme government has ordered that all foreigners taken with arms in their hands, making war upon the nation, shall be treated as pirates. . . . I therefore order that you should give immediate effect to the said ordinance. . . . I trust that in reply to this, you will inform me that public vengeance has been satisfied. . . ." (Weems, 83-84) Also killed are Ward's Georgia Battalion men.

March 28

New Orleans newspapers report the fall of the Alamo.

March 29

Houston abandons San Felipe de Austin. Although this move leaves the surrounding countryside defenseless, he is unwilling to risk a fight before he is ready. Critics of this unpopular retreat dub it "The Runaway Scrape."

March 31

Santa Anna leaves the Alamo to join General Ramirez y Sesma's army.

April 2

Santa Anna reaches Gonzales.

April 7

Santa Anna arrives at San Felipe de Austin.

April 11

New York papers print the news of the fall of the Alamo.

April 12

Boston papers print the news of the fall of the Alamo.

April 14

Houston leaves Groce's Plantation and marches southeastward in order to stay ahead of the Mexican army.

Hearing that President Burnet and other officials are in Harrisburg, only thirty miles away, Santa Anna takes a hand-picked force of 750 men and tries to catch them by surprise. Burnet and the Texian officials are warned, and manage to flee in time to avoid capture. Santa Anna burns Harrisburg to the ground, and orders the presses of the town newspaper thrown into Buffalo Bayou.

April 16

Finally ready to fight, Houston leads his men toward Harrisburg, and the Mexican forces that are known to be nearby.

April 17

At New Washington, Interim President David G. Burnet is nearly captured. A patrol of Mexican Dragoons rides up just as he embarks into Galveston Bay in a small rowboat to be picked up by the Texas Navy ship *Flash.* Burnet is accompanied by his wife and several aides. In an act of chivalry, Col. Juan Almonte refuses to let his men fire on the rowboat for fear of hitting Mrs. Burnet. Almonte does, however, order that the settlement of New Washington be put to the torch.

Texian scouts Deaf Smith and Henry Karnes capture a Mexican courier bearing dispatches from Santa Anna, destined for Mexico City. The dispatches are carried in a leather saddlebag stamped "William Barret Travis." The courier claims he got the saddlebags in San Antonio de Bexar after the fall of the Alamo.

April 18

Houston's army reaches Buffalo Bayou, near Harrisburg. The Texians are now between Santa Anna's detached force and the main Mexican army.

April 19

Houston's army marches through the ashes of Harrisburg. About 250 sick men, most of whom have the measles, are left camped near the ruins of the town. Thanks to recent additions to his army, Houston is still left with about 1,000 effective fighting men.

April 20

Santa Anna's division of the Mexican army is about 900 strong. His scouts report that Houston is only eight miles away. The Mexicans mount a brief attack on the Texian positions, then withdraw when Houston's men refuse to come out and fight in the open. Both sides set up artillery positions, and an artillery duel commences. The day's engagement ends indecisively, and the Mexicans set up camp only 1,000 yards from the Texian positions.

April 21

Gen. Martín Perfecto de Cos joins Santa Anna with 400 reinforcements, bringing Mexican strength to about 1,500.

The Mexicans are placed on alert early in the day but by afternoon allow their security to become incredibly lax. At 4:00 P.M. the Texians mount a surprise attack on the Mexican camp. In eighteen minutes the battle is over and the Mexican army is completely defeated, but Santa Anna escapes.

April 22

A Texian patrol captures Santa Anna, dressed in a Mexican private's uniform. His identity is revealed when he is brought into camp, and captured Mexican soldiers shout, *"El Presidente!"* Houston demands that all remaining Mexican troops in Texas withdraw south of the Rio Grande. Santa Anna agrees, and for the time being, at least, the threat to Texas independence is over.

Alamo defenders on the gun ramp at the rear of the chapel.

Alamo defenders in the southwest corner of the compound.

Top left: *During the siege, the marksmanship skills of the Alamo defenders kept the Mexicans from coming too close to the Alamo's walls.*

Top right: *One of the most famous Alamo legends is that Lt. Col. William Barret Travis asked all of those who would stay in the Alamo and fight to the end to cross over a line that he drew in the sand with his sword. We do not know if this legend is true or not. If it is, the incident probably happened on March 5, when Travis did call the garrison together to give them the option of staying to fight or trying to escape.*

Bottom left: *One of the bravest of the Alamo defenders, James Butler Bonham, twice rode out of the Alamo with dispatches but returned to fight and die in the final battle.*

PART 2: WEATHER LOG

As is often the case in military operations, the weather played a significant part in Santa Anna's Texas Campaign. The Texians underestimated the ability of the Mexican army to march during the winter months, and were caught off guard when the first elements of the Army of Operations arrived in San Antonio de Bexar about six weeks before they were expected. From the Mexican standpoint, this march was not accomplished without cost. Cold weather, rain, and even snowstorms caused much suffering and death among the *soldados,* who were ill-clothed and not equipped for a cold weather campaign.

Today the average temperature range in San Antonio for mid-February is from 45 to 65 degrees Fahrenheit. In early March it varies from 47 to 70 degrees. In this section we have used a variety of sources to compile a "weather log" of conditions from early February through mid-March 1836 in order to help readers understand how the weather conditions may have affected the actions of both sides.

February 5, Friday

At Monclova, 59 degrees, rained at night. Per Juan Almonte. (Chariton: *100 Days,* 211)

February 6, Saturday

At Monclova, 59 degrees and cloudy. Per Juan Almonte. (Chariton: *100 Days,* 212)

February 7, Sunday

At Monclova, 62 degrees and clear. Per Juan Almonte. (Chariton: *100 Days,* 216)

February 13, Saturday

At Presidio de Rio Grande, 51 degrees and stormy. Per Juan Almonte. (Chariton: *100 Days,* 226)

A severe snowstorm strikes Santa Anna's army while it is on the march, causing much suffering and even some deaths. The heavy snow reached a depth of 15-16 inches, up to the knees of the suffering *soldados.* (Lord: *A Time to Stand,* 71; Filisola, Vol II: 157; and Sanchez Lamego, 22)

February 14, Sunday

At Presidio de Rio Grande, 46 degrees, weather moderates. Per Juan Almonte. (Chariton: *100 Days,* 231)

February 15, Monday

At Presidio de Rio Grande, 56 degrees, "fine weather for travellng." Per Juan Almonte. (Chariton: *100 Days,* 295)

February 17, Wednesday

At the Neuces River, "exceedingly hot at mid-day." Per Juan Almonte. (Chariton: *100 Days,* 243)

February 20, Saturday

At the Rio Frio, night clear and pleasant, 72 degrees, cloudy and misty but no rain during the day. Per Juan Almonte. (Chariton: *100 Days,* 247)

February 21, Sunday

At Arroyo Hondo, "not cold," cloudy, light showers, SE winds, heavy rain begins at 5:00 P.M., starts to clear by midnight. Per Juan Almonte. (Chariton: *100 Days,* 249)

February 22, Monday

At the Rio Medina, cloudy, cleared at 10:00 A.M.. Per Juan Almonte. (Chariton: *100 Days,* 249)

Numerous sources state that a sudden rainstorm in the evening forced cancellation of a Mexican plan to stage a surprise attack on the Texians in San Antonio de Bexar, while they were celebrating Washington's Birthday.

February 23, Tuesday

No information found.

February 24, Wednesday

No information found.

February 25, Thursday

At San Antonio de Bexar, a strong north wind comes up at 9:00 P.M. Per Juan Almonte. (Chariton: *100 Days,* 270) A "brisk norther" blew up, per Vicente Filisola. (Filisola: Vol. II:171)

Temperatures dropped from "summertime heat during the afternoon to near freezing after sunset." (Weems, 67)

Near San Patricio, a cold north wind hits at 7:00 P.M., and six soldiers of the Yucatan Battalion die from exposure. Per José Urrea. (Chariton: *100 Days,* 276)

February 26, Friday

At San Antonio de Bexar, strong north winds, temperature dropped to 39 degrees, then climbed back up to 60 degrees. Per Juan Almonte. (Chariton: *100 Days,* 276) The north wind continued, per Vicente Filisola. (Filisola, Vol. II:171)

At Washington-on-the-Brazos, it was excessively cold after yesterday's "summer heat." Per William Fairfax Gray. (Chariton: *100 Days,* 277)

On Urrea's line of march up the Gulf Coast, the night was excessively raw and cold, with a cold rain that "looked like snow" beginning at 3:00 A.M. "the dragoons, who were barely able to dismount, were so numbed by the cold that they could hardly speak . . ." Per José Urrea. (Chariton: *100 Days,* 277)

February 27, Saturday

At San Antonio de Bexar, 39 degrees with a strong north wind. Per Juan Almonte. (Chariton: *100 Days,* 277)

February 28, Sunday

At San Antonio de Bexar, the weather moderates; 40 degrees at 7:00 A.M. Per Juan Almonte. (Chariton: *100 Days,* 284) There was a "dreary drizzle." (Lord: *A Time to Stand,* 117)

At Washington-on-the-Brazos, cold and drizzle. Per William Fairfax Gray. (Chariton: *100 Days,* 284)

February 29, Monday

At San Antonio de Bexar, 55 degrees at night with a hard west wind. Per Juan Almonte. (Chariton: *100 Days,* 286) Another norther struck at midnight. (Lord: *A Time to Stand,* 124)

At Washington-on-the-Brazos, a warm day with the threat of rain from the south. Per William Fairfax Gray. (Chariton: *100 Days,* 287)

At the Rio Frio, "bitter cold brought on by a blustery norther." Per José Enrique de la Pena. (De la Pena, 35)

March 1, Tuesday

At San Antonio de Bexar, continued cold, 36 degrees in the morning, clear day with diminishing winds, 34 degrees at night. Per Juan Almonte. (Chariton: *100 Days,* 291)

With Duque's column at the Tinaja de Arroyo Hondo, the snowfall was "rather abundant" at night. Per José Enrique de la Pena. (De la Pena, 36)

At Washington-on-the-Brazos, a cold wind came up at night, bringing thunder, lightning, rain, and hail, temperature down to 33 degrees. Per William Fairfax Gray. (Chariton: *100 Days,* 293)

At San Patricio, "The north wind was very strong and the cold extreme." Per José Urrea. (Castaneda, 223)

March 2, Wednesday

At San Antonio de Bexar, 34 degrees but a clear and pleasant day with no wind. Per Juan Almonte. (Chariton: *100 Days,* 296)

With Duque's column at the Tinaja de Arroyo Hondo, it was so cold that written messages could not be sent because the ink froze, and a soldier of the Toluca Battalion died from the extreme cold. Per José Enrique de la Pena. (De la Pena, 36)

March 3, Thursday

At San Antonio de Bexar, 40 degrees, clear and calm. Per Juan Almonte. (Chariton: *100 Days,* 303)

At Washington-on-the-Brazos, cold in the morning, then warming, a clear day. Per William Fairfax Gray. (Chariton: *100 Days,* 303)

March 4, Friday

At San Antonio de Bexar, 42 degrees, windy, "not cold." Per Juan Almonte. (Chariton: *100 Days,* 309)

March 5, Saturday

At San Antonio de Bexar, 50 degrees and clear, 68 degrees at midday. Per Juan Almonte. (Chariton: *100 Days,* 310)

March 6, Sunday

At San Antonio de Bexar, in the early morning, it was very cold, per an unknown Mexican soldier. (Chariton: *100 Days,* 317)

At San Antonio de Bexar, it was three days past the full moon. Between 3:00 A.M. and 6:00 A.M. the moon was 88% full. (Von Schmidt, 65)

March 7, Monday

At San Antonio de Bexar, the wind was from the north. Per Juan Almonte. (Chariton: *100 Days,* 345)

March 8, Tuesday

At San Antonio de Bexar, it was cold, but a "fine clear day." Per Juan Almonte. (Chariton: *100 Days,* 347)

March 9, Wednesday

At San Antonio de Bexar, it was not very cold, but a violent north wind continued all niqht. Per Juan Almonte. (Chariton: *100 Days,* 351)

March 10, Thursday

At San Antonio de Bexar, it was clear and mild, but a north wind began blowing early. Per Juan Almonte. (Chariton: *100 Days,* 354)

March 11, Friday

At San Antonio de Bexar, it was pleasant but "somewhat windy." Per Juan Almonte. (Chariton: *100 Days,* 357)

March 12, Saturday

At San Antonio de Bexar, the "Day broke mild—became windy—but clear and temperate." Per Juan Almonte. (Chariton: *100 Days,* 362)

At Washington-on-the-Brazos, it was warm and pleasant. Per William Fairfax Gray. (Chariton: *100 Days,* 362)

March 13, Sunday

At San Antonio de Bexar, it was windy but clear, 85 degrees in the afternoon. Per Juan Almonte. (Chariton: *100 Days,* 363)

March 14, Monday

At San Antonio de Bexar, it was windy and warm. Cloudy early, then clearing, with wind abating a little. Per Juan Almonte. (Chariton: *100 Days,* 367)

At Washington-on-the-Brazos, it was "gloomy and warm, indicating rain." Per William Fairfax Gray. (Chariton: *100 Days,* 367)

March 15, Tuesday

At San Antonio de Bexar, it was windy and warm. Per Juan Almonte. (Chariton: *100 Days,* 368)

March 16, Wednesday

At San Antonio de Bexar, the wind continued. Per Juan Almonte. (Chariton: *100 Days,* 372)

CHAPTER THIRTEEN

Through Their Own Eyes

HOW THE PARTICIPANTS SAW THE SIEGE OF THE ALAMO AND THE TEXAS REVOLUTION

"You ask me if I remember it. I tell you yes. It is burned into my brain and indelibly seared there. Neither age nor infirmity could make me forget."

Enrique Esparza, 1907

(Enrique was the young son of defender Gregorio Esparza, and was present throughout the siege and final battle of the Alamo.)

NOTE: In this section, we have maintained the authors' original spelling, punctuation, grammar, syntax, etc. Also, we have included the specific source from which we obtained each of these quotations, although most are available from a number of different documents.

* * * * *

There is no better way to study an event than through the eyes of the actual participants. Even though all of those who took part in the Texas Revolution and the Siege of the Alamo are long dead, their legacy lives on in the written words that they left behind.

As in any human endeavor, not every participant sees the entire picture, or records the details 100% accurately. Bias and self-interest are inevitably entwined in all human events. With these cautions in mind, the following quotations are presented to give the reader a better insight into the thoughts and feelings of those who actually took part in these momentous events.

Although we have drawn the quotations used here from a number of sources, there is one book that stands above all others in this regard. It is Wallace O. Chariton's *100 Days in Texas: The Alamo Letters.* We heartily reccommend it as a first choice for those interested in reading primary documents about the Alamo.

* * * * *

Probably the most famous document related to the Siege of the Alamo is William Barret Travis' famous "Victory or Death" letter, sent out by courier on February 24. Here it is in its entirety:

To the people of Texas & all Americans in the world—

Fellow citizens and compatriots—I am besieged by a thousand or more of the Mexicans under Santa Anna—I have sustained a continual Bombardment & cannonade for 24 hours & have not lost a man—The enemy has demanded a surrender at discretion, otherwise, the garrison are to be put to the sword, if the fort is taken—I have answered the demand with a cannon shot, & our flag still waves proudly from the walls—I shall never surrender or retreat. Then, I call on you in the name of Liberty, of patriotism, & everything dear to the American character to come to our aid, with all dispatch—The enemy is receiving reinforcements daily & will no doubt increase to three or four thousand in four or five days. If this call is neglected, I am determined to sustain myself as long as possible & die like a soldier who never forgets what is due his own honor & that of his country—

VICTORY OR DEATH
William Barret Travis
Lt. Col. Comdt.

P.S. The Lord is on our side—When the enemy appeared in sight we had not three bushels of corn—We have since found in deserted houses 80 to 90 bushels and got into the walls 20 or 30 head of Beeves—

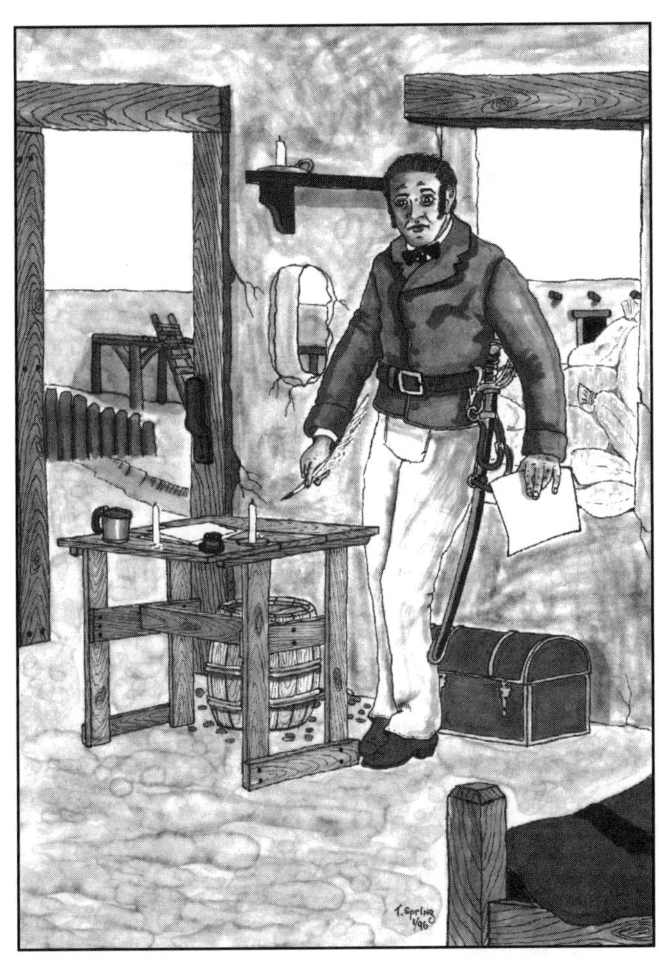

Lt. Col. William Barret Travis was a gifted orator and writer, and he penned many inspiring dispatches during the course of the Siege of the Alamo. The most famous of these he wrote on February 24, "To the people of Texas & all Americans in the world—." Here Travis has just finished writing his historic plea for help in his quarters in the northwest corner of the Alamo compound.

(Chariton: *100 Days*, 267)
Travis died at the Alamo, March 6, 1836

* * * * *

War is our only recourse—there is no other remedy but to defend our rights, our country, and ourselves by force of arms.

—Stephen F. Austin, in a widely circulated letter September 19, 1835
(Daughters of the Republic of Texas: *The Alamo*, 14)

* * * * *

The following document, a proclamation by Mexican Minister of War José María Tornel y Mendivil, is important because it brands all foreigners fighting in Texas as "pirates." From the Mexican viewpoint, this is part of the justification for the no-quarter policy at the Alamo, and for the executions of the prisoners at Goliad.

Ministry of War and Marine
Central Section
Desk No. 1

CIRCULAR

Most Excellent Sir:

Under this date I have notified all commandants-general and the principal governors and political chiefs of departments and territories as follows:

"The supreme government has positive information that in the United States of the North public meetings are being held with the avowed purpose of arming expeditions against the Mexican nation, of helping those who have rebelled against this government, of encouraging civil war, and of bringing upon our territory all those evils attendant upon civil war. Some expeditions have already been organized in that republic—our former friend—such as the one conducted by the traitor Jose Antonio Meija to Santa Anna [The town Santa Anna] in Tamaulipas and others on their way to the coast of Texas. All kinds of war supplies have been sent to the said coast; and, due to this censurable procedure, the rebellious colonists have been able to carry on a war against the nation that has showered so many favors upon them. The supreme government has the most positive assurance that these acts, censured by the wise laws of the United States of the North, have merited the consequent disapproval of that government with which we maintain the best understanding and an unalterable harmony. The speculators and adventurers have succeeded in evading the punishment that awaited them in that republic, but we hope that it will still overtake them. His Excellency, the President *ad interim,* who cannot see with indifference these aggressions that attack the soveignty of the Mexican nation, has seen proper to command that the following articles be observed with regard to them. 1st. All foreigners who may land in any port of the republic or who enter it armed and for the purpose of attacking our territory shall be treated and punished as pirates, since they are not subjects of any nation at war with the republic nor do they militate under any recognized flag. 2nd. Foreigners who introduce arms and munitions by land or by sea at any point of the territory now in rebellion against the government of the nation for the purpose of placing such supplies in the hands of its enemies shall be treated and punished likewise. I have the honor of transmitting these instructions to you for their publication and observance."

I have the honor of transmitting the foregoing circular to Your Excellency for your information, assuring you of my sincere affection.

GOD AND LIBERTY

José María Tornel

Mexico, December 30, 1835.

To His Excellency, the President, General-in-Chief of the Army of Operations, Antonio Lopez de Santa Anna, Benefactor of his Country.

(Castaneda: *The Mexican Side*, 55-56)

* * * * *

The narrative of José Enrique de la Pena, of the Zapadores Battalion, is one of the most controversial documents to come out of the Texas Revolution. While there are some serious questions about its authenticity, a number of respected historians and authors believe it is legitimate. (See the sidebar essay accompanying de la Pena's biography in Chapter Eleven.) We have included a few quotations from the de la Pena narrative in this section, so that the reader at least gets a feel for the document.

> Comrades in arms, our most sacred duties have brought us to these uninhabited lands and demand our engaging in combat against a rabble of wretched adventurers to whom our authorities have unwisely given benefits that even Mexicans did not enjoy, and who have taken possession of this vast and fertile area, convinced that our unfortunate internal divisions have rendered us incapable of defending our soil. Wretches! Soon they will become aware of their folly! Soldiers, our comrades have been shamefully sacrificed at Anahuac, Goliad, and Bejar, and you are those destined to punish these murderers. My Friends: we will march as long as the interests of the nation that we serve demand. . . .

—Gen. Antonio López de Santa Anna
to his soldiers
February 17, 1836
(De la Pena: *With Santa Anna in Texas,* 40)

* * * * *

In this war you know that there are no prisoners.

—Gen. Antonio López de Santa Anna to
Gen. Joaquin Ramirez y Sesma,
San Antonio de Bexar
February 29, 1836
(Filisola: *Memoirs,* Volume II:173)

* * * * *

Permit me, through you, to volunteer my services in the present struggle of Texas without conditions. I shall receive nothing, either in the form of service pay, or lands or rations.

—James Butler Bonham to
Gen. Sam Houston
December 1, 1835
(Groneman: *Alamo Defenders,* 129)
Bonham died at the Alamo, March 6, 1836

* * * * *

If we succeed the Country is ours. It is immense in extent, and fertile in its soil and will amply reward all our toil. If we fail, then death in the cause of liberty and humanity is not cause for shuddering. Our rifles are by our side, and choice guns they are, we know what awaits us, and are prepared to meet it.

—Daniel Cloud to I. B. Cloud
December 26, 1835
(Chariton: *100 Days in Texas,* 71)
Daniel Cloud died at the Alamo, March 6, 1836

* * * * *

David Crockett's final letter:

Saint Agusteen Texas 9th January, 1836
My Dear Sone & daughter,

This is the first I have had an opertunity to write you with convenience. I am now blessed with excellent health and am in high spirits although I have been received by everybody with open ceremony of friendship. I am hailed with a hearty welcome to this country. . . . I must say as to what I have seen of Texas it the garden spot of the world. The best land and the best prospects for health I ever saw. . . .

. . . I am rejoiced at my fate. I had rather be in my present situation than to be elected to a seat in Congress for life. I am in hopes of making a fortune yet for myself and my family bad as my prospect has been.

. . . I hope you will all do the best you can and I will do the same. Do not be uneasy about me I am among my friends—I must close with great respect.

Your affectionate father
Farewell. David Crockett
(Foreman: *Crockett: The Gentleman from the Cane,* 44)
Crockett died at the Alamo, March 6, 1836

* * * * *

I have left the garrison at Bexar 100 men under command of Lt. colonel Neill. This force I consider to be barely sufficient to hold the post and will require at least fifty additional troops to place it in a strong defensive position. I have ordered all the guns from the town into the Alamo and the fortifications in the town to be destroyed.

—Frank W. Johnson to the
General Council of Texas
January 3, 1836
(Chariton: *100 Days,* 100)

* * * * *

We have 104 men and two distinct fortresses to garrison, and about twenty four pieces of artillery. You doubtless have learned that we have no provisions or clothing since Johnson and Grant left. If there has ever been a dollar here, I have no knowledge of it. The clothing sent here by the aid and patriotic exertions of the honorable Council, was taken from us by arbitrary measures of Johnson and Grant, taken from men who endured all the hardships of winter and who were not even sufficiently clad for summer, many of them having but one blanket and one shirt . . .

—Lt. Col. James C. Neill to the
Governor and General Council
January 6, 1836
(Chariton: *100 Days,* 105)

* * * * *

This place [San Antonio de Bexar] is an ancient Mexican fort & Town divided by a small river which eminates from Springs. The town has two Squares in and the church in the centre, one a military and the other a government square. The Alamo or the fort as we call it, is a very old building, built for the purposes of protecting the citizens from hostile Indians.

—Capt. William R. Carey,
San Antonio de Bexar
January 12, 1836
(Groneman: *Alamo Defenders,* 134)
Carey died at the Alamo, March 6, 1836

* * * * *

I have become one of the most thorough going men you ever heard of. I go the whole Hog in the cause of Texas. I expect to help them gain their independence and also to form their civil government, for it is worth risking many lives for. From what I have seen and learned from others there is not so fair a portion of the earth's surface warmed by the sun.

—Micajah Autry to his wife, from Nacogdoches
January 13, 1836
(Groneman: *Alamo Defenders,* 139)
Autry died at the Alamo, March 6, 1836

* * * * *

I can say to you with Confidence, that we can rely on great aid from the Citizens of this town [San Antonio de Bexar] in case of an attack, they have no money here, but Don Gasper Flores, and Louisiana Navaro, have offered us all their goods Groceries, and Beeves, for the use and support of the army. . . .

—Lt. Col. James C. Neill to
Maj. Gen. Samuel Houston
January 14, 1836
(Chariton: *100 Days,* 145)

* * * * *

Colonel Bowie will leave here in a few hours for Bexar, with a detachment of from thirty to fifty men. . . . I have ordered the fortifications in the town of Bexar to be demolished, and if you should think well of it, I will remove all the cannon and other munitions of war to Gonzales and Copano, blow up the Alamo, and abandon the place, as it will be impossible to keep up the Station with volunteers.

—Gen. Sam Houston to Governor Henry Smith
January 17, 1836
(Chariton: *100 Days,* 152)

* * * * *

You can rely on aid from the citizens of this town in face of siege, Saguine [Juan Seguin] is doing all for the cause he can, as well as many of the most wealthy and influential citizens.

You can plainly see by the plat [Jameson drew a detailed map of the Alamo's defenses] that the Alamo was not built by a military people for a fortress . . .

If the men here can get a reasonable supply of clothing, provisions and money they will remain the balance of the 4 months, and do duty and fight better than fresh men, they have all been tried and have confidence in themselves.

—Maj. Green B. Jameson, Chief Engineer,
to Gen. Sam Houston
January 18, 1936
(Chariton: *100 Days,* 155)
Jameson died at the Alamo, March 6, 1836

* * * * *

Remember, soldiers, in civil war triumphant victories must always be accompanied by mourning and by the tears of widows and orphans. . . .

—From a proclamation by Minister of War José María Tornel y Mendivil printed in the newspaper *El Mosquito Mexicano* on January 22, 1836. The proclamation establishes a "Legion of Honor" for soldiers who "have made the Texas campaign or serve in Tampico or other points of foreign aggression."

Candidates for the award must kneel and "swear to be faithful to the country, the Government, and to honor and do all that constitutes the duty of a reliant loyal gentleman of the Legion of Honor!"

(Chariton: *100 Days,* 166)

* * * * *

If teams could be obtained here by any means to remove the Cannon and Public Property I would immediately destroy fortifications and abandon the place, taking the men I have under my command here, to join the commander in shief at Copano. . . .

—Lt. Col. James C. Neill to the Governor and General Council, January 23, 1836
(Chariton: *100 Days,* 168)

* * * * *

In obedience to my orders, I have done everything in my power to get ready to march to the relief of Bexar, but owing to the difficulty of getting horses and provisions, and owing to desertions, I shall march to-day with only about thirty men, all regulars except four. I shall, however, go on and do my duty, if I am sacrificed, unless I receive new orders to countermarch. Our affairs are gloomy indeed—the people are cold & indifferent—they are worn down by & exhausted with the war, & in consequence of dissentions between contending & rival chieftans, they have lost all confidence in their own govt. & officers. You have no idea of exhausted state of the country—volunteers can no longer be had or relied upon—A speedy organization, classification & draft of the Militia is all that can save us now. A regular army is necessary—but money, & money only can raise & equip a regular army—

—Lt. Col. William Barret Travis to Governor Henry Smith
January 28, 1836
(Groneman: *Alamo Defenders,* 144-145)

* * * * *

The following letter shows a definite change in the attitudes of both Neill and Bowie, as they are now clearly committed to defending the Alamo rather than destroying and abandoning it.

All I can say of the soldiers stationed here is complimentary to both their courage and their patience . . . I cannot eulogise the conduct & character of Col Neill too highly: no other man in the army could have kept men at this post, under the neglect they have experienced. . . .

It does however seem certain that an attack is shortly to be made on this place & I think & it is the general opinion that the enemy will come by land. The Citizens of Bejar have behaved well. Col. Neill & Myself have come to the solemn resolution that we will rather die in these ditches than give it up to the enemy. These citizens deserve our protection and the public safety demands our lives rather than to evacuate this post to the enemy—again we call aloud for relief . . .

—Col. James Bowie to Governor Henry Smith
February 2, 1836
(Groneman: *Alamo Defenders,* 147)
Bowie died at the Alamo, March 6, 1836

* * * * *

. . . many soldiers sickened with diarrhoea, and some with blistered feet; plenty of water, but no fodder . . .

—Col. Juan Almonte
February 3, 1836
(Chariton: *100 Days,* 206)

* * * * *

His Excellency himself attends to all matters whether important or most trivial. I am astonished to see that he has personally assumed the authority of major general . . . of quartermaster, of commissary, of brigadier generals, of colonels, of captains, and even of corporals. . . .

The members of the army in general have no idea of the significance of the Texas war, and all of them believe that they are merely on a military excursion.

It is pitiful and despairing to go looking for provisions and beasts of burden, money in hand when there is plenty of everything in the commissaries. . . . Consequently, we are perishing from hunger and misery in the midst of plenty.

—Lt. Col. José Juan Sanchez Navarro,
diary entries February 1836
(Hunnicutt:
A Mexican View of the Texas War, 60-61)

* * * * *

When we arrived in this city [Monclova], His Excellency the President had left for Rio Grande the day before. He is going to Bexar with inconceivable, rather astonishing haste. Why is His Excellency going in such haste? Why is he leaving the entire army behind? Does he think that his name alone is sufficient to overthrow the colonists?

—Lt. Col. José Juan Sanchez Navarro
February 9, 1836
(Chariton: *100 Days,* 221)

* * * * *

Santa Ana by the last accounts was at Satillo, with a force of 2500 men & guns. Sesma was at the Rio Grande with about 2000—He has issued his proclamation denouncing vengeance against the people of Texas—and threatens to exterminate every white man within its limits—This being the Frontier Post nearest the Rio Grande, will be the first to be attacked—We are illy prepared for their reception, as we have not more than 150 men here and they in a very discouraged state—Yet we are determined to sustain it as long as there is a man left; because we consider death preferable to disgrace, which would be the result of giving up a Post which has been so dearly won, and thus opening the door for the invaders to enter the sacred Territory of the colonies.

In consequence of the sickness of his family, Lt. Col. Neill has left this post, to visit home for a short time, and has requested me to take the Command of the Post—In consequence of which, I feel myself delicately and awkwardly situated—I therefore hope that your Excelly will give me some definite orders, and that immediately—

—Lt. Col. William Barret Travis to
Governor Henry Smith, February 12, 1836
(Chariton: *100 Days*, 225-226)

* * * * *

Much has been made of the personality conflict between Col. James Bowie and Col. William Barret Travis. While some authors, and particularly some Hollywood movies, might overdramatize that conflict, the following letter shows that there definitely were some difficulties between the two. The letter shows, too, that Travis joined Bowie and Neill in the conviction that the Alamo had to be defended against the advancing Mexicans.

My situation is truly awkward & delicate —Col Neill left me in command—but wishing to give satisfaction to the volunteers here & not wishing to assume any command over them I issued an order for the election of an officer to command them with the exception of one company of volunteers that had previously engaged to serve under me. Bowie was elected by two small companey's; & since his election he has been roaring drunk all the time; he has assumed all command—& is proceeding in a most disorderly & irregular manner—interfering with private property, releasing prisoners sentenced by court martial & by the civil court & turning every thing topsy turvy—If I did not feel the honor & that of my country compromitted I would leave here instantly for some other point with the troops under my immediate command—as I am unwilling to be responsible for the drunken irregularities of any man. I hope you will immediately order some regular troops to this place—as it is more important to occupy this Post than I imagined when I last saw you—It is the key of Texas from the Interior without a footing here the enemy can do nothing against us in the colonies now that our coast is being guarded by armed vessels—I do not solicit the command of this post. . . . I will do it if it be your order for a time until an artillery officer can be sent here.

—Lt. Col. William Barret Travis to
Governor Henry Smith, February 13, 1836
(Groneman: *Alamo Defenders*, 152-153)

* * * * *

It is my duty to inform you that my department is nearly destitute of medicine and in the event of a siege I can be of very little use to the sick. . . .

—Chief Surgeon Dr. Amos Pollard to
Governor Henry Smith, February 13, 1836
(Groneman: *Alamo Defenders*, 153)
Dr. Pollard died at the Alamo on March 6, 1836

* * * * *

The following letter shows that Bowie and Travis apparently reached a quick resolution of their differences, realizing that if they were to be effective commanders, they could not let petty quarrels stand in the way of their common duty.

From all the information we have received there is no doubt but that the enemy will shortly advance upon this place, and that this will be the first point of attack we must therefore urge the necessity of sending reinforcements, as speedily as possible to our aid.

By an understanding of today Col. J. Bowie has the command of the volunteers of the garrison, and Col. W. B. Travis of the regulars and volunteer cavalry. All general orders and correspondence will henceforth be signed by both until Col. Neill's return.

—Col. James Bowie & Lt. Col. William B. Travis
to Governor Henry Smith, February 14, 1836
(Chariton: *100 Days*, 231)

* * * * *

. . . a sudden attack was expected on our garrison here. . . . It is however fully ascertained that we have nothing of the kind to apprehend before a month or six weeks as the Enemy have not yet crossed the Rio Grande 180 mi. distant from this place nor are they expected to make any movement this way until the weather becomes warm or until the grass is sufficiently up to support their horses we conceive it however important to be prepared as a heavy attack is expected from Santa Ana himself in the Spring as no doubt the despot will use every possible means and strain every nerve to conquer and exterminate us from the land—in this we have no fear. . . .

We want only men who can undergo hardships and deprivation. Otherwise they are only a pest and expense to their fellow Soldiers . . .

—David P. Cummings to his father
February 14, 1836
(Groneman: *Alamo Defenders,* 154)
Cummings died at the Alamo, March 6, 1836

* * * * *

We have removed all the men to the Alamo where we make such resistance as is due our honor, and that of the country, until we can get assistance from you, which we expect you to forward immediately. In this extremity, we hope you will send us all the men you can spare promptly. We have one hundred and forty six men, who are determined never to retreat. We have but little provisions, but enough to serve us till you and your men arrive. We deem it unnecessary to repeat to a brave officer, who knows his duty, that we call on him for assistance.

—Col. James Bowie and
Lt. Col. William Barret Travis to
Col. James Fannin, February 23, 1836
(Chariton: *100 Days,* 263)

* * * * *

In a few words there is 2000 Mexican soldiers in Bexar, and 150 Americans in the Alamo. Sesma is at the head of them, and from the best accounts that can be obtained, they intend to show no quarter. If every man cannot turn out to a man every man in the Alamo will be murdered.

—Launcelot Smither, Alamo courier Gonzales
February 24, 1836
(Groneman: *Alamo Defenders,* 157-158)

Smither survived the Alamo, but was killed on September 11, 1842 by Mexican soldiers who were part of General Woll's expedition into Texas.

* * * * *

Sir; on the 23rd of Feb. the enemy in large force entered the city of Bexar, which could not be prevented, as I had not sufficient force to occupy both positions. Col. Bartes, the Adjutant-Major of the President-General Santa Anna, demanded a surrender at discretion, calling us foreign rebels. I answered them with a cannon shot. . . .

. . . Two or three of our men have been slightly scratched by pieces of rock, but have not been disabled. I take great pleasure in stating that both officers and men conducted themselves with firmness and bravery. Lieutenant Simmons of cavalry acting as infantry, and Captains Carey, Dickinson and Blair of the artillery, rendered essential service, and Charles Despallier and Robert Brown gallantly sallied out and set fire to houses which afforded the enemy shelter. . . . The Hon. David Crockett was seen at all points, animating the men to do their duty. . . . Give me help, oh my country! Victory or Death!

—Lt. Col. William Barret Travis to
Gen. Sam Houston
February 25, 1836
(Chariton: *100 Days,* 270-271)

* * * * *

If you execute your enemies, it saves you the trouble of having to forgive them.

—Gen. Antonio López de Santa Anna
February 1836
(Time Life: *The Spanish West,* 104)

* * * * *

With a forlorn hope of 320 men, we will start tonight or tomorrow morning at the dawn of day to relieve the gallant little garrison, who have so nobly resolved to sustain themselves until our arrival. Our force is small compared with that of the enemy. It is a desperate resort, but we hope the God of Battles be with us—

—Capt. John Brooks to his sister, from Goliad
February 25, 1836
(Chariton: *100 Days,* 273)

* * * * *

After taking Fort of the Alamo, I shall continue my operations against Goliad and other fortified places, so that before the rains come, the campaign shall be terminated completely as far as the Sabine River which forms the dividing line between our Republic and the one of the North.

—Gen. Antonio López de Santa Anna to
Gen. Vicente Filisola
February 27, 1836
(Filisola: *Memoirs,* Volume II:168-169)

* * * * *

While initially many Texians believed that a return to the precepts of the Mexican Constitution of 1824 was the most desirable goal of their struggle, by the time of the Siege of the Alamo, most were convinced that a complete break from Mexico was the only way to insure the rights to which they believed they were entitled. On March 2, 1836, the Convention at Washington-on-the-Brazos ratified a Declaration of Independence from Mexico:

> We, therefore, the delegates, with plenary powers, of the people of Texas, in solemn convention assembled, appealing to a candid world for the necessities of our condition, do hereby resolve and declare, that our political connection with the Mexican nation has forever ended, and that the people of Texas do now constitute a FREE, SOVEREIGN, and INDEPENDENT REPUBLIC and are fully invested with all the rights and attributes which properly belong to independent nations; and conscious of the rectitude of our intentions, we fearlessly and confidently commit the issue to the supreme Arbiter of the destinies of nations.
>
> —Texas Declaration of Independence from the Convention at Washington-on-the-Brazos, March 2, 1836 (Chariton: *100 Days,* 297)

* * * * *

Contrast the above sentiments with those of Santa Anna, and it is not hard to understand why war between Texas and Mexico was inevitable:

> A hundred years to come, my people will not be fit for liberty. A despotism is the proper government for them.
>
> —Antonio López de Santa Anna (Time Life: *The Spanish West,* 96)

* * * * *

Fortunately, not all Mexicans agreed, and some saw Santa Anna as being as much of a danger to Mexico as he would be to Texas:

> This young man will cause all Mexico to weep.
>
> —Gen. Juan O'Donojo, 1821 (Time Life: *The Spanish West,* 98)

* * * * *

Although some may assume that Davy Crockett's legendary status began with the Walt Disney TV series in the 1950s, the following quotation shows that he was already well on his way to becoming a folk hero in 1836:

> We have just received additional intelligence from Bexar. The Mexicans have made two successive attacks on the Alamo in both of which the gallant little garrison repulsed them with some loss. Probably Davy Crockett "grinned" them off.
>
> —Capt. John Brooks to his mother, from Goliad, March 2, 1836 (Chariton: *100 Days,* 299)

* * * * *

> The power of Santa Anna is to be met here or in the colonies; we had better meet them here, than to suffer a war of desolation to rage our settlements. A blood red banner waves from the church of Bexar, and in the camp above us, in token that the war is one of vengeance against rebels; they have declared us as such, and demanded that we should surrender at discretion or this garrison should be put to the sword. Their threats have no influence on me or my men, but to make all fight with desperation, and that high-souled courage which characterizes the patriot, who is willing to die in defense of his country's liberty and his own honor.
>
> —Lt. Col. William Barret Travis to the President of the Convention at Washington-on-the-Brazos, March 3, 1836 (Chariton: *100 Days,* 305)

* * * * *

> I am still here, in fine spirits and well to do. With 140 men, I have held this place 10 days against a force variously estimated from 1,500 to 6,000, and I shall continue to hold it till I get relief from my countrymen, or I will perish in its defense. We have had a shower of bombs and cannon balls continually falling among us the whole time, yet none of us has fallen. We have been miraculously preserved.
>
> All our couriers have gotten out without being caught, and a company of 32 men from Gonzales got in two nights ago, and Col. Bonham got in to-day by coming between the powder house and the enemy's upper encampment. . . . Let the Convention go and make a declaration of independence; and we will then understand, and the whole world will understand what we are fighting for. If independence is not declared, I shall lay down my arms, and so will the men under my command. But under the flag of independence, we are ready to peril our lives a hundred times a day, and dare the monster who is fighting us under the blood red flag. . . .
>
> —Lt. Col. William Barret Travis to Jesse Grimes March 3, 1836 (Groneman: *Alamo Defenders,* 160-161)

Travis was obviously unaware that Texas had declared its independence on March 2.

* * * * *

Take care of my little boy. If the country should be saved, I may make for him a splendid fortune; but if the country be lost and I should perish, he will have nothing but the proud recollection that he is the son of a man who died for his country.

—Lt. Col. William Barret Travis to David Ayers
March 3, 1836
(Chariton: *100 Days,* 307)

* * * * *

The reputation Texans have for marksmanship is well deserved.

—Lt. José Enrique de la Pena, commenting on the death of his friend José María Heredia, a fellow officer in the Zapadores Battalion
(De la Pena: *With Santa Anna in Texas,* 63)

* * * * *

Since it is necessary to act with decision against the enemies who are defending the Alamo, His Excellency the general in chief has ordered that tomorrow at 4:00 A.M. the attack columns shall be ready within rifle range of the first trenches in order to undertake the assault which is to be carried out at the signal which His Excellency shall order to be sounded by trumpet from the North battery.

—Gen. Antonio López de Santa Anna to generals, section leaders, and corps commanders
March 5, 1836
(Filisola: *Memoirs,* Volume II:175)

* * * * *

On the 6th of March I received orders to go to San Antonio with my company and a party of American citizens, carrying provisions for the defenders of the Alamo on their horses.

Arriving at the Cibolo and not hearing the signal gun which was to be discharged every fifteen minutes as long as the place held out, we retraced our steps to convey to the general-in-chief the sad tidings.

—Alamo courier Capt. Juan Seguin, who was returning to the fortress on the day of its fall
(De la Teja: *A Revolution Remembered,* 80)

* * * * *

Long live our country, the Alamo is ours!

—Lt. Col. José Juan Sanchez Navarro
March 6, 1836
(Hunnicutt: *A Mexican View of the Texas War,* 62)

* * * * *

Army of operations—Most Excellent Sir—Victory marches with the army, and this moment of 8:00 A.M. it has just achieved the most complete and glorious outcome which will perpetuate its memory.

—Gen. Antonio López de Santa Anna to Minister of War José María Tornel y Mendivil
March 6, 1836
(Filisola: *Memoirs,* Volume II:180)

* * * * *

A siege of a few days would have caused its [the Alamo's] surrender, but it was not fit that the entire army should be detained before an irregular fortification hardly worthy of the name. Neither could its capture be dispensed with, for bad as it was, it was well equipped with artillery, had a double wall, and defenders who, it must be admitted, were very courageous. . . .

—Gen. Antonio López de Santa Anna, 1837
(Castaneda: *The Mexican Side,* 13)

* * * * *

Our soldiers, it was said, lacked the cool courage that is demanded by an assault, but they were steadfast and the survivors will have nothing to be ashamed of.

—Lt. José Enrique de la Pena
(De la Pena: *With Santa Anna in Texas,* 45)

* * * * *

I could not desist from visiting the cemetery where the remains of my friends were buried during the time I remained in Bejar, and the most tender emotions were with me as I contemplated the end of miserable human existence. Health, talents, courage, happiness and love may all be ended at once by a lead bullet. Only the memory of virtues survives him who possessed them.

—Lt. José Enrique de la Pena
(De la Pena: *With Santa Anna in Texas,* 63)

* * * * *

So Jim is dead?. . . . I'll wager they found no wounds in his back.

—Mrs. Elve Bowie, on hearing of her son's death at the Alamo
(Daughters of the Republic of Texas: *The Alamo,* 28)

* * * * *

After the fall of the Alamo, Lieutenant Colonel Sanchez Navarro proposed to General Cos that the following verse be inscribed on a monument to the Mexican soldiers killed in the siege:

The bodies that lie here at rest
Were those of men whose souls elate
Are now in Heaven to be blest
For deeds that time cannot abate.
They put their manhood to the test,
And fearlessly they met their fate;
No fearful end, a patriot's fall.

(Hunnicutt: *A Mexican View of the Texas War,* 63)

* * * * *

In our opinion all that bloodshed of our soldiers as well as of our enemies was useless, having as its only objective an inconsiderate, childish and culpable vanity so that it might be proclaimed that Bexar had been reconquered by force of arms. . . .

—Gen. Vicente Filisola
(Filisola: *Memoirs,* Volume II:179)

* * * * *

Though the bravery and intrepidity of the troops was general, we shall always deplore the costly sacrifice of 400 men who fell in the attack. Three hundred were left dead on the field and more than a hundred of the wounded died afterward as a result of the lack of proper medical attention and medical facilities in spite of the fact that their injuries were not serious.

—Ramon Martínez Caro,
Secretary to Santa Anna, 1837
(Castaneda: *The Mexican Side,* 105)

* * * * *

Colonel Fannin should have relieved our brave men in the Alamo. He had 430 men with artillery under his command, and had taken the line of march with a full knowledge of the situation of those in the Alamo, and owing to the breaking down of a wagon abandoned the march, returned to Goliad and left our Spartans to their fate.

—Gen. Sam Houston to Henry Raguet
March 13, 1836
(Chariton: *100 Days,* 365-366)

* * * * *

Since I have had the honor to address you from Gonzales, the lady of Lieutenant Dickenson, who fell at the Alamo, has arrived and confirms the fall of that place, and the circumstances, pretty much as my express detailed them.

—Gen. Sam Houston to James Collinsworth
March 15, 1836
(Chariton: *100 Days,* 368)

* * * * *

After the fall of the Alamo, sentiment against Santa Anna ran as high in the United States as it did in Texas. The following is from a newspaper article reporting on the exhibition of a portrait of Santa Anna in the Mississippi Hotel. The writer is either the most perceptive art critic that ever lived, or he has let his evaluation of the painting be colored by his political feelings:

The expression of his [Santa Anna's] eye and the lower part of his face is that of a cold blooded assassin, smiling scornfully at the victims of his cruelty and bent upon the execution of his purpose with no other design than the gratification of a morbid ambition stimulated by the predominance of the animal propensities. The first impression of the portrait, uninfluenced by a knowledge of his deeds, is that of a man destitute of the finer feelings of the human heart, and evincing a contempt for every thing that serves not to gloat his unnatural appetite.

—*The Detroit Democratic Free Press*
November 9, 1836

* * * * *

The army underwent great privations during its march, and consequently deserves the highest praise for its constancy and resignation, qualities characteristic of the Mexican soldier.

—Minister of War José María Tornel y Mendivil
1837
(Castaneda: *The Mexican Side,* 360)

* * * * *

On February 25, 1837, Juan Seguin, by then a lieutenant colonel in the Regular Texas Cavalry, presided at the burial of the remains of the defenders of the Alamo at San Antonio de Bexar. Here is the English translation of the words that he spoke that day:

Bexar, February 25, 1837

Companions in Arms! These remains which we have the honor of carrying on our shoulders are those of the valiant heroes who died in the Alamo. Yes, my friends, they preferred to die a thousand times rather than submit themselves to the tyrant's yoke. What a brilliant example! Deserving of being noted in the pages of history. The spirit of liberty appears to be looking out from its elevated throne with its pleasing mien and pointing to us, saying: "there are your brothers, Travis, Bowie, Crockett, and others whose valor places them in the rank of my heroes." Yes soldiers and fellow citizens, these are the worthy beings who, by the twists of fate, during the present campaign delivered their bodies to the ferocity of their enemies; who, barbarously treated as beasts, were bound by their feet and dragged to this spot, where they were reduced to ashes. The venerable remains of our worthy companions as witnesses, I invite you to declare to the entire world, "Texas shall be free and independent, or we shall perish in glorious combat."

(De la Teja: *A Revolution Remembered,* 156)

* * * * *

Let us weep at the tomb of the brave Mexicans who died at the Alamo defending the honor and the rights of their country. They won a lasting claim to fame and the country can never forget their heroic names.

—Antonio López de Santa Anna, 1837
(Castaneda: *The Mexican Side,* 15)

CHAPTER FOURTEEN

Places to Visit and Other Resources

"We in America do not build monuments to war. We do not build monuments to conquest. We build monuments to commemorate the spirit of sacrifice in war—reminders of our desire for peace."

Franklin Delano Roosevelt (Edsall, 59)

PLACES TO VISIT

HISTORIC SITES RELATED TO THE ALAMO AND THE TEXAS REVOLUTION

People come from all over the country, indeed from all over the world, to visit the Alamo in San Antonio. For those interested in the Alamo and the Texas Revolution, there are many other sites of related interest within reasonable traveling distance of San Antonio. This section will discuss some of them, but is not meant to be an all-inclusive listing. Additional and up-to-date information may be obtained from:

Texas Department of Transportation
Division of Travel and Information
P.O. Box 5064
Austin, Texas 78763-5064
1-800-452-9252

San Antonio Visitors and Convention Bureau
P.O. Box 2277
San Antonio, Texas 78298
(210) 270-8700

THE ALAMO
San Antonio, Texas

The first and foremost historical site to visit is, of course, the Alamo itself. Only part of the original Alamo compound remains. It has been swallowed up by modern San Antonio, but is nonetheless well worth a visit. Not only is it *the* place where the historic events of the Alamo battle took place, the Alamo is very interesting and scenic in spite of its modern surroundings.

The Alamo is administered by the Daughters of the Republic of Texas (DRT) and is open to the public without charge. Two of the original buildings remain: the chapel and the long barracks. Both are now museums containing displays and artifacts pertaining to the siege and to Texas history. The beautifully maintained Alamo grounds, and the adjacent "Alamo Plaza," cover most of the area that was once the Alamo compound.

Two modern buildings on the grounds blend in very well, and are worthy of note. The gift shop contains an excellent selection of books, prints, and other Alamo memorabilia. It is also a museum in itself, containing a number of displays and exhibits relating to the Alamo and to Texas history. The other modern building is the Daughters of the Republic of Texas Library. It contains books, maps, manuscripts, prints, and artwork related to the Alamo and the Texas Revolution. The library's resources are available for use by serious students of Texas history.

There has been considerable discussion recently about what should be done to preserve and restore the Alamo. Proposals have ranged from maintaining the staus quo up to reconstructing the entire Alamo compound. As of the time of this writing, it does not appear that there will be any major rebuilding. Rather, existing structures will be repaired and stabilized. Museum displays will be updated and expanded to tell more of the history of San Antonio. Artist/historian Gary Zaboly was commissioned to produce several large-scale paintings as a part of the new "Wall of History."

The national press has recently given much attention to a claim that the silver treasure from the fabled San Saba mine had been hidden in the Alamo's well by Jim Bowie. After much fanfare, and no small amount of controversy, a dig into the well came up with nothing.

It should be noted that the Daughters of the Republic of Texas receive no public funds to maintain the Alamo. They do it solely through donations and from the proceeds of the gift shop.

The Alamo
P.O. Box 2599
San Antonio, Texas 78299

THE ALAMO IMAX THEATER
ALAMO . . . THE PRICE OF FREEDOM
San Antonio, Texas

No visit to the Alamo is complete without viewing the IMAX motion picture *Alamo . . . The Price of Freedom.* It is shown several times daily at the Alamo IMAX Theater, located adjacent to the Alamo compound in the Rivercenter Mall.

The forty-five-minute IMAX movie is shown on a screen that is six stories tall. Six-track magnetic stereo sound resounds from thirty-two strategically placed speakers, giving the audience an experience that will not soon be forgotten.

Alamo . . . The Price of Freedom is the most historically accurate Alamo movie ever made. (See Chapter Sixteen: Alamo Movies & Music.) It was filmed at the John Wayne Alamo movie set at Brackettville, Texas, during the summer of 1987. Wayne's Alamo set was reconditioned and updated, using some of the most knowledgeable Alamo historians in the country as consultants. Historical reenactors played the parts of both the Texians and the Mexican *soldados.* The widely acclaimed film was awarded the 1988 Wrangler Award for the Best Historic Western Movie.

In addition to *Alamo . . . The Price of Freedom,* other current films are shown on the Alamo IMAX Theater's giant screen. But the IMAX is more than just an outstanding theater. It is also a mini-museum with an excellent gift shop and bookstore. The IMAX gift shop offers one of the best selections of books on Alamo and Texas history that you will find anywhere. Prints, posters, and other related items are also offered for sale. The Plaza de Valero Exhibit Gallery in the theater lobby contains a number of interesting exhibits on the making of *Alamo . . . The Price of Freedom.* It also has displays and artifacts pertaining to the history of early San Antonio and the Siege of the Alamo.

There is no admission charge for the gallery or the gift shop. If you make it to the Alamo, do not even think of leaving without a stop at the IMAX!

Alamo IMAX Theater
Rivercenter Mall
849 E. Commerce, Suite 483
San Antonio, Texas 78205
(210) 225-4629

THE ALAMO CENOTAPH
San Antonio, Texas

The Alamo Cenotaph, dedicated in 1939, is a large marble monument by noted sculptor Pompeo Coppini. Located in Alamo Plaza, in front of the Long Barracks Museum, the Cenotaph honors those who gave their lives in defense of the Alamo.

THE BRICK WALK
San Antonio, Texas

The San Antonio Brick Walk is an avenue of bricks that are inscribed with the names of the defenders of the Alamo. Patriotic citizens may also purchase bricks inscribed with their own names and have them laid into the walk. The Brick Walk begins at the intersection of East Houston Street and Alamo Plaza, at the approximate location of the northwest bastion of the original Alamo, and extends westward from there.

The Brick Walk was dedicated with fitting ceremony on March 5, 1990. The two authors, along with essayist Dr. Todd Harburn, had the honor of participating, by setting in place a brick honoring one of the Alamo defenders as the names were read to the assembled crowd. Each of the other bricks were laid in a similar manner, until all of the valiant defenders were so honored.

San Antonio Brick Walk
P.O. Box 1980
San Antonio, Texas 78297
(210) 82-BRICK

LA VILLITA
San Antonio, Texas

At the time of the siege, La Villita was an area of run-down huts, or "*jacales*," located a short distance to the southeast of the Alamo. These *jacales* provided some cover for Santa Anna's men, until they were burned by the Texians. La Villita was rebuilt as San Antonio grew. Today, many of La Villita's historic buildings have been restored, and it is now an area of quaint restaurants, stores, and craft shops. The house where General Cos surrendered to the Texians, on December 9, 1935, is one of the restored buildings. La Villita also includes an outdoor theater along the beautiful San Antonio Riverwalk.

THE TEXAS ADVENTURE SPECIAL EFFECTS THEATER
San Antonio, Texas

The Texas Adventure Special Effects Theater is a relatively new Alamo attraction. It provides an action-packed, thirty-minute multi-media show that tells the story of the Siege of the Alamo and Texas' struggle for independence. It uses state of the art special effects techniques, including 3-D ghostlike images, lifelike animatronic characters, and electrifying sound and lighting. There is also a magnificent 54mm diorama of "Crockett's Last Stand," which depicts the brutal action in front of the chapel during the final assault on the Alamo.

The Texas Adventure is located between the Alamo and the Riverwalk.

The Texas Adventure
307 Alamo Plaza
San Antonio, Texas 78205
(210) 227-8224

THE AFRICAN AMERICAN MONUMENT
San Antonio, Texas

Dedicated on July 15, 1994, the African American Monument is one of the newest Alamo area attractions. Located at the corner of Congress Avenue and 11th Street, it honors the African Americans who took part in the Siege of the Alamo, and who served at Goliad and other places during the Texas Revolution.

THE SAN FERNANDO CATHEDRAL
San Antonio, Texas

In 1836 Santa Anna placed his blood-red flag of no quarter in the tower of the San Fernando Cathedral. Today's cathedral stands on the original site, and is the center of an active Catholic parish. The walls behind today's altar area date from the 1750s, while the modern church has expanded forward, now covering over twice its original area.

On February 25, 1837, Lt. Col. Juan Seguin of the Regular Texas Cavalry returned to the Alamo and held a burial service for what was left of the ashes of the Alamo defenders. There is some dispute over where the ashes were eventually buried. According to one legend, they were placed in a common casket and buried beneath the floor of the sanctuary of the San Fernando Cathedral.

During church renovation in 1936, human remains were recovered from this spot. In 1938 these remains were reinterred in a marble crypt in the front of the church, and credited as being those of the Alamo defenders. Visitors are welcome to stop in and pay their respects, but are asked to remember that this is still an active place of worship.

San Fernando Cathedral
115 Main Plaza
San Antonio, Texas 78205

JOSÉ ANTONIO NAVARRO STATE HISTORIC SITE
San Antonio, Texas

José Antonio Navarro was a Tejano loyal to the cause of freedom, and was among the signers of the Texas Declaration of Independence. Three of the limestone structures of his *hacienda*—the home, the office, and the kitchen—all have been restored to their 1850 appearance.

José Antonio Navarro State Historic Site
South Laredo Street
San Antonio, Texas
(210) 226-4801

THE SAN ANTONIO MISSIONS
San Antonio, Texas

The Alamo, as the Mission San Antonio de Valero, was the first of six missions established in the San Antonio area. Today the other five missions make up what is known as San Antonio Missions National Historic Park. They include Mission Concepción, the site of the Mission Najera, Mission San José, Mission San Juan, and Mission Espada. Each mission is different, and each tells a slightly different story about early Texas history. All are within about six miles of the Alamo. They are excellent examples of the Catholic faith and Spanish culture in early San Antonio, and are well worth visiting. Four of the missions are still active Catholic parishes.

San Antonio Missions National Historic Park
2202 Roosevelt Avenue
San Antonio, Texas 78210

THE CAMPO SANTO
San Antonio, Texas

The Campo Santo, or Catholic Cemetery, was established in 1808, and closed in 1860. It was located near modern Milam Square, where the Santa Rosa Hospital now stands.

The Tennessee Mounted Volunteers, including the famous Davy Crockett, paused here while they sent word ahead of their pending arrival in San Antonio de Bexar.

The Campo Santo is the final resting place for many of the Mexican soldiers killed in the Siege of the Alamo, including Lt. José María Torres, of the Zapadores Battalion, who was killed while trying to take down the Alamo flag.

THE PROTESTANT CEMETERY
San Antonio, Texas

A Protestant Cemetery was once located across the street from the Campo Santo, where Milam Square Park now stands. Col. Benjamin Rush Milam, killed during the Siege of Bexar in December 1835, was originally buried where he fell on the Veramendi property. On December 7, 1848, he was reburied in the Protestant Cemetery, by members of the Alamo Masonic Lodge #94. Human remains uncovered during a recent construction project have been positively identified as Milam's. Plans are currently under way to reinter them in a suitable burial vault marked by a state historical marker.

CITY CEMETERY NUMBER 1
San Antonio, Texas

City Cemetery Number 1 was established in 1854, and is located just east of downtown San Antonio, near the intersection of Commerce and Monumental streets. It is the final resting place of many famous Texans, including Samuel Maverick and artist Theodore Gentilz.

During the Siege of the Alamo, the area was known as "Powder House Hill," named after a three-story stone arsenal built by early Spanish soldiers. A Mexican artillery battery was erected there during the siege.

ENRIQUE ESPARZA GRAVESITE
Losoya, Texas

Enrique Esparza was the young son of Alamo defender Gregorio Esparza, and he was present during the entire Siege of the Alamo. In 1905 the *San Antonio Express* published an interview with Enrique, detailing his recollections of the siege.

Enrique Esparza died on December 10, 1917, and was buried in the churchyard of El Carmen Church, today Our Lady of Mount Carmel, northwest of the town of Losoya. A Texas State Historical Marker has been placed in front of the old church bell tower.

Losoya is located just south of the Medina River, about twelve miles from downtown San Antonio.

ALAMO VILLAGE
Brackettville, Texas

Few readers of this book are not familiar with John Wayne's epic 1960 motion picture *The Alamo.* (See Chapter Sixteen.) For the movie, Wayne contracted with James T. "Happy" Shahan to build authentic replicas of the Alamo Mission and the village of San Antonio de Bexar on Shahan's cattle ranch. Alamo Village, as the set is known, took almost two years to complete. It is located about 125 miles west of San Antonio on Highway FM 674, seven miles north of Brackettville.

Alamo Village still exists, and in fact is frequently used for filming movie and television productions, and even for commercials. The area covered by the movie set's compound is approximately three-fourths the size of the original Alamo. The front of the chapel is full scale, and the rest of the buildings are also approximately the correct size.

The Alamo Village set was updated to bring it up to current standards of authenticity for the 1987 film *Alamo . . . The Price of Freedom.* Other notable movie and television productions filmed there include *Bandolero, Two Rode Together, Barbarosa, Lonesome Dove, Thirteen Days to Glory, Houston—The Legend of Texas, Seguin, Gunsmoke II,* and James Michener's *Texas.*

Alamo Village is open to the public, and is a must place to visit for any serious Alamo student. While the original Alamo is now surrounded by a modern city, the Brackettville set has the feel and appearance of what San Antonio and the Alamo were like in 1836.

Visitors can explore every nook and cranny of the Alamo compound. They can also enjoy lunch and a cool drink in the same *cantina* where John Wayne and his men attended a *fandango* in *The Alamo.* During the summer months, there is regularly scheduled western melodrama and musical entertainment. There is also a gift shop that is well stocked with treasures for Alamo buffs.

Alamo Village
Box 528
Brackettville, Texas 78832
(512) 563-2580

FORT CLARK SPRINGS

Brackettville, Texas

Located near Brackettville, Fort Clark was a cavalry post from the Indian War period until it was deactivated in 1946. While it has no direct connection to the Alamo or to the Texas Revolution, we include it here for several reasons.

One of the advantages of using Happy Shahan's ranch for John Wayne's movie was its remote location. Overnight accommodations in Brackettville are still somewhat limited. Staying at Fort Clark Springs is one of the available options.

Another reason for including Fort Clark in this section is because during the filming of *The Alamo,* John Wayne used the old post commandant's quarters as his residence. All visitors can do today is view the outside of the building and read the commemorative sign, but it is still worth the trouble.

Readers familiar with western history will remember Fort Clark as the headquarters of Col. Ranald S. Mackenzie's Fourth Cavalry during the post-Civil War Indian conflicts. Using Fort Clark as a base, Mackenzie's men made a number of daring but unauthorized sorties into Mexico in pursuit of Indians who raided on U.S. soil, then fled across the border to sanctuary. Some readers may recall the 1950s TV series *Mackenzie's Raiders,* in which Richard Carlson played Colonel Mackenzie. Carlson also played Lt. Col. William Barret Travis in the 1955 movie *The Last Command.* (See Chapter Sixteen.)

Another very important reason why we have included Fort Clark in our book is to recognize what we consider to be a unique and outstanding effort to preserve this historic site. When Fort Clark was deactivated, it could easily have fallen into decay like many other abandoned military posts. However, due to the creative efforts of private investors, the facility was adapted to profitable civilian use, while its historical significance was largely preserved.

Today Fort Clark is a thriving membership resort community in which many of the original military buildings have been preserved and converted into housing for both permanent residents and temporary guests. Overnight guests can either stay in motel-like accommodations in the old cavalry barracks, or camp in their own rigs in the modern RV park. While some facilities are restricted to members only, nonmember guests are allowed use of the restaurant, bar, swimming pool, golf course, and tennis courts. The "Guardhouse Cavalry Museum" has exhibits depicting the fort's history, and is open to the public.

Fort Clark Springs was developed entirely with private funds; no tax subsidies were involved. The authors visited the site during our 1990 trip to Texas, and were thoroughly impressed by this example of how the private sector can tastefully and profitably preserve historic sites that otherwise would fall into ruin. While a little bit outside of the main focus of this book, we feel that the Fort Clark story is a story worth telling. If you visit Brackettville, be sure to visit Fort Clark Springs as well!

Fort Clark Springs Association, Inc.
P.O. Box 345
Brackettville, Texas 78832
(512) 563-2493

GOLIAD

There are actually three sites of interest near Goliad, which is located about ninety-five miles southeast of San Antonio. They are:

1. Presidio Santa Maria del Loreto de la Bahía
2. Goliad State Historical Park
3. La Coleto Creek Battlefield

PRESIDIO SANTA MARIA DEL LORETO DE LA BAHÍA

Goliad, Texas

Commonly known as Presidio La Bahía, this is the presidio occupied by Col. James Fannin and his men while Santa Anna besieged the Alamo. The presidio was first established in 1721, and moved to its present site in 1749. La Bahía is the oldest restored fort in the United States west of the Mississippi River. It actually played a part in the American Revolution, when soldiers from its garrison, allied with the Americans, fought against the British in several Gulf Coast battles.

The first Texian offensive action of the Revolution took place at La Bahía, when it was captured from the Mexicans on October 9, 1835. La Bahía's most famous, and most tragic, claim to historical significance is that Fannin's army was brought back there after surrendering at La Coleto Creek. On Palm Sunday, after being told that they were to be paroled, most of the Texians were marched a short distance from the presidio and then summarily executed by the Mexicans. Fannin and other wounded soldiers were killed inside the mission walls. He and 324 of his men are buried in a common grave on the spot where most of them died, just a few hundred yards from the presidio.

The Presidio La Bahía is restored to its 1836 appearance, with the exception of the church bell tower, which was not added until the twentieth century. The site hosts living history programs, and limited rental rooms for overnight guests are available in the restored priest's quarters. La Bahía is still an active Catholic parish, owned and operated by the Diocese of Victoria, Texas.

Presidio La Bahía
P.O. Box 57
Goliad, Texas 77963
(512) 645-3752

GOLIAD STATE HISTORICAL PARK

Goliad, Texas

Goliad State Historical Park is located just a few miles from Presidio La Bahía. It is the site of Mission Nuestra Señora del Espíritu Santo de Zuniga, commonly known as Mission Espíritu Santo, and is still an active Catholic parish.

Mission Espíritu Santo was once one of the largest and most successful of the Spanish missions in Texas. It was also Texas' first large cattle ranch. In addition to the restored mission, Goliad State Historical Park includes a campground, a picnic area, and fishing along the San Antonio River.

Goliad State Historical Park
P.O. Box 727
Goliad, Texas 77963
(512) 645-3405

LA COLETO CREEK BATTLEFIELD

Near Goliad, Texas

When Fannin's army started out from La Bahía to fall back to Victoria, they made it as far as La Coleto Creek. There they ran into the southern column of the Mexican arrny, under Brig. Gen. José Urrea. On March 20, after two days of battle, Fannin surrendered when the Mexicans promised him honorable terms. Marched back to Goliad, the Texians were imprisoned at La Bahía for a week, then were marched out and executed under Santa Anna's direct order.

The La Coleto Battlefield is part of Goliad State Historical Park. The site of the battle is marked by a small park and a stone monument. It is located about ten miles northeast of Goliad, and can best be reached by following State Highway 59 out of town.

ANAHUAC

Anahuac, Texas

Largely ignored in most accounts of the Alamo, the coastal city of Anahuac played an important part in the early events of the Texas Revolution. (Many of the early scenes of the movie *The Last Command* correctly take place there.)

Anahuac was a port of entry for American settlers and goods. A small fort was built there about 1831. This fort, and its garrison, were captured by William Barret Travis in June 1835. It was one of the first, and somewhat embarrassing, acts of resistance by the Texians. Today, a park on the site contains an historical marker, some traces of the old fort, and camping and picnic areas.

THE SAM HOUSTON REGIONAL LIBRARY AND RESEARCH CENTER

Liberty, Texas

The Sam Houston Regional Library and Research Center in Liberty, Texas, is a repository for many books and documents on early Texas history. It's also a mini-museum, with a number of historical artifacts on display.

SAN JACINTO BATTLEGROUND STATE HISTORIC PARK

La Porte, Texas

Six weeks after the fall of the Alamo, Sam Houston's Texas Army was finally ready to fight. Pursued by Mexican forces under Santa Anna, Houston withdrew all the way to the coast, using the time to organize and train his army. Then, in a sudden surprise attack, the Texians decisively defeated the Mexicans in a battle that lasted only twenty minutes. The next day, Santa Anna was captured and was forced to sign a treaty granting Texas its independence.

Today the San Jacinto Battleground State Historical Park, located twenty-two miles east of downtown Houston, contains a museum and a large monument commemorating the battle that won Texian independence. Also of interest, moored in a permanent slip in the park, is the battleship *Texas,* the sole surviving example of a pre-World War I dreadnaught.

San Jacinto Monument State Historical Park
3800 Park Road 1836
La Porte, Texas 77571
(713) 979-2019

TEXAS STATE CEMETERY

Austin, Texas

The State Cemetery in Austin was established in 1851. A number of important figures from the Texas Revolution are buried there, including Stephen F. Austin, Edward Burleson, and Robert "Three-Legged Willie" Williamson. There is also a plaque honoring Susannah Dickinson, who is buried in nearby Oakwood Cemetery.

The Texas State Cemetery is located on Comal Avenue, between 7th and 11th streets, in Austin.

OTHER ALAMO RESOURCES

THE ALAMO SOCIETY

The Alamo Society is an international organization whose members share a common interest in the history of the Alamo and the Texas Revolution.

Members share their knowledge on a wide range of subjects in *The Alamo Journal,* which is published five times yearly. Articles deal with such diverse topics as the Alamo's "true" history, myths about the Alamo, reviews and commentary on Alamo books and movies, and stories about, and interviews with, the actors that appeared in them.

Famous author Walter Lord, who wrote *A Time to Stand,* is a member. Fess Parker, Walt Disney's Davy Crockett, often contributes a column, "Talkin' with Fess." Society member Ashley Ward of Ohio was responsible for the discovery of a print of the long lost UNCUT version of John Wayne's *The Alamo.* (See Chapter Sixteen.)

If you have a serious, or even just a casual, interest in Alamo history and lore, then you should be a member of the Alamo Society. Write for information on dues and other aspects of the Society.

William R. Chemerka
The Alamo Society
7 Heritage Drive
East Hanover, NJ 07936

THE SAN ANTONIO LIVING HISTORY ASSOCIATION

The San Antonio Living History Association Inc. (SALHA) is a non-profit, educational organization of historical reenactors that was founded in 1986. Its members specialize in reenacting events of the 1830s, and in particular the events and lifestyles of the Texas War of Independence. SALHA sponsors a number of different annual battle reenactments and other special events for the general public, as well as cultural and educational programs for schoolchildren in the San Antonio area.

SALHA attempts to give a balanced picture of Texas history, and its members portray a wide range of civilian and military historical impressions. Regular Texian and Mexican soldiers, militia and auxiliary units, Tejanos, American and European immigrants are all represented. SALHA is a family oriented group, and women and children also play appropriate roles. Authenticity in interpretation, clothing, and equipment is a high priority.

Most SALHA members hail from Texas, and in particular from South Texas, but there are members from coast to coast, Canada, Mexico, and abroad. For additional information on membership or activities, contact:

THE SAN ANTONTlO
LIVING HISTORY ASSOCIATION, c/o:

Robert E. Carrier	or	Ed Miller
3938 Heritage Hill Dr.		9950 Timber Trace
San Antonio, TX 78247		San Antonio, TX 78250
(210) 496-5937		(210) 521-7594

THE ALAMO BATTLEFIELD ASSOCIATION

The Alamo Battlefield Association is an organization dedicated to the preservation and study of the Alamo and the Texas War of Independence, from 1718 until the present. Members receive a newsletter and an annual, scholarly journal. The association also sponsors an annual conference, with speakers on a wide range of historical topics. For more information, write:

THE ALAMO BATTLEFIELD ASSOCIATION
P.O. Box 697
San Antonio, Texas 78293

THE ALAMO LEGACY AND MISSION ASSOCIATION

The Alamo Legacy and Mission Association (ALMA) is an organization that is dedicated to promoting the rich and varied heritage of San Antonio and the state of Texas through living history interpretation.

Through historical reenactments and educational programs, ALMA members tell Texas' history from the Spanish colonial period through 1900. In addition to educational activities at established historic sites, ALMA provides color and honor guard details, as well as historical Texas interpreters, for ceremonial and civic occasions and other special events.

ALAMO LEGACY & MISSION ASSOCIATION
c/o Charles Lara
Rt. 3 Box 3112
Lakehills, Texas 78063
(210) 612-3457

JOHN WAYNE MOVIE SET. The John Wayne movie set from The Alamo *still exists, and can be visited at Alamo Village, on the ranch of James T. "Happy" Shahan, near Brackettville.*

LA BAHÍA. The Presidio La Bahía at Goliad has been restored the way it appeared during the Texas Revolution, with the exception of the church bell tower, which was not added until the twentieth century.

CHAPTER FIFTEEN

Uniforms, Weapons, and Equipment of the Alamo

PART 1: INTRODUCTION TO ALAMO-ERA FIREARMS

NOTE: For the benefit of those readers who do not have a background in historic weapons, a brief explanation of the firearms used at the Alamo, and how they worked, is provided here.

Despite the general popularity of the American longrifle, most of the firearms used at the Alamo were smoothbores. Although the percussion ignition system had been invented about 1816, its use was still limited, and most of the weapons on both sides used the flintlock ignition system.

The first thing that must be understood is the difference between a smoothbore and a rifle. Smoothbores are just what the name implies—the barrel is nothing more than a smooth tube. A rifle, on the other hand, has a barrel with a series of gently twisting "lands and grooves" milled into it.

Most authorities agree that the principle of rifling was invented by German gunmakers in the late fifteenth or early sixteenth centuries. (Kauffman, 1) When a soft lead ball, covered with a cloth patch, is fired from a rifled barrel, it is gripped by the lands and grooves, which cause the ball to spin with the twist of the rifling. This spin greatly improves the accuracy of the shot compared to that of a ball fired from a smoothbore. Both the accuracy and the maximum effective range of a rifle are significantly greater than that of a smoothbore musket.

On the negative side, when trying for accuracy, a rifle is slower and more difficult to load than a smoothbore. However, it is a misconception that this always need be the case. If the shooter is in a hurry, by omitting patch, the undersized ball can be rammed down a rifled barrel just about as quickly as down a smoothbore. Accuracy suffers, however. A major reason why the rifle was slow to gain acceptance as a military arm was the fact that it was not generally fitted for a bayonet, and in 1836 the bayonet was still an important military weapon.

All of the firearms used at the Alamo were muzzleloaders, which meant that the powder and ball had to be placed down the barrel from the muzzle end. The procedure for loading a muzzleloading firearm was essentially the same in the 1830s as it is for today's black powder shooters.

Smoothbore muskets were often loaded from prepared paper cartridges, where the ball was wrapped with the powder. The tip of the cartridge was torn off, and a small amount of powder was poured into the pan of the lock for priming. The rest of the powder was then poured down the barrel, and the ball was rammed down on top of it. The paper from the cartridge was usually used as wadding between the powder and the ball.

In most cases with rifles, and when prepared cartridges were not used with smoothbores, the loading sequence was slightly different. Ball and powder were carried separately—the balls in a leather hunting bag or military cartridge box, and the powder in a powder horn or flask.

In loading, the powder was first poured into a measure, for both safety reasons and to insure an accurate charge. The powder was then poured down the barrel from the measure. In spite of the popular Hollywood image, it was, and *is,* very dangerous to load *directly* from a horn or flask. Except in extreme emergencies, the powder was poured into a measure first, and then down the barrel.

For maximum accuracy, a rifle ball had to be "patched" before being rammed down the barrel. A piece of linen or cotton patching was placed over the muzzle, and the ball was forced down just below the rim of the muzzle, with the patching wrapping itself around the ball. The excess patching, if any, was cut away, and the ball was then rammed the rest of the way down until it was seated on the powder charge. To facilitate the ramming, and to help keep the bore cleaner, the patch was usually lubricated with grease or tallow. For a quick shot, human saliva worked just fine.

When loading was done from a horn or flask, instead of from a premade cartridge, the pan of the lock was primed as the last step, again as a safety measure. Riflemen often carried a second, smaller horn, with finer grained powder, for priming.

The flintlock is a simple, reliable ignition system that has been around since 1630. (Kauffman, 4) A flintlock is nothing more than a mechanical flint and steel device that sends a shower of sparks into the priming pan when the trigger is pulled. The priming powder ignites and burns through a small "touch hole," setting off the main charge. The resulting explosion sends the ball on its way out the barrel and toward its target.

The main components of the flintlock are the hammer, or cock, the frizzen, or battery, and the pan. The pan holds the priming powder, and it is securely covered by the frizzen until the gun is fired. The hammer is a serpent-like device with two jaws that tightly hold a small piece of sharpened flint in place. When the trigger is pulled, the hammer springs forward, striking the flint against the frizzen, which is hardened steel. The flint striking the frizzen causes a shower of sparks, which is directed downward into the pan, igniting the priming powder. This powder burns through the touch hole into the barrel, causing the main charge to ignite. The resulting pressure drives the ball out of the end of the barrel and on its way toward the target.

A newer system known as percussion ignition existed in 1836, but it was not yet in wide use. In the percussion system, the pan was replaced by a hollow "nipple," over which a brass cap containing a small amount of fulminate of mercury was fitted. When the hammer on a percussion lock struck the nipple, the resulting spark was driven down through the hollow nipple and into the main charge, causing the gun to fire.

While the percussion system would eventually replace the flintlock, it is doubtful that many were used at the Alamo by either side. As late as 1843, the percussion system was still looked upon with suspicion by military authorities. That year, U.S. Army Col. Sylvanus Thayer, an innovative thinker best remembered as "The Father of West Point," was sent on a fact-finding trip to Europe. Three of the eight areas of military science that he was ordered to gather information on had to do with the percussion lock. Thayer was specifically asked to "Note all of the objections that have been found against them that are well authenticated." (Dupuy, 242)

There is evidence that at least a few percussion guns were used by the Texians, however. The Muse-

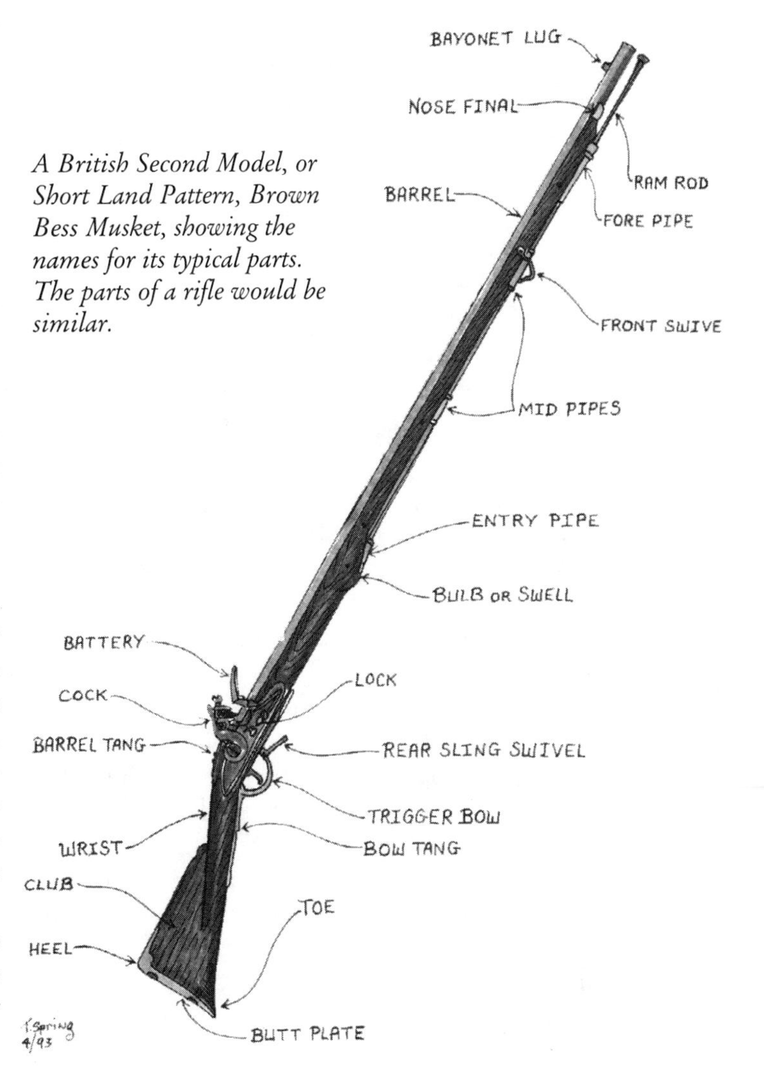

A British Second Model, or Short Land Pattern, Brown Bess Musket, showing the names for its typical parts. The parts of a rifle would be similar.

um of Insurrection in Mexico City has a display of U.S. Model 1833 Springfield percussion rifles labeled "Batalla Del Alamo 1836." If this attribution is correct, then percussion weapons were not entirely unknown at the Alamo. (Bourdage, 14) It is also possible that a few of the wealthier Mexican officers could have carried personally owned percussion weapons.

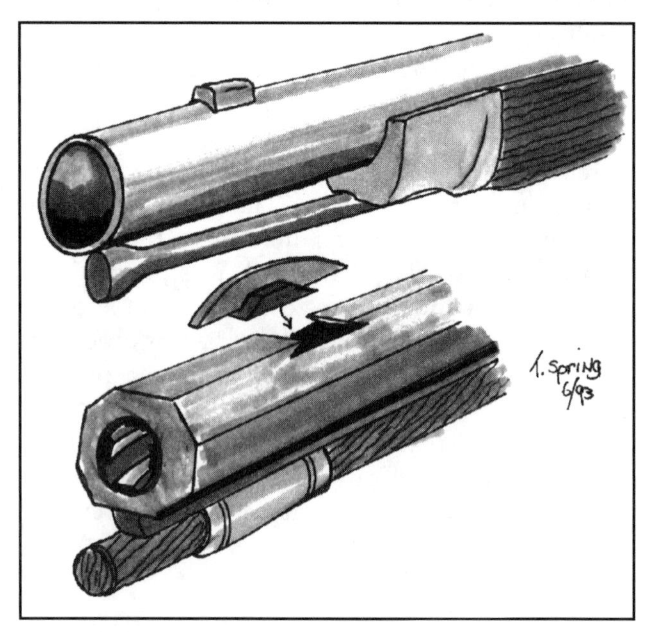

THE DIFFERENCE BETWEEN RIFLED AND SMOOTHBORE BARRELS

TOP: *A smoothbore barrel with a bayonet lug affixed to the top.*

BOTTOM: *An octagon rifle barrel, showing the lands and grooves. Unlike most smoothbores, rifles had front sights. This one is dovetailed in place, and can be adjusted for windage to improve accuracy.*

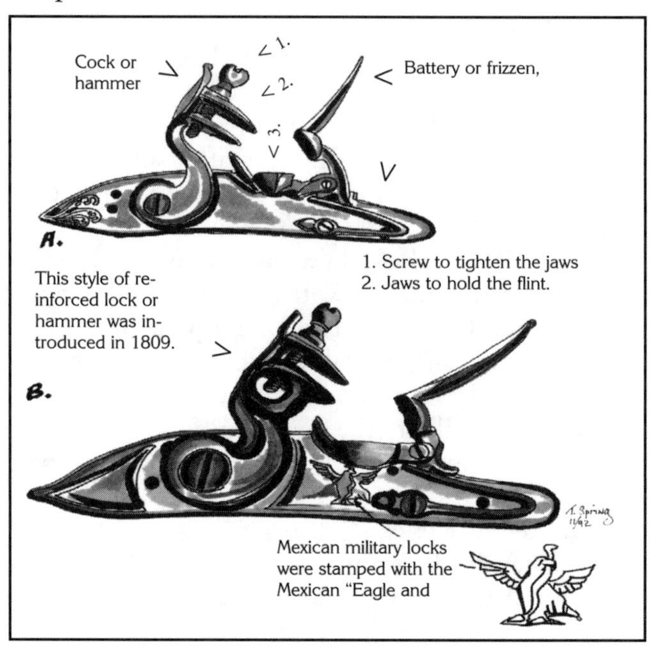

TYPICAL RIFLE AND MUSKET FLINTLOCKS

A. *A typical American rifle lock, circa 1810-1814.*

B. *A British surplus Third Model Brown Bess or "India Pattern" lock, used by the Mexican army, and undoubtedly by some Texians as well.*

Musket locks were typically larger than rifle locks.

PART 2: UNIFORMS, WEAPONS, AND EQUIPMENT OF THE ALAMO DEFENDERS

There was no such thing as an "official" uniform for the Texas Army. Lt. Col. William Barret Travis is known to have ordered a uniform before he went to the Alamo, but it was never delivered, and we have no idea what it would have looked like.

Most of the Alamo defenders wore typical civilian clothing of the period. Some who had prior military service may have worn parts of their old uniforms and used pieces of their old equipment. Even volunteers with no prior service may have had military clothing and equipment, because the United States government occasionally sold surplus goods at public auction. Undoubtedly, there was a liberal mixture of civilian clothing and gear. Some Texians may have worn buckskin clothing, as popularized by Hollywood movies, but most would have been dressed in garments of manmade fabrics such as wool, linen, and cotton. The Tejanos, of course, would have worn clothing typical of their Mexican heritage.

There was one unit at the Alamo, the New Orleans Greys, that was officially uniformed at one time. Before they left New Orleans, they were issued uniforms similar to the gray U.S. Army fatigue uniforms. However, they had fought through the Siege of Bexar, and by the time of the Alamo, their uniforms would have been well worn. The very latest research also suggests that most or all of the "Greys" were equipped with rifles rather than smoothbored muskets.

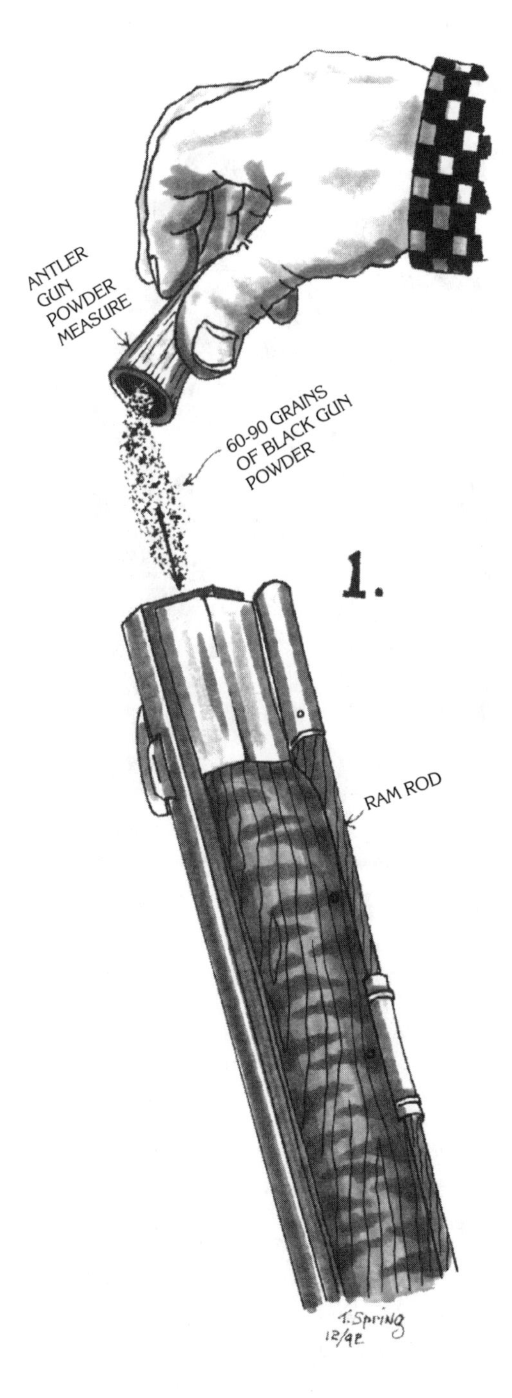

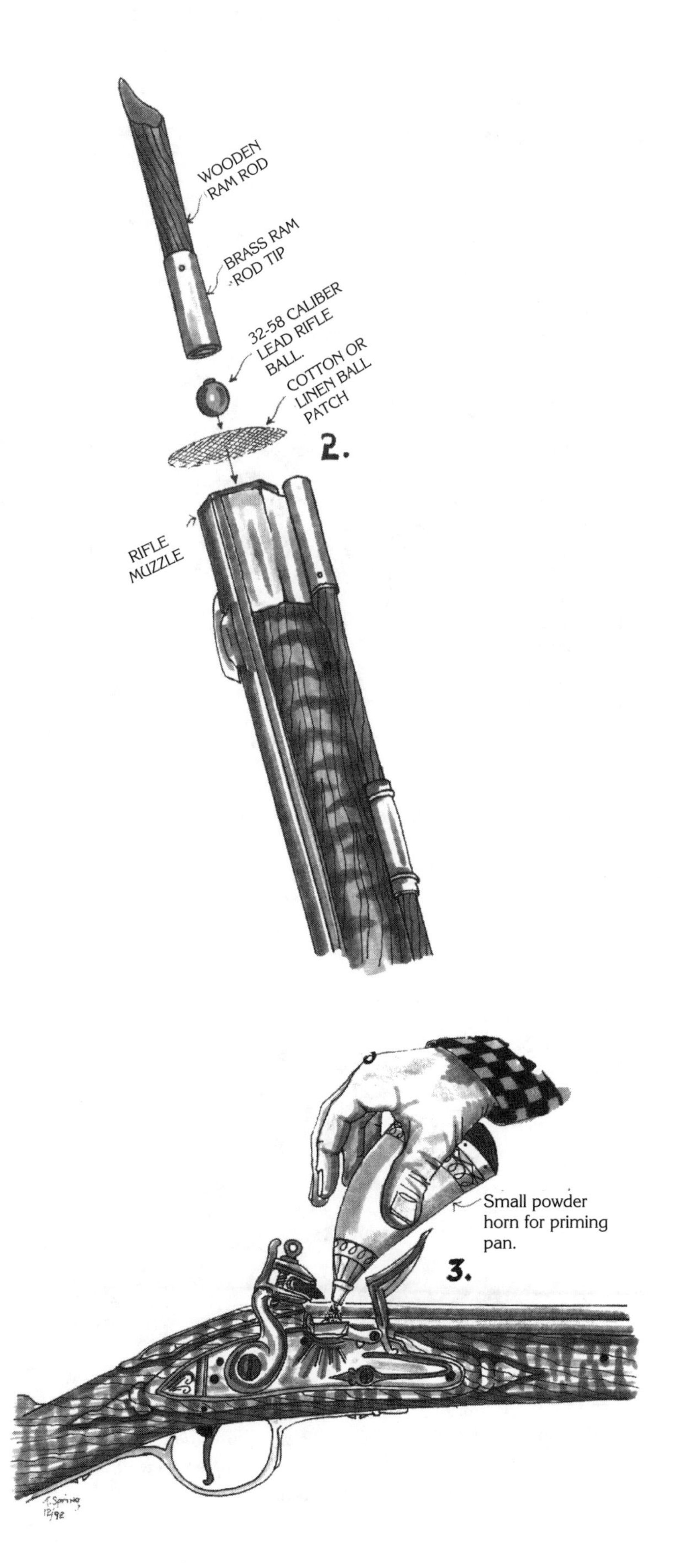

Loading the muzzle-loading rifle

ALAMO DEFENDERS. *These two figures show examples of civilian dress that would have been worn at the Alamo. The defender on the left wears a warm wool coat, trousers, and leather boots. He gives the appearance of being well to do, and is probably from an American or European background. The defender on the right is a Tejano who supports the Revolution. He wears clothing that is typical of that worn on the Mexican frontier.*

A "COW'S KNEE." *Leather lock covers, or "cow's knees," such as these were used to protect the locks of both civilian and military weapons during wet weather.*

ALAMO DEFENDERS. *The defender on the left belongs to one of the companies of New Orleans Greys. Their uniform was similar to the field uniform of the U.S. Army at the time. It consisted of a short gray coatee, gray trousers, and a forage cap, which came in several styles. This man wears his military coat with non-uniform civilian trousers, which replace his issued ones that have worn out. His forage cap is the leather 1833 model. He carries a Model 1816 U.S. Military Musket, and is holding a canvas haversack. (Note that the latest research, uncovered since these sketches were completed, suggests that the Greys probably were equipped with rifles rather than muskets.) The volunteer on the right wears civilian clothing typical of a fairly well-to-do gentleman of the period. He carries a side by side, double-barreled flintlock shotgun, and wears a brass powder flask over his shoulder. Both of these indicate that he is a man of some means. The view of this sketch is looking toward the northwest corner of the Alamo compound.*

TEJANO DEFENDERS. The Tejano on the left is a member of Juan Seguin's company of Regular Texas Cavalry. He wears traditional vaquero *clothing that is ideal for mounted activity. The man on the right is dressed in the more simple, yet functional, manner of a Mexican peasant.*

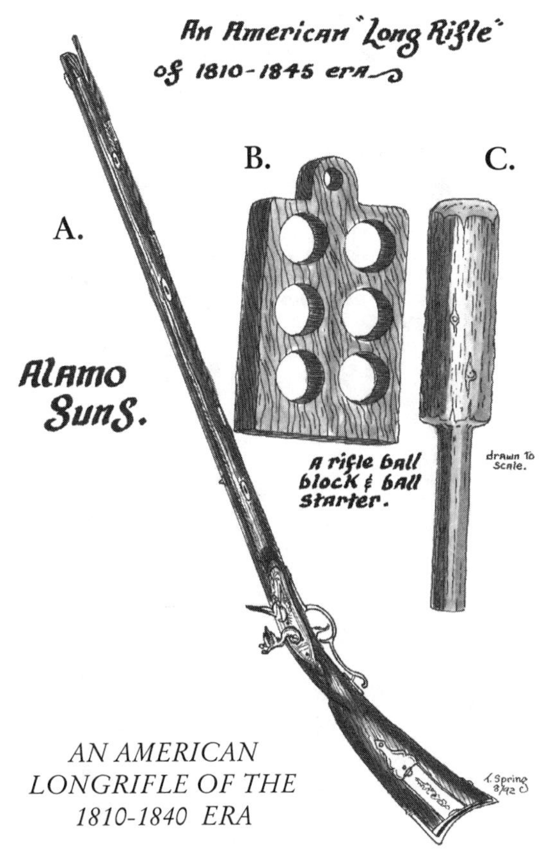

AN AMERICAN LONGRIFLE OF THE 1810-1840 ERA

A. *A typical Kentucky or Pennsylvania Longrifle of the period. These were some of the most beautiful firearms ever made and generally had octagonal barrels, fine steel locks, brass and/or German silver hardware, and curly maple stocks.*

B. *A hardwood loading block. Loading blocks were sometimes used to speed up the loading process. Lead balls with greased patches around them were set in the holes in the block. When needed, a ball was centered over the muzzle of the rifle and pushed down through the block and into the bore.*

C. *A short starter. Short starters were sometimes used to get the ball started down the barrel, both with and without the use of a loading block. A short starter provided better leverage than the long ramrod. Once the patch and ball were three or four inches into the barrel, the regular ramrod was used to push them the rest of the way down.*

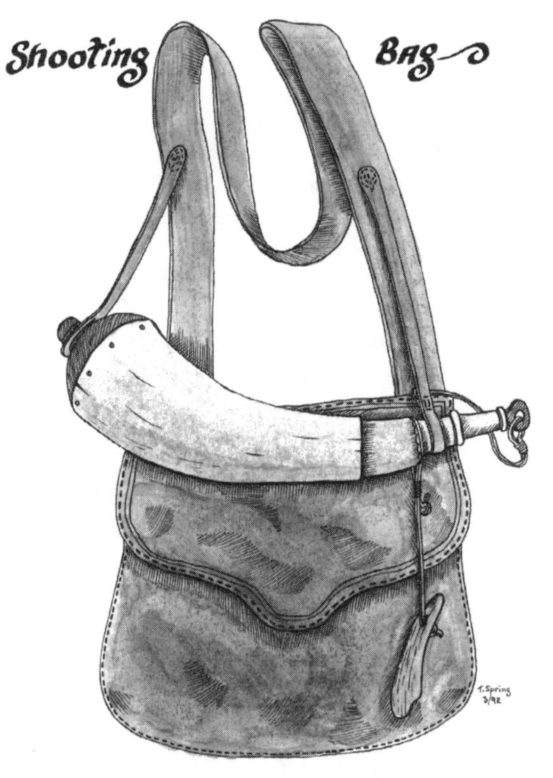

LEATHER HUNTING POUCH AND POWDER HORN. Riflemen carried their shooting supplies in leather pouches such as this one. The pouches contained lead balls, patching material and grease, extra flints, a short starter, and simple tools to keep the gun functioning properly. Riflemen also usually carried a ball mold and pieces of bar lead either in their shooting pouch or elsewhere in their kit. If the person had a smoothbore instead of a rifle, he most likely would carry buckshot in addition to round balls. The hunting pouch illustrated here has a powder horn attached to its strap. The horn could also be carried on a strap all by itself, depending on the owner's preference. An antler tip powder measure also hangs from a leather thong.

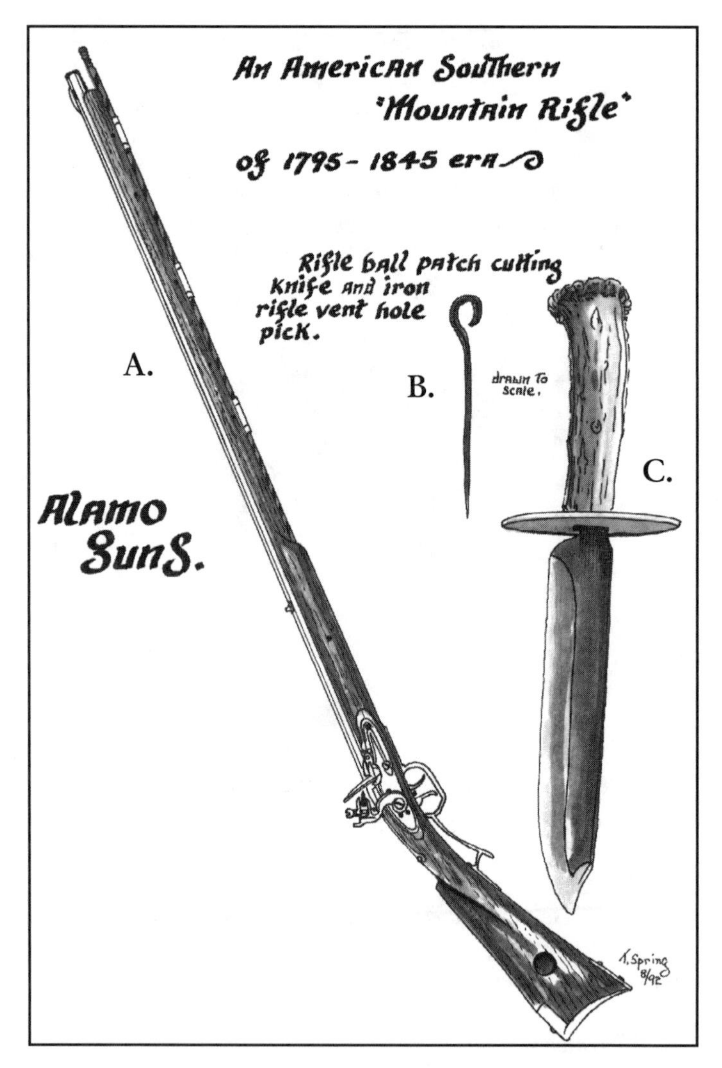

AN AMERICAN SOUTHERN MOUNTAIN RIFLE, 1795-1845

A. *The Southern Mountain Style Rifle shown here was less ornate, and less expensive, than the fancier Kentucky and Pennsylvania longrifles, but very functional nonetheless. Mountain rifles generally had iron hardware, less expensive wood, and a plainer design than the longrifles. Instead of brass patchboxes, they usually just had a grease hole in the stock. The hole was filled with grease or tallow, which was used as lubricant for the patches.*

B. *A touch hole pick. The forged touch hole pick was a small needle-like device that was used to keep the touch hole free of powder fouling.*

C. *A patch knife. Many riflemen carried small knives that were used to cut away the excess patching when the ball was seated flush with the end of the muzzle.*

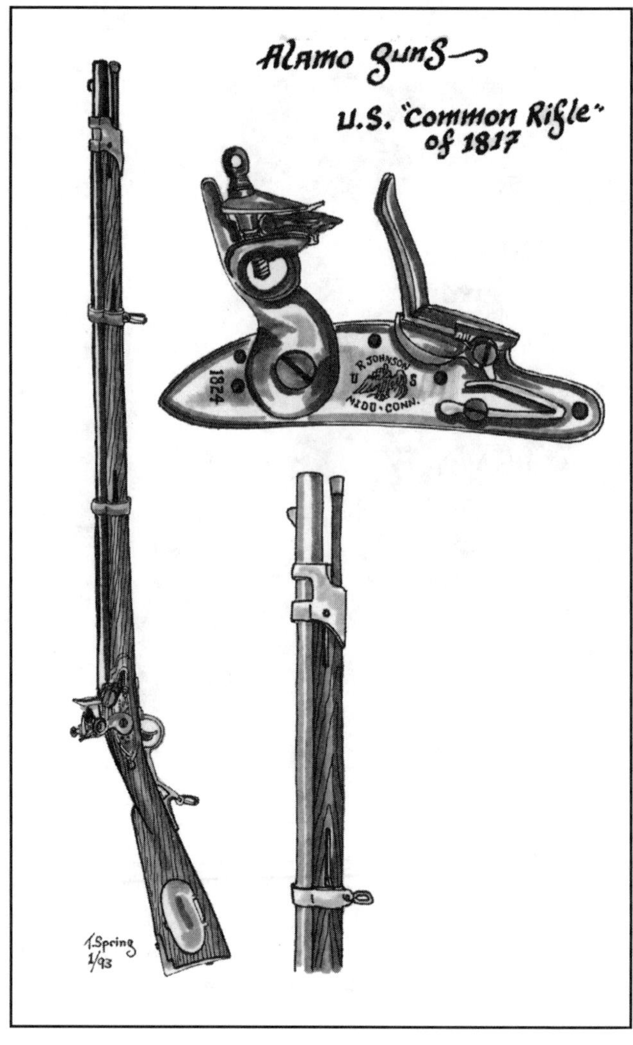

THE U.S. MODEL 1817 "COMMON RIFLE"

This early American military rifle was in common use on the frontier by 1836, and was undoubtedly used by some of the Alamo defenders. It was one of the few U.S. military rifles to use a paper cartridge with a pre-patched ball.

The date 1824 on the lock indicates that the lock was made in that year. Unless the lock was a replacement, the rifle itself would have been assembled in 1824 or later.

The lock had a unique detachable brass pan, and was made by Henry Deringer and Simon North.

MODEL 1816 U.S. MILITARY MUSKET
The U.S. Model 1816 Military Musket was one of the surplus American weapons that saw use at the Alamo. This model of musket was first introduced in 1816, and with minor variations, it remained in production for many years. The way that the sling swivel is attached to the stock indicates that the one illustrated is the 1822 version. The locks were manufactured separately from the guns, and were stamped with their date of manufacture. The lock illustrated here was made in 1816, and kept in storage until 1822, when the musket shown was assembled. The 1816 Musket was fitted with traditional triangular-style bayonet.

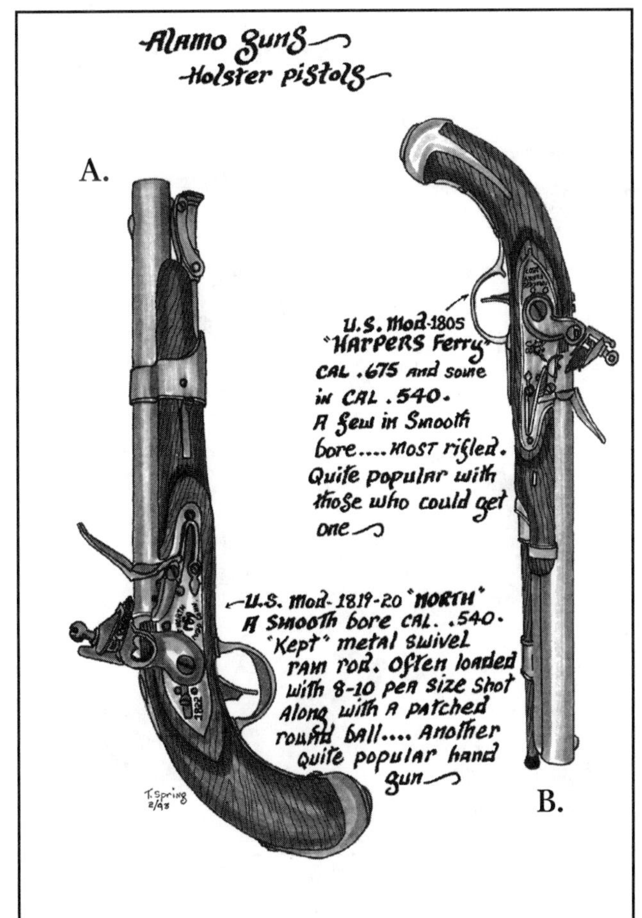

Above right:
HOLSTER PISTOLS. While pistols were not as common on the frontier as long guns, many people did carry them. In the military, pistols were especially popular with officers and mounted troops. The two pistols illustrated here are U.S. military models.
A. *The U.S. Model 1819 "North" pistol was a smoothbore of .54 caliber. It could be loaded with a solid lead ball, buckshot, or both. The swivel ramrod was permanently attached so that cavalrymen could reload without fear of dropping it.*
B. *This .54-caliber Model 1805 "Harper's Ferry" pistol was one of a long line of firearms to bear that name. They were named for the federal arsenal at Harper's Ferry, West Virginia, where they were made. Most of this model were smoothbore, but a few were rifled.*

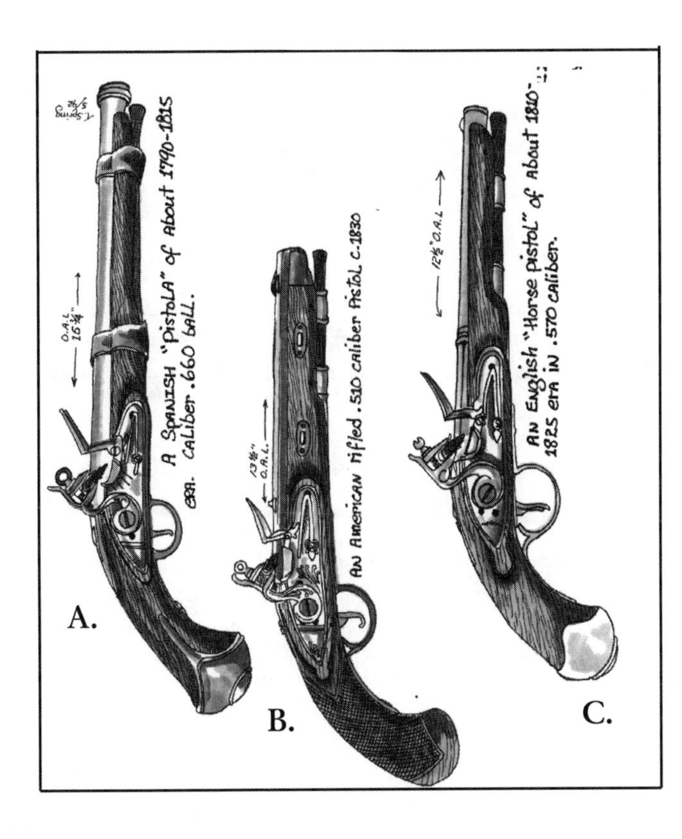

Left:
Pistols of Spanish, English, and American manufacture could have been carried by the Alamo defenders.
A. *A Spanish-style, .66-caliber smoothbore pistol, circa 1790-1815.*
B. *An American "Kentucky"-style rifled pistol, .51 caliber, circa 1830.*
C. *An English, .57-caliber smoothbore horse pistol, circa 1810-1825.*

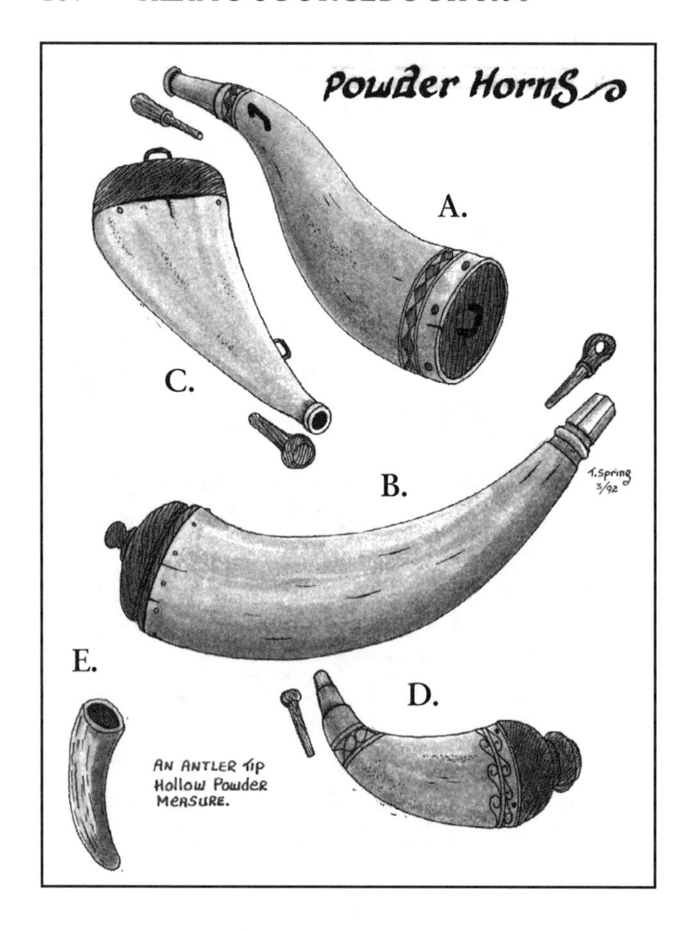

POWDER HORNS

Powder horns were usually made from hollowed out cow or steer horns, and were often elaborately carved and decorated. They were used to carry a supply of black powder, and usually had a capacity of one-half to one pound. They could either be carried on a separate shoulder strap or affixed to the shooting bag.

A. & B. *Typical round horns of modest quality.*

C. *A smaller, flat powder horn. Horns could be made soft by boiling, and then gently bent into any shape desired. This one has been flattened and fitted with a narrow wooden end plug to make it easier to carry.*

D. *A small priming horn, filled with a finer grain powder, was used to prime the pan on a flintlock.*

E. *A powder measure. A hollowed out deer antler made a good powder measure. Use of a powder measure not only made loading safer, but also insured that the powder charges were of a consistent size.*

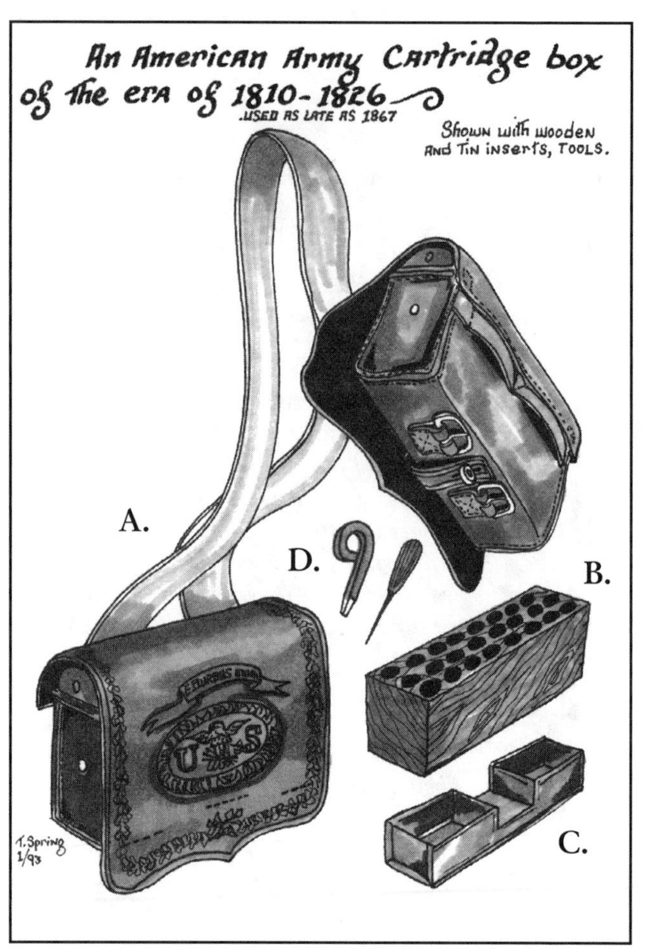

A TYPICAL AMERICAN
MILITARY CARTRIDGE BOX

A. *A Model 1808 cartridge box, front and rear views. The military cartridge box was to the soldier what the shooting bag and powder horn were to civilian hunters and riflemen. Although this is a Model 1808 box, the design stamped on the flap shows that it was made in 1835. Most similar boxes had plain flaps.*

B. *Pre-rolled paper cartridges containing both powder and ball were stored in the holes of a drilled wooden block. The block fit down inside the leather box, loosely enough so that it could be easily removed.*

C. *A tin insert was often used underneath the cartridge block to hold extra flints, tools, and cleaning materials.*

D. *Examples of two tools that might have been carried in a cartridge box: a hand-forged screwdriver that also could be used as a "flint knapper" to keep the edge of the flint sharp, and a non-issue pick to keep the touch hole clear.*

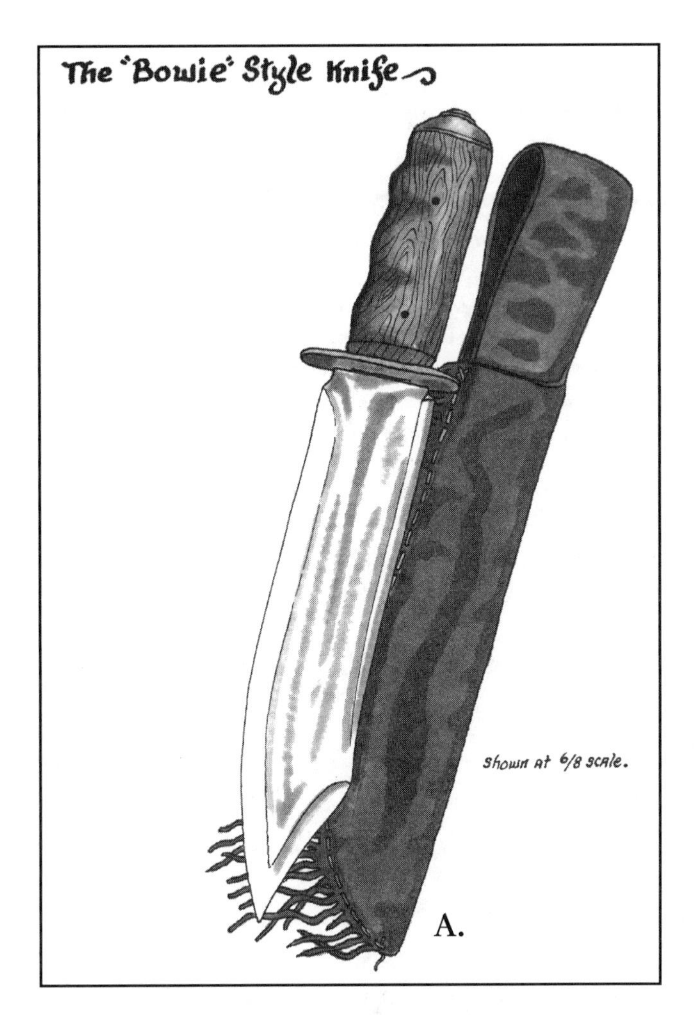

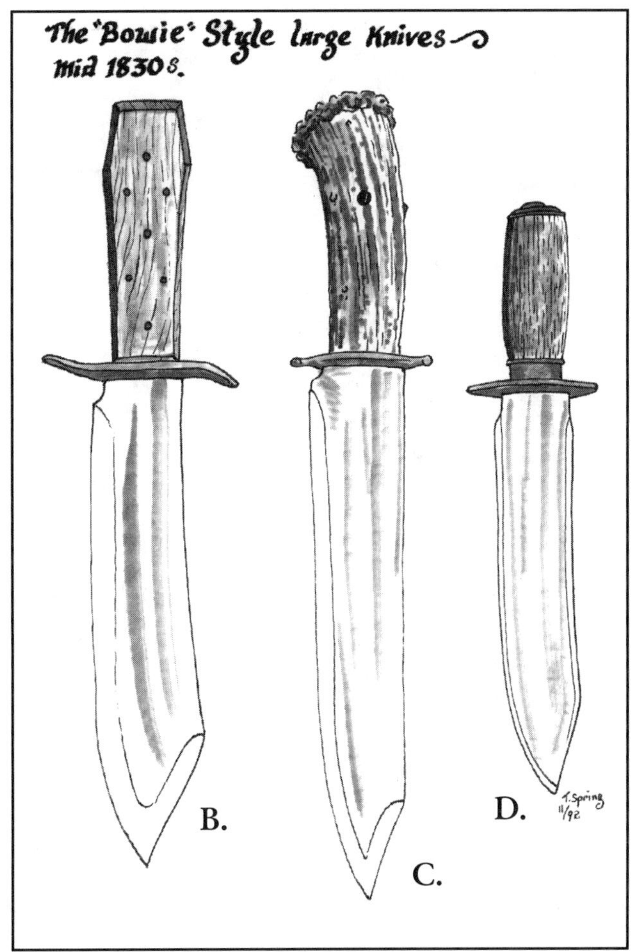

BOWIE KNIVES

Bowie knives were made famous by James Bowie long before the Siege of the Alamo. Large and heavy, "Bowie"-style knives were more suited for fighting than for regular chores. Blacksmith Rezin Bowie, James' brother, made the one that James carried during the Siege of the Alamo. More than likely it was taken as a trophy by a Mexican soldier after the battle, and its current whereabouts is unknown. Several knives that could possibly be Bowie's have surfaced over the years, but none have been positively authenticated.

The examples shown here are typical Bowie-style knives of the 1830s period:

A. *This Bowie knife has a wooden "finger grooved" handle, a style of handle that dates back at least to the War of 1812.*
B. *A Bowie knife with a wooden "coffin shaped" handle.*
C. *A similar blade with an antler handle.*
D. *A smaller blade with an oval-shaped wooden handle.*

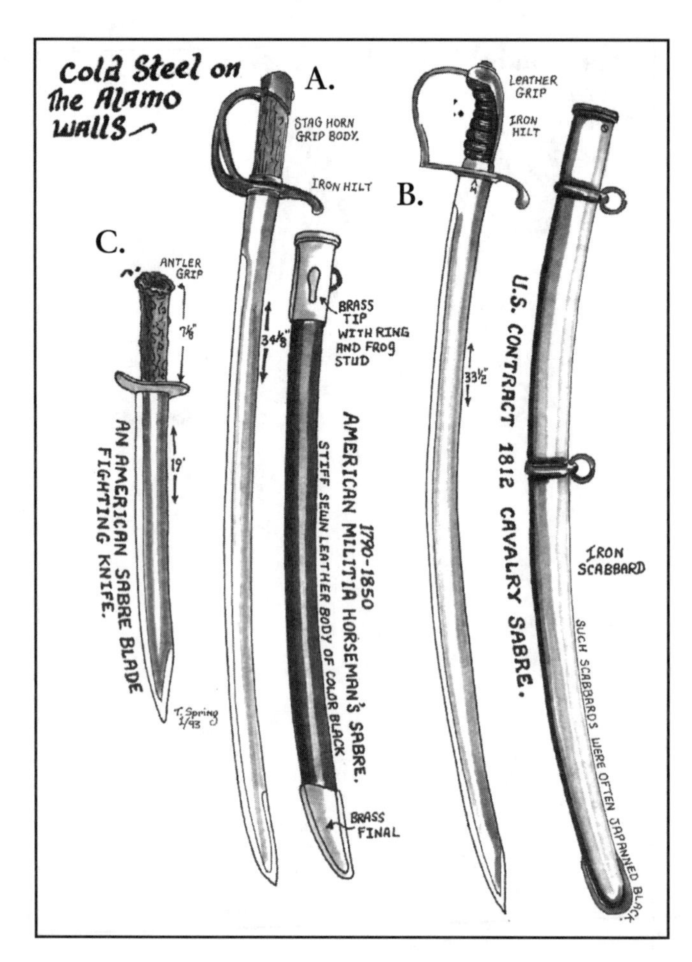

SWORDS

In the 1830s, swords were still in common use by the military, especially by horsemen and officers. Col. William Barret Travis and some of the other officers at the Alamo undoubtedly had swords, and it is possible that a few of the NCOs and enlisted men also carried them.

A. *An example of an American militia cavalry sabre, circa 1790-1850. This is a plain, simple sword that could have been made by a local blacksmith. It has a forged steel blade, an iron hilt with stag grip, and a black leather scabbard with brass hardware.*

B. *The U.S. Model 1812 Cavalry Sabre had a steel blade, an iron hilt, a leather-covered grip, and an iron scabbard. This model sabre had been in use for over twenty years, and it is very possible that some found their way to the Alamo.*

C. *A locally made hunting sword, which was in reality a large knife with an antler handle and a slightly curved iron blade.*

PART 3: UNIFORMS, WEAPONS, AND EQUIPMENT OF THE MEXICAN ARMY

UNIFORMS

The Mexican Army of Operations is often depicted as a magnificently uniformed, well-equipped body of men. This perception is both true and false. As with most armies in the field, what the regulations said, and what really existed, were often two very different things.

In theory, the Mexican army was uniformed along Napoleonic lines and was equipped with a wide variety of surplus French and English weapons and accoutrements. One thing is undoubtedly clear—the Mexican army was definitely uniformed better than the Texian army that opposed it.

The official Mexican army uniforms for the Texas Campaign were prescribed by the Dress Contracts of 1832 and 1833. However, at any given time, and within any given unit, uniform parts and equipment from the 1821, 1823, and 1827 warrants could also be found.

Two images of the Mexican soldier popularized in Alamo art and movies are definitely erroneous, and should be corrected. The first error is the infantry shako with the "bull's eye" design painted on the top. This design was used briefly in the 1820s, but that particular shako was very poor quality and fell apart quickly in bad weather. Even at the time they were used, these bull's eyes were not perfectly concentric circles that we see depicted today. In reality, they were poorly hand painted, and the circles were uneven and even elongated. By 1836, this style of shako had long since been replaced by a sturdier model with a plain black top. (See illustration on page 170.)

The second mistake that is often made is showing the puffy "wings" on the shoulders of the uniform coats, similar to those worn by grenadiers in many armies of the time. There is no evidence that these wings were worn by any Mexican troops during the Texas Campaign.

STANDARD UNIFORM ISSUE FOR A MEXICAN INFANTRY SOLDIER

Every thirty months:

—A dark blue dress coat of Queretaro cloth, with a scarlet collar, lapels, cuffs, and turnbacks, white piping, and brass buttons. (The exact definition of Queretaro cloth is elusive, but evidence indicates that it was a coarse woolen cloth manufactured at the textile mill in the town of Queretaro, Mexico.)
—Two sailcloth waistcoats, with red collars and cuffs. During the Texas Campaign, the waistcoat was often worn as a fatigue coat.
—Two pairs of sailcloth trousers.
—Two linen shirts.
—Two black velveteen neck stocks.
—Two pair of shoes. Mexican soldiers were issued both low- and high-cut leather shoes. Sandals were also worn, and on some occasions the soldiers even went barefoot.
—One fatigue cap, with band, tassel, and visor.

Every sixty months:

—A black cowhide shako, slightly bell topped with a brass plate and chinscales, cotton cords, and wool pompon. The cords were yellow for fusiliers, red for grenadiers, and green for chasseurs. At least some units are believed to have had white canvas covers for their shakos, designed to protect them while on the march and during bad weather.
—A blue-gray overcoat of Queretaro cloth, with a red collar, cuffs, piping, and brass buttons.
—A leather or canvas knapsack with leather straps and metal buckles.

Without time consideration:

—Leather crossbelts, with a black leather, tin-lined cartridge box, bayonet, and frog. The crossbelts were generally white leather, but some of the elite troops were issued black ones.
—A canteen with strap.
—A blue-gray burlap blanket with leather strap, worn on top of the knapsack.
—A burlap ration bag.

A supplementary warrant of June 1833 authorized a single-breasted, dark blue infantry coat, while the 1832 model was double-breasted with white piping. The 1833 model had a red collar, cuffs, and piping. The unit designation was embroidered on the collar of this coat. This unit designation was probably a number prior to 1835, with letter combinations thereafter. (For example, "BM" for the Battalion Matamoros.) Crimson epaulettes without fringe may have been worn with this coat.

Dark blue or white canvas trousers were also specified with the 1833 warrant. As a general rule, white trousers were worn during the summer. When authorized, dark blue, sky blue, or gray trousers would have been worn during the cooler months, but this was not an absolute rule. White, dark blue, and blue-gray trousers with red piping were all worn during the Texas Campaign.

After 1833, single or double "*sardinetas,*" or vertical cuff flashes, were authorized for the preference companies; that is, the grenadiers and light infantry.

Mexican field officers wore bicorn hats, with red, white, and green feathers over a tricolored cockade. Company officers were required to wear shakos when serving with their units, but were authorized plain bicorns without lace or feathers for other wear.

Infantry militia uniforms, while officially the same as for the regulars, often varied widely, with some units having no uniform at all.

STANDARD UNIFORM ISSUE FOR A MEXICAN CAVALRY TROOPER

Every thirty months:

—A dark blue, single-breasted tailcoat with red facings and white metal buttons. An earlier version of scarlet Queretaro cloth, with green collar, lapels, cuffs, and turnbacks, was probably not worn during the Texas Campaign.
—One pair of blue Queretaro cloth riding pants, with antelope skin inserts, a red seam stripe, and cordovan bells at the bottom of the legs.
—One pair of cloth trousers with stripes for dismounted wear.
—One sailcloth jacket.
—One pair sailcloth trousers.
—Two velveteen neckstocks.
—Two pair of shoes.
—One fatigue cap, the same as for the infantry.

Every sixty months:

—A cowhide helmet with brass shield, comb,

and chinscales, a goatskin, bearskin, or horsehair crest, and a wool plume or pompon.
—A cape of yellow Queretaro cloth, with a green collar and white metal buttons.
—A shabrak (saddle blanket) of Queretaro cloth with a wide cotton band and two tassels, and a lining of sailcloth or coarse brown linen.
—A saddle roll of green Queretaro cloth, trimmed with a cotton band and lined with sailcloth.
—Leather crossbelts, with a black leather, tin-lined cartridge box with loops for the cartridges, a waistbelt, and a bandoleer.
—A canteen with strap.
—A pair of leather gauntlets. (In reality, although gauntlets may have been common among the officers, they were probably relatively rare among the private soldiers.)
—One grain bag of sailcloth or coarse brown linen.
—Horse furniture.

(NOTE: If the cavalry followed the infantry pattern, some of the above items were probably issued without regard to a time schedule, but even Joseph Hefter's classic work *El Soldado Mexicano* does not clearly define this.)

Militia cavalry units, by regulation, wore uniforms similar to the regulars, but with reversed colors. This means that the milltia cavalry coats would have been red with a dark blue collar, lapels, cuffs, and turnbacks.

The presidial cavalry companies generally wore dark blue coatees with red facings, sometimes with a unit number embroidered on the collar. Blue trousers, with a red stripe and black leather reinforcement, were worn for garrison duty. In the field, loose-fitting blue or gray overalls with red stripes were often worn *over* protective leather gaiters.

Rather than the leather helmets of the regular cavalry, the presidial troopers wore a black, wide-brimmed hat with a flat crown. For dress, the right side was turned up. A wide white band, white or silver cords, and a tricolored plume were added. On campaign, the brim was worn flat, and all decoration except the white band was removed.

Another unique characteristic of these units was that their presidial name was often stitched onto their crossbelts.

Light cavalry units, created in 1835, were issued dark blue coatees with red facings and white metal buttons. They wore medium blue, leather-reinforced overalls with a red stripe on the seam. In addition to the traditional cavalry headgear, they sometimes wore a fur busby with cords and chinscales. They were armed with .65-caliber British Paget Carbines, sabres, and lances.

UNIFORMS OF OTHER MEXICAN UNITS

Mexican artillery uniforms were similar to infantry uniforms, with yellow grenade insignia on their red collars. The cuffs were blue, with red slashes, and the turnbacks were also red.

The elite Zapadores, or engineers, wore uniforms like those of the artillery, but with black facings and dark red piping. Their shakos had red lace, with a tufted red pompon resembling a bursting grenade.

THE MEXICAN UNIFORM OF 1833

The blue 1833 contract coatee was single-breasted and had a red collar, cuffs, and piping. A unit designation would have been embroidered in the collar. White canvas broadfall trousers, as specified in the warrant, are shown. Dark blue ones could also have been worn.

Top left:
TWO MEXICANS DRESSED FOR FIELD SERVICE
The veteran campaigner on the left wears a standard infantry uniform with full, if somewhat modified, field gear. He is armed with a surplus British India Pattern Brown Bess Musket. In addition to his issued equipment, he carries a large, personally owned knife on his right side. His cartridge box is not an issued model, and his blanket is tied to his pack in a nonregulation manner. The "muleteer" on the right has no uniform; he merely wears his own everyday clothing. Muleteers were civilians contracted to handle the army's mules, carts, and wagons that made up the supply trains.

Top right:
MEXICAN INFANTRY PRIVATE
This Mexican infantryman wears the 1833 single-breasted coatee, with white canvas trousers over his gaiters.

Bottom left:
A MEXICAN LIGHT CAVALRY TROOPER
This Mexican light cavalry trooper wears a dark blue jacket with red facings, and gray riding trousers. He also wears the crested cavalry helmet. Fur busbies and shakos with cords and chin scales were also sometimes worn by cavalry troopers. The trooper has dismounted to inspect a powder horn that was possibly dropped by an Alamo courier. He is armed with a surplus British carbine and an eight-foot, iron-tipped lance.

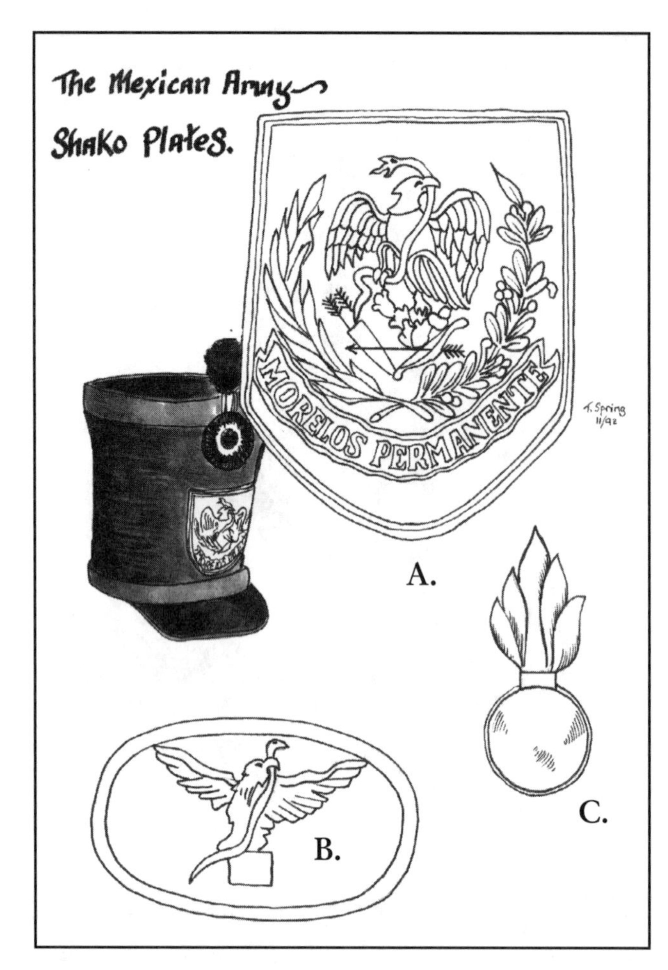

MEXICAN SHAKO AND SHAKO PLATES

Shown here is a plain, typical Mexican infantry leather shako. Those worn in the Texas Campaign were made of cowhide, and belled out slightly at the top. They were similar to the French 1825 Model. For regular regiments, the shakos were often decorated with pompons, dangling cords, and had fancy brass chinscales to hold them on the soldier's head. Militia shakos, on the other hand, had plain leather chinstraps and no decorative cords.

All shakos had a brass plate on the front. Three different types are shown here:

A. *The plate of the Morales Permanente Battalion. This sketch is based on a partial original plate recovered during an archeological dig.*

B. *A light infantry shako plate.*

C. *A grenadier's shako plate.*

Contrary to the image often projected in art and movies Mexican shakos did not have a "target" of concentric circles painted on the top. This design was used briefly in earlier years, but was definitely obsolete by the Texas Campaign.

MEXICAN CAVALRY HELMET. This Mexican cavalry helmet, with its long horsehair mane, is similar to the "crested" one shown on the cavalryman on page 169, except that the crest has been replaced by the horsehair mane.

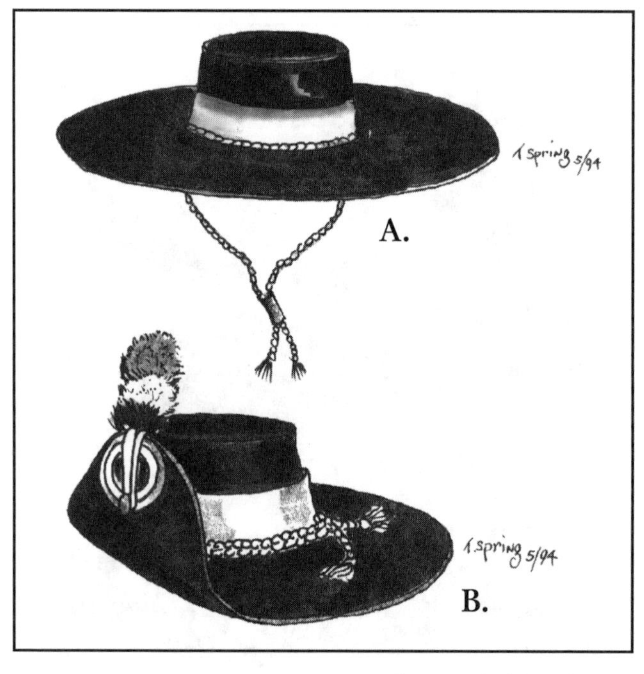

PRESIDIAL CAVALRY HATS. The presidial cavalry hat is shown in both the campaign (A) and dress (B) modes. For dress, the hat was worn with the cockade, plume, and hat cords, with the side turned up. On campaign, the cords, cockade, and plume were removed, and the brim was worn flat.

MEXICAN ARMY WEAPONS

The Mexican infantry generally carried surplus British Third Model, .75-caliber, Brown Bess Muskets. Most of these weapons were veterans of the Napoleonic Wars.

The elite light infantry troops were issued the more modern .62-caliber English Baker Rifle.

Dragoons carried British Paget carbines, Tower pistols, and British sabres.

THE BRITISH BROWN BESS MUSKET

At one time, Mexico had its own factory capable of manufacturing fine quality firearms, but by the time of the Texas Revolution, it was no longer in production. (Hefter, 53) The most common long gun of Santa Anna's army was the English Brown Bess .75-caliber smoothbore musket.

Although the Brown Bess lacked the range and accuracy of the rifles used by some of the Texians, this military musket was still a formidable weapon in the hands of well-disciplined troops. With proper training, a soldier could fire four rounds per minute with his musket, but few of the Mexican *soldados* were that proficient.

The Brown Bess was a rugged and reliable weapon that served the British army well for over a hundred years. The three main variations are now classified by collectors and historians as the First, Second, and Third Models.

The Long Land Pattern Musket, or "First Model," was introduced in 1717. This basic design survived in the British army until it was replaced by percussion ignitions and rifled barrels in the 1830s. Surplus "Besses" continued to see service with foreign armies, including that of Santa Anna, for many years.

Under the British Ordnance System, the locks, barrels, and furniture were all purchased separately, and then assembled into finished muskets as the need arose. Because of this, and due to repairs made after the gun entered service, any given Brown Bess could contain a mixture of parts from earlier models.

The First Model Brown Bess was eventually replaced by the "Second Model," or Short Land Pattern Musket. This version incorporated a number of changes that evolved during the Seven Years War, or as it was called in North America, the French and Indian War, 1754–1763. The most obvious differences between the First and Second Models was that the Second Model had a shorter barrel, and the wooden ramrod of the First Model was replaced by a steel one in the Second Model.

The Second Model also underwent continuous modification, until officially replaced by the "Third Model," or India Pattern, in 1793. The quality of the Third Model Brown Bess was somewhat inferior to that of the Second Model, but it was also cheaper to produce. The barrel was shorter, the stock was made from cheaper wood, and greater tolerances were allowed in the fitting of the parts. The Third Model remained in production through the Napoleonic Wars, until 1815. The only major modification was the addition of a reinforced cock in 1809.

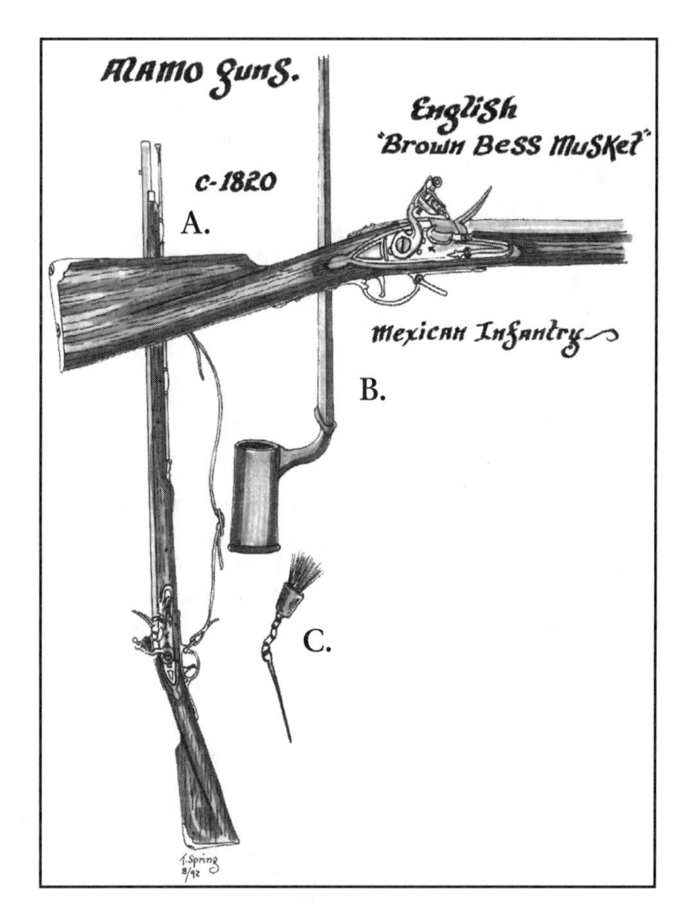

A. *A typical India Pattern Brown Bess musket of the kind purchased by the Mexican army. This example has a lock with the pre-1809 cock. See illustration on page 158 for an example of the reinforced cock that was introduced in 1809.*
B. *The Brown Bess was fitted with a triangular-shaped socket bayonet. It left a terrible wound that was very difficult for surgeons to close up. The triangular bayonet was eventually banned by many nations because of this.*
C. *A military style brush and pick that was used to keep the pan and touch hole free of powder fouling. It hung from the cartridge box shoulder strap, so that it was readily accessible.*

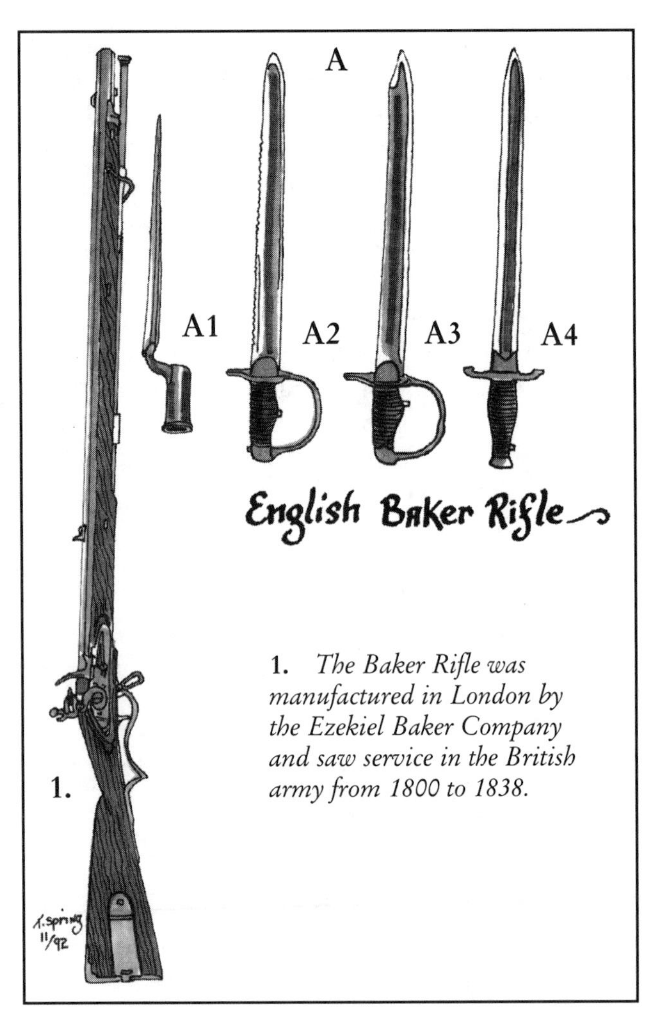

1. *The Baker Rifle was manufactured in London by the Ezekiel Baker Company and saw service in the British army from 1800 to 1838.*

The Baker Rifle was .62 caliber, and fired a .615 ball. It was 46 inches overall, and weighed 9.5 pounds. A carbine model, for mounted troops, was 36 inches in length and weighed 6.5 pounds. The barrel had a hooked breech and was held in place by three keys, which made it considerably easier to clean than the Brown Bess. The Baker Rifle had a folding rear sight that was calibrated to 300 yards.

In the Mexican army, many of the elite light troops were equipped with Baker rifles. Units so equipped included the light infantry, the Zapadores, and the Jiminez and Matamoros battalions. It is believed that a shot from a Baker Rifle killed Ben Milam during the Texians' siege of San Antonio de Bexar on December 6, 1835.

Some Baker Rifles were used by the Texian army after they were captured in the Battle of San Jacinto.

BAKER RIFLE BAYONETS

Top left: *Four versions of the Baker Rifle bayonet. The Baker Rifle originally was equipped with a triangular bayonet much like the Brown Bess (A1). This was soon replaced by a unique "sword bayonet," of which two variations are shown (A2 & A3). The rifle could not be fired with the sword bayonet in place, so a later version of the bayonet eliminated the sword grip (A4).*

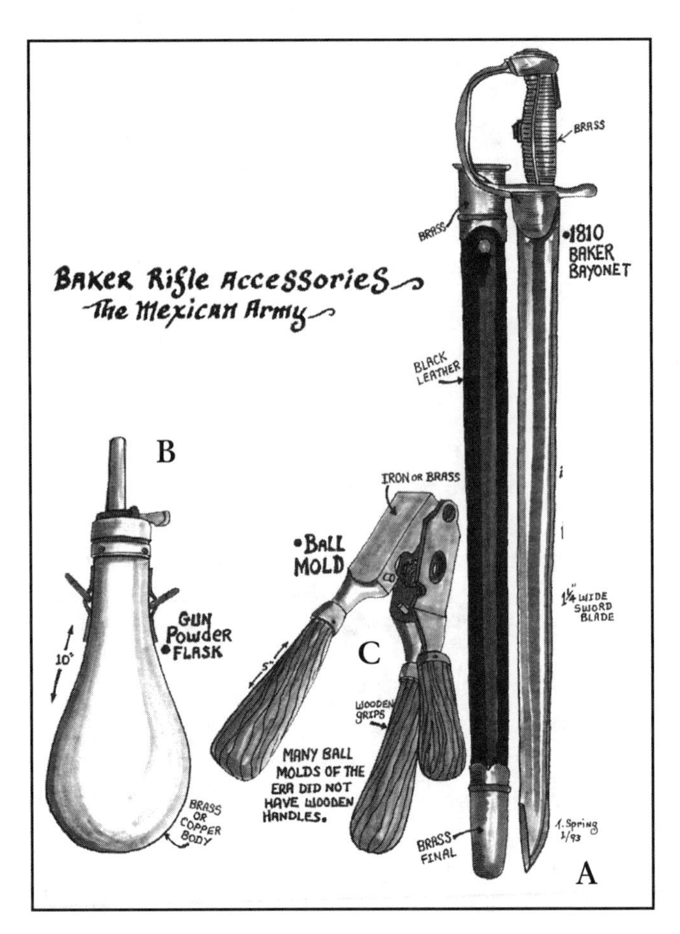

Top right:

A. *A detailed sketch of the Model 1810 sword bayonet and leather scabbard for the Baker Rifle. The bayonet blade was 1¼ inches wide and approximately 22 inches long. The scabbard was made of black leather with brass furniture.*

B. *A powder flask. Powder flasks were made of brass, copper, tin, zinc, or German silver. They were becoming popular in the 1830s, and were used to carry gunpowder just like the powderhorn was. (Kauffman, 137) Flasks may have been used by some of the Mexican officers, and even by some of the Texians, but it is unlikely that any of the common Mexican soldiers would have possessed them.*

C. *A mold for musket or rifle balls. The mold was made of iron or brass, and sometimes, but not always, had wooden handles.*

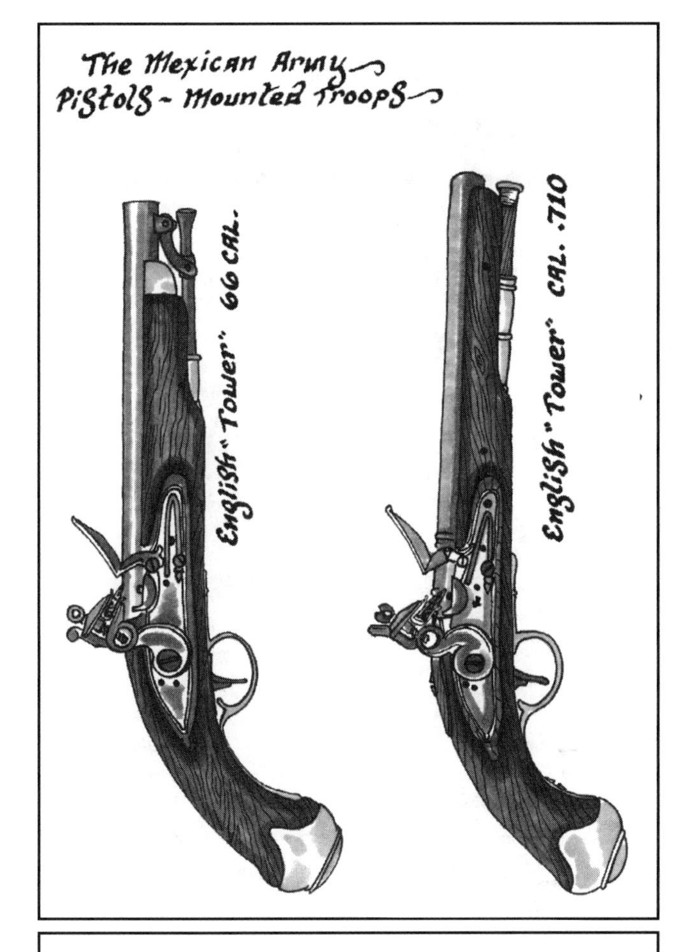

Top left:

MEXICAN PISTOLS

The use of pistols in the Mexican army would have been primarily by officers and mounted troops. These show two versions of the English "Tower" pistol. Both are flintlock, although it is possible that a few of the wealthier officers might have had personally owned percussion pistols in 1836.

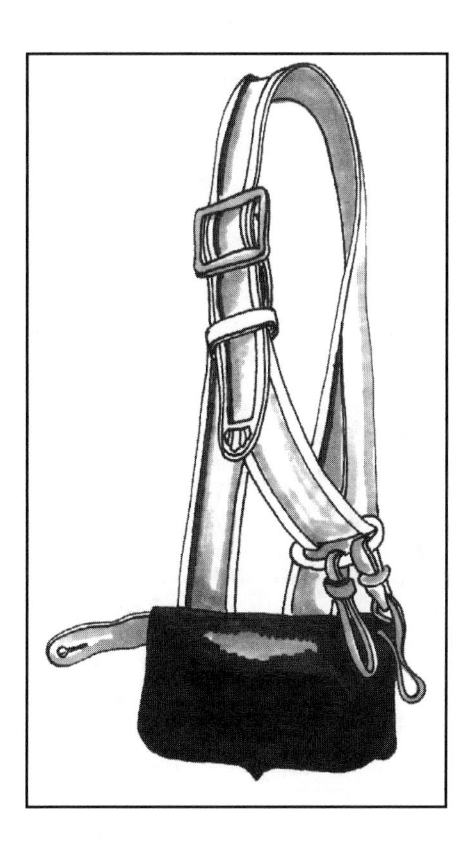

Above:

A FRENCH STYLE DRAGOON CARTRIDGE BOX

A French style dragoon cartridge box as used by mounted troops. The hook on the shoulder strap attached to a ring on the trooper's carbine. This allowed him to carry the carbine ready for use, but still left both of his hands free.

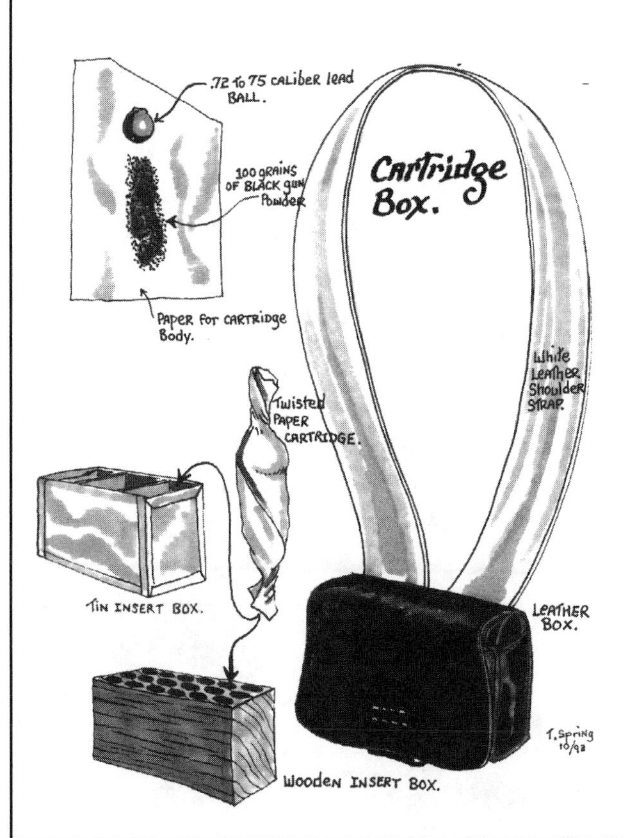

Left:

A TYPICAL BRITISH CARTRIDGE BOX

This sketch shows a British cartridge box, which, like the French, was made of black leather. For regular companies, the shoulder straps were white leather, but the light infantry, and possibly other elite units, had black straps. This box also had a wooden or tin insert for the cartridges.

Paper cartridges combined the powder charge with the lead musket ball in a paper wrapper, greatly increasing the loading speed. Generally, a musket cartridge contained about 100 grains of black powder, but Mexican powder was often of such poor quality that up to 400 grains were used.

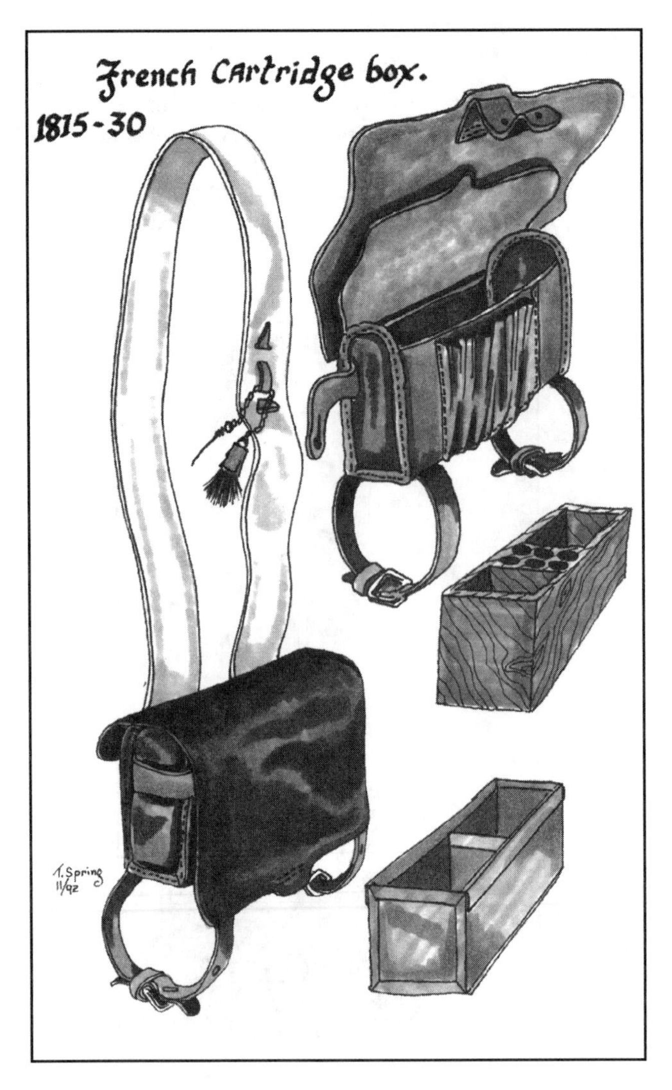

TYPICAL FRENCH CARTRIDGE BOX

Since the Mexican uniforms were based on French military fashion, many of the accoutrements were French surplus or the French pattern. Also, since most of the firearms were purchased from Britain, some British equipment saw service as well. This illustration shows a typical French cartridge box of the 1815-1830 period. It was made of black leather, with a white leather shoulder strap. The box was fitted with a wooden or tin insert to hold the cartridges. The small pouch on the front, under the flap, was for extra flints and cleaning tools. A brush and pick hung from the shoulder strap. The straps on the bottom of the box were used to carry the soldier's fatigue cap when the shako was worn.

Right:

OTHER WATER CONTAINERS

When official military issue canteens were not available, the soldiers improvised.

A. & B. *Examples of canteens made from common gourds.*

C. *A canteen made from a glass bottle with a leather carrying harness.*

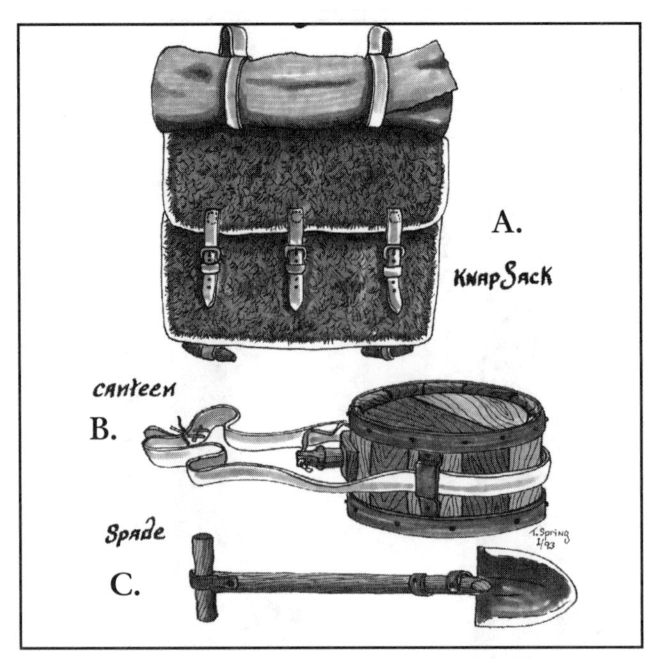

MEXICAN ARMY FIELD EQUIPMENT

A. *A French-style Mexican army knapsack. It was made from cowhide with the hair left on, and had white leather straps with wooden "torpedo" keepers underneath. The soldier's blanket of coarse bluegray wool was rolled up and strapped on top. The Mexicans also used the British Trotter knapsack, which was made of canvas over a wooden frame, with white leather straps and brass buckles.*

B. *A wooden canteen with leather strap.*

C. *A spade made from wood and hand-forged iron.*

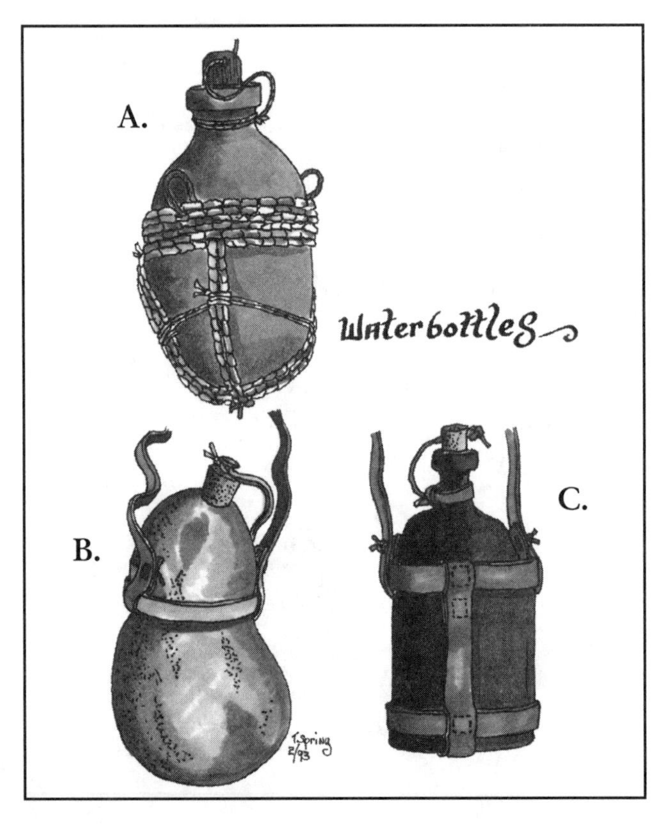

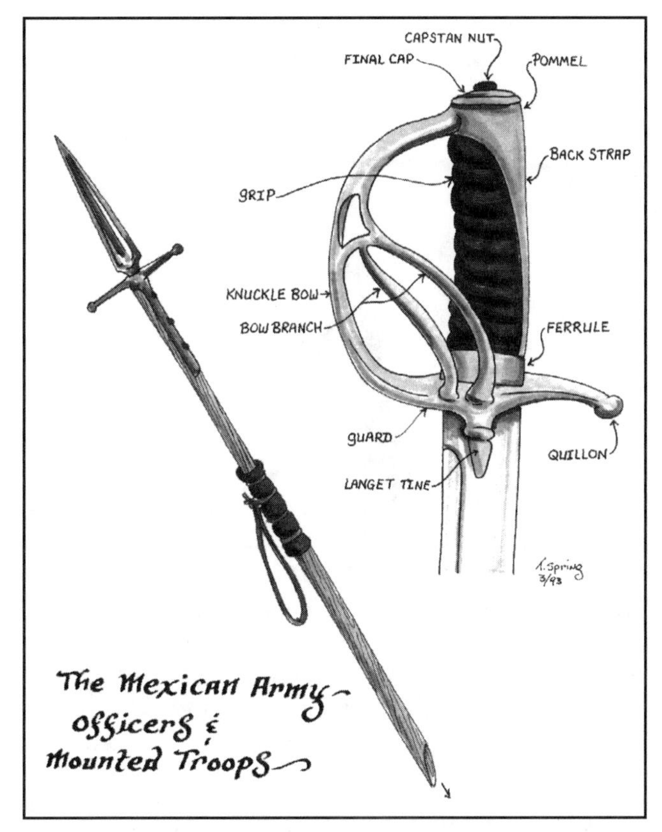

Top left:

MEXICAN ARMY SWORDS

Mexican swords would probably have been purchased from European suppliers. Shown here is sword nomenclature that would have been used by both the Mexican and the Texian armies.

A MEXICAN CAVALRY LANCE

Many Mexican mounted soldiers were armed with lances in addition to their carbines and swords. The lance was a psychologically intimidating weapon, if not terribly effective in a practical sense. The shaft was eight feet long, and made of nutwood. The iron blade was over eight inches long. The iron crossbar was designed to prevent "over penetration."

MILITARY TENTS

Nineteenth-century military tentage was quite universal in design, with most armies using similar styles. Most tents were made from heavy linen cloth. Both the Mexican and Texian armies would have used tents while in the field when they were available.

When armies on the march encamped, the tents were laid out according to a specific plan that considered both the makeup of the army and the lay of the land. The art of "measuring, arranging, and ordering camps" was known as castramentation (Lochee, 1), and the idea was to keep the army constantly organized and ready to fight in case the camp was attacked.

As in so many other areas, the officers fared better than the enlisted men when it came to tentage. Beginning on this page are examples of the most common types of tents used in the Texas Campaign.

COMMON WEDGE TENT

The wedge tent is one of the oldest and simplest styles of tent, and is similar to a modern pup tent. Wedge tents often sheltered five or six men in very close quarters. They were most likely used by both sides during the Texas Campaign.

Bottom left:

AN OFFICER'S MARQUEE

The marquee was a very comfortable style of tent generally reserved for officers. During the Texas Campaign, some Mexican officers brought along folding metal beds for their marquees to add to their personal comfort. The marquee dates back at least as far as the Middle Ages, and the basic design is similar to a modern circus tent.

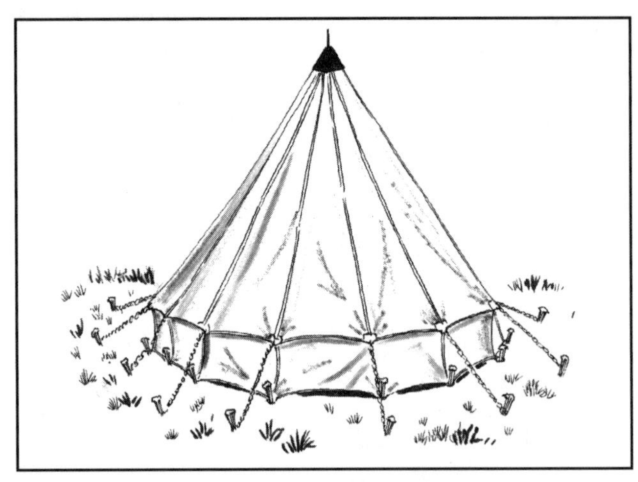

BRITISH BELL TENT
The British-style bell tent dates back at least to the Napoleonic period. This unique tent required only one nine-foot pole for support, and could shelter twelve men. The bell tent was officially adopted by the Mexican army, and was used by the common Mexican soldiers during the Texas Campaign.

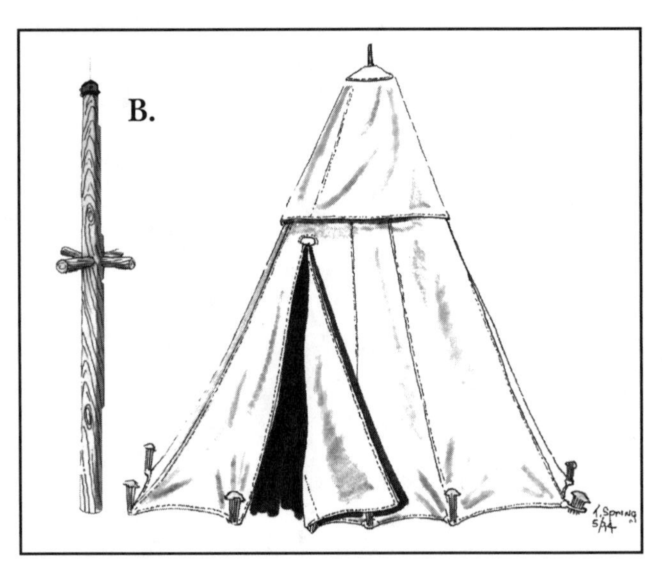

THE BELL OF ARMS
The bell of arms was a small, cone-shaped tent used to store and protect an army's muskets while it was in the field. The single upright pole of a bell of arms (at left) had crossbars to support the muskets when they were stored inside.

SANTA ANNA'S RED STRIPED MARQUEE
During the Texas Campaign, Santa Anna used a red striped marquee, although it was not set up while he was in San Antonio de Bexar. During the Siege of the Alamo, he occupied quarters in the town.

PART 4: ARTILLERY AT THE ALAMO

An old saying holds that "Artillery lends dignity to what might otherwise be a vulgar brawl." (Peterson, Preface) Artillery played an important part in the Siege of the Alamo, and, in fact, during the entire Texas Revolution. The opening confrontation of the Revolution occurred at Gonzales, when a force of Texians defied Mexican soldiers sent to reclaim a cannon that had been given to them by the Mexican government for defense against Indians. The Alamo contained a large and valuable collection of cannon, and the lack of a means to carry them away was one of the factors that led to the decision to defend, rather than destroy and evacuate, the fortress.

Inability to move his artillery also influenced Col. James W. Fannin, and accounted for part of his reluctance to leave Goliad and come to the defense of the Alamo. During the Battle of San Jacinto, two light artillery pieces known as the "Twin Sisters" played an important part in the route of Santa Anna's army. On the Mexican side, Santa Anna's decision to storm the Alamo before the arrival of his heavy siege guns has made him the subject of heavy criticism, both by some of his own officers and also by latter day historians.

The muzzleloading artillery used by both sides at the Alamo operated on much the same principle as the muzzleloading firearms of the infantry and cavalry, only on a much larger scale. The art of artillery was really quite advanced by the 1830s. Artillerists were considered to be among the elite of the army, and generally received higher pay than the common footsoldier. "The oldtime gunner was not only an artist, vastly superior to the average soldier, but, when circumstances permitted, he performed his wizardry with all due ceremony." (Manucy, 79) The mathematics involved in artillery calculations would be a challenge to today's college math majors.

Both the operational principles and the equipment itself were similar for both sides during the Texas Revolution. A good case can be made for the argument that the Texian artillery was superior to, and more effective than, the Mexican artillery during the Siege of the Alamo. The defenders were relatively well supplied with artillery, while Santa Anna brought his army in action with only his light guns present. The Mexican siege guns lagged behind the main army, and Santa Anna is often criticized for not waiting for them to arrive. Had he waited, he could have used the siege guns to pound the Alamo into submission, rather than take it by storm as he did, with the resulting high casualties on the Mexican side.

In the 1830s, the term "cannon" meant the barrel or "tube" of the gun only. The entire gun was referred to as a "piece of ordnance." (Gooding, 2) There were four main types of artillery pieces in use at the time:

1. GUNS: Fired shot or shells horizontally or at low angles over long distances.
2. CARRONADES: Lightweight pieces with shorter barrels that could fire at a higher elevation; used for defensive works and aboard ships.
3. HOWITZERS: Had short barrel that could fire either horizontally or at high angles.
4. MORTARS: Shell guns with short, heavy barrels. Mortars fired exploding shells with time fuses at high angles. Mortar shells were designed to drop into the enemy's defensive works, rather than blast through the walls. (Gooding, 3-14)

A piece of ordnance was classified by the size of the projectile that it shot; i.e., a six-pound gun fired a six-pound ball. Field guns were generally considered to be twelve-pounders or less, while larger guns were classified as siege and garrison guns.

Artillery barrels, or tubes, were made of either iron, brass, or bronze. For the latter two styles, various alloys of copper, brass, tin, and zinc were used, and the terms brass and bronze were practically interchangeable. (Peterson, 45) Artillery tubes could be mounted on three main types of carriages:

1. GARRISON CARRIAGES: Heavy carriages designed for permanent fortifications where weight was not a factor. They could be made of wood or iron.
2. SIEGE CARRIAGES: Similar to garrison carriages, but used by the attackers in a siege. Weight was not usually a factor. Siege gun carriages were generally of wooden construction.
3. FIELD CARRIAGES: Lighter weight carriages designed for mobility. Field carriages were designed to hook up to limbers and be moved about by animal or human power. They were almost always of wooden construction.

A "wheel" on an artillery carriage had spokes and was over twenty inches in diameter. Wheels were designed for field use. "Trucks" were under twenty inches in diameter, and could either be solid or have spokes. Solid trucks could be made of either iron or wood, with iron generally preferred for garrison duty and wood for shipboard use.

There were two main types of trails on artillery carriages. Double trails, also called flask, split or bracket trails, were becoming obsolete by the 1830s. They were being replaced by a single or "block" trail design from about the 1790s on.

Other artillery rolling stock consisted of limbers, to assist in hauling the carriages, ammunition and powder wagons, and traveling blacksmith forges for repairs.

Whenever possible, in both garrison or siege use, artillery was fired from wooden platforms that allowed normal recoil and minimized stress on the carriages. (Gooding, 27-33)

Artillery pieces were fired much like a musket. First, the charge of black powder was rammed down the barrel. The powder was generally premeasured and sealed in a bag of flannel, serge, or sometimes, paper. Flannel bags were preferred because they burned cleaner and were safer. (Peterson, 63-64) To anchor the powder, a wad of hay, straw, or oakum was rammed down on top of it. The projectile was rammed down last. This could be solid shot with a sabot attached, an exploding shell, or an anti-personnel round such as grapeshot, cannister, or case shot.

Once the piece was loaded, it had to be primed, just like the musket. Priming was accomplished either by filling the touch hole with fine, loose powder, or by the use of a fuselike device called a "priming tube." This was a hollow piece of tin or reed filled with gunpowder moistened with linseed oil.

After priming, the gun was ready for firing. This was done by touching a piece of smoldering wick, called "slowmatch," or a device called a portfire, which burned like a flare, to the priming charge. For the gunner's safety, both devices were held on long staffs called "linstocks."

After the gun was fired, it had to be carefully cleaned out and damp sponged to be sure that no sparks or other debris remained in the barrel. Failure to do so could have disastrous consequences.

Very little is known about the types or sizes of the guns that Santa Anna used at the Alamo. Spanish artillery of the eighteenth century resembled the French styles. (Peterson, 60) It would therefore seem logical that Mexican artillery in use in 1836 would also follow French and Spanish patterns, with many of the tubes dating back to the eighteenth century.

According to Gen. Vicente Filisola, the artillery accompanying the Army of Operations consisted of the following:

Two 12-pounders
Four 8-pounders
Four 6-pounders
Seven 4-pounders
Four 7-inch howitzers

There were also six "reserve gun carriages," two "campaign forges," and two transport carts. (Filisola: Vol. II:152)

It is known that Santa Anna ordered the assault on the Alamo before the arrival of his heavier siege guns. Therefore, it is believed that the Mexican guns that actually played a part in the Siege of the Alamo were four- and six-pounders and some of the howitzers. They were on field carriages, most likely with a combination of split and block trails. Both a map by Lt. Col. José Juan Sanchez-Navarro and modern archeological evidence indicate that the Mexicans actually did try to set up siege works for these guns, even though they were too light to inflict serious damage on the Alamo's walls.

More is known about the ordnance used by the Texian defenders. Estimates of the number of guns at their disposal range from fifteen to forty pieces. At the Alamo Society Symposium held at the Alamo IMAX Theater on March 6, 1992, Texas historian Thomas Ricks Lindley delivered a paper on Alamo artillery. (This paper was published in the July 1992 issue of the *Alamo Journal*, and the author eventually plans to publish a book on the subject.)

Lindley's is probably the most thorough study on the subject to date. He argues that there were twenty-one guns at the Alamo during the siege. He arrives at this figure by adding up the total number of guns available to the Texian army, and then accounting for the location of each. Collaborating this figure, Lt. Col. James Neill, commander of the Texian Artillery Corps, recorded that he had twenty-four guns at San Antonio, three of which he soon after sent to Goliad.

As further proof, Lindley states that twenty-one guns agrees with the number quoted both by Santa Anna and Lieutenant Colonel Sanchez-Navarro. He states that probably only eighteen of these guns were mounted and used during the siege, a figure that Santa Anna, Sanchez-Navarro, and Susannah Dickinson all agree with.

Exactly what type of guns were these used by the men of the Alamo? The most famous was the eighteen-pounder that was mounted in the southwest bastion. It was brought to the Alamo from San Felipe de Austin, by way of Dimmitt's Landing, arriving a few days after General Cos' surrender. The party that brought the gun was led by Capt. Thomas K. Pearson, and included Damacio Jiminez, the most recently identified defender of the Alamo. The eighteen-pounder may have originally been left in Brazoria in 1832 by a ship that needed to lighten its load in order to cross a sandbar. (Shearring: *The Alamo's Eighteen Pounder,* 1)

Probably the most unique piece of the Texians' ordnance was a nine-inch "Pedrero gun." This was an old-style gun with a light, thin-walled barrel, designed to fire stones rather than iron shot. (Manucy, 37)

There also was a Spanish sixteen-pounder, and an iron twelve-pounder that Lindley calls a "gunade." This was apparently an atypical carronade. There were two iron 8-pounders, six 6-pounders, three iron 4-pounders, one other 4-pounder, two 3-pounders, two smaller brass guns, and one iron gun of unknown size. These smaller guns were the ones that were probably not used during the siege.

Most of the Alamo's guns were on field carriages, but the three at the rear of the chapel are believed to have been on garrison carriages.

It is interesting to note that in contrast to the "no quarter" treatment received by the Texian defenders of the Alamo and Goliad, the paroled Mexican *soldados* from the Battle of Bexar were given a four-pounder and ten rounds of ammunition to defend themselves against hostile Indians on their return to Mexico.

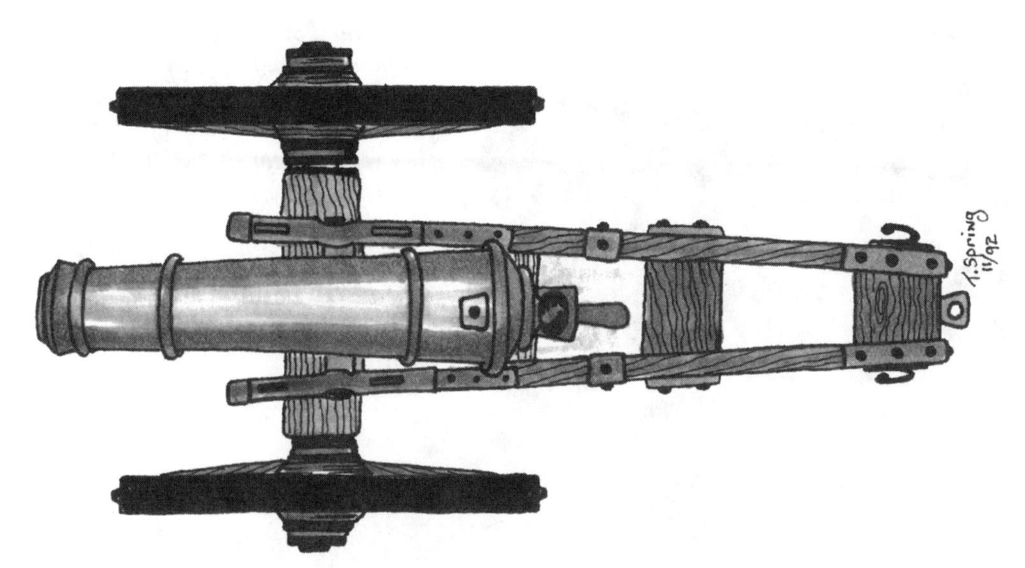

A typical field gun that could have been used by either side. Double trailed carriages (also called split or bracket trails) such as this were becoming obsolete by the 1830s, but were probably still in use on the Texas frontier. There is very little reliable information about the actual carriages used by either side during the Texas Revolution, so these illustrations are based on what was typical for the period.

A simple but functional artillery piece with a wooden axle and solid wooden wheels. Wheels such as these were sometimes used in the Southwest.

A field gun with a single, or block trail, carriage, typical of those used during the Texas Revolution.

The eighteen-pounder

A conjectural view of what the Alamo's most famous gun, the eighteen-pounder, may have looked like. Although damaged by the Mexicans, and also from many years of being buried in the ground, the barrel still survives and is on display at the Alamo. The carriage is based on a typical single trail carriage for the period. The eighteen-pounder would be classified as a siege gun.

A cutaway view of a loaded cannon barrel.

The implements used to load an artillery piece were called sidearms, and were almost always double-ended:

A. *A wooden rammer, used to ram down the powder, wadding, and ball.*

B. *A sheepskin sponge, used damp to insure that no sparks remained in the barrel.*

C. *A gun worm, used to clear the barrel of any solid debris.*

D. *A powder ladle, used to place a premeasured powder charge down the barrel. By the 1830s, most powder charges were prewrapped in flannel bags, and the ladle was unnecessary.*

A typical garrison mounted cannon with wooden trucks. Although iron trucks were preferred for garrison carriages, they were difficult to obtain on the frontier, and wooden ones were often substituted.

A very crudely mounted cannon tube. Such a mounting would have only been used when a lack of time, or a lack of skilled carpenters and blacksmiths, made the construction of a more traditional carriage impossible.

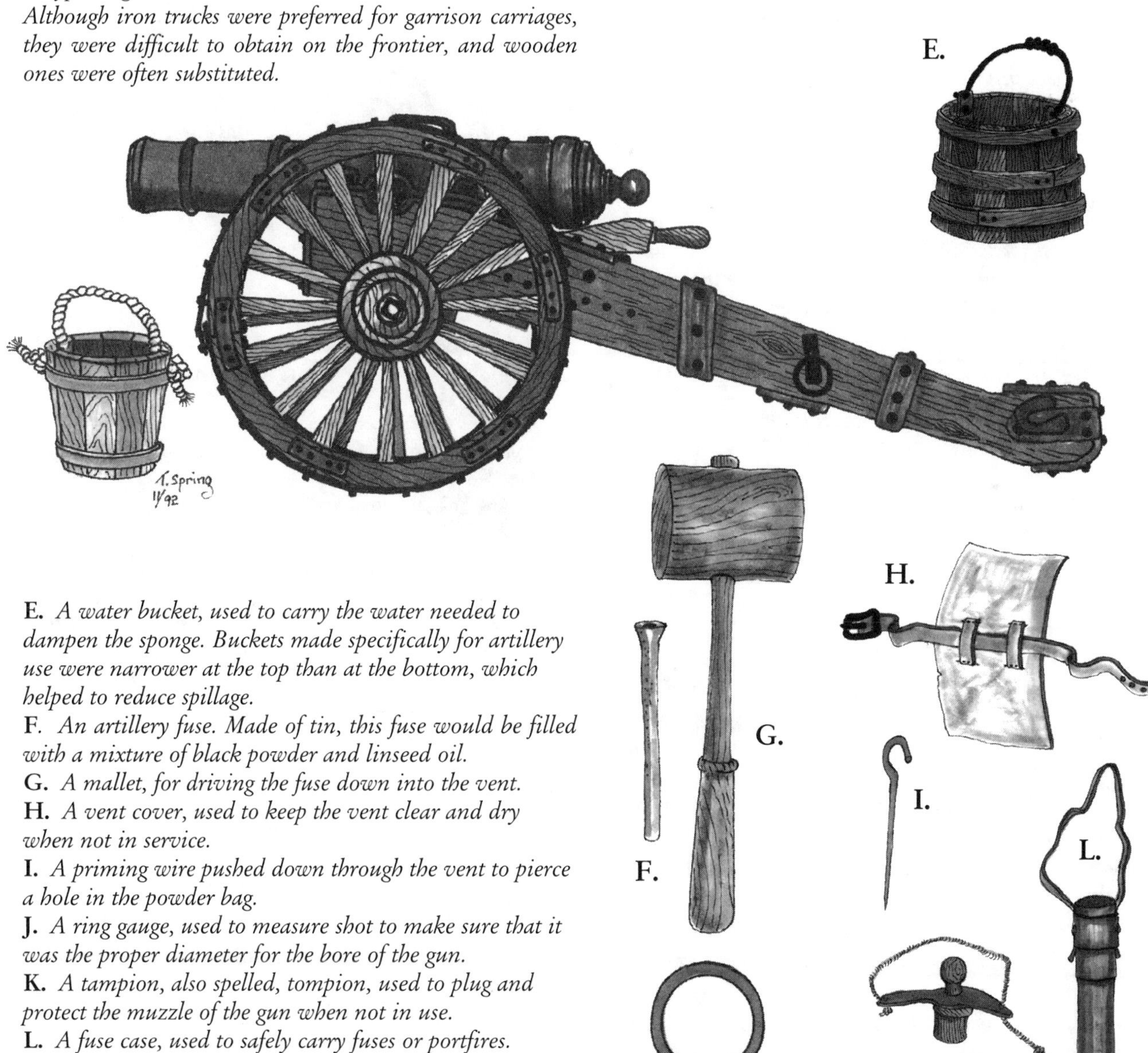

E. *A water bucket, used to carry the water needed to dampen the sponge. Buckets made specifically for artillery use were narrower at the top than at the bottom, which helped to reduce spillage.*
F. *An artillery fuse. Made of tin, this fuse would be filled with a mixture of black powder and linseed oil.*
G. *A mallet, for driving the fuse down into the vent.*
H. *A vent cover, used to keep the vent clear and dry when not in service.*
I. *A priming wire pushed down through the vent to pierce a hole in the powder bag.*
J. *A ring gauge, used to measure shot to make sure that it was the proper diameter for the bore of the gun.*
K. *A tampion, also spelled, tompion, used to plug and protect the muzzle of the gun when not in use.*
L. *A fuse case, used to safely carry fuses or portfires.*
M. *A linstock, with a piece of slowmatch attached. The linstock was used to ignite the priming charge and fire the gun.*

NOTE: Items are not drawn to scale.

ARTILLERY PROJECTILES

A. *Solid shot*

B. *A bomb or exploding shell. The shells were generally fired one of two ways:*

1. *"Firing at one stroke": The shell was fired with the fuse facing out. The muzzle flash enveloped the shell and ignited the fuse as it left the barrel.*
2. *"Firing at two strokes": The shell was fired with the fuse facing out. The fuse was lit, and then the gun was fired. Obviously, this produced unhappy results when there was a malfunction with the main charge.*
3. *A third but rarely used option was to fire the shell with the fuse facing down. This method was dangerous, because the fuse could sometimes be blown into the shell while it was still in the gun, causing an explosion.*

C. *Bar shot.*

D. *Chain shot.*

E. *Grape shot.*

F. *Scrap shot. Sometimes old scrap items would be loaded for shot. Except in moments of extreme desperation, these would be first loaded into some type of a container, for if they were fired loose, they could easily damage the bore of the gun. Some examples of scrap items that were used:*

1. *Chopped up sections of horseshoes.*
2. *Old nails.*
3. *Links, or chopped up links of chain.*
4. *Chopped up brass and iron parts from broken or non-serviceable weapons (not illustrated).*

NOTE: Items are not drawn to scale.

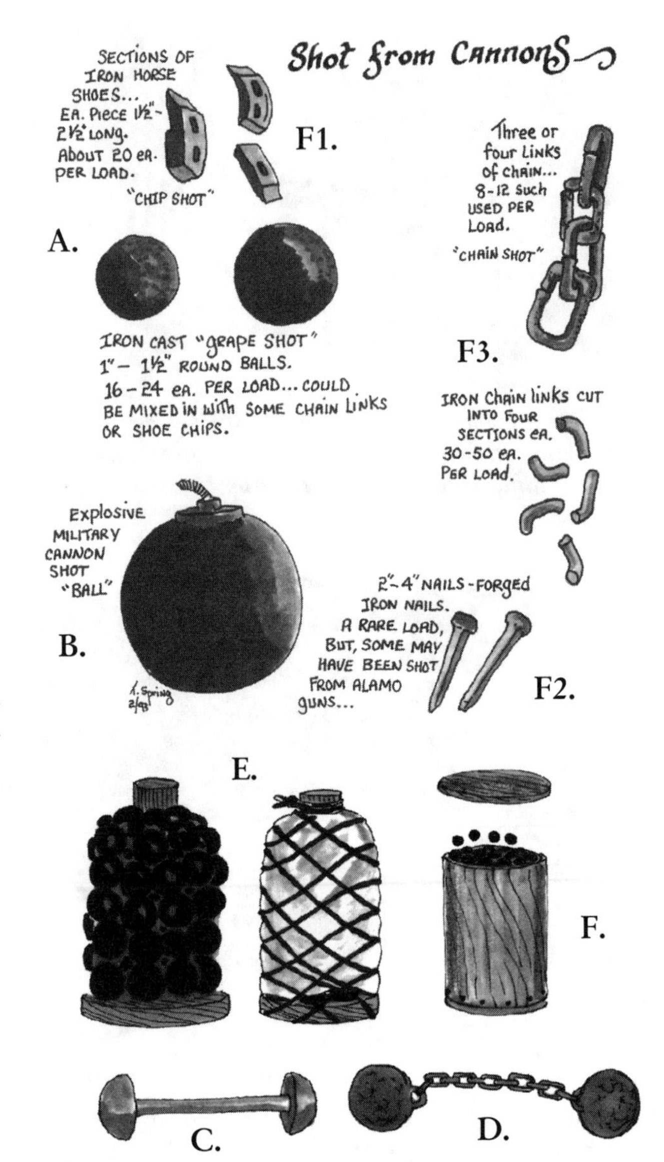

PART 5: FLAGS OF THE TEXAS REVOLUTION

"Let the old men tell the story, let the legend grow and grow,
Of the thirteen days of glory at the siege of Alamo.
Lift the tattered banner proudly, let the eyes of Texas shine,
Let the fort that was a mission be an everlasting shrine.
Once they fought to give us freedom, that is all we need to know,
Of the thirteen days of glory at the siege of Alamo."

From: "The Ballad of The Alamo"
Lyrics by Paul Francis Webster
Music by Dimitri Tiomkin
From the John Wayne Movie *The Alamo*

"Lift the tattered banner proudly." Flags have been used to inspire and rally people for thousands of years, and they certainly were so used during the Siege of the Alamo and the Texas Revolution. There are many different flags associated with this conflict, and in this section we will take a look at some of them.

On January 21, while on his way to the Alamo, William Barret Travis purchased a flag in San Felipe de Austin. We know that he paid $5 for this flag, but nothing is known about its design. Mexican General Miguel A. Sanchez Lamego, in his 1968 book *The Siege and Taking of the Alamo*, suggests that this flag may have had "thirteen stripes of red and white with a large five-pointed white star surrounded by the word TEXAS." He adds that the white star may have been in a blue or green field. (Sanchez Lamego, 48) Sanchez Lamego claims that this information comes from a note written by Davy Crockett, but does not give enough information for this to be verified. (See illustration on page 75 for the artist's concept of what this flag may have looked like.)

It can be reasonably assumed that, whatever Travis' flag looked like, it made it to the Alamo, and that it was flown during the siege.

The following are some of the other flags that are known to have been in use during the Texas Revolution.

THE MEXICAN NATIONAL COLORS

The red, white, and green tricolor, with the eagle and serpent in the center, was the national flag of Centralist Mexico. It has survived until this day with only minor changes. Variations of this flag were carried by the different units of Santa Anna's army. Often the name of the unit was added to the flag. At least four period examples still exist: an 1832 contract cavalry flag, and the colors of the battalions of Toluca, Matamoros, and Guerrero. They were all captured by Sam Houston's forces during the Battle of San Jacinto.

The flag of the Toluca Battalion is on display at the San Jacinto Museum. Those of the Matamoros and Guerrero battalions are in storage at the Texas State Archives, while the cavalry flag is held by the Dallas Historical Society.

THE FLAG OF THE FIRST COMPANY OF NEW ORLEANS GREYS

Only one flag is known with absolute certainty to have been at the Alamo. That flag is the azure blue banner of the First Company of the New Orleans Greys. The 45" x 34" flag is made of silk, and has metallic gold fringe on its borders. Strangely, the design on the flag is slightly off center.

The provenance of this flag is firmly established, because it was captured and sent back to Mexico City by Santa Anna as proof of the United States' involvement in the Texas Revolution. It is possible that this is the flag that Lt. José María Torres, of the Zapadores Battalion, was trying to take down when he was killed. However, modern photos of the flag show that it is clean, with no signs of battle damage. Therefore, the possibility that it was not flying during the battle must also be considered.

At different times, the Greys' Flag has been displayed at the Mexican Artillery Museum, the museum at Chapultepec Castle in Mexico City, and, most recently, at the Museum of Interventions in the Churubusco Convent. Unfortunately, the flag has not always been properly cared for. Walter Lord reported that when he was researching his book A Time to Stand, *the Greys' flag was crumbling away in a file drawer, wrapped in brown wrapping paper. (Lord, 212) In 1964 the flag underwent major restoration by Chapultepec Museum restoration experts María de la Luz Peredo de Vazquez and Carmen Velasco Abreko. (Sanchez Lamego, 48)*

Shortly after the signing of the recent North American Free Trade Agreement (NAFTA), there were reports of talks between U.S. and Mexican officials discussing the return of the Greys' Flag in exchange for colors of the Matamoros, Toluca, and Guerrero battalions that were captured at the Battle of San Jacinto. Mexican authorities are now denying that these talks ever took place, and officials at the museums at Curubusco and Chapultepec are claiming that they do not have the flag or know its whereabouts. The cause of this sudden turnabout is unknown. We can only hope that the Mexican government is taking the necessary steps to properly preserve this important relic, whether they wish to exchange it with us or not.

THE "SEGUIN FLAG"

Another flag that was possibly at the Alamo is one that has often been called the "Seguin Flag," because of its probable association with the Tejano members of the Alamo garrison. This flag consists of the familiar Mexican tricolor, with two gold stars in the white center section in place of the Mexican Eagle. The stars represent the two Mexican states of Coahuila and Texas. Like the 1824 Flag, this design reflects loyalty to the constitutional government of Mexico.

Col. Juan Almonte reported in his diary that as the first Mexicans approached San Antonio de Bexar, the enemy hoisted "the tri-colored flag with the two stars, designed to represent Coahuila and Texas." (Chariton: Alamo Legends, *230) The flag was lowered when the Texians fled into the Alamo, and it is not known for sure what became of it. A contemporary sketch of the Alamo by Lt. Col. José Juan Sanchez Navarro shows this flag flying from what is probably the long barracks. (Sanchez Lamego, 45)*

THE 1824 FLAG

Perhaps the flag most commonly associated with the Alamo is the 1824 Flag. The design again includes the red, white and green tricolor. The Mexican Eagle is replaced by the date "1824" in the white center section, signifying loyalty to the Mexican Constitution of 1824. The first recorded mention of this flag flying over the Alamo is in Reuben Potter's article in the Magazine of America History *in January 1878. Since then, many other historians have followed Potter's lead and credited this flag as having flown over the Alamo.*

The 1824 Flag was probably designed by Capt. Philip Dimmitt shortly after the Battle of Gonzales on October 2, 1835. He was in command of Presidio La Bahía at Goliad at the time. Dimmitt's version reportedly had "Constitution of 1824" in the center, instead of just "1824." Then, in November, the Texas General Council ordered that all vessels of the Texas Navy "shall carry the flag of the Republic of the United States of Mexico, and shall have the figures 1,8,2,4, ciphered in large Arabics on the white ground thereof." (Young: Dimmitt's 1824 Flag, 10) Captain Dimmitt was in San Antonio de Bexar in the later part of February, and it is possible that he had his 1824 Flag with him at that time.

It is possible that both the Seguin flag and the 1824 flag were flown at the Alamo, yet Santa Anna chose the Greys' Flag to send home. Santa Anna himself wrote that "The bearer carries with him one of the flags of the enemy battalions taken that day . . ." (Sanchez Lamego, 44) This wording certainly implies that more than one flag was flown over the Alamo.

General Sanchez Lamego explains very clearly why Santa Anna chose to send the Greys' flag, rather than one of the Mexican tricolor variations, back to Mexico City. "Had he sent the green-white-red 1824 flag to Mexico, it would have been an inconvenient reproach to himself and a reminder of his illegal usurpation of power. It would also serve as a striking proof that he was fighting not against mutinous foreigners, but against Mexican nationals upholding the rightful constitution of 1824." (Sanchez Lamego, 47)

Yet, to be completely fair and objective, one must also consider the possibility that neither the Seguin nor the 1824 flags were flown over the Alamo. By February and March of 1836, most sentiment was for independence from Mexico, rather than continued alliance with it. While both of these flags may have flown over Bexar earlier, this feeling for independence may have precluded them being used at the Alamo. We will probably never really know for sure.

THE COME AND TAKE IT FLAG

The white banner with the words "Come and Take It" under a single star and a cannon barrel was carried by the Texians at the Battle of Gonzales on October 2, 1835. There, a band of rebels defied Mexican soldiers who were sent to retrieve a six-pound cannon that had been given to them for defense against Indians.

Capt. Almeron Dickinson, an artillery officer at the Alamo, participated in the Battle of Gonzales. It is possible that he brought the Come and Take It Flag to the Alamo with him.

DIMMITT'S "BLOODY ARM FLAG"

This flag was also designed by Capt. Philip Dimmitt. It dropped any pretense of continued loyalty to Mexico—in fact, the severed arm implied quite the opposite. This flag probably dates to December 1835, when the Goliad garrison under Dimmitt signed its own declaration of independence from Mexico. This unilateral action was not favorably received by the Texian government at large, and Dimmitt was eventually forced to stop flying his flag over Goliad.

This flag is known to have been at Washington-on-the-Brazos on March 2, 1836, when Texian independence was finally declared, so it could not have been at the Alamo.

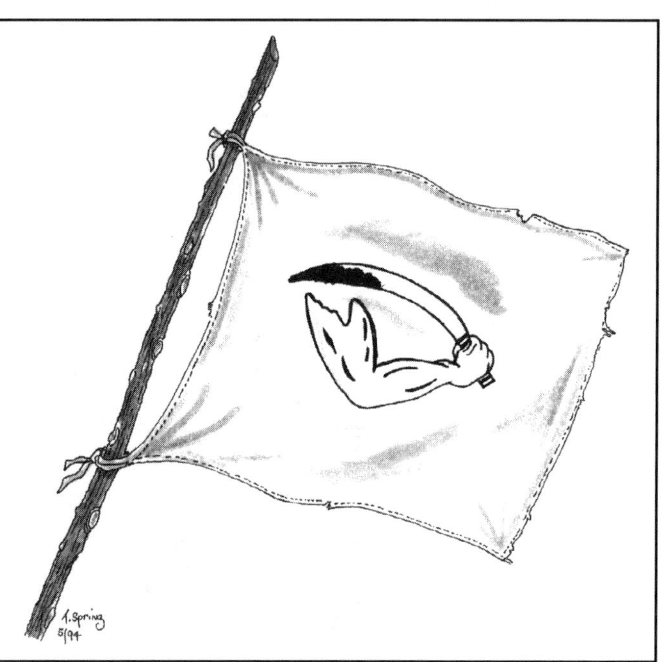

THE DODSON FLAG

Archaelaus Bynum Dodson was the first lieutenant of Andrew Robinson's volunteer company when the Texas Revolution broke out. The Dodson Flag was designed and made by his young wife, Sarah Bradley Dodson. The Dodson Flag was at the Battle of Concepción, and was the first flag to be raised over San Antonio de Bexar after the city was captured in December 1835. It also was one of the flags flying at Washington-on-the-Brazos on March 2, 1836, when Texas declared its independence.

The Dodson Flag was an elongated red, white, and blue tricolor, with a large white star in the blue section. It bears an amazing resemblance to the later "Lone Star Flag," but it is not known if it had any influence on that design.

THE AUSTIN FLAG

The Austin flag was created by Stephen F. Austin for his Texas colony. The British ensign in the upper left corner signified the roots that many of the colonists had in England and the United States. The sixteen alternating green and blue stripes (starting with green on top) showed the blending of the cultures of Mexico and the United States in Austin's Colony.

THE LORENZO DE ZAVALA FLAG

This flag was designed by Lorenzo de Zavala, the first provisional vice-president of the Republic of Texas. On May 11, 1836, it was adopted as the first official flag of the Republic. The flag was blue, with a white star in the center. White letters around the points of the star spelled out the word "Texas."

THE LONE STAR FLAG

On December 11, 1836, a second flag, designed by President David G. Burnet, was adopted as the official flag of the Republic. It was like the de Zavala flag, except that the star was gold, and the word "Texas" was omitted.

The Lone Star Flag, the third and final flag of the Republic, was adopted on January 22, 1839. It was designed by Dr. Charles B. Stewart, who was the second signer of the Texas Declaration of Independence. Stewart's design is similar to that of the Dodson Flag, but it is not known if he based it on that or not.

After Texas was admitted to the United States, the Lone Star Flag became its official state flag. It is probably the most widely recognized of any state flag in the entire union.

CHAPTER SIXTEEN

Alamo Movies and Music

PART 1: ALAMO MOVIES

"Gimme something allegorical."

John Wayne
(Thompson, 72)

IF ANYONE IN AMERICA was asked prior to the mid-1950s who was the greatest frontiersman of all, most likely their answer would have been Daniel Boone. Even the standard biography of Boone basically made this claim in its title: *Daniel Boone, Master of the Wilderness.* But ever since three Sunday evenings in December 1954 and January and February of 1955, most Americans know that Davy Crockett was the "King of the Wild Frontier." This "fact" is, of course, ridiculous. While Crockett was a successful hunter in his youth, and undoubtedly was comfortable in the woods and fields of the Trans-Appalachian wilderness, he could in no way be compared to the explorer and adventurer Daniel Boone. But the combined genius and talent of Walt Disney and Fess Parker made this historical reality so insignificant that when Disney got around to telling the story of Daniel Boone, it barely registered on the national psyche. And, although John Wayne claimed while making *The Alamo* that he was going to play the real Crockett, that is, Col. David Crockett of Tennessee, and leave the coonskin cap to Fess Parker, when the time came for Davy, or, David, to meet his end battling the Mexican hordes, he was wearing a coonskin cap!

Probably the ultimate irony occurred years later, when Parker again donned buckskins and a coonskin cap, picked up a longrifle, and took to playing Daniel Boone in a TV series. As can be expected, the character was virtually indistinguishable from Parker's Crockett. Maybe, in the end, it is Fess Parker who is the real "King of the Wild Frontier."

All joking aside, there can be little doubt that most Americans have probably formed many of their opinions on what occurred at the Alamo not from books, but from the various movies made about the battle. Almost every generation since the advent of film has produced at least one movie about the Alamo. Not every one of these will be discussed here. Anyone interested in a comprehensive account of all the Alamo movies is encouraged to read Frank Thompson's wonderful *Alamo Movies,* which describes each film and is illustrated with many photos. Here we will simply examine several major Alamo films and themes.

Returning to Disney's effort, it is interesting to note how many nice historical touches there are in what is basically an attempt to put folklore on film. The approach of the movie, with the ongoing verses of the song "The Ballad of Davy Crockett," the pages apparently taken from a folksy autobiography, and the line drawings introducing the various segments, all show that the major inspiration was not any objective biography but the Crockett of the almanacs. Still, this is one of the few Alamo movies where you really get a sense that the Alamo is besieged, with the bombardment and sense of impending death taking their toll on the defenders' spirits and bodies. Bowie seems genuinely sick, not just from an accident or wound as is often shown, but from the wasting illness described by Dr. Sutherland. The authentic "Deguello" is used, and the Mexican assault begins in the dark, just as the real one did. Unfortunately, there are so few Mexicans attacking that the battle scenes, while well choreographed, are fairly unconvincing. Still, the movie holds up well as entertainment even after forty years, due in no small part to Fess Parker's natural decency and charm, which, according to those who have met him, is not an act.

At about the same time that Disney's Davy Crockett was fighting for Texas independence on the small screen, another Alamo movie with a rather strange history was hitting the big screen. For years, while under contract to Republic Pictures, John Wayne had been developing a film on the Alamo. At one point he went so far as to have "teaser" posters made, copies of which were recently offered for sale by the aforementioned Frank Thompson. They show a typically heroic Wayne clutching a generic heroine in one arm while his opposite hand fires a pistol. In a corner the modern Alamo facade is assaulted by nondescript figures, while a banner across the top proclaims "Coming Soon! Herbert J. Yates Presents THE ALAMO! Starring John Wayne! With one of the greatest casts ever assembled!" Strictly speaking, these are posters for a movie that never was made. Instead, two others were.

After years of being put off by Herb Yates, head of Republic Studios, Wayne finally went independent so that he could begin making his dream film on his own. He had already been working on ideas for the film at Republic, and a partial script had to be left behind.

Whether to spite Wayne, or just not wanting an opportunity to go to waste, Yates had the script completed and hired Frank Lloyd, director of the classic *Mutiny On the Bounty* to direct the film. Instead of Davy Crockett, *The Last Command,* as the movie came to be called, featured Jim Bowie as the central character. Sterling Hayden was cast as Bowie, with Richard Carlson as Travis. Two veteran character actors turned in the two best performances of the film. Arthur Hunnicutt played a bearded, drawling Davy Crockett straight out of the almanacs, and J. Carroll Naish, who had played everything from demented hunchbacks and mad scientists to a French Canadian trapper and Gen. Phil Sheridan, played a surprisingly sympathetic Santa Anna. In many ways this is the most ambitious Alamo film, going into the background of the Texas Revolution in some detail, but it has a lot of problems. Hayden virtually sleepwalks through the film as Bowie, and there is a ridiculous romantic subplot involving a Mexican girl who is infatuated with him. Despite these faults, many Alamo buffs and historians regard this as the best of the theatrical Alamo films, and Hunnicutt's Crockett is very popular. The more modest budget gives some idea of what would have been the outcome if Wayne had stayed at Republic and not sunk his personal fortune into what would be the next Alamo movie.

John Wayne's dream of making a major film based on the story of the Alamo drove him through most of the 1950s. Although the film was first announced by Wayne's mentor, John Ford, there was little doubt in Hollywood that *The Alamo* was John Wayne's project.

When he left Republic, Wayne's scriptwriter, James Edward Grant, was forced to leave his first draft of the Alamo script behind, which certainly accounts for the many similarities in characters and incidents between *The Last Command* and *The Alamo.* Undaunted, Grant set out to create a screenplay that would do justice to both Wayne's vision and the Alamo story. How well, or how badly, he did has been a source of argument ever since the movie premiered.

As Frank Thompson has pointed out, there is not a single scene in *The Alamo* which corresponds to an historically verifiable incident. Despite the hours of research Grant said he did (he claimed to have read over 100 books on the Alamo), the story is basically made out of whole cloth. Eminent Texas historians J. Frank Dobie and Lon Tinkle were both on the set frequently as historical advisors, but when they saw the finished film, they demanded that their names be removed from the credits. Especially galling to them was the unlikely romance between Flaca and Crockett, who was actually a married man looking for a new home for his wife and family. This fictional romance takes up much of the first half of the film, and adds little to the real drama.

On the other hand, there is much to like about *The Alamo.* William Clothier's cinematography is superb. Almost every shot, if frozen, is a fine work of art. Dimitri Tiomkin's rousing score received a well-deserved Academy Award nomination. The large scale set, called Alamo Village, is quite accurate and has been used for many movie and television productions since. (See Chapter Fourteen.) The battle scenes contain many exciting and memorable sequences. A number of the actors who worked

BRAVEHEART IN SOUTH TEXAS

While work on this chapter was progressing, a Hollywood film was released that dealt with a handful of brave men risking everything to be free, who were opposed by a tyrannical foe determined to make them submit or die. This was not a film about the Alamo. It was Mel Gibson's hit film *Braveheart,* the story of the medieval Scottish patriot and rebel William Wallace, and his successor, Robert the Bruce.

The connection between the stories of Wallace and the Alamo defenders is deeper and more revealing than just the thematic one mentioned. Many of the Anglo settlers in Texas were of Scottish, Irish, or Scots-Irish stock. These Celts had been the main ethnic group to settle in America before the American Revolution, and had continued the centuries-old wars to be free of domination from the Vikings, the Normans, and the English.

Just how important this heritage was to the Texians is shown by a recruiting poster issued in 1835. Across the top, in banner letters, it proclaims "NOW'S THE DAY AND NOW'S THE HOUR!" This is a line from a Robert Burns poem called "Scots Wha Ha'e." It is a battle cry that evokes the memory of Wallace and the Bruce. The poem ends:

"Lay the proud usurper low,
Tyrants falling, every foe,
Liberty's in every blow,
Let us do or die !"

Wallace would have agreed . . . and so did the defenders of the Alamo.

on the film said that, although Wayne had his limitations with the dramatic scenes, he was one of the best action directors they had ever worked with.

Several of the performances are excellent. Especially effective is Laurence Harvey as the aristocratic Lt. Col. William Barret Travis. (When Harvey, an Englishman, told his wife he had won a starring role in *The Alamo,* she replied, "That's wonderful dear. What's an alamo?") Hank Worden, a frequent Wayne costar who usually played characters that might be considered "intellectually challenged" in current parlance, is very good as the thoughtful, insightful "Parson." Richard Boone's Sam Houston is outstanding. Originally, Wayne had wanted to play Houston himself as a cameo, but was forced to take a starring role in order to get financing. Needing someone who could make an impact in just one or two scenes, he reportedly first sought screen icon Charlton Heston. At that point in his career, Heston wanted lead roles so Wayne turned to Boone, a popular TV star and movie character actor. It was a fortuitous choice. Boone's first scene sets the stage for the story, and the speech to his officers predicting the fall of the Alamo is extremely moving. "Tomorrow morning, when your men start to bellyache, tell them . . . fellow Texicans . . . are dying to buy them this precious time. I hope they remember. I hope Texas remembers . . ."

Wayne's performance as Crockett has been frequently criticized, but as some historians have pointed out, "the Duke," like Davy Crockett, was part self-made man and part media creation. Wayne may have had special insight into Crockett's personality.

Viewed in this light, some of the Crockett/Wayne dialogue takes on special relevance. "A man has to do a lot of things to get elected"—and also to get a movie made. "They named me Davy after an uncle who didn't give us the farm after all," Wayne says as Crockett. Wayne's birth name, Marion Michael Morrison, was inspired by a wealthy relative. And Crockett's concerns about the price of living up to his public image probably mirrored Wayne's personal financial risk.

Two scenes also show a rare insight into the two Crocketts, the private person and the media creation. When word comes that Fannin's reinforcements won't be coming after all, Bowie decides he's taking his company out, and asks if Crockett will do the same. Ruefully, Crockett responds, "It seems like the better part of valor." He knows the Almanac Davy would stay no matter what. But he also feels responsible for his Tennesseans, who he knows will follow him to their deaths. Then, after Travis has bid farewell to those leaving, thanking them for their ten days of heroic service, Bowie and the rest of his men dismount and rejoin Travis. Then Crockett's men begin to join those staying. Crockett stays mounted until all his men have begun to move toward the rest. He even looks a little surprised, and although he joins Bowie and Travis at the front of the doomed garrison, you get the feeling that if even one of his men had chosen to leave,

Crockett would have gone with him so they would not feel they had betrayed him.

John Wayne's *The Alamo* was the last cinematic word on the subject for many years. Then, in the early to mid-1980s, as the 150th anniversary of the Texas Revolution approached, several projects of varying quality appeared. The made-for-TV movie, *The Alamo: Thirteen Days to Glory,* based on Lon Tinkle's book, was probably the least successful effort. The cast, featuring Alec Baldwin as Travis, James Arness as Bowie, and Brian Keith as Crockett, was acceptable at best. Considering that both Andy Griffith and Rip Torn were first considered for the Tennessean, Keith's miscasting is especially disappointing. The one bright spot in the film is the performance by the then almost unknown stage actor Raul Julia as Santa Anna. Although not as sympathetic as J. Carroll Naish, Julia presents a complex and human Santa Anna. Filmed on a very tight budget, with some stock scenes repeated to an extreme, and some hilarious invented incidents, *Thirteen Days to Glory* is probably the most disappointing Alamo movie, at least since the early talkies.

Three other TV productions have been more successful. *Seguin!,* made for PBS, was a revisionist view of the Tejano hero, but featured strong performances by A. Martinez and Henry Darrow as Juan and Don Erasmo Seguin respectively. Interestingly, although the film championed the ill-fated Tejanos and was somewhat hard on the Anglos, it presented one of the most totally evil Santa Annas ever, played by Edward James Olmos.

More recently, the miniseries of James Michener's *Texas* centered on the cultural clash that occurred from the early days of the Austin colony into the Republic. While it does a good job of showing the respect between the early settlers and the increasing tension that developed, there is little understanding of the Mexican Centralist/Federalist controversy. The performances are fine if not exceptional, and at last there's a movie that gives Stephen Austin something resembling his due. The Alamo scenes are few and somewhat confusing, but Bowie (David Keith) has a great line when Travis makes his speech. "Hell, I'm dying anyway. I might as well go cuttin'," he says.

Unfortunately, the movie also contains perhaps the silliest Alamo scene ever filmed. Several hours after the fall, Rick Schroeder's character rides into the now deserted mission and finds his friends' bodies on the funeral pyre, and a friend's hat on the ground. There is no sign of the Mexican army anywhere! Apparently they only wanted to take San Antonio, not hold it.

A better TV movie about the Revolution is *Houston, The Legend of Texas,* available on video as *Gone to Texas.* Benefitting from the help of historical reenactors, and featuring a strong performance by the charismatic Sam Elliott as Houston, this is perhaps the best overall account of the Texas Revolution. The December 1835 Battle of Bexar is well handled, if truncated, and its Alamo scenes are limited but evocative and haunting. Although she is much too old for the character, the casting of Elliott's wife Katherine Ross as Susannah Dickinson adds a resonance to the scene where she describes the fall of the Alamo that makes the casting choice hard to criticize. Overall, this is a very good effort.

Unfortunately, what may be the best theatrical film ever made about the Alamo is also the most difficult to see. *Alamo . . . The Price of Freedom,* which shows several times a day at a theater across the street from the Alamo, was filmed in the IMAX format, requiring a special facility to show it. Made with only a few professional actors, the film relies heavily on historical reenactors for its authentic look.

The excellent screenplay was written by Keith Merrill and George A. McAlister. Merrill also produced and directed the film, while McAlister served as executive producer. One of Hollywood's finest historical producers, Ray Herbeck, Jr., a reenactor himself, served as associate producer. Texas historian Kevin R. Young acted as technical advisor and also served as director of the IMAX Theater for many years after the film's debut. The film also received support from the custodians of the Alamo, the Daughters of the Republic of Texas, with their then director, Bernice Strong, acting as historical advisor.

Shown on a 61 x 84-foot screen, and utilizing a 32-speaker, six-track stereo sound system, the IMAX format makes *Alamo . . . The Price of Freedom* visually stunning. The movie contains some of the most vivid battle scenes ever filmed. Ray Herbeck later worked as a producer on *Glory,* and was involved in some of the preproduction work for *The Last of the Mohicans. Alamo . . . The Price of Freedom* has intense combat sequences similar to those in these two well-known movies. Due to its special format, the film only runs about forty-five minutes, and it lacks dramatic depth. It also lacks the fictional padding that has afflicted so many longer versions. Filmed at Happy Shahan's Alamo Village, with Wayne's Alamo restored to a very accurate appearance, and with an attention to detail and intensity that are remarkable, *Alamo . . . The Price of Freedom* is probably as close to being at the Alamo as most of us would want to get.

As this book goes to press, there are more projects in the works. There is talk of another heavily revisionist version of the Texas Revolution. And, just as John Wayne worked for years to get his version of the Alamo made, David Zucker, a well-known Hollywood director, is fighting an uphill battle to get his dream film produced, an authentic biography of Davy Crockett.

Apparently in Hollywood, as in Texas, they still remember the Alamo!

In the movie The Last Command, *veteran character actor Arthur Hunnicutt plays a Davy Crockett right out of the Almanacs—half bear, half alligator, and all frontiersman. It is a wonderful performance, and very popular among Alamo buffs.*

Two more figures right out of the movies. Many of the Tennesseans in John Wayne's The Alamo *wear coonskin caps, and many of the others look like a cross between mountain men and cowboys—like the other defender in this figure. Although we know from Smithwick that coonskin caps were worn, they probably were not common. They simply were not too practical or comfortable in the Texas heat.*

This sketch shows graphically how Hollywood has affected our perception of history. The second-floor balcony and staircase on the long barracks did not exist at the time of the siege. They were not added until the 1840s, but Wayne included them in his Alamo so Travis would have a high spot from which he could look down on the garrison. Almost every movie since Wayne's has included this anachronism. Now the building hardly looks right without it!

Almost every Alamo movie has a scene where some character dramatically proclaims that the Mexicans have "breached" the north wall. In fact, no such breach was made— the Mexicans were finally just able to go over the top of the wall. But again, since no popular work on the Alamo seems complete without the breach in the north wall, here it is.

"Thimblerig," the gambler, first appeared in the fictional account of Crockett's adventures in Texas supposedly written by Crockett himself. He appears both in Walt Disney's "Davy Crockett," played by Hans Conreid, and in John Wayne's The Alamo, *played by Denver Pyle. This illustration is closer to Conreid's portrayal. Although there is no real historical evidence for his presence at the Alamo, he has become an integral part of the Alamo legend.*

PART 2: ALAMO MUSIC — AN INCOMPLETE LISTING

"A time to be reapin', a time to be sowin',
The green leaves of summer are callin' me home.
'Twas so good to be young then in the season of plenty,
When the catfish were jumpin' as high as the sky.

A time just for plantin', a time just for plowin'
A time to be courtin', a girl of your own.
'Twas so good to be young then, to be close to the earth,
And to stand by your wife at the moment of birth."

From: "The Green Leaves of Summer"
Lyrics by Paul Francis Webster
Music by Dimitri Tiomkin
From the John Wayne movie *The Alamo*

As in so many other areas, the saga of the Alamo has inspired a significant body of songs and music. Some of it, like the song "The Green Leaves of Summer," has enjoyed a popularity well beyond its connection to the Alamo. It is virtually impossible to compile a complete list of Alamo-related music from all conceivable sources. For example, in addition to the hit version by The Brothers Four, "The Green Leaves of Summer" has been recorded by countless groups and individuals over the years. However, we feel that this *Sourcebook* would be incomplete without at least a partial list of Alamo music.

MUSIC RELATING TO WALT DISNEY'S *DAVY CROCKETT— KING OF THE WILD FRONTIER*

Song Title: "The Ballad of Davy Crockett"
Artist: Fess Parker
Label & Number: Columbia 40449
Date: March 12, 1955
Chart Information: On pop charts for 17 weeks; peaked at number 5.
Comments: The complete song had twenty stanzas of six lines each. Re-released many times, including on the albums *Songs About Zorro,* Disneyland Records No. MM-28, and "Walt Disney's Wonderful World of Color: All Time Children's Favorite Stars and Songs," Disneyland Records No. DQ-1245.

Song Title: "The Ballad of Davy Crockett"
Artist: The Wellingtons
Label & Number: Disneyland DL-557 (3373)
Date:
Chart Information:
Comments:

Song Title: "The Ballad of Davy Crockett"
Artist: The Mellomen
Label & Number: Disneyland
Date: 1955
Chart Information:
Comments: Re-released as part of the special CD boxed set *The Music of Disney: A Legacy in Song,* Walt Disney Records, 1992. (No. 60957-2)

Song Title: "The Ballad of Davy Crockett"
Artist: Bill Hayes
Label & Number: Cadence 1256
Date: February 26, 1955
Chart Information: On charts for 20 weeks; peaked at number 1.
Comments: "Farewell to the Mountains" (called simply "Farewell") is on the reverse or flip side.

Song Title: "The Ballad of Davy Crockett"
Artist: Tennessee Ernie Ford
Label & Number: Capitol 3058
Date: March 26, 1955
Chart Information: On country charts for 16 weeks; peaked at number 4.

Comments:

Song Title: "The Ballad of Davy Crockett"
Artist: Mac Wiseman
Label & Number: Dot 1240
Date: May 28, 1955
Chart Information: On country charts for 2 weeks; peaked at number 10.
Comments:
Song Title: "The Ballad of Davy Crockett"
Artist: The Sons of the Pioneers
Label & Number: RCA Victor FICW1659
Date:
Chart Information:
Comments:

Song Title: "The Ballad of Davy Crockett"
Artist: The Kentucky Headhunters
Label & Number: Mercury 868122
Date: March 30, 1991
Chart Information: On country charts for 11 weeks; peaked at number 49.
Comments:

Song Title: "Farewell to the Mountains"
Artist: Fess Parker
Recorded on: The Album *Walt Disney's Three Adventures of Davy Crockett*
Label & Number: Disneyland ST-1926
Date:
Chart Information:
Comments: This version is very similar to the soundtrack of the original TV show.

Song Title: "Farewell to the Mountains"
Artist: Fess Parker
Recorded on: The Album *Walt Disney's Wonderful World of Color: All Time Children's Favorite Stars and Songs*
Label & Number: Disneyland DQ-1245
Date: 1963
Chart Information:
Comments: This version of "Farewell to the Mountains" is fully orchestrated. The album also included "The Ballad of Davy Crockett" by Fess Parker.

Song Title: "Old Betsy (Davy Crockett's Gun)"
Artist: The Sons of the Pioneers
Label & Number: RCA Victor FICW3488
Date:
Chart Information:
Comments:

Album Title: *Walt Disney's Three Adventures of Davy Crockett*
Artists: Fess Parker, Buddy Ebsen, et al
Label & Number: Disneyland ST-1926
Date:
Chart Information:
Comments: A story record, containing narrations of "Davy Crockett Indian Fighter," "Davy Crockett Goes to Congress," and "Davy Crockett at the Alamo." Also contains the songs "The Ballad of Davy Crockett" and "Farewell to the Mountains."

FROM THE MOVIE *THE LAST COMMAND*

Song Title: "Jim Bowie"
Artist: Gordon MacRae
Label & Number: Capitol F3191
Date: 1955
Chart Information:
Comments:

FROM THE *JIM BOWIE* TELEVISION SERIES

Song Title: "Jim Bowie — Adventurin' Man"
Artist: The Prairie Chiefs
Label & Number: RCA Victor H2WW-0793
Date:
Chart Information:
Comments:

FROM JOHN WAYNE'S *THE ALAMO*

Album Title: *The Alamo* Soundtrack
Artist: Dimitri Tiomkin, et al
Label & Number: Mono: Columbia CL1558
Stereo: Columbia CS8358
Date: 1960
Chart Information: Includes two songs, "The Ballad of the Alamo" by Marty Robbins and "The Green Leaves of Summer," by The Brothers Four, that charted as singles on the pop music charts.
Comments:

CD Title: *The Alamo* Soundtrack: Japanese Release

Artist: Dimitri Tiomkin, et al
Label & Number: Sony SRCS7073
Date:
Chart Information:
Comments: The same music as the 1960 LP record.

CD Title: *The Alamo* Soundtrack: U.S. Release
Artist: Dimitri Tiomkin, et al
Label & Number: Sony CK66138
Date: 1995
Chart Information:
Comments: Contains additional music from the soundtrack that was not included on previous releases.

Song Title: "The Ballad of the Alamo" (Single Release)
Artist: Marty Robbins
Label & Number: Columbia 41809
Date: October 10, 1960
Chart Information: On pop charts for 13 weeks; peaked at number 34.
Comments:

Song Title: "The Ballad of the Alamo"
Artist: Bud & Travis
Recorded on: *Folksong Festival* cassette tape
Label & Number: EMI (A Division of Capitol Records) 4XLL-57218
Date: 1989
Chart Information:
Comments:

Song Title: "The Green Leaves of Summer" (Single Release)
Artist: The Brothers Four
Label & Number: Columbia 41808
Date: October 31, 1960
Chart Information: On the pop music charts for 7 weeks; peaked at number 65.
Comments:

Song Title: "The Green Leaves of Summer"
Artist: Los Indios Tabajaras
Label & Number: Reader's Digest RD6A-065 & RDK5358
Date: 1981
Chart Information:
Comments: Released on the Reader's Digest set *Easy Listening Folk;* available on LP record, cassette, and 8-track stereo.

Song Title: "The Green Leaves of Summer"
Artist: Montovani
Recorded on: The album *Montovani Plays Music from Exodus and Other Great Themes*
Label & Number:
Date: 1961
Chart Information:
Comments: Re-released on the Time Life CD *Instrumental Favorites: Montavani.* Time Life No. R986-05.

FROM THE IMAX MOVIE *ALAMO . . . THE PRICE OF FREEDOM*

Cassette Tape Title: *Alamo . . . The Price of Freedom* Soundtrack
Produced by: Merrill Jenson & Kevin R. Young
Label & Number: Rivertheater Associates Ltd.; no number
Date: 1993
Chart Information:
Comments: Contains the song "The Price of Freedom" by Sergio Salinas.

FROM THE *TEXAS ADVENTURE* SPECIAL EFFECTS THEATER

CD Title: "Songs for the Alamo"
Artist: Various
Label & Number: Stage Door Productions SD03061836
Date: 1994
Chart Information:
Comments: Executive producer Bob Flick was an original member of The Brothers Four, who recorded the hit version of "The Green Leaves of Summer."

MISCELLANEOUS

Cassette Tape Title: *Remember the Alamo! Mexican & Texian Music of 1836*
Produced by: Ray Herbeck, Jr.
Label & Number: Starline Productions, Inc. SGC5020
Date: 1989
Chart Information:
Comments: Contains excellent liner notes about music of the period.

Song Title: "Remember the Alamo"
Artist: The Kingston Trio
Recorded on: The album *The Kingston Trio at Large*
Label & Number: Capitol T-1199
Date:
Chart Information:
Comments:

Song Title: "Remember the Alamo"
Artist: Johnny Cash
Recorded on: *We The People* CD
Label & Number: Folk Era Productions FE2055CD
Date:
Chart Information:
Comments:

Song Title: "Letter from the Alamo"
Artist: Billy Elder
Label & Number: Capitol 4452 (45-34433)
Date:
Chart Information:
Comments:

Song/Video Title: "You're Going to Miss Me (When I'm Gone)" — Music Video
Artist: Brooks & Dunn
Label & Number:
Date:
Chart Information:
Comments: Although the subject matter of this country and western song is not Alamo related, the music video was filmed at Alamo Village in Brackettville, Texas, and contains some beautiful photography of the site.

CHAPTER SEVENTEEN

The Embattled Shrine

"Let the old men tell the story, let the legends grow and grow,
Of the 13 days of glory at the siege of Alamo."

From "The Ballad of the Alamo"
From the John Wayne movie *The Alamo*
Lyrics by Paul Francis Webster
Music by Dimitri Tiomkin

"The Mission that became a fortress, the fortress that became a shrine . . ."
John Wayne

IN THE YEARS SINCE the Battle of the Alamo, the mission-turned-fortress has been revered as a shrine of freedom by many, but the ongoing story of the Alamo as shrine has also been marked by frequent controversy. As with many cultural icons, groups have praised or attacked what they claim the Alamo stands for.

Following the fall of the Alamo, Mexican troops once again garrisoned the old mission. After San Jacinto, they tore down many of the walls, filled in the trenches, and burned down the palisade that had been defended by Crockett and his Tennesseans. The artillery ramp in the chapel had been set afire, perhaps in an unsuccessful attempt to burn down the structure. Artillery and ammunition were dumped in the river to make them useless.

Several sections of the barracks were used by local families for living quarters, as they had been before the start of hostilities. Stones and rock were carried off by others to build new homes. During the time of the Republic, San Antonio was occupied twice by invading Mexicans, but there was no more combat at the Alamo.

The annexation of Texas by the U.S. in 1845 led to the War with Mexico. By this time, the only buildings left in the compound were the chapel, the old convent or long barracks, and the low barracks, at the south end of the compound where Bowie had been. Taken over by the U.S. Army as a supply depot, the two-story convent was re-roofed and strengthened. The overhanging roof and outside staircases familiar to viewers of John Wayne's *The Alamo* actually date from this renovation.

Meanwhile, the Catholic Church and the City of San Antonio were involved in a dispute over ownership of the chapel. Despite this controversy, the army began renovating the old church. Eventually, the Texas Supreme Court ruled in favor of the Catholic Church, but rather than try to reconsecrate the battle-scarred building, the church contented itself with collecting a monthly rent from the army.

In the late 1840s, the military bureaucracy almost accomplished what two sieges and a violent battle had failed to do. Plans were laid for demolishing the remaining Alamo buildings and replacing them with more contemporary and possibly utilitarian structures. Ultimately, this plan was rejected and once again the Alamo escaped utter destruction.

It was during this period of controversy that the most famous part of the Alamo buildings came to be. In 1849 the hump, or gable, which today is the most recognizable symbol of the Alamo, was added. The army continued to use the barracks and chapel as a supply depot until the Civil War, when the Confederate Army took the buildings over and put them to the same use. Following the war, the Federal Army again reclaimed the supply depot and maintained it until 1879, when Fort Sam Houston was built.

The historic shrine was now in the midst of a

busy tavern district. The north and west walls were gone, and the rooms along the south wall which had escaped destruction before were razed in the 1860s. A city plaza now sat where Jim Bowie had faced death from illness and Mexican bayonets.

When the army moved out, the Catholic Church sold the old *convento* to storeowner Honore Grenet, who also leased the chapel. For the first time a museum was established to honor the historic site. It amounted to one small corner of the convent building. Grenet also added a new facade to the convent, with turrets and fake artillery, apparently designed to invoke the building's martial past.

In 1882 Grenet died and the convent was sold to the firm of Hugo and Schmeltzer. The chapel was purchased by the State of Texas, which did little to preserve or restore it. At this point the venerable memory had little relation to the gaudy, commercial architectural curiosity that stood in Alamo Plaza.

At the turn of the century, controversy about the Alamo began in earnest. An unsuccessful attempt to purchase the Hugo and Schmeltzer building was made by the San Antonio Chapter of the Daughters of the Republic of Texas. The chapter was headed by Adina de Zavala, whose grandfather, Lorenzo de Zavala, had been a Tejano patriot and the first vice-president of the Republic. This attempt to save the Alamo was countered by a proposal to raze the structure and replace it with a hotel. Perhaps surprisingly, many Texans were in favor of this proposal. But before anything was done to destroy the historic landmark, a wealthy rancher's daughter, Clara Driscoll, came forward and offered to buy the buildings with her own money. Chagrined, the Texas Legislature bought the property, then appointed the Daughters guardians of the site.

As one controversy ended, another began, one which continues to the present day. In 1913 the remnants of the second floor of the convent building were removed under questionable circumstances. The reason given was that the second-floor ruins hindered people's view of the shrine, as the chapel was now called. While the shrine became a major tourist destination and a source of patriotic emotion, and while new buildings and monuments were erected, the long barracks/convent ruins became overgrown with flora and suffered from a benign neglect. In time a museum and gift shop building, a library, and memorial gardens were added to the grounds, and a huge statue, the Alamo Cenotaph, was erected opposite the convent. Finally, during the 1968 Hemisfair, a roof was added to the ruins of the convent, and a museum tracing the history of the mission was established. Critics point out that the so-called Long Barracks Museum in no way resembles the original structure. Although this is true, it has saved another part of the original compound from complete obliteration.

In fact, it is the proposed reconstruction of parts of the original compound that has given rise to current controversy. On one side is a group of historians, civic leaders, and others who would like to see many of the original buildings reconstructed. Some (though certainly not all) even advocate tearing down existing buildings, some of which are historic in themselves, and replacing them with full-scale representations of the original structures. Others only want to see reconstructions where there are currently no buildings, such as where the palisade and main gate were in the present Alamo Plaza.

Those opposed to the plan, also including historians and some Alamo buffs, point out the irony of tearing down known historic buildings to replace them with conjectures of what might have been. They oppose the reconstructions in Alamo Plaza for the same reason. Only an educated guess can be made as to the true appearance of the original structures, so it would be better to interpret the site with other means than costly new buildings that might be proven wrong in a few years of additional research. Adding to the intensity of the debate are old questions of how much emphasis each part of the Alamo's history should be given, how various persons and groups should be interpreted, and concerns of race. Modern disputes over "political correctness" add to the controversy.

Also adding to the controversy are concerns over the future of the former Alamo mission *campo santo,* or cemetery, directly in front of the chapel. Native American activists have pointed out that this area holds the remains of American Indians who lived and died at the mission, and any construction runs the risk of disturbing their burial grounds, even though continued use as a city park means tourists are regularly walking over and around their ancestors' graves.

While verbal and political battles are being waged over the future of the physical site of the Alamo, a war of words rages over the written record of the history of the Alamo. Some of the skirmishes are rather good natured, as buffs joust over disputed eyewitness accounts and engage in the type of textual analysis usually associated with Shakespearean and biblical scholars.

Other arguments are more acrimonious, again reflecting current debates over ethnic rivalries, accusations of racism, and political correctness. Among the issues in dispute are the fate of Davy Crockett and the authenticity of a controversial account of the Siege and Battle of the Alamo by Mexican Lt. José Enrique de la Pena.

According to some accounts, there were a handful of Texans taken alive following the final assault on the Alamo. If these stories are to be believed, then there is some evidence that among these unfortunates was Crockett. The story of Crockett surviving and being executed later has appeared often over the years, and in some accounts, the Tennessean was taken alive as a slave to Mexican silver mines. In fact, Crockett's son, John Wesley, made a trip to Texas in the late 1830s hoping to find proof his father was still alive. But this mystery became a source of controversy in the past few years, first when an English translation of de la Pena's account was publicized, and more recently, when a revisionist history of the Texas Revolution used that account, and others, to portray Crockett as a loudmouthed, bragging coward who hid during the battle and then lied and begged for his life before being executed. Jeff Long's *Duel of Eagles,* which works hard to portray every major character on both sides of the Revolution in the worst possible light, blends several Mexican accounts to achieve its revisionist view of Crockett's death, while ignoring the fact that every Mexican account that deals with the alleged executions states that the victims died bravely. In some cases they are trying to kill Santa Anna even as they are killed.

José Enrique de la Pena was an officer of the Mexican army who severely criticized Santa Anna's conduct of the Texas campaign following the return of the army to Mexico. In Mexico in the 1950s, a book appeared that was accepted by both Mexican and American historians as de la Pena's long lost narrative, originally published but then quickly suppressed in the nineteenth century. Its authenticity was unquestioned for years, until Long's book caused some Crockett supporters to begin an in-depth analysis of the Mexican accounts. As a result of this probing, inconsistencies in de la Pena's account led some to theorize that the work was a forgery. In 1994, Alamo buff and historian Bill Groneman published *Defense of a Legend,* outlining his reasons for suspecting the Mexican officer's account was a fake. Others came to the defense of the de la Pena account, and the battle is far from over.

And so, the mission-turned-fortress, and the fortress-turned-shrine, continues to be a battleground. So be it, if that's what it takes to remember the Alamo.

El Soldado Mexicano

A TRIBUTE TO THE MEXICAN SOLDIER

EARLIER IN THIS BOOK we offered a tribute to the defenders of the Alamo, Anglo and Tejano alike, that was written by our artist, Ted Spring. Before we end, we feel compelled to also honor the courage of *LOS SOLDADOS MEXICANOS*, the common Mexican soldiers who fought and died in the same campaign.

The political motivations of Santa Anna, who was as unpopular with many Mexicans as he was with the Texians, should not prevent us from recognizing the bravery shown, and the sufferings endured, by these *soldados,* who were just trying to do their duty to their country.

Joseph Hefter, an Austrian engineer who lived and worked in Mexico for many years, compiled a body of research on the Mexican soldier that is unequaled. It is fitting that we use his words to express our tribute:

On his final retreat through rain and mud, carrying his wounded with him on improvised stretchers, followed by a caravan of soldier—women with their pots and kids, the Mexican soldier could look back on 120 months of fighting against Texans, Frenchmen, Americans and against hostile factions of his own citizens; 120 months with 23 changes in government . . . The years of warfare had brought only tragedy and loss, although the man and the officer in the firing line had borne the burden of sacrifices with unbowed head, and discharged well their duty to the tricolor flag. . . .

Above the wreckage of these battlefields, behind the haze of a century of neglect by history, there still looms silent and dignified, the ghost of the common Mexican soldier. . . .

(Hefter: *El Soldado Mexicano,* 78)

Bibliography

A variety of sources have been consulted in the preparation of this text, including books, periodicals, personal correspondence, and unpublished manuscripts. To make it easier for the reader to identify a source cited, all entries in this bibliography are listed alphabetically by the author's last name.

Baker, Karle Wilson. "Trailing the New Orleans Greys." In *Southwest Review,* Volume 22, Number 3, April 1937.

Baugh, Virgil E. *Rendezvous at the Alamo: Highlights in the Lives of Bowie, Crockett, and Travis.* Bison Books, University of Nebraska Press, Lincoln & London, 1985.

Bekker, Bob. *Fourth Is a Badge to Great Americans.* Sports Editorial in the *Grand Rapids* (Michigan) *PRESS,* July 4, 1991.

Benavides, Robert M. *The Alamo Low Barracks and Main Gateway.* Unpublished manuscript. Copy in the author's possession.

Bivins, John. "Crockett Redivivus: A Painstaking Recreation of Davy's First Rifle." In *MUZZLELOADER* Magazine, January 1989.

Borroel, Roger. *The Texas Revolution of 1836: A Concise Historical Perspective Based on Original Sources.* La Villita Publications, East Chicago, Indiana, 1989.

Bourdage, John. "Percussion Weapons at the Alamo?" In *The Alamo Journal,* February 1988.

Boyd, Bob. *The Texas Revolution: A Day by Day Account.* Edited by Soren W. Nielsen. *The San Angelo Standard-Times,* San Angelo, TX, 1986.

Bradfield, Jane. *Take One Cannon: The Gonzales Come and Take It Cannon of October 1835.* Patrick J. Wagner Research and Publishing Company, Shiner, TX, 1981.

Burke, James W. *David Crockett, Man Behind the Myth.* Eakin Press, Austin, TX, 1984.

Casso, Raul IV. "Damacio Jiminez: The Lost and Found Alamo Defender." In the *Southeastern Historical Quarterly,* Volume XCVI, Number 1, July 1992.

Castaneda, Carlos E. *The Mexican Side of the Texas Revolution (1836) by the Chief Mexican Participants.* Graphic Ideas Inc., Austin & Dallas, 1970. Originally published in 1928. Contains the following accounts:

1. Gen. Antonio López de Santa Anna
2. D. Ramon Martinez Caro (secretary to Santa Anna)
3. Gen. Vicente Filisola
4. Gen. José Urrea
5. Gen. José María Tornel (secretary of war)

Chariton, Wallace O. *Exploring the Alamo Legends.* Wordware Publishing Inc., Plano, Texas, 1990.

———. *100 Days in Texas: The Alamo Letters.* Wordware Publishing, Inc., Plano, Texas, 1990.

———. *Unsolved Texas Mysteries.* Wordware Publishing, Inc., Plano, Texas, 1991.

Chartrand, Rene. "Organization and Uniforms of the Mexican Army, 1810–1838." In *Military Collector & Historian, the Journal of the Company of Military Historians,* Westbrook, CT, Vol. XLVII, No. 1, Spring 1996.

Chemerka, William R. *Alamo Almanac & Book of Lists.* Eakin Press, Austin, Texas, 1997.

———. "Alamo Flag to be Returned?" An item in the "Alamo News" column in *The Alamo Journal,* October 1994.

———. "Courage Under Fire: The Mexican Army at the Battle of the Alamo." In *The Alamo Journal,* August 1989.

Clark, Donald, and Andersen, Christopher. *John Wayne's The Alamo: The Making of John Wayne's 1960 Epic Film.* Midwest Publishing, in connection with R&G Productions, Hillside, Illinois, 1994.

Company of Military Historians. *Mexican Army 1835.* Uniform plate and text by H. Charles McBarron and Detmar H. Finke. The Company of Military Historians, Westbrook, CT, date unknown.

———. *Mexican Army Riflemen, Texas Campaigns, 1835–1836.* Uniform plate and text by Gary Zaboly. The Company of Military Historians, Westbrook, CT, 1995.

———. *New Orleans Greys at San Antonio de Bexar, 1835.* Uniform plate and text by Peter Stines and Edward L. Miller. The Company of Military Historians, Westbrook, CT, 1996.

———. *Republic of Texas Rangers, 1839.* Uniform plate and text by Randy Steffen. The Company of Military Historians, Westbrook, CT, date unknown.

Connally, Thomas Lawrence. "Did David Crockett Surrender at the Alamo?" In *The Journal of Southern History,* XXVI, August 1960. The complete text and a full discussion of the famous "Dolson Letter."

Courtney, Jovita. *After the Alamo—San Jacinto: From the Notes of Doctor Nicholas Decomps Labadie.* Vantage Press, New York, 1964.

Crimmins, Col. M. L. "The Storming of San Antonio de Bexar in 1835." Printed in the *West Texas Historical Association Yearbook,* October 1946.

Crisp, James E. "Davy in Freeze-Frame: Methodology of Madness?" In *The Alamo Journal,* Issue 98, October 1995.

———. "The Little Book That Wasn't There: The Myth and Mystery of the de la Pena Diary." In *The Southwestern Historical Quarterly,* Volume XCVIII, No. 2, October 1994.

———. "Trashing Dolson: The Perils of Tendentious Interpretation." In *The Alamo Journal,* Issue 99, December 1995.

Crockett, David. *A Narrative of the Life of David Crockett, By Himself.* University of Nebraska Press, Lincoln, 1987. Originally published in Philadelphia by E. L. Carey and A. Hart in 1834.

Curtis, Gregory. "Forgery Texas Style: Highly Suspect—A Famous Letter from the Alamo May Very Well Be a Twentieth Century Fraud." In *Texas Monthly,* Volume 17, Issue 3, March 1989.

———. "Seer and Scholar." In *Texas Monthly,* December 1993. Details the efforts of two current Alamo scholars, Frank Buschbacher, who is attempting to locate treasure that Bowie possibly buried at the Alamo, and Tom Lindley, who is coming up with some amazing new information in his intense study of who the Alamo defenders really were.

Darling, Anthony D. *Red Coat and Brown Bess.* The Museum Restoration Service, Ottawa, Canada, 1970.

Daughters of the Republic of Texas. *The Alamo Long Barrack Museum.* Taylor Publishing Company, Dallas, Texas, 1986.

———. *1836: The Alamo.* Details of the construction of the Alamo as it was in 1836. Daughters of the Republic of Texas, 1983.

Davidson, Richard A. "The Incredible and the Credulous: Another Look at De La Pena and Nunez." In *The Alamo Journal,* December 1992.

De la Pena, José Enrique. *With Santa Anna in Texas: A Personal Narrative of the Revolution.* Translated and edited by Carmen Perry, Texas A&M University Press, College Station, 1975.

De la Teja, Jesus F. *A Revolution Remembered: The Memoirs and Selected Correspondence of Juan N. Seguin.* State House Press, Austin, Texas, 1991.

Dobie, J. Frank. "Jim Bowie, Big Dealer." In *The Southwestern Historical Quarterly,* Volume LX, No. 3, January 1957.

Downey, Fairfax. *Texas and the War with Mexico.* American Heritage Publishing Company, New York, 1961.

Dubravsky, Ed. "Alamo Timetable." In *The Alamo Journal,* September 1992. Using scientific data, the author analyzes the amount of daylight present for the different phases of the final assault on the Alamo.

———. "The Baker Rifle." In *The Alamo Journal,* October 1994.

———. "North Wall!" In *The Alamo Journal,* July 1993. An analysis of the action at the north wall during the final battle.

Dupuy, R. Ernest, Lt. Col., F.A., U.S.A. *Where They Have Trod: The West Point Tradition in American Life.* Frederick A. Stokes Company, New York, 1940.

Edsall, Margaret Horton. *A Place Called THE YARD: Guide to the United States Naval Academy.* The Douglas W. Edsall Company, Annapolis, MD, 1976; 6th edition, 1986.

Elting, Col. John R., Retired, Editor. *Military Uniforms in America, Volume II: Years of Growth, 1796–1851.* The Company of Military Historians, Presidio Press, San Rafael, California, 1977.

Esparza, Enrique. "The Story of the Massacre of the Heroes of the Alamo." In *The San Antonio Express,* March 7, 1905.

Filisola, Vicente. *Memories for the History of the War in Texas.* Two Volumes. Translated by Wallace Woolsey. Eakin Press, Austin, Texas, 1985. Originally published in Mexico City, 1848.

Fisher, David J. *The Music of Disney: A Legacy in Song.* The Walt Disney Company, 1992. (The commemorative book accompanying the special boxed CD music set of the same name.)

Foreman, Gary L. *Crockett, Gentleman from the Cane—A Comprehensive View of the Folkhero Americans Thought They Knew.* Taylor Publishing Company, Dallas, Texas, 1986.

Fox, Anna A., with contributions by Susan W. Dial, Samuel Nesmith, and Herbert G. Uecker. *Archeological Investigations in Alamo Plaza, San Antonio, Bexar County, Texas, 1988 and 1989.* The Center for Archeological Research, The University of Texas at San Antonio, Archeological Survey Report Number 205, 1992.

Gaddy, Jerry J., Editor. Illustrated by Joseph Hefter. *Texas in Revolt: Contemporary Newspaper Accounts of the Texas Revolution.* The Old Army Press, Fort Collins, Colorado, 1973.

Gooding, S. James. *An Introduction to British Artillery in North America.* Historical Arms Series No. 4, Museum Restoration Service, Ottawa, Ontario, Canada, 1972.

Gray, Ruthann E., and Laura S. Lara. *A Woman's Guide to 1830's Fashion, Finery, and Practical Pursuits.* Privately printed by the San Antonio Living History Association, 1989.

Green, Michael R. "To the People of Texas & All Americans of the World." In *The Southwestern Historical Quarterly,* XCI, April 1988.

Groneman, Bill. *Alamo Defenders—A Genealogy: The People and Their Words.* Eakin Press, Austin, Texas, 1990. Updated Fourth Printing, 1995.

———. "Anthony Wolf: Tracing an Alamo Defender." In *The Journal of South Texas,* Volume 3, Number 1, Spring 1990.

———. "A Witness to the Executions." In *The Alamo Journal,* October 1993.

———. "The Controversial Account of Jose Enrique de la Pena." A paper delivered at the 99th Annual Meeting of the Texas State Historical Association, San Antonio, Texas, March 1995. Copy in the author's possession.

———. *Defense of a Legend: Crockett and the de la Pena Diary.* Republic of Texas Press, An Imprint of Wordware Publishing, Inc., Plano, Texas, 1994.

———. "De la Pena and the Alamo Mystery Victim." In *The Alamo Journal,* February 1993.

———. *Eyewitness to the Alamo.* Republic of Texas Press, Plano, Texas, 1996.

———. *Galba Fuqua: A Question of Evidence.* Unpublished manuscript, October 1990. Copy in the author's possession.

———. "Some Comparisons to the de la Pena Diary." In *The Alamo Journal,* July 1994.

———. "Some Problems with the Almonte Account." In *The Alamo Journal,* February 1994.

———. "Some Problems with the Urriza Account." In *The Alamo Journal,* July 1993.

———. Untitled follow-up explanation to Kevin Young's article "A Re-evaluation of a Re-evaluation," written in response to his "Some Problems with the Urriza Account." In *The Alamo Journal,* February 1994.

Guerra, Mary Ann Noonan. *The Alamo.* The Alamo Press, 1983, no further information given.

Hamilton, Allen Lee. "The Alamo Avenged: Pathway to Retreat Ignored." In *Military History* Magazine, October 1988.

Harburn, Dr. Todd E., D.O. *The Alamo: A Trip Back in Time.* A miscellaneous package of information assembled for the authors' first trip to the Alamo in March 1990. In addition to Dr. Harburn, our group, dubbed "The Michigan Contingent of the Tennessee Mounted Volunteers," included Tim and Terry Todish, Jerry A. Olson, Barry A. Lewis, and Chuck Spring. Our experiences on this trip gave us the inspiration to attempt this book.

Harburn, Dr. Todd E., D.O. "The Crockett Death Controversy: A Commentary and Opinion Regarding the Same As Contained in Duel of Eagles, The Mexican and U.S. Fight for the Alamo." In *The Alamo Journal,* April 1991.

———. *Davy Crockett's Beaded Buckskin Vest: A Recreation.* Unpublished outline for a talk presented at the Alamo Society Symposium, at the Alamo IMAX Theater, San Antonio, March 6, 1992. Copy in the author's possession.

———. "If You Can Tolerate One More Comment On . . ." In *The Alamo Journal,* June 1966.

Hardin, Stephen L., Editor. "The Felix Nunez Account and the Siege of the Alamo." In *The Southwestern Historical Quarterly,* Volume XCIV, No. 1, July 1990.

Hardin, Stephen L., with paintings by Richard Scollins. "Gallery: David Crockett." In *Military Illustrated* Magazine, February/March 1990.

Hardin, Stephen L., with illustrations by Gary Zaboly. *Texian Illiad: A Military History of the Texas Revolution.* University of Texas Press, Austin, 1994.

Hartman, R. G. *The Alamo: Historical Map of the Battle and Preceding Events.* Richardson, Texas, 1968.

Hauck, Richard B. *Crockett—A Bio-Bibliography.* Greenwood Press, Westport, CT and London, 1982. Reprinted as *Davy Crockett—A Handbook.* The University of Nebraska Press, Lincoln, NE, and London, 1986.

Haythornethwaite, Philip. *The Alamo and the War of Texas Independence 1835–1836.* Plates by Paul Hannon. Osprey Publishing, London, 1986. Part of the *Osprey Men-at-Arms* Series.

———. Letter to Kevin Young regarding Edward Edwards, September 18, 1992. Copy in the author's possession.

Hefter, Joseph, editor, with Francisco Ferrer Llul. *Bibliografia Iconografica del Traje Militar de Espana* (Pictorial Bibliography of Spanish Military Dress). Limited, numbered edition privately published by Francisco Ferrer Llul and Joseph Hefter, Mexico City, 1963.

Hefter, Joseph, with Mrs. Angelina Nieto and Mrs. John Nicholas Brown. *El Soldado Mexicano (The Mexican Soldier) 1837–1847: Organization, Dress, Equipment Compiled from original Sources.* Monograph 1, Military Historical Documents, Editions Nieto-Brown-Hefter, Mexico City, 1958.

Hefter, Joseph. *Los Soldados de la Independencia y de la Revolucion Mexico: 1810–1820 & 1910–1920.* Military Monographs Number 2, Mexico City, 1960.

Herbeck, Ray Jr., Producer, and Kevin R. Young, Historical Advisor. *Remember the Alamo! Mexican & Texian Music of 1836.* Star Line Productions Inc., Glendale, California. Extensive liner notes to the audio music cassette.

Huffines, Alan C. "A Mexican Shako Plate." In *Military Collector & Historian, the Journal of the Company of Military Historians,* Westbrook, CT, Vol. XLVIII, No. 1, Spring 1996.

Huneycutt, C. D. *The Alamo: An In-Depth Study of the Battle.* Gold Star Press, New London, North Carolina, 1986.

Hunter, Butch. "James Bowie's Knife." In *Wild West* Magazine, June 1994.

Hutton, Paul Andrew. "The Alamo: An American Epic." In *American History Magazine—Texas and the Alamo: Texas Sesquicentennial Issue,* March 1986.

———. "Continuing Battles for the Alamo." In *American History Magazine—Texas and the Alamo: Texas Sesquicentennial Issue,* March 1986.

———. "Davy Crockett. An Exposition on Hero Worship." In *Crockett at Two Hundred,* University of Tennessee Press, Knoxville, TN, 1989.

———. "Davy Crockett—He Was Hardly King of the Wild Frontier." In *TV Guide* Magazine, February 4, 1989.

———. *Forward to a Narrative of the Life of David Crockett, of the State of Tennessee.* University of Nebraska Press, Lincoln, NE, and London, 1987.

Ivey, Jake. "Southwest & Northwest Gun Emplacements." In the *Journal of the Alamo Lore and Myth Organization,* Volume 3, Issue 3, September 1981.

Jackson, Jack. *Los Tejanos: The True Story of Juan N. Seguin and the Texas-Mexicans During the Rising of the Lone Star.* Fantagraphics Books, Inc., Stamford, CT, 1982.

Jackson, Ron. *Alamo Legacy: Alamo Descendants Remember the Alamo.* Eakin Press, Austin, Texas, 1997.

Johnson, Allen, & Dumas Malone, editors. *The Dictionary of American Biography.* Charles Scribner's Sons, New York, 1930. 1958 edition.

Joslin, E. C. *Spink's Catalogue of British and Associated Orders, Decorations and Medals with Valuations.* Webb & Bower (Publishers) Limited, Exeter, England, 1983.

Joslin, E. C., A. R. Litherland, and B. T. Simpkin. *British Battles & Medals.* Spink & Sons Limited, London, England, 1988.

Katcher, Philip R. N. *The Mexican American War.* Plates by Gerry A. Embleton. Osprey Publishing, London, 1976. Part of the *Osprey Men-at-Arms* Series.

Kauffman, Henry J. *The Pennsylvania Kentucky Rifle.* Bonanza Books, New York, 1960.

Kilgore, Dan. *How Did Davy Die?* Texas A&M University Press, College Station, 1978.

———. "Why Davy Didn't Die." In *Crockett at Two Hundred,* University of Tennessee Press, Knoxville, TN, 1989.

Lindley, Thomas Ricks. "A Correct List of Alamo Patriots." In *The Alamo Journal,* December 1993.

———. "Alamo Artillery: Number, Type, Caliber, and Concussion." In *The Alamo Journal,* July 1992. Text of a paper delivered at the Alamo Society Symposium at the Alamo IMAX Theater in San Antonio, March 6, 1992.

Lindley, Thomas Ricks, Editor. "The Cannon Tale: A New Alamo Account." In *The Alamo Journal,* December 1994. A letter from William James Cannon to Governor J. S. Hogg, Austin, Texas, June 9, 1893, in which Cannon claims to have been at the Alamo.

Lindley, Thomas Ricks. "Drawing Truthful Conclusions." In

the *Journal of the Alamo Battlefield Association,* Volume 1, Number 1, Summer 1995.

———. "Killing Crockett." Published in *The Alamo Journal,* in three parts:
I. "It's All in the Execution," in Issue #96, May 1995
II. "Theory Paraded as Fact," in Issue #97, July 1995
III. "Lindley's Opinion," in Issue #98, October 1995

Lochee, Lewis. *An Essay on Castramentation.* London, 1778. Reprinted by the King's Arms Press, Oldwick, New Jersey, 1990.

Lofaro, Michael A. *Davy Crockett, the Man, the Legend, the Legacy.* University of Tennessee Press, Knoxville, Tennessee, 1989.

Lofaro, Michael A., and Cummings, Joe, Editors. *Crockett at Two Hundred.* University of Tennessee Press, Knoxville, Tennessee, 1989.

Long, Jeff. *Duel of Eagles: The Mexican and U.S. Fight for the Alamo.* William Morrow and Company, New York, 1990.

Loranca, Manuel. *Santa Anna's Last Effort: The Alamo and San Jacinto.* From *The San Antonio Express,* June ??, 1878. An interview with a former sergeant in the Mexican army, originally printed by the Corpus Christi *Free Press.*

Lord, Walter. *A Time to Stand: The Epic of the Alamo.* Bonanza Books, New York, 1987. (Originally published in 1961.)

———. "Update to Myths and Realities of the Alamo." An essay in *The Republic of Texas,* published by the Texas State Historical Association, American West Publishing Company, Palo Alto, California, 1968.

Mahoney, Bob. "Flags of the Alamo." In *The Alamo Journal,* December 1986.

Manucy, Albert. *Artillery Through the Ages: A Short Illustrated History of Cannon, Emphasizing Types Used in America.* Division of Publications, National Park Service, 1949. 1985 Edition.

Marks, Paula Mitchell. "The Men of Gonzales." In *American History Magazine—Texas and the Alamo: Texas Sesquicentennial Issue,* March 1986.

Matovina, Timothy M. *The Alamo Remembered: Tejano Accounts and Perspectives.* University of Texas Press, Austin, 1995.

McDonald, Archie P. "Lone Star Rising—Texas Before & After the Alamo." In *American History Magazine—Texas and the Alamo: Texas Sesquicentennial Issue,* March 1986.

McEvoy, Harry S. "The Original Bowie? A Bowie Buff Has Highest Hopes." In *Muzzleloader* Magazine, January/February 1982.

Miller, Edward L. "The Texas Revolution, Civilian Suits, Whiskey-Loving Foreigners and the New Orleans Greys." In *Military Collector & Historian, the Journal of the Company of Military Historians,* Westbrook, CT, Vol. XLVIII, No. 1, Spring 1996.

Montejano, David. *Anglos and Mexicans in the Making of Texas 1836–1986.* University of Texas Press, Austin, 1987.

Morris, Roy Jr. "Filibusters, American and European Soldiers of Fortune Plagued Many Latin American Countries." In *Wild West Magazine,* October 1993.

Musso, Joseph. "A Bowie Knife." In *The Alamo Journal,* December 1992.

Myers, Cindi. "The Alamo: What You Want to Know About Texas' Famous Site." In *Historic Traveler* Magazine, May/June 1995.

Myers, John Myers. *The Alamo.* Bison Books Edition, The University of Nebraska Press, Lincoln & London, 1973.

Newell, Rev. C. *History of the Revolution in Texas, Particularly the War of 1835 & '36.* Wiley & Putnam, New York, 1838.

Niderost, Eric. *San Antonio, Texas.* The *Travel* feature in *Military History,* February 1994.

Nofi, Albert A. *The Alamo and the Texas War for Independence.* Combined Books, Conshohocken, Pennsylvania, 1992.

Olson, Jerry O., Editor. *The Alamo: March 6, 1836.* The Olson Press, Dearborn, Michigan, 1990. An anthology of material pertaining to the Alamo and the Texas Revolution prepared especially for the Michigan Contingent of Tennessee Mounted Volunteers' trip to the Alamo in March of 1990. Published in a numbered, limited edition.

Peterson, Harold L. *Round Shot and Rammers: An Introduction to Muzzler-loading Land Artillery in the United States.* South Bend Replicas, Inc., South Bend, Indiana, 1969.

Pohl, James W. *The Battle of San Jacinto.* The Texas State Historical Association, 1989.

Potter, Reuben M. "Captain R. M. Potter's Account of the Fall of the Alamo." Reprinted in *Chronology and Documentary Handbook of the State of Texas,* Oceana Publications, Inc., Dobbs Ferry, NY, 1979. A revised version of the 1860 article below.

———. *The Fall of the Alamo: A Reminiscence of the Revolution of Texas.* Fuller Printing Company, Bryan, Texas, 1979. Originally published by the Herald Steam Press, San Antonio, 1860.

Ramsdell, Charles. "The Storming of the Alamo." In *American Heritage* Magazine, February 1961. Ramsdell is Susannah Dickinson's great-grandson.

Randle, Kevin D. "Santa Anna's Signal." In *Military History* Magazine, April 1985.

Reid, Jan. "Davy Crock?" In *Texas Monthly,* May 1995.

Rivertheater Associates Ltd. *Alamo . . . The Price of Freedom.* The story of the making of the movie. Rivertheatre Associates Ltd., San Antonio, 1993.

Robinson, Cecil. *Flag of Illusion: The Texas Revolution Viewed As a Conflict of Cultures.* An essay in Walter Lord's *Update to Myths and Realities of the Alamo.* In *The Republic of Texas,* published by the Texas State Historical Association, American West Publishing Company, Palo Alto, California, 1968.

Rosenthal, Phil. *Alamo Soldiers: An Armchair Historian's Guide to the Defenders of the Alamo.* A-Team Productions, 1989. (No publisher's address given.)

Rosenthal, Phil, and Bill Groneman. *Roll Call at the Alamo.* The Old Army Press, Fort Collins, Colorado, 1985. A limited edition of 500 autographed, numbered copies.

Rubio, Abel G. *Stolen Heritage, A Mexican-American's Rediscovery of His Family's Lost Land Grant.* Eakin Press, Austin, Texas, 1986.

Ruiz, Francisco. Account of the fall of the Alamo by the *alcalde* (mayor) of San Antonio de Bexar, reprinted in *Message of Governor O. B. Colquitt to the Thirty-Third Legislature Relating to the Alamo Property,* Von Boeckmann-Jones Printers, Austin, Texas, 1913.

Sanchez Lamego, Gen. Miguel A. *The Siege and Taking of the Alamo.* Translated by Consuelo Velasco, with some comments on the battle by Joseph Hefter. English edition printed by the Blue Feather Press for the Press of the Territorian, Santa Fe, New Mexico, 1968.

Sanchez Navarro, Lt. Col. José Juan. *A Mexican View of the Texas War: Memories of a Veteran of the Two Battles of the*

Alamo. In *The Library Chronicle* of the University of Texas, Austin, Volume IV, Number 2, Summer 1951.

Sandweiss, Martha A., Rick Stewart, and Ben W. Huseman. *Eyewitness to War: Prints and Daguerreotypes of the Mexican War, 1846–1848.* Amon Carter Museum, Fort Worth, Texas, and the Smithsoniam Institution Press, Washington, DC, 1989.

Santos, Richard G. *Santa Anna's Campaign Against Texas.* Texian Press, Waco, Texas, 1968.

Schoelwer, Susan Pendergast, with Tom W. Glaser. *Alamo Images: Changing Perceptions of a Texas Experience.* The DeGolyer Library and Southern Methodist University Press, Dallas, 1985.

Schoelwer, Susan Pendergast. "Alamo Images." In *American History Magazine—Texas and the Alamo: Texas Sesquicentennial Issue,* March 1986.

Shackford, James Atkins. *David Crockett: The Man and the Legend.* University of North Carolina Press, Chapel Hill, 1956.

Shearring, Howard G. *The Alamo's Eighteen Pounder.* Unpublished manuscript; copy in the author's possession.

———. Letter to the Daughters of the Republic of Texas Library, the Alamo, regarding Edward Edwards, November 16, 1990. Copy in the author's possession.

———. Letter to the Daughters of the Republic of Texas Library, the Alamo, regarding Edward Edwards, December 13, 1990. Copy in the author's possession.

———. Letter to Bill Groneman, regarding Edward Edwards, October 21, 1992. Copy in the author's possession.

———. Letter to Bill Groneman, regarding Edward Edwards, November 19, 1992. Copy in the author's possession.

———. Letter to Robert Lancaster, regarding Edward Edwards, June 8, 1995. Copy in the author's possession.

———. *The Career and Mysterious Death of Edward Edwards.* Unpublished manuscript; copy in the author's possession.

Smith, Richard Penn. *Col. Crockett's Exploits and Adventures in Texas . . . Written by Himself.* Published by T. K. and P. G. Collins, Philadelphia, 1836. Although attributed to Crockett, this book was actually written by Smith. William Snell Smith, who was also involved in its publication, did correspond with Crockett, so parts of it may be valid.

Sovereign Publications, Hollywood, California, 1960. *The Alamo.* Color booklet commemorating the release of the John Wayne film *The Alamo.*

Sterling, Susan Griffith. "Letter of February 17, 1926." Sterling, Angelina Dickinson's daughter, disavows the claim of William James Cannon that he was a survivor of the Alamo. In *The Alamo Journal,* October 1995.

Stines, Peter. "The Baker Rifle." "From the Stein" column in *The Bexar Dispatch,* the newsletter of the San Antonio Living History Association, May/June 1992.

———. "Pretty Betsey: Davy Crockett's Fancy Rifle." In *The Alamo Journal,* February 1988.

Sullivan, David M. "The Republic of Texas Marine Corps." In *Military Collector & Historian, the Journal of the Company of Military Historians,* Westbrook, CT, Vol. XLVIII, No. 1, Spring 1996.

Telegraph and Texas Register, Volume I, Number 21. San Felipe de Austin, Thursday, March 24, 1836. Facsimile reprint of the original newspaper containing some of the first news of the fall of the Alamo.

Thompson, Frank, with a Foreword by Fess Parker. *Alamo Movies.* Old Mill Books, East Berlin, Pennsylvania, 1991.

Tijerna, Andres. *Tejanos & Texas Under the Mexican Flag 1821–1836.* Texas A&M University Press, College Station, 1994.

Tinkle, Lon. *The Alamo: 13 Days to Glory.* Signet Books, New York, 1960. Originally published in 1958.

Time Life Books. *The Old West Series—The Texans.* Time Life, Alexandria, Virginia, 1975.

———. *The Old West Series—The Spanish West.* Time Life, Alexandria, Virginia, 1976.

———. *The Old West Series—The Mexican War.* Time Life, Alexandria, Virginia, 1978.

Todish, Tim J. "An Alamo Odyssey." In *Muzzleloader* Magazine, March/April 1992.

———. "Davy Crockett: Frontiersman . . . Congressman . . . Poet?" In *The Alamo Journal,* April 1991.

Turner, Jerry. "Jim Bowie and His Knife." In *Muzzleloader* Magazine, September/October 1995.

Utterback, Martha. Letter from the Daughters of Republic of Texas Library at the Alamo, to Howard G. Shearring, regarding Edward Edwards, December 4, 1990. Copy in the author's possession.

Vexler, Robert I., and William F. Swindler, Editors. "Captain R. M. Potter's Account of the Fall of the Alamo." In the *Chronology and Documentary Handbook of the State of Texas.* Oceana Publications, Inc., Dobbs Ferry, New York, 1979. This version of Potter's account is taken from *America: Great Crises in Our History Told By Its Makers,* published by the Veteran of Foreign Wars, Chicago, 1925. It is a revised version of Potter's 1860 article.

Von Schmidt, Eric. "The Alamo Remembered—From a Painter's Point of View." *Smithsonian* Magazine, March 1986.

Wayne, Pilar, with Alex Thorleifson. *John Wayne: My Life with the Duke.* McGraw-Hill, New York, NY, 1987.

Webster, Paul Francis, and Dimitri Tiomkin. *The Ballad of the Alamo.* Sheet music for the song from the John Wayne movie. Distributed by Leo Feist Inc., 1960, New York, NY.

———. "The Green Leaves of Summer." Sheet music for the song from the John Wayne movie. Distributed by Leo Feist Inc., 1960, New York, NY.

Weems, John Edward, and Ron Stone, with illustrations by Tom Jones. *The Story of Texas.* Shearer Publishing, Fredericksburg, Texas, 1986.

Weems, John Edward, with Jane Weems. *Dream of Empire: A History of the Republic of Texas 1836–1846.* Reprinted by Barnes & Noble Books, New York, 1995; first published in 1971 by Simon & Schuster, NY.

Williams, John Hoyt. *Sam Houston: The Life and Times of the Liberator of Texas, an Authentic American Hero.* Simon & Schuster, NY, 1993.

Whitburn, Joel. *The Billboard Book of Top 40 Hits 1955 to the Present.* Billboard Books/Watson-Guptill Publications, New York, 1989.

———. *Top Country Singles 1944–1993.* Record Research Inc., Menomonee Falls, Wisconsin, 1994.

———. *Top Pop Singles 1955–1993.* Record Research Inc., Menomonee Falls, Wisconsin, 1994.

Whitmarsh, L. M. "A Welsh Mexican?" An article about Edward Edwards in *Family Tree* Magazine, October 1990.

Winter, Butch. "James Bowie's Knife." In *Wild West* Magazine, June 1994.

Young, Kevin R. "A Re-evaluation of a Re-evaluation." In *The Alamo Journal,* December 1994. A critique of Bill Groneman's "Some Problems with the Urriza Account."

———. "Dimmitt's 1824 Flag." In *The Alamo Journal,* December 1986.

———. "Edward Edwards: Mystery Man of the Alamo." In *The Alamo Journal,* May 1993.

———. "Mexican Army Infantry and Cavalry Battalions, 1835–1836." Unpublished manuscript. Copy in the author's possession.

———. "Mexican Flags of the Texas War for Independence Period." Unpublished manuscript. Copy in the author's possession.

———. "Understanding the Mexican Army." Unpublished manuscript. Copy in the author's possession.

———. "Who Is Who in the Mexican Army." Unpublished manuscript. Copy in the author's possession.

Zaboly, Gray. *Crockett's Company Riding the Camino Real on Their Way to San Antonio.* Original watercolor (1970) and personal letter to Tim Todish describing the scene (1990), both in possession of Tim Todish.

———. "Crockett Goes Into Texas: A Newspaper Chronology." In the *Journal of the Alamo Battlefield Association,* Volume 1, Number 1, Summer 1995.

———. *Travis' Line.* 1990. Limited edition art print and copies of notes from the artist's personal journal kept while completing the painting, both in the possession of Tim Todish.

Zuber, W. P. "Letter to Charlie Jeffries, August 17, 1904." In *In the Shadow of History,* Texas Folk-Lore Society Publications Number XV, Folklore Associates Inc., Hatboro, Pennsylvania, 1966. Recollections of the fall of the Alamo and the death of Crockett.

Index

Author/Artist Biographies

Timothy J. Todish

TIM TODISH is a native of Grand Rapids, Michigan. He has a bachelor's degree in management from Michigan State University. A sergeant and twenty-seven-year veteran of the Grand Rapids Police Department, he has served in nearly every area of the organization during his career.

Tim has had an interest in history since childhood, and specializes in Rogers' Rangers, the French and Indian War, and the Alamo and Texas Revolution. In addition to a successful book on the French and Indian War, he has written many magazine and journal articles on historical subjects. He has provided background research for a number of movie and television productions, including the 1992 film *The Last of the Mohicans,* and the Learning Channel's *Archeology* television show. In addition, he and his son Tim R. appeared as reenactor-extras in *The Last of the Mohicans.*

Tim is a member of the Company of Military Historians and is on the Special Features Staff of *Muzzleloader Magazine.* An avid historical reenactor, he is also a member of the Living History Hall of Fame, at the Museum of the Old Northwest, Galveston, Indiana. He currently resides in Grand Rapids with his wife, Colleen, and son, Tim R. Todish.

Terrence S. Todish

TERRY TODISH is author Tim Todish's younger brother, and is also a Grand Rapids native. He has a history degree from Aquinas College, and works for a company that does specialized research for law firms. Terry has also worked as a museum curator and archivist, edited a national living history newspaper, and participated in some of the background work for the film *The Last of the Mohicans.*

Terry has published a number of short historical articles, but *Sourcebook 1836* is his first major literary effort. He is largely responsible for Chapters One, Three, Five, Eight, Seventeen, and Part One of Chapter Sixteen. Chapter Seven is a joint effort by Tim and Terry. Terry is also a historical reenactor. Recently, he served as historical consultant on the History Channel series *Frontier* and portrayed a character in the "Pontiac" episode. He currently resides in Grand Rapids with his wife, Marian, and daughter, Bree.

Ted M. Spring

Artist TED SPRING is a native of Ticonderoga, New York, which accounts for his interest in Rogers' Rangers and the French and Indian War. He credits his fascination with the Alamo to Walt Disney, John Wayne, and the U.S. Army. A former army medic with one and one-half tours in Vietnam, Ted first got to see the real Alamo while taking his medic training at Fort Sam Houston.

Largely a self-taught artist, Ted has taken classes at Oscar Rose College in Midwest City, Oklahoma. Currently employed as a truck driver, Ted uses his travel opportunities to visit historic sites, museums, and libraries across the country to do research for his artwork. He has written and illustrated a series of highly successful historical sketchbooks. Ted's interest in historic firearms and in leatherwork helps him with the historic detail in his sketches. For *Sourcebook 1836,* he created over 140 original pen and ink sketches, as well as a thoroughly researched, full-color overview of the Alamo compound.

Ted currently lives in Nicoma Park, Oklahoma, with his family.

Dr. Todd E. Harburn, D.O.

DR. TODD HARBURN, who contributed the essay on the controversial death of Davy Crockett, is a man of many skills and interests. A native of Flint, Michigan, Todd attended Hope College, where he majored in pre-med and earned all-conference honors in football. He graduated from the Chicago College of Osteopathic Medicine, and in addition to his orthopedic surgery practice, he is the football team physician for Alma College.

Todd has had a lifelong interest in history, especially in the French and Indian War and the Alamo. His first book, *Of Scarlet and Blue: The 60th Royal American Regimental Coat 1755-1768* (with R. Scott Stephenson), set the standard for the uniform coats used by most British French and Indian War reenactors today, and was the basis for the patterns for the British uniforms in the movie *The Last of the Mohicans.*

Todd has written a number of historical articles for various magazines and journals, and has also co-authored two sports history books: *MIAA FOOTBALL: The Illustrated Gridiron History of the Michigan Intercollegiate Athletic Association* (with his father, Gerald E. Harburn), and *Alma College Football: A Centennial Salute to the Champions, 100 Years of Alma College Football 1894-1994* (with Dr. Charles A. Gray). Todd currently resides in Okemos, Michigan, with his wife, Shirley, and daughters Shannon and Stacey.

Other Books of Interest

By Tim J. Todish . . .

Lodge History: Jibshe Wanagan Lodge 79, Order of the Arrow, Boy Scouts of America. (With Rick Lanning)
Print-Craft Press, Grand Rapids, MI, 1975

America's FIRST First World War: The French and Indian War 1754-1763.
Hardcover: Dickinson Brothers, Grand Rapids, MI, 1982.
Softcover: Eagle's View Publishing Co., Ogden, Utah, 1988.

By Ted Spring . . .

The SKETCHBOOK 56 Series, published by Track of the Wolf, Inc., Osseo, MN:
Volume 1: The Book of Rogers' Rangers; 1984
Volume 2: The French Marines 1754-1761 (with Bill Hofstetter); 1984
Volume 3: The Highlanders and Provincial Rangers (with George A. Bray III); 1984
Volume 4: The Spanish Colonial Era Infantry 1739-1781; 1990
Volume 5: The Women of the French War Era 1750-1769; 1991
Volume 6: Indian Allies of the French War Era 1756-1761; 1992

A SHINING TIME Series, published by Track of the Wolf, Inc., Osseo, MN:
Volume 1: The Fur Trade; 1992
Volume 2: The Hunters, Scouts, and Plainsmen 1835-1875; 1994
Volume 3: The Horse Soldiers: Part 1 — The Dragoons 1776–1849; 1995